The Tylos Period Burials
in Bahrain

The Tylos Period Burials in Bahrain
Volume 1
The Glass and Pottery Vessels

Søren Fredslund Andersen © 2007

ISBN 978 87 7934 373 3

Copyediting and revision: Helen Knox
Layout: Hanne Kolding
Cover: Hanne Kolding
Drawings: Søren Fredslund Andersen, Karsten Mikkelsen and Ali Omran
Photographs: Søren Fredslund Andersen, Bahrain National Museum and Moesgård Museum
Printed by: Narayana Press

Published by:
Culture & National Heritage
Kingdom of Bahrain
in association with
Moesgård Museum and
Aarhus University

Distributed by
Aarhus University Press
Langelandsgade 177
DK-8200 Aarhus N
Denmark
www.unipress.dk

Gazelle Book Services Ltd.
White Cross Mills,
Hightown
Lancaster,
LA1 4XS
www.gazellebooks.co.uk

The David Brown Book Company (DBBC)
P.O. Box 511
Oakville CT 06779
USA
www.oxbowbooks.com

The Tylos Period Burials in Bahrain

VOLUME 1

The Glass and Pottery Vessels

by Søren Fredslund Andersen

Kingdom of Bahrain

Culture & National Heritage

مملكة البحرين

الثقافة والتراث الوطني

Acknowledgements

The material presented in this study was excavated by the Bahrain National Museum and I am most grateful to Shaikha Mai bint Mohammad Al Khalifa, Assistant Undersecretary for Culture & National Heritage and Dr. Abdullah Yateem, former Assistant Undersecretary for Culture & National Heritage in the Ministry of Information for giving me permission to analyse the fascinating finds from the Tylos period.

My warm thanks also go to Mr. Khaled Al-Sindi, former Acting Director of Archaeology and Heritage for paving the way for some very efficient months in Bahrain together with Mr. Yousif Bumtai, Acting Director of Archaeology and Heritage and Mr. Fuad Noor, Acting Director of Museums. Without Mr. Mustafa Ibrahim Salman, this study would never have been completed; his assistance in the daily work in the stores and archives in Bahrain and his continued data collection, when I was in Denmark, have been invaluable. I am also thankful to: Mr. Isa A. M. Abdelrahim, Storeroom Manager, Mr. Ali Omran, Surveyor and Draftsman, Mr. Muhammed Saleh, Mr. Muhammed Rashid, Mr. Karsten Mikkelsen, Draftsman, Mr. Saleh Ali, Photographer and Ms. Thuraya Ali Bualai, Secretary, who together with a large number of friends and colleagues at the Bahrain National Museum have helped in many ways and with their good humour made my visits to Bahrain enjoyable.

The project was made possible with a three-year PhD scholarship from the Danish PhD School in Archaeology, with additional financial support from the following individuals and institutions: the Ministry of Information, Kingdom of Bahrain, the Elisabeth Munksgaard Foundation, Shaikha Noora bint Ibrahim Al Khalifa, Shaikha Mai bint Muhammad Al Khalifa and the Danish Institute in Damascus, Syria. Moesgård Museum and Aarhus University has provided a base for my work.

Dr. Lise Hannestad, Dept. of Classical Archaeology, University of Aarhus has been my supervisor assisted by Dr. Flemming Højlund, Oriental Department, Moesgård Museum and Dr. St John Simpson, Department of The Ancient Near East, the British Museum; I am very grateful to them for their interest in the project and for useful suggestions and discussions. I am also indebted to a large number of friends and colleagues, who have commented and discussed the work, with special thanks to Prof. Ernie Haerinck, University of Ghent, Dr. Derek Kennet, Durham University and Ms. Birte Poulsen, University of Aarhus for useful critique and comments during the evaluation of my thesis.

Table of contents

Introduction

Over the last decades, our knowledge about the late pre-Islamic period on Bahrain has increased with the publication of old and new discoveries. We can now begin to write in more detail about the history of Bahrain from the period when Alexander the Great's scout expeditions in 324 BC reported the existence of two islands called "Tylos" and "Arados" – which are now known to be the main islands of Bahrain – until the people living on these islands embraced Islam in the seventh century AD. This period extends over nearly 1000 years and is now generally known as "the Tylos period" on Bahrain. However, very few ancient authors and inscriptions refer to Bahrain in the Tylos period, which has made it extremely difficult to establish a history by traditional means. We therefore depend on archaeology with the limits and pitfalls thereby involved, to form

a knowledge of the people who lived on Bahrain before the coming of Islam and the contexts within which they functioned. Although significant progress has been made, the published finds and written sources only provide a sporadic picture. The aim of this study is to supply further knowledge of the period by bringing significant archaeological material excavated by Bahraini archaeologists into play.

Thousands of objects were recovered during rescue excavations of burial mounds dating to the Tylos period and the material is stored in the Bahrain National Museum. During preliminary investigations in 2001 and 2002, it became clear that very significant archaeological material was available and accessible for studies of the Tylos period (Andersen 2002; Andersen *et al.* 2004). It also became clear that an attempt to carry out a study based on *all* finds and contextual

Figure 1. Shakhoura Mound A1, Season 1996-97 during excavation.

documentation from the Bahraini excavations would not be possible within the time limits and conditions for a PhD thesis. Two categories of finds were therefore selected (presented in this volume) together with excavation data from selected mounds from two areas (see Salman & Andersen (forthcoming)). It was obvious that the pottery found in the tombs should be studied for a number of reasons: 1) it is a common grave good; 2) it is suitable for creating a relative chronology; 3) the pottery would create a link between the tombs and the few known settlements on Bahrain from the Tylos period; 4) stylistic studies of pottery have proved to be a trustworthy indicator of foreign influence during the period in the Gulf region (e.g. Hannestad 1983; Andersen 2002).[1] The glass vessels became the second group to be studied in more detail. Many of the glass vessels are of well-dated and well-distributed types and are often found with pottery vessels and thus able to provide the pottery sequence with absolute dates. Furthermore, the glass illustrates a clear stylistic development, supplementing that of the pottery. The stylistic development of the glass and pottery vessels is therefore most suitable for creating a chronological system, which can link archaeological remains with historical evidence. However, the vessels contain further information that is not purely chronological. By extending the temporal analysis of the archaeological remains with a spatial dimension, the typological developments are believed to reflect interactions between contemporary cultures in terms of influence and choice.

The study presented in this volume is therefore not a study of burial practices, but will concentrate on the glass and pottery vessels found in the tombs and use the interpretation of these objects to write more of the history of Bahrain in the Tylos period.

The glass vessels are the first to be presented and discussed in Chapter 2, followed by the pottery in Chapter 3. In Chapter 4 the chronological development of the assemblage will be discussed, including the topographical situation. In Chapter 5 the results of the study of the glass and pottery vessels will be discussed in the light of other sources.

Research history
It was not until 1925 that the first possible reference to burials from the Tylos period was made, although a number of archaeological investigations were conducted in Bahrain earlier (see Frifelt 1984–1985: 11 for a summary of the early works). The archaeolo-

gist Ernest Mackay worked as others before him on the huge Bronze Age mounds in Ali, but reported on the excavation of a tumulus near Janussan carried out by Major Daly (Lombard & Salles 1984: 24). Mackay dated the finds to around 300 BC or slightly earlier and illustrated three of the pottery vessels found by Daly (Mackay, Harding & Petrie 1929: 29, pl. VII/26–28). Daly later presented the objects to the Department of Assyrian and Egyptian Antiquities at the British Museum and the museum bought a plaster figurine. In 1950, on behalf of the Peabody Museum/Harvard Expedition, Henry Field conducted a reconnaissance of south-western Asia with an archaeological, anthropological, botanical and zoological aim. Assisted by T.G. Bibby, who later became the field director of the Danish Gulf Expeditions, Field carried out a survey of various archaeological sites in Bahrain and excavated a tumulus with multiple burials.[2] The recovery of blue-green glazed vessels was reported, and the lack of similarity between the graves in this tumulus and those at Ali, where previously opened tumuli could be studied, was noted (Field 1951).

The Danish Gulf Expeditions from the Aarhus/Moesgaard Museum made the final breakthrough in the exploration of the Tylos period during the 1950s and 60s. Although initially attracted by the Bronze Age tumuli as so many before them, the Danes investigated numerous archaeological sites in order to find and explore the settlements. They carried out extensive excavations at the site of Qala'at al-Bahrain, which appears to be the ancient capital of Bahrain, and managed for the first time to establish a sound chronological framework for the pre-Islamic and Islamic periods in Bahrain, and describe the characteristics of six successive periods (Bibby 1958; 1996). The full publication of these excavations is now at an advanced stage. Based on the stratigraphy at Qala'at al-Bahrain and the typology of the pottery, a chronological system for part of the Tylos Period has been developed using the description of the pottery from four distinctive sub-periods covering the period from c. 300 BC to c. AD 200 (Højlund & Andersen 1994). In addition there is a small collection of imported beakers, probably dating to the third century AD (Højlund & Andersen 1997: 213–215). The assemblage of local pottery illustrates a change in fashion in the

---

[1] Storage jars have been used for infant burials in the Tylos period, but these vessels are not included in this study, which focus on the gravegoods.

[2] This tumulus was situated in a group of six, where a Danish team excavated the remaining five in 1959. These mounds were part of the larger mound field south of Qala'at al-Bahrain, but their exact position can no longer be established (Jensen 2003: 127–128).

period just after the Greek conquest of the Achaemenid Empire by the adoption of Greek shapes by local potters. However, the new shapes such as the fish plate and the echinus bowl hardly indicate any changes in habit, since small, open bowls were also very common in the Achaemenid period. Sometime later in the Tylos period vessels inspired by Mediterranean pottery and intended for wine drinking were introduced (Andersen 2002). The pottery from Qala'at al-Bahrain thus indicates changes in the material culture just after 325 BC, followed by a long, uniform period until a break sometime in the centuries after the beginning of our era.

Probably the most important find from the Tylos period at Qala'at al-Bahrain was a coin hoard of *c.* 300 silver coins dating to the end of the third century BC. These coins were local east Arabian imitations of Alexander the Great's tetradrachms and they indicate that some sort of political entity was established in east Arabia towards the end of the third century BC. It has been suggested that this entity may have had its centre on Bahrain (Callot 1994), but the ancient city of Gerrha, with its own mint, could also have been the centre in north-east Arabia (Mørkholm 1973; Potts 1990: 85). The great majority of the remaining published finds from Qala'at al-Bahrain can be interpreted as domestic rubbish, which does not necessarily provide information on religious or ethnic conceptions and groupings in the pre-Islamic society of Bahrain.

During the first season of the Danish Gulf Expeditions in 1953–1954, the two distinctive kinds of burials, which were noted by Field, were investigated as two tumuli situated in north-west Bahrain between the villages of Janabia and Saar were excavated together with another three tumuli in the area south of Qala'at al-Bahrain. The two tumuli near Saar were dated to the Bronze Age, but the other three tumuli were from the Iron Age. In Bibby's account of these excavations (1954), the characteristics of the Tylos period tombs were described, i.e. an internally plastered, rectangular cist, slightly larger than the deceased, with a plaster frame creating the base for the large capstones covering the tomb. He also mentions iron "nails" in the frame, which may have served a purpose during the covering of the tomb, the reuse of one of the excavated tombs and secondary burials in one of the other tombs. The finds, however, were rather limited, as tomb robbers had entered the tombs before the archaeologists. The difference in the shape of the tumuli of the two periods was also described for the first time, as it was noted that the tumuli of the Iron Age were "wider and not always completely circular, while several are built into one, forming irregular shapes"

(Bibby 1954: 137–141). During the 1959–1960 seasons, the Danish Gulf Expeditions excavated five small tumuli belonging to the same group as the one investigated by Field, and one tumulus near the village of Saar. A final tumulus was excavated at the turnoff from the Budaiya Road to Qala'at al-Bahrain as a rescue operation. All these tumuli are dated to the Tylos period and a full account has been published (Jensen 2003; Littleton 2003; MacDonald 2003).

The Danish Gulf Expeditions also uncovered a Bronze Age temple complex at Barbar (Andersen & Højlund 2003) where more recent layers overlaid the Bronze Age remains. The pottery indicates activity at the site from around the third century AD until the ninth or tenth century. The recovery of some stone sculpture fragments from a human-sized figure and part of a possible dedicative inscription suggest that it was not just a settlement of local peasants working in the surrounding gardens. The site could therefore have been a place of some religious or secular importance, possibly in the third or fourth century AD (Frifelt 2001; Andersen & Kennet 2003; Curtis & Andersen, forthcoming).

From the late nineteenth century until the present law of antiquities was passed in 1969, it was mainly Europeans working in the administration or the oil industry, who explored the mounds, and a vast number of tumuli were bulldozed without prior investigations in order to clear land for the rapid development of the country. The Advisor to the Government of Bahrain, Sir Charles Belgrave had a small collection of Parthian pottery found in 1937, when the road from Manama to Budaiya was constructed. He believed, however, that the graves were Phoenician (Bibby 1954: 137–138; Herling & Salles 1993: 164). Most of these excavations and clearings have left us with very little useful information, if any at all. The exception is an excavation carried out by Captain Higham. He worked for the British Army in Bahrain and excavated a tumulus with ten graves in the late 1960s. He deposited his findings in the British Museum[3] and the collection was published (During-Caspers 1972–1974; 1980).

The establishment of the Bahraini Directorate of Antiquities in 1969 changed the picture, as most of the private bulldozing stopped and leisure diggings were banned. All legal excavations have since then been conducted or supervised by the Directorate. Already in its first years, the excavations conducted by the Directorate produced new and major discoveries, as tombs were found, which were datable to

---

[3] The British Museum later bought the collection.

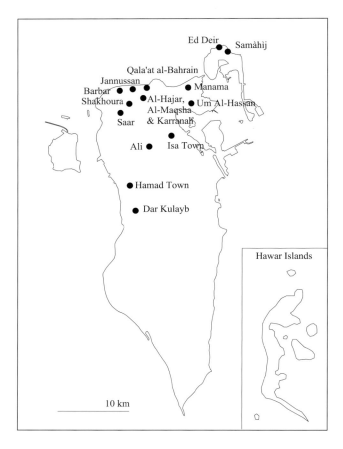

Figure 2. Map of Bahrain with sites mentioned in the text.

the intermediate period between the well-known Bronze Age and Tylos burials (Rice 1972).

Although the Directorate of Antiquities has itself conducted a large number of excavations, foreign expeditions were still welcomed and teams from Britain, Australia, France, Germany and Belgium have excavated tumuli from the Tylos period. In 1975 a British team investigated a mound north of Janussan (McNicoll & Roaf 1975); in 1979–1980 an Australian team excavated some mounds in the Saar area (Petocz & Hart 1981); in 1980–1981 a French Mission excavated parts of the large mounds south of the village of Janussan (Lombard & Salles 1984) and in 1986–1987 a cemetery near Abu Saybi and another near Karranah (unpublished). A German team carried out investigations in Karranah and Saar in the early 1990s (Herling *et al.* 1993; Herling & Velde 1994; Herling 2003) and a Belgian team excavated two mounds in Shakhoura in 1999 and 2000 (Daems & Haerinck 2001; Daems, Haerinck & Rutten 2001). Some of these excavations are published in full, others are well described in unpublished reports, which have been widely circulated and the remainder are still unpublished. Based on limited material, mainly excavated by foreign teams, a chronological sequence of pottery has been

presented with a subdivision of the Tylos period into three ceramic phases, i.e. Early Tylos = "Failaka horizon", Middle Tylos-1 = "Bahrain Horizon" and Middle Tylos-2 = "ed-Dur horizon", covering the period from 300 BC to the second century AD (Herling & Salles 1993). A recent review of the chronology of the earliest Tylos period indicates, however, that the earliest burials attributed to the Tylos period should not be dated earlier than the late third/early second century BC by comparing the large selection of pottery from the tombs excavated by the Bahraini authorities with the pottery sequence from Qala'at al-Bahrain. An overall lack of burials from the earliest Tylos period, which is also evident in the Achaemenid period, indicates that a burial custom without much material splendour was practised among the majority of the population and that this practice, which has left us with no evidence, was replaced by a more elaborate style sometime in the Tylos period (Andersen 2002).

An analysis of the skeletal remains for two populations on Bahrain, i.e. one from the Hamad Town DS3 area and the other one from Mound 5, 1987–1988 in Saar, has been published and a significant difference was noted between the two societies. High infant/child morbidity was documented in both areas, but heavy workloads and infectious diseases marked the skeletal remains of both males and females in DS3, whereas in Saar it would appear that the females were not heavily involved in physical work. The analysis was applied to a model of living in small agricultural settlements, and the differences in the standard of living between the two populations were understood to be the result of the two populations responding in a slightly different way to slightly different conditions (Littleton 1998).

The last settlement site, which is known from the Tylos period, was excavated by the Directorate of Antiquities. In the area south of the village of Saar, an isolated house or possibly a fire temple was cleared on top of a Bronze Age burial complex. Within a rectangular building a coin dating to the fifth century AD and a few sherds were recovered, but the amount of finds from this site is very limited (Crawford, Killick & Moon 1997: 20; Lombard & Kervran 1993: 138; Killick & Moon 2005: 2).

Since the establishment of the Directorate of Antiquities, large-scale rescue excavations in a number of areas have been carried out and more than 100 tumuli, each containing up to 200 tombs, have been excavated. The complete objects are stored in the Bahrain National Museum and a small selection of these objects has previously been presented in museum and exhibition catalogues (Lombard & Kervran 1989; Vine 1993; Lombard 1999), whereas fragments and bones have been brought to external stores, often stored by tumulus rather than tomb. The huge archaeological material recovered during the Bahraini excavations and the documentation produced is, together with published reports from foreign expeditions, the empirical foundation for this study.

Terminology

Before proceeding further, the terms used to describe places and periods should briefly be presented to prevent any misunderstandings. Different terms have been used by various scholars in the past and will be used in this study, most of them implying various levels of precision.

Geographical terms

The modern name of *Bahrain* will be used as the name of the geographic unit, i.e. the Bahrain archipelago, whereas the modern state of Bahrain will be referred to as the Kingdom of Bahrain. The ancient names of *Dilmun* and *Tylos* will be used to describe periods rather than areas. The ancient name of *al-Bahrain* covers the area of Bahrain and the adjacent coastal regions, but will not be used since the general and neutral term north-east Arabia will be preferred. A rich archaeological record from the Oman peninsula (the United Arab Emirates (UAE) and Sultanate of Oman) has been published and that area will be termed south-east Arabia or the Oman peninsula, when the modern names are not used. Modern Yemen will be called either by that name or by South Arabia. It is intended that locations that are more specific will be termed by modern geographical names, whereas vague terms such as north-east Arabia will be preferred for ancient "cultural regions". *Mesopotamia* covers the river plains of the Euphrates and Tigris and thus modern Iraq and part of Syria. *Iran* is the area of modern Iran and *the North* is approximately the area of Iran and Iraq, which are the main areas of the empires of the period. The *East* or *Near East* will be used as a general term covering the area from the borders of the Roman Empire in Jordan and Syria at around the beginning of our era, over the Arabian Peninsula and Iraq, Iran and Afghanistan to the Indus. The *West* is thus the area controlled by the Romans, but often the term "the Mediterranean region" will be used, as it is believed that developments and traditions in the north-west part of the Roman Empire are not that relevant for this study. The east Mediterranean region is equivalent to the Syro-Palestinian region and thus excludes Egypt, which will be referred to independently.

Chronological terms

Absolute dates will only be used with caution and must be regarded as suggestions. They will therefore consequently be given as round figures of a quarter of a century except when dates are cited from others or are of a nature where more precise figures can be used, e.g. inscribed dates or coins. They will always be given in the Christian era and it will always be noted if a date is before Christ (BC) or after (AD). Historical eras of the region will often be used as chronological terms and they are not meant to indicate any political affiliations. Table 1 lists these periods and their approximate lifespan.

Period	From	To
Achaemenid	500 BC	300 BC
Seleucid	300 BC	150 BC
Parthian	150 BC	AD 225
Sasanian	AD 225	AD 650
Islamic	AD 650	

Table 1. Historical periods used as chronological terms in the region.

Material and documentation

The material presented in the following chapters is the result of excavations carried out by the staff of the Directorate of Antiquities as rescue excavations, although foreign teams have worked in cooperation with the Directorate in a few cases. It has not been the aim of these excavations to solve specific academic problems, but rather to try to recover as many objects and as much information as possible with the resources available. This does not create an ideal set of data, and information that requires specialized training or equipment is not likely to have been recognized during excavation.

A team of labourers, who did not have any formal training in archaeology, but may have participated in archaeological work over a period, normally conducted the excavations. One or two archaeologists from the Directorate supervised them. The excavations are named in rather descriptive terms as follows: 1) Area, named after the nearest village; 2) Mound number; and 3) Excavation season. An example is Shakhoura, Mound 1, Season 1992–1993, which in the following will be abbreviated to Shakhoura, Mound 1–92–93. The combination of mound number and season is important, since a mound called number 1 etc. exists in more than one area, but two mounds with the same number in the same area were not likely to have been excavated in the same season (although this cannot be completely excluded either). No systematic archive has been maintained for the excavations carried out by the Directorate and an excavation that has taken place over more than one season may thus sometimes be counted as two. The lack of a systematic archive and appropriate procedures for saving the information recorded during excavations makes it impossible to provide any figures for the number of mounds, tombs, burials etc. that have been excavated. A total number of tombs that have been excavated against which to view numbers of specific objects or details simply does not exist and cannot be reconstructed. Furthermore, objects were lost in transit from the excavation to the museum and during storage in the museum, so the total figures for glass and pottery vessels provided in the study refer to the number studied and not to the number excavated.

The excavations were normally conducted in 5 x 5 m squares laid out in a grid system or by dividing the mound into quarters. Sometimes the baulks between the squares were left to give access to the work across the site and provide a section. When a tomb was encountered, it was normally numbered in sequence[4] and very often the tomb number was painted on the frame of the tomb to ensure consistency. When the capstones of a tomb were cleared, the tomb was opened. Photographs or drawings were sometimes made of the contents of the tomb. The grave goods and skeletal remains were then removed and most often, a list of the contents and general measurements and characteristics of the tomb was made in a notebook by the excavation supervisor. Grave goods have often been found outside a tomb, but in clear relation to a specific tomb. The objects recovered were then transported to the museum, with a little note specifying the context of that object following the system mentioned above, with the tomb number added and sometimes the square number. Furthermore, the objects were often given a find number in the field, but such numbers were rarely used in the notebooks. Burial jars were treated in a similar way but following a different numbering system, e.g. Jar no. 1, 2 etc. For the description of objects in the notebooks, general terms have been used and often different terms by different supervisors for similar objects. This makes it extremely difficult to make a detailed comparison of the contexts recorded from the field notes with the objects in the storeroom, although it is possible to get an idea of the quality of the information.

When the objects were brought to the museum from the excavations, they were most often cleaned, although that will have removed all the remains of the contents of the containers. Finally, the objects were placed in the stores. Complete vessels and rare objects were placed in the Main Store at Bahrain National Museum within a controlled environment, whereas pottery fragments and skeletal remains were placed in external stores without climate control. The note filled by the supervisor at the excavation followed the object. A numbering system for the objects in the Main Store was introduced at a very early stage after the foundation of the Museum in the 1970s and maintained until the 1990s. Over the past few years, while this study has been going on, a new numbering system with "A-numbers" (i.e. numbers starting with an "A") has been introduced. This means that the museum number, which is recorded with each object, presented in the catalogue will be a number in the old series, a field number if no other number has been assigned, or a new "A-number".

Methodology

The glass and pottery vessels presented in the next two chapters were found in tombs, but the aim of these excavations and the archiving of the objects and documentation, as described above, means that the primary source for this study is the collection of vessels in the Bahrain National Museum and not specific tomb assemblages. Some of the vessels have their context information preserved, which makes it possible to reconstruct find combinations, but it must be emphasized that the vessels studied are the ones in the museum store.

Although glass and pottery vessels are similar in many aspects, there are some significant differences in the study of the two categories. This mainly refers to modern research and the ancient distribution of the vessels. It is apparent that most glass vessels find exact parallels that are from well-dated contexts and were discovered over a very large area. The great majority of glass types can therefore be dated by external means. The find combinations in the Bahraini tombs are used to verify these datings. For the pottery, the situation is very different. Only very few types find good and well-dated parallels in the published literature and in a much smaller area, where relatively little archaeological research has been made. The find combinations with the relatively well-dated glass vessels and the contextual relations between different types of pottery vessels are therefore the primary dating evidence. To get an initial overview, the tombs that combine more than one type were seriated. The datings provided by the

---

[4] There are a few examples of numbering within squares, e.g. Hamad Town, Mound 1–94–95.

Bahraini evidence were then verified by the external parallels, which in most cases fitted quite well. In a few cases, the Bahraini and the external datings did not correspond. In these situations the external dat- ings were often based on relatively long sequences with very few absolute datings or with question- able dating evidence, and the Bahraini evidence can therefore be regarded as superior.

The Glass Vessels

2

Over the last thirty-five years more than 300 complete glass vessels have been found in the tombs dating to the Tylos period in Bahrain and since the study of pre-Islamic glass vessels in eastern Arabia is still in its infancy, the collection of glass from Bahrain should make a significant contribution. The collection may also throw light on aspects of trade and distribution of glass in the region in the period from the beginning of our era until the coming of Islam.

East Arabia

No glass fragments from the pre-Islamic period from either the Danish or French excavations at Qala'at al-Bahrain have been published and so far only a few collections from excavations in eastern Arabia are known, e.g. from ed-Dur and Kush in the UAE (Whitehouse 1998; 2000; Price & Worrell 2003; Worrell & Price 2003). A few fragments have been reported from burials from the so-called Samad culture in Oman (Yule 2001: 79) and the presence of glass vessels from the excavations at Mleiha has been mentioned (Whitehouse 2000: 117; Mouton 1999: 17–19). A single vessel has been reported from Dhahran in north-east Arabia (Potts *et al*. 1978: pl. 10/48). Some of the vessels from the Bahraini tombs have also been presented before in museum and exhibition catalogues (Boucharlat & Salles 1989; Vine 1993; Nenna 1999).

The excavations at Ed-Dur were conducted by teams from four nations in the late 1980s and early 1990s. The site is believed to be a rather short-lived settlement founded in the early years of the Christian era and abandoned in the early second century AD, except for a fortress situated at a high sand dune between the coast and the main settlement.

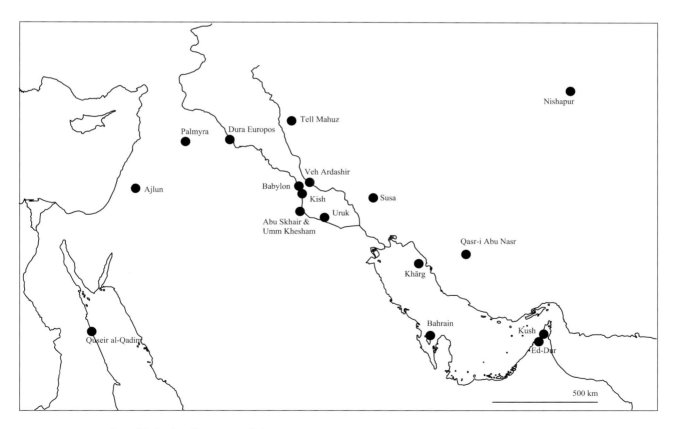

Figure 3. Sites with published collections of glass.

The fortress has been dated to the third century AD and was reused as a burial ground in the late third to fourth century AD (Lecomte 1993). The main settlement had a rural character where houses and tombs were scattered over a large area. Some of the tombs were simple cists for single burials, not unlike the ones from Bahrain but generally lacking the tumulus, other tombs were underground vaults with a dromos-like entrance and a vaulted burial chamber built in well-cut ashlars. These chambers were used for multiple burials. As on Bahrain, the deceased was often accompanied by grave goods, and glass vessels were rather common gifts (Haerinck 2001). The glass fragments and vessels from the Danish and Belgian excavations in ed-Dur have been published and discussed in detail by David Whitehouse (1998; 2000) and some of the glass vessels from the French excavation in the fortress and graves have also been presented (Lecomte 1993: fig. 14).

The ed-Dur assemblages published by Whitehouse consist of 227 complete vessels and glass fragments. Both the stylistic evidence and a compositional analysis suggest that the great majority of the assemblage was of east Roman origin, though a few vessels from both excavations may be of Parthian or Sasanian manufacture (Whitehouse 2000: 116–117). The earliest vessels are cast bowls, which according to Whitehouse should be dated to the period from *c*. 25 BC to the early second century AD. He argues, however, that the lack of two distinctive types of the late first to the early second century AD, i.e. the colourless bowls and plates with overhanging rims and the facet-cut beakers, suggests that the majority of the glass from ed-Dur should be dated to the period between 25 BC and AD 75 (*ibid*. 119–120). In his discussion of the glass, Whitehouse does not separate vessels found in graves from fragments believed to originate from the settlement. This is partly due to later activities in and around the tombs, which have mixed the material from settlement and tombs (Haerinck, pers. comm. 2006).

A preliminary report on the glass from the settlement at Kush has also been published. Roman, Sasanian and Islamic assemblages were identified. The vessels from the Roman and Sasanian period were dominated by tableware, with little evidence of vessels being used as storage vessels for foodstuffs and cosmetics (Price & Worrell 2003: 155).

Whitehouse addressed the question of how vessels produced within the Roman Empire ended up in eastern Arabia and listed three possible trade routes: 1) that the vessels arrived by sea from Egypt; 2) that they were exported from Egypt to India and re-exported to the Gulf; and 3) that they were carried overland to the head of the Gulf and shipped to the Oman peninsula. He concludes that the last possibility probably accounts for the majority of the vessels (2000: 120–122). Several sites along the routes suggested by Whitehouse have been excavated and from some of them glass studies have been published. In the following, I will briefly introduce some of the most important of these sites.

The Red Sea

From the Red Sea coast of Egypt evidence has been published from Quseir al-Qadim, which initially was believed to be the ancient town of Leukos Limen (Meyer 1992), but recently the site has convincingly been identified as the ancient city of Myos Hormos, one of the two major Roman ports along the Red Sea (Peacock 1993). Quseir al-Qadim is situated at the mouth of a caravan track linking it with the Nile valley where the distance between the coast and the Nile is short. The site itself could not provide provisions for a large settlement due to the barren land and a lack of substantial water sources, but during the period from *c*. AD 25 and to the second or early third century AD the site was active. The activities at Quseir al-Qadim were related to the Roman trade with India and on the Indian Ocean in the same period. The site was reoccupied in the late Ayyubid period until the early Mamluk period (late twelfth to early fourteenth century AD) where trade again flourished. The glass assemblage published consists of 373 diagnostic fragments of both open and closed vessels of which a large amount can be described as luxury tableware (Meyer 1992).

Recent excavations in Berenike, which was the other major Roman port at the Red Sea, have revealed a material similar to that presented from Quseir al-Qadim, but the site remained occupied in Late Antiquity (Nicholson 1999; 2000; Sidebotham 2004).[5]

The Levant and Mesopotamia

Glass vessels found along the overland route from the Levant to Mesopotamia are well represented. The first city along the route coming from southern Syria was Palmyra, from where a museum collection has been presented (Gawlikowski & As'ad 1994). Massive archaeological investigations have been carried out in the town of Dura-Europos situated beside the Euphrates from where goods could be shipped down to central and southern Mesopotamia and the Gulf via the river. Excavations carried out in Dura-Europos and in cemeteries outside the city, together with written sources, document that

---

[5] Only preliminary reports have been published so far.

the city was founded in the early Hellenistic period and vanished in the middle of the third century AD (Perkins 1973). The glass was published in one volume and divided into a Hellenistic, early Imperial and middle Imperial assemblage mainly on stylistic grounds, rather than on contextual evidence (Clairmont 1963). Studies and presentations of better-dated material have indicated that the chronological attributions made by Clairmont are not definite and should be treated with caution.[6] The tombs and their grave goods were published in another volume (Toll 1946). In the tombs there seems to have been a preference for unguentaria, in contrast with a large variety of open-shaped vessels from the settlement.

From Mesopotamia, several collections of glass from funerary and other contexts have been published. Negro Ponzi published a collection of glass from the Abu Skhair cemetery in central Iraq (1972). She suggested a late Parthian date for the vessels, based on the accompanying pottery and the possible use of "slipper-coffins" in the cemetery and noted some stylistic differences between this assemblage and well-known east Roman types, indicating an independent Mesopotamian production (*ibid.* 218). Recently Negro Ponzi has questioned the association with the pottery, since later excavations have revealed that the cemetery consisted of various grave groups and the graves containing the late Parthian pottery were not in the same groups as the ones containing the glass (Negro Ponzi 2005). A slightly later date than initially proposed for the glass from Abu Skhair was suggested for the use of the cemetery at Tell Mahuz in northern Iraq, where both glass vessels and eleven coins were found in the graves. Three of the coins were illegible, whereas the remaining eight coins were issues of early Sasanian emperors (third to fourth century AD) (Negro Ponzi: 1968–1969: 308–309 and Appendix A).

Recently four find groups from the Umm Khesham cemetery have been presented. This site is situated in central Iraq and close to the Abu Skhair cemetery. The four groups have been dated to the fourth and fifth century AD, due to similarities between some of the vessels and the Abu Skhair assemblage (Negro Ponzi 2005).

A small group of Parthian and Sasanian period glass has also been excavated in the graves and the settlement at Uruk in southern Mesopotamia (Boehmer, Pedde & Salje 1995; van Ess & Pedde 1992). From Seleucia, glass vessels from both settlement and graves have been published and discussed in de-

tail by Negro Ponzi (1970–1971; 2002). She argues that the lack of tableware in the settlement is because the earlier levels have not been reached in the excavations and the upper social classes had moved to the new capital of Ctesiphon in the middle and late Parthian periods from which the majority of finds belong (*ibid.* 109–110). From the settlement at Choche, where levels dating from the mid-third to the sixth century have been excavated,[7] a selection of both bottles and tableware has been published (Negro Ponzi 1984).

The manufacture of glass vessels in the Near East is indicated by finds from the Achaemenid period, where high-quality vessels were used for the table of the higher classes, although the majority of the production may have taken place in the West (Triantafyllidis 2003: 15). It seems unlikely that a production was maintained in the East during Hellenistic and early Parthian times and no findings of glass production facilities have been reported east of the Roman frontiers in these periods either, whereas evidence for large-scale glass production is reported for the late Sasanian and/or early Islamic periods (Adams 1981: 211–213).

It is the aim of this chapter to present the glass vessels found in the Bahraini tombs and to discuss the assemblage in light of the above collections. It is clear, however, that glass was traded over vast distances, and relevant material from many additional sites and museum collections has been consulted. The study of the glass will provide the chronological foundation for the study of the pottery vessels in Chapter 3. The glass catalogue is organized in a formal typological classification, where each type has been given a type code. For the great majority of types I have followed generally accepted type classifications, with an attempt to use the classification and terminology of Isings (1957) whenever appropriate. In a few cases, I have chosen to join types, which have been separated by other scholars (i.e. Type 6, Type 18 and Type 41), because the dating and possible place of production is the same and they share some easily identifiable features. My ambition has not been to create a very refined typology, but to create a useful tool for further analysis of the Bahraini material, which in this case is the pottery. Questions about specific workshops and the distribution of their

---

[6] Isings 1957, which has become the foundation for most glass studies, seems to have been unknown to Clairmont.

---

[7] The earliest layers contained coins of Ardashir and Sapur I (AD 224–272) and the latest dwelling blocks were dated by coins of Bahram V (AD 420–438). These blocks were overlaid by slightly younger debris containing coins of the second half of the fifth century AD (Negro Ponzi 1984: 33).

products have not been the focus of the analysis of the Bahraini material, since there is no evidence of a production of glass on Bahrain in the Tylos period. I have therefore assumed that all glass vessels were imported. By far the majority of the types are quite well dated in other studies and I have therefore been able to date most of the Bahraini vessels by external means.

The Bahraini glass vessels were recorded in the Main Store of the Bahrain National Museum during two visits to Bahrain in 2003 and 2004. During the first visit a brief recording of c. two thirds of the vessels was made with some basic notes and digital photographs. In the following season a more detailed recording was made and all vessels were photographed and some drawn. Basic manufacturing details, which are not obvious on the photographs, were recorded but extensive descriptions of shape, preservation and colour have been omitted, since these features appear on the colour table. Due to the reorganization of the Main Store, a few vessels recorded in the 2003 campaign could not be found the following year and some information and illustrations may thus be lacking.

The catalogue is organized chronologically, as it appeared that four distinctive assemblages could be described on the basis of stylistic evidence, which were confirmed by find combinations when the registrations of contexts were entered into the database. It was also clear that time was a significant factor separating the four assemblages. The underlying reasons for the changes in the assemblages over time are also partly embedded in the presentation, since the glass from the Bahraini tombs reflects technological invention, changes in trade and distribution patterns and cultural orientations, which are central topics in the description and discussion of the individual types.

Within each period, the specific types have been grouped according to production technique, since this is a common approach and will ensure easy accessibility to the catalogue. Within this overall grouping, the vessels have been grouped according to function. Unguentaria are defined as small bottles suitable as containers for liquids, such as perfumed oils and other substances for personal adornment. No vessels have preserved any of their possible content and a more precise function cannot be established for the Bahraini vessels. Bowls, cups, plates and beakers are believed to have served as tableware, although a bowl of Type 42 was found with a content of shells and beads, indicating that some vessels may have been used as containers for objects used for personal adornment.

The catalogue numbers used in the glass and pottery chapters are made as a combination of the type code and a sequence number (i.e. cat. no. 2.4 is vessel number 4 of type 2).

For each type of vessel, two tables have been produced. The first list contains descriptive information regarding the vessels and the second list provides the context information and references to earlier publication of the vessel. It is also noted if the vessel has not been illustrated here. For the descriptions, the following terms have been used. "Length/height" is used for the maximum length or height of the vessel when fully preserved. If the vessel does not have a resting surface that allows it to stand on its own, the bottom of the vessel can have an attached knob (e.g. as seen on cat. no. 1.2), it can be pointed (cat. no. 11.3) or rounded (cat. no. 1.3). The term "rounded" is used rather broadly, since it is applied not only to globular vessels (cat. no. 13.1) but also to date-flasks and other vessels without a base. Most common is a concave base where the bottom has been pushed in. If a mark from a pointed tool is visible, the term "kicked" has been used. Often a pontil scar is visible (abbreviated in the table to w. ps: with pontil scar). A few vessels have an applied disc as a base, which has been called a "pad base" (cat. no. 46.1), others have pinched-out knobs (cat. no. 45.1) or a coil base (cat. no. 34.18). Very few vessels have bases that are more elaborate. The rim is very often outsplayed (abb. Outsp.) or flaring, most often with a rolled-in lip (abb. rolled-in, e.g. cat. no. 26.3). On some vessels, the lip has been sheared off without any further treatment, although this term has also been used if it has been impossible to clarify the finish of the lip, due to weathering or the general state of preservation. Some have been cracked off and others fire-polished (abb. fp). On a very few vessels, traces of mechanical polishing are evident. The original colour of the vessels was often difficult to determine due to weathering, but often a few spots of what was likely to have been the original colour were visible. The terms greenish, bluish, greyish etc. are used when a tint of that colour is present, whereas blue, purple and green are used for strongly coloured vessels. In a few cases, it may be the colour of the weathered surface that was recorded. Further information regarding the preservation of the vessels and decoration is listed under remarks. In some cases, a well-defined type has been thoroughly discussed in a recent publication and I have only made that single reference together with a very brief summary. In addition to the external chronological evidence are find combinations from the Bahraini tombs and for each type of glass vessel; tombs combining a certain type with others will be referred to and discussed.[8] In this way it is possible to verify the external dating evidence.

All illustrations of glass vessels are in scale 1:2 (50%) unless otherwise stated.

---

[8] Tombs combining types of pottery and glass are listed in Appendix 1. In the discussion it is the catalogue number that is most often mentioned, and in order to find the types related to the vessel in question the second table, which provides the context information, should be used.

The pre-blowing assemblage and early blown types (first century BC to the first decades of the first century AD)

Glass vessels dating to the time around the invention of glass-blowing just before the beginning of the Christian era are only represented by a few vessels in the Bahraini tombs. Some of these vessels were made by pre-blowing techniques, i.e. casting and core-forming, and others in early blown traditions, i.e. Type 2 marbled unguentarium. The types presented in the following are predominately defined by techniques, rather than shape, due to the relatively low numbers.

Unguentaria

Two types of unguentaria belong in this phase. They are both characterized by their manufacturing technique rather than by their shape.

Type 1: Core-formed bottle

The technique of making a glass bottle around a core of clay, mud and/or sand by trailing threads around it or dipping the core into the hot glass was probably invented in Mesopotamia in the middle of the second millennium BC (Grose 1989: 45–47). Until the invention of glass-blowing in the first century BC (Israeli 1991), core-forming was the technique used for making closed vessels. Only three core-formed bottles are recorded. Two of them were found in Shakhoura, Mound A1–96–97 (cat. nos 1.1 and 1.2) and both in the earliest phase of the necropolis. All three vessels have two threads attached to the shoulder and neck as handles.

 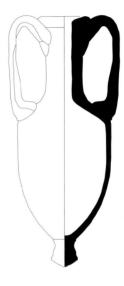

Figure 4. Cat. no. 1.1.   *Figure 5. Cat. no. 1.1*

Dating evidence and discussion

The two amphoriskoi in the shape of a transport amphora of the late Hellenistic period (cat. nos 1.1 and 1.2) are common in collections (e.g. Fossing 1940: 118–123; Hayes 1975: nos 34–37; Harden 1981: nos 352–361; Grose 1989: nos 168–176), whereas very few seem to have been reported from excavations (Kunina 1997: cat. nos 37 and 38 were excavated in the Pantikapaion necropolis in the

Cat. no.	Length	Max dia.	Rim dia.	Rim	Resting surface	Colour	Remarks
1.1	13.9	5.3	2.7	Outsp.	Attached knob	Black, white	Base knob and handles made of clear greenish glass.
1.2	14.2	5.8	2.5	Outsp.	Attached knob	Blue, yellow	
1.3	7.2	4.1	1.7	Outsp.	Round	Blue, yellow, red	

Table 2. Description of vessels of Type 1. Measurements in centimetres.

Cat. no.	BNM No	Area	Mound	Square	Context	Number	Remarks
1.1	A489	Shakhoura	A1-96-97	E10	Tomb	2	
1.2	A11265	Shakhoura	A1-96-97	D13	Tomb	47	Nenna 1999: no 271.
1.3	A11268	Saar	4-91-92	11	Tomb	14	Nenna 1999: no 272.

Table 3. Context information for vessels of Type 1.

Figure 6. Cat. no. 1.2.

Figure 7. Cat. no. 1.3.

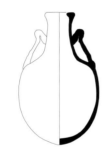

Figure 8. Cat. no. 1.3

early twentieth century). They are a very late type of core-formed vessels and are believed to have been produced between the late second and the end of the first century BC. A production in Cyprus has been suggested (Hayes 1975:14), in Aleppo in Syria (Fleming 1999: 12) and in the eastern Mediterranean/Syro-Palestinian area (Grose 1989: 169–174). The contextual relation of cat. no. 1.2 to a linear incised bowl (Type 3) supports a dating to the first century BC.

The little blue amphoriskos with marvered and festooned red and yellow decoration (cat. no. 1.3) finds no parallels, but the use of core-forming and red glass indicates a dating in the second century BC, which is supported by the find combinations with glazed and plain ware pottery, which can be dated to the period from *c.* 200–50 BC.

Type 2: Marbled unguentarium
The marbled unguentaria are made from a gather of multicoloured glass, similar to the blanks used for casting mosaic bowls. When the multicoloured gather was inflated, it showed veins of colours.

Dating evidence and discussion
The marbled unguentaria are believed to be early variants of blown vessels, since they rely on techniques used for casting mosaic bowls and also for blowing. Multicoloured vessels also appear to have been in fashion in the first half of the first century AD, but were replaced by naturally coloured (tinted) or colourless vessels in the 60s or 70s AD (Grose 1989: 261–262). The find combination of cat. no. 2.1 with a Type 4 vessel supports a dating in the first half of the first century AD, whereas the ves-

Cat. no.	Length	Max dia.	Rim dia.	Rim	Resting surface	Colour	Remarks
2.1	12	4.2	1.9		Pointed	Blue/white	Amphoriskos, One handle missing.
2.2	6.5	3.6	2	Outsp. & rolled-in	Concave		Similar to Type 6.
2.3	11.8	5	2.4	Outsp. & rolled-in	Concave	Blue	Fragmented. Similar to Type 6.
2.4	11.9	6.8				Blue/yellow/white	Similar to Type 6.

Table 4. Description of vessels of Type 2. Measurements in centimetres.

Cat. no.	BNM no.	Area	Mound	Square	Context	Number	Remarks
2.1	BM	Unplaced	Higham		Tomb	36	During-Caspers 1972/74: 152–55, During-Caspers 1980: 16. Not illustrated.
2.2	A11229	Hamad Town	1-94-95	C8	Tomb	5-C8	Nenna 1999: no 280.
2.3	A9523	Saar	11-95-96		Tomb	25	
2.4		Al-Hajar	2-1971		Tomb	1B	Boucharlat & Salles 1989: no 208, Vine 1993: 68. On display, BNM. Not illustrated.

Table 5. Context information for vessels of Type 2.

Figure 9. Cat. no. 2.2.

Figure 10. Cat. no. 2.2

Figure 11. Cat. no. 2.3.

Figure 12. Cat. no. 2.3

and purple glass arranged in a mosaic of spirals, creating a lively colour effect when cast. This vessel also has the ribbed decoration characterizing the pillar moulded bowls.

Type 3: Linear incised bowl
Only one so-called linear incised bowl has been recorded from the Bahraini tombs.

Dating evidence and discussion
Cat. no. 3.1 is a so-called cast monochrome linear incised bowl (Isings 1957: Form 1). These bowls are widely distributed and date from the last decades of the first century BC to the early years of our era (Grose 1989: 249; Isings 1957: Form 1). They are well attested at ed-Dur (Whitehouse 1998: nos 5–15; 2000: nos 4 and 11) and the contextual relation with a core-formed bottle (Type 1) supports this dating.

Figure 13. Cat. no. 3.1.

sels found together with cat. no. 2.4 in Al-Hajar, Mound 2–1971, Tomb 1B indicate that marbled unguentaria were still circulated probably into the second half of the first century AD.

Open vessels
The three bowls dating to this period are cast. Two of them are made of monochrome glass, where one has a ribbed decoration made in the casting process (pillar moulded bowl), and the other has incised lines applied after the casting. The last vessel, now in the British Museum, was made of black, white

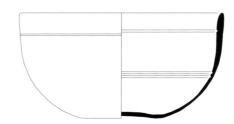

Figure 14. Cat. no. 3.1

Cat. no.	Length	Rim dia.	Rim	Resting surface	Colour	Remarks
3.1	5.7	11.5	Straight & polished	Concave	Clear brownish	Decorated with internal incised lines.

Table 6. Description of the vessel of Type 3. Measurements in centimetres.

Cat. no.	BNM no.	Area	Mound	Square	Context	Number	Remarks
3.1	A284	Shakhoura	A1-96-97	D13	Tomb	47	

Table 7. Context information for the vessel of Type 3.

Type 4: Pillar moulded bowl
The pillar moulded bowls are made in a double mould with the use of a monochrome blank or fragments of multicoloured canes creating a mosaic pattern.

Dating evidence and discussion
Cat. no. 4.1 is a so-called mosaic pillar moulded bowl dating to the very late first century BC and early first century AD (Isings 1957: Form 3a; Grose 1989: 279–282). They are widely distributed and fragments are reported from ed-Dur (Whitehouse 1998: nos 52–61; 2000: 96–98).

Monochrome pillar moulded bowls such as cat. no. 4.2 are very well represented among the finds from ed-Dur and are also a widely distributed type. They have been found in dated contexts spanning the period from the early first century BC, although the examples dating to the first half of the century are less symmetrical than the examples from ed-Dur and Bahrain, and brown to yellowish green in colour. A group of eight bowls are reported from Herculaneum, where they were waiting to be sold, when Vesuvius erupted and lava and ashes covered the city in AD 79. These bowls provide evidence that the type was still traded at that time (White-

Figure 15. Cat. no. 4.2.

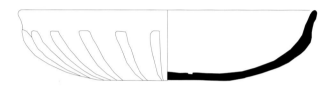

Figure 16. Cat. no. 4.2.

house 2000: 93–96; Isings 1957: 18–19). The contextual relation between cat. no. 4.1 and cat. no. 2.1 supports a dating in or around the first half of the first century AD.

Cat. no.	Length	Rim dia.	Rim	Resting surface	Colour	Remarks
4.1	4.6	13	Straight & polished		Purple/white	Mosaic.
4.2	4	15.5			Bluish	Monochrome.

Table 8. Description of vessels of Type 4. Measurements in centimetres.

Cat. no.	BNM no.	Area	Mound	Square	Context	Number	Remarks
4.1	BM 1999	Unplaced	Higham		Tomb	36	During-Caspers 1972/74: 152–55, During-Caspers 1980: 14. Not illustrated.
4.2		Abu-Saybi	1983	98	Tomb	2	On display BNM.

Table 9. Context information for vessels of Type 4.

Cat. no.	Length	Rim dia.	Rim	Resting surface	Colour	Remarks
5.1	6.5	7.8		Flat	Milky white	

Table 10. Description of the vessel of Type 5. Measurements in centimetres.

Cat. no.	BNM no.	Area	Mound	Square	Context	Number	Remarks
5.1	BM	Unplaced	Higham		Tomb	36	During-Caspers 1972/74: 152–55, During-Caspers 1980: 16. Not illustrated.

Table 11. Context information for the vessel of Type 5.

Type 5: Unique bowl
This bowl was made of translucent white glass.

Dating evidence and discussion
No parallels have been found, but the contextual relation with a Type 4 bowl and a Type 2 unguentarium indicates an early first-century AD date for this vessel.

The early Roman imperial period assemblage (first and second century AD)

The invention of glass-blowing, possibly in the later half of the first century BC, made a significant change to the production of glass vessels, since the production time for each vessel was reduced, especially for unguentaria. During the first decades of the first century AD, the vessels produced using the new technique became dominant in trade and distribution and core-made vessels were no longer produced. Cast bowls remained in production, but were supplemented with blown open forms. Free-blown unguentaria are the most frequent group found in the Bahraini tombs, but small mould-blown bottles are also common. Open shapes are less frequent in the tombs and only a few mould-blown and free-blown vessels are recorded.

Free-blown unguentaria
Unguentaria were common glass vessels in the early Roman Imperial period. They are all blown; the majority are free-blown, but many mould-blown small bottles have also been recorded.

Type 6: Plain unguentarium
Type 6 is the most common type of glass vessel from the Bahraini tombs with forty-three pieces recorded. The vessels are made of thin glass, mostly blue, green or brown or with a tint of these colours although one has a marvered white pattern (cat. no. 6.9). A cylindrical neck accounting for up to about half of the height of the vessel characterizes Type 6. Most often the transition between the neck and the body is well marked, although a few are more sloping, which is regarded to be a later feature (Isings 1957: 40). The rim is outsplayed with a rolled-in lip in most cases; only two specimens have an outsplayed, sheared rim (cat. nos 6.7 and 6.38). The body is bulbous or conical and the resting surface rounded, flat or slightly concave, sometimes with a pontil scar. Although the vessels forming this group have slight variations and further subdivisions of the type have been made by various scholars (see references below), such a division does not seem to reflect function, dating or origin[9] and is therefore not attempted in this study.

Figure 17. Cat. no. 6.1.

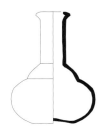

Figure 18. Cat. no. 6.1

Figure 19. Cat. no. 6.2.

Figure 20. Cat. no. 6.2

Figure 21. Cat. no. 6.3.

---

[9] The variations may, however, reflect workshops, but this topic will not be pursued in this study, since it seems rather unlikely that glass workshops were set up in Bahrain in the pre-Islamic period and all vessels are thus assumed to be imports.

Figure 22. Cat. no. 6.4.

Figure 23. Cat. no. 6.5.

Figure 24. Cat. no. 6.6.

Figure 25. Cat. no. 6.6

Figure 26. Cat. no. 6.7.

Figure 27. Cat. no. 6.8.

Figure 28. Cat. no. 6.9.

Figure 29. Cat. no. 6.10.

Figure 30. Cat. no. 6.11.

Figure 31. Cat. no. 6.12.

Figure 32. Cat. no. 6.13.

Figure 33. Cat. no. 6.14.

Figure 34. Cat. no. 6.15.　　*Figure 35. Cat. no. 6.16.*　　*Figure 36. Cat. no. 6.17.*　　*Figure 37. Cat. no. 6.18.*

Figure 38. Cat. no. 6.19.　　*Figure 39. Cat. no. 6.19*　　*Figure 40. Cat. no. 6.20.*　　*Figure 41. Cat. no. 6.21.*

Figure 42. Cat. no. 6.22.　　*Figure 43. Cat. no. 6.23.*　　*Figure 44. Cat. no. 6.24.*　　*Figure 45. Cat. no. 6.24*

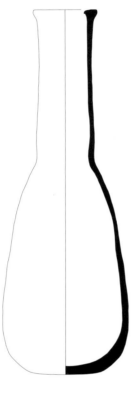

Figure 46. Cat. no. 6.25. *Figure 47. Cat. no. 6.26.*

Figure 48. Cat. no. 6.27.

Figure 49. Cat. no. 6.28. *Figure 50. Cat. no. 6.28* *Figure 51. Cat. no. 6.29.* *Figure 52. Cat. no. 6.29*

Figure 53. Cat. no. 6.30. *Figure 54. Cat. no. 6.31.* *Figure 55. Cat. no. 6.32.*

Figure 56. Cat. no. 6.33.   *Figure 57. Cat. no. 6.33.*   *Figure 58. Cat. no. 6.34.*   *Figure 59. Cat. no. 6.35.*

 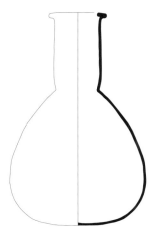  

Figure 60. Cat. no. 6.36.   *Figure 61. Cat. no. 6.36*   *Figure 62. Cat. no. 6.37.*   *Figure 63. Cat. no. 6.37*

Figure 64 and 65. Cat. no. 6.38   *Figure 66. Cat. no. 6.40.*   *Figure 67. Cat. no. 6.41.*   *Figure 68. Cat. no. 6.42.*

Cat. no.	Length	Max dia.	Rim dia.	Rim	Resting surface	Colour	Remarks
6.1	6.2	4.5	1.8	Outsp. & rolled-in	Concave	Blue/white	
6.2	6.2	5.5	2.6	Outsp. & rolled-in	Round	Brownish	
6.3	13.6	3.2			Flat w. ps	Clear bluish	Neck and rim missing.
6.4	12.8	7.9	3.7	Outsp. & rolled-in	Flat	Bluish	Thick walled fabric.
6.5	6.1	4.3	1.7	Outsp. & rolled-in	Flat	Bluish	
6.6	7.3	2.5	1.8	Outsp. & rolled-in		Brownish	Base missing.
6.7	7.6	5.6	2.3	Outsp. & sheared	Concave w. ps	Whitish	
6.8	10.9	6.3	2.3	Outsp. & rolled-in	Flat	Clear white	
6.9	7.4	5.6			Concave	Black/white	Neck and rim missing.
6.10	11.6	6.8	2.7	Outsp. & rolled-in	Concave	Greenish	
6.11	4.5	4.1			Convex	Clear greenish	Rim missing.
6.12	9.2	4.6	2	Outsp. & rolled-in	Concave	Clear greenish	
6.13	7.7	4.6	2.8	Outsp. & rolled-in	Round	Clear	
6.14	7.3		3	Outsp. & rolled-in	Concave w. ps	Greenish	Half.
6.15	4.5	2.9	1.5	Outsp. & rolled-in	Concave	Blue	
6.16	4.3	3	1.5	Outsp. & rolled-in	Round w. ps	Whitish	
6.17	12	6.9	2.2	Outsp. & rolled-in	Flat	Greenish	
6.18	10.5	3.5	2.6	Outsp. & rolled-in	Concave w. ps	Greenish	
6.19	7.7	2.9	1.6	Outsp. & rolled-in	Concave	Brownish	
6.20	10.4	4.7	2	Outsp. & rolled-in	Concave	Clear greenish	
6.21	7.3	6.3	2.7	Outsp. & rolled-in	Concave w. ps	Clear	
6.22	5.6	3.3	1.7	Outsp. & rolled-in	Round	Clear	
6.23		2.4			Concave	Green	Neck and rim missing.
6.24	4.4	2.9	1.5	Outsp. & rolled-in	Round w. ps	Clear greenish	
6.25	3.8	2.7	1.3	Outsp. & rolled-in	Round	Brownish	
6.26	3.4	2.6	1.2	Outsp. & rolled-in	Round	Brownish	
6.27	15.8	7.2	3.9	Outsp. & rolled-in	Flat w. ps	Clear brownish	Thick-walled fabric.
6.28	20	6.9	3	Outsp. & rolled-in	Flat w. ps	Clear greenish	Partly restored.
6.29	7.5	3.6	1.9	Outsp. & rolled-in	Concave	Blue	
6.30	6.4	2.4	2.1	Outsp. & rolled-in	Convex w. ps	Decayed to white	
6.31	10.1	3.9	2.3	Outsp. & rolled-in	Flat w. ps	Brownish	
6.32	11	3.1	2.6	Outsp. & rolled-in	Concave w. ps	Brownish	
6.33	6	5.2	2.1	Outsp. & rolled-in	Concave		
6.34		4.1			Concave w. ps		Neck and rim missing.
6.35	11.2	6.8	2.9	Outsp. & rolled-in	Concave		
6.36	11.5	7.3	3.1	Outsp. & rolled-in	Flat	Clear bluish	
6.37	8.6	4.9	1.9	Outsp. & rolled-in	Flat	Clear greenish	
6.38	5.5	3	1.6	Outsp. & Sheared	Flat	Clear greenish	Rim partly missing.
6.39				Outsp. & rolled-in			Decayed rim fragment.
6.40	8.2	4.7	2.8	Outsp. & rolled-in	Flat	Clear bluish	
6.41	6.5	4.3	2.3	Outsp. & rolled-in	Flat w. ps	Clear brownish	
6.42	3.7	2.5	1.4	Outsp. & rolled-in	Round w. ps	Clear brownish	
6.43	16.2	9				Greenish	

Table 12. Description of vessels of Type 6. Measurements in centimetres.

Cat. no.	BNM no.	Area	Mound	Square	Context	Number	Remarks
6.1	A8929	Shakhoura	7-93	F4	Tomb	82	
6.2	A11037	Shakhoura	1-92-93	I3	Tomb	175	
6.3	A8934	Al-Maqsha	2-92		Tomb	13	
6.4	1655-2-91?						No context information.
6.5	A8938	Hamad Town	1-94-95	B7	Tomb	2-B7	
6.6	A8905	Saar	11-95-96		Tomb	25	
6.7	A14387	Hamad Town	1986-87	A1	Tomb	1	
6.8	815-2-88						No context information.
6.9	A9066	Shakhoura	A1-96-97	C3	Tomb	87	
6.10	A9045	Saar	7-95-96	I4	Tomb	49	
6.11	A9069	Hamad Town	1-94-95	C8	Tomb	5-C8	
6.12	A9516	Saar	11-95-96		Tomb	25	
6.13	A9041	Hamad Town	10-89-90	I4			
6.14	A9076	Saar	12-91		Tomb	18	
6.15	A9072	Saar	7-95-96	C2	Tomb	137	
6.16	A9071	Saar	8-90-91		Tomb	6	
6.17	A9055	Saar	7-95-96	C4	Tomb	7	
6.18	10248-2-2000						No context information.
6.19	A9531	Shakhoura	2-91		Tomb	3	
6.20	A9525	Saar	7-95-96	C5	Tomb	78	
6.21	5708						No context information.
6.22	A9522	Saar	5-96-97	C3	Tomb	7	
6.23	A9521	Saar	7-95-96	I4	Tomb	49	
6.24	A9520	Hamad Town	1-94-95	E2	Tomb	2-E2	
6.25	A9527	Saar	1995	A3	Tomb	4	
6.26	A9527	Saar	1995	A3	Tomb	4	
6.27	A177						No context information.
6.28	A580	Al-Hajar	2-1971		Tomb	1B	Boucharlat & Salles 1989: no. 206.
6.29	A273	Saar	4-91-92	8	Tomb	36	
6.30	A619	Shakhoura	25-01		Outside tomb	17	
6.31	A2068	Saar	10-99-01	B	Tomb	46	
6.32	A943	Saar	1996-97	C5	Tomb	48	
6.33	A9002	Shakhoura	2-91-92		Tomb	47	
6.34	A1927	Saar	6-96	E3	Tomb	41	
6.35	A10348	Saar	1997	D1	Tomb	19	
6.36	A1119	Saar	7-95-96		Tomb	5	
6.37	A15076	Hamad Town	1-94-95	D9	Tomb	1-D9	Nenna 1999: no 294.
6.38	IMA 30	Hamad Town	1-94-95	B6	Tomb	5-B6	Nenna 1999: no 290.
6.39	A11134	Shakhoura	1-92-93	I2	Tomb	166	Not illustrated.
6.40	A798	Shakhoura	1-92-93	D6	Tomb	108	
6.41	A1608	Shakhoura	2-01-02	AE1	Tomb	57	
6.42	A12072	Saar	8-90-91		Tomb	6	
6.43		Al-Hajar	2-1971		Tomb	1B	Boucharlat & Salles 1989: no. 207. On display, BNM. Not illustrated.

Table 13. Context information for vessels of Type 6.

Dating evidence and discussion

Type 6 vessels were very common throughout the Roman Empire in the first century AD, and the type has been subdivided into several subtypes (i.e. Isings 1957: Forms 6, 8, 9, 26a, 28a; de Tommaso 1990: Types 38, 76; Cool & Price 1995: 159–162, 212–220; Vessberg & Westholm 1956: Flasks A.I.α, A.III.α, A.III.γ.1, A.VI, tubular unguentarium). In the East examples are published from ed-Dur (Whitehouse 1998: nos 68–71, 102; 2000: nos 38–40, 88 with marvered decoration), Seleucia (Negro Ponzi 2002: nos 7–8), numerous tombs in Dura Europos (Toll 1946) and fragments have been reported from Quseir Al-Qadim (Meyer 1992: nos 169, 192), whereas the type is generally absent from sites dated to the third century AD onwards, e.g. the necropolis at Tell Mahuz (Negro Ponzi 1968–1969), the late phases at Choche (Negro Ponzi 1984) and the necropolis at Abu Skhair (Negro Ponzi 1972). A

dating to the first and possibly into the second century AD is thus likely and supported by the many find combinations with well-dated mould-blown types of the first and early second century AD (see Appendix 1).

Type 7: Plain unguentarium

Type 7 is made of thicker glass than Type 6, which may reflect a different place of production. It is not a very common type in the Bahraini tombs with only five vessels recorded. The body is squat and accounts for only about one third of the total height of the vessel. The resting surface is concave with a pontil scar, except on one specimen where the underside is smooth (cat. no. 7.4). On cat. no. 7.1 the base has been kicked with a pointed tool before the pontil was applied. The neck is cylindrical and the transition between the body and the neck is well marked in this group. The rim is outsplayed with a rolled-in lip.

Figure 69. Cat. no. 7.1.

Figure 70. Cat. no. 7.2.

Figure 71. Cat. no. 7.3.

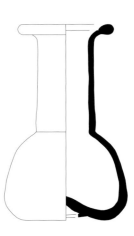

Figure 72. Cat. no. 7.3

Figure 73. Cat. no. 7.4.

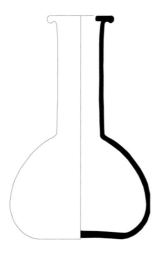

Figure 74. Cat. no. 7.4

Figure 75. Cat. no. 7.5.

Cat. no.	Length	Max dia.	Rim dia.	Rim	Resting surface	Colour	Remarks
7.1	12	6			Kicked	Whitish	Rim missing.
7.2	10.9	7.7	6.2	Outsp. & rolled-in	Concave w. ps	Green	
7.3	10.9	6.7	4.8	Outsp. & rolled-in	Concave w. ps	Turquoise	
7.4	12.3	7.6	3.6	Outsp. & rolled-in	Flat	Clear greenish	
7.5	11.8	7.9	5.6	Plain	Concave w. ps	Clear greenish	

Table 14. Description of vessels of Type 7. Measurements in centimetres.

Cat. no.	BNM no.	Area	Mound	Square	Context	Number	Remarks
7.1	A9059	Shakhoura	1-92-93	B7	Tomb	51	
7.2	A14378	Al-Hajar	2-1971		Tomb	1A	Boucharlat & Salles 1989: no. 205.
7.3	A543						No context information.
7.4	A15073	Abu-Saybi	1983	85	Tomb	1	Nenna 1999: no. 293.
7.5	A15077	Hamad Town	73-85-86		Tomb	27	Nenna 1999: no. 291.

Table 15. Context information for vessels of Type 7.

Dating evidence and discussion

Type 7 does not find close parallels in the West, or in the corpus from Cyprus presented by Vessberg & Westholm (1956), but is related to Isings' Form 28b (1957). Vessels similar to the ones from Bahrain are found in Dura Europos in tombs 7, 13, 40-IX and 46. Apart from Tomb 40-IX these tombs also contained vessels of Isings' Form 28b (1957) and vessels related to the later candlestick type, indicating a second century dating (Toll 1946; Isings 1957: 43). Other vessels of Type 7 are known from Karanis (Harden 1936: no. 805) and some of the thick-walled bases from Seleucia and Quseir al-Qadim may also be remnants of this variant (Negro Ponzi 2002: figs 5, 6, 9; Meyer 1992: nos 194–195). These eastern find spots could indicate that Type 7 may derive from a Mesopotamian (or Egyptian) production. The similarities with Type 6 and the contextual relation between cat. no. 7.2 and a mould-blown vessel, together with the external evidence strongly indicate a first or second century date for Type 7.

Figure 76. Cat. no. 8.1.

Type 8: "Baby feeding" bottle
One bottle with a spout has been recorded.

Dating evidence and discussion
Bottles with spouts are well known, although their function is not well understood. They have been labelled baby feeding bottles, but may rather have

Cat. no.	Length	Max dia.	Rim dia.	Rim	Resting surface	Colour	Remarks
8.1	6.9	5.5	3.5	Outsp. & rolled-in	Flat w. ps	Green	Spout 3.4 cm long. Opening 0.4 cm.

Table 16. Description of the vessel of Type 8. Measurements in centimetres.

Cat. no.	BNM no.	Area	Mound	Square	Context	Number	Remarks
8.1	A11251	Saar	7-95-96	A4	Tomb	44	Nenna 1999: no. 303.

Table 17. Context information for the vessel of Type 8.

Figure 77. Cat. no. 9.1.

Figure 78. Cat. no. 9.2.   *Figure 79. Cat. no. 9.2.*

been used as sprinklers. The similarity with Type 6 and the contextual association with a Type BD stemmed cup with handles in glazed ware, suggest a first-century AD date for the Bahraini example.

Type 9: Miniature jug
This type is typologically closely related to Type 6 and Type 13, but it has only one handle. Two vessels of this type have been recorded from the Bahraini tombs.

Dating evidence and discussion
A complete example was found in the necropolis in ed-Dur, where the majority of finds dates to the first century AD (Whitehouse 1998: no. 75). The type is known from Cyprus (Vessberg & Westholm 1956: Jug A.1.α) but it seems generally to have been rather uncommon. The stylistic relation with the more common and thus better-dated Types 6 and 13 supports a first-century AD date. Cat. no. 9.2 was also found with a Type 6 unguentarium.

Type 10: Amphoriskos
Six amphoriskos with a piriform body have been recorded. One example (cat. no. 10.4) has splashed decoration made by applying bits of glass in various colours to the gather and then reheating and inflating the vessel. This technique has only been used for this one vessel from Bahrain.

Dating evidence and discussion
The type is well represented throughout the Roman Empire and beyond (Isings 1957: Form 15; Kunina 1997: cat. nos 187–192; Whitehouse 1997: nos 293, 294; Grose 1974: 50). In the Near East examples are reported from the necropolis at ed-Dur (Whitehouse 1998: no. 77) and Dura Europos, Tomb 55 (Toll 1946: 94, no. 23). The vessels from dated contexts indicate a first-century AD date for this type (Isings 1957: 32–34; Whitehouse 1997: no. 293), which is supported by cat. no. 10.6 that was found with a number of first-century AD types.

Type 11: Amphoriskos with pointed base
This is a small group with only three vessels recorded. Two of the vessels (cat. nos 11.1–11.2) have a rounded base rather than the sharply pointed one of the last vessel.

Dating evidence and discussion
Type 11 is related to Isings' Form 60 (1957), although the vessels mentioned by Isings are larger. The shape of cat. no. 11.3 recalls the core-formed

Cat. no.	Length	Max dia.	Rim dia.	Rim	Resting surface	Colour	Remarks
9.1	7.4	5.8	2.7		Concave	Blue	The rim is folded out, up, in and up, making a fold below the vertical lip.
9.2	6.5	5.2	2.6	Outsp. & rolled-in	Flat	Purple	

Table 18. Description of vessels of Type 9. Measurements in centimetres.

Cat. no.	BNM no.	Area	Mound	Square	Context	Number	Remarks
9.1	A11266	Saar	7-96	B3	Tomb	42	Nenna 1999: no. 274.
9.2	A12743	Saar	7-95-96	B4	Tomb	5	

Table 19. Context information for vessels of Type 9.

36

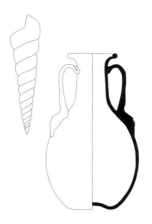

Figure 80. Cat. no. 10.1.   *Figure 81. Cat. no. 10.2*   *Figure 82. Cat. no. 10.2*

Figure 83. Cat. no. 10.3.   *Figure 84. Cat. no. 10.3.*   *Figure 85. Cat. no. 10.4*   *Figure 86. Cat. no. 10.5.*

Cat. no.	Length	Max dia.	Rim dia.	Rim	Resting surface	Colour	Remarks
10.1	8.3	5.5	2.5		Flat	Irrisident	Rim missing.
10.2	8.4	4.8	2.6	Outsp. & rolled-in	Concave	Blue	Body partly restored.
10.3	10.3	5.3	2.6	Outsp. & rolled-in	Concave	Blue & purple	Blue handles and purple body.
10.4	12.7	6.7	3.4	Outsp. & rolled-in	False ringfoot	Blue & yellow	Yellow and blue splat decoration. Body partly restored.
10.5	11.6	5.4	2.9			Blue	
10.6	8	5		Outsp. & rolled-in		Purple	

Table 20. Description of vessels of Type 10. Measurements in centimetres.

Cat. no.	BNM no.	Area	Mound	Square	Context	Number	Remarks
10.1	A9075	Abu Arshira			Tomb	120	
10.2	A14398	Hamad Town	83-85-86		Tomb	14	
10.3	A335	Saar	7-95-96	B4	Tomb	3	
10.4	A11272	Hamad Town	73-85-86		Tomb	54	
10.5	A11261	Saar	4-91-92	7	Tomb	44	
10.6		Al-Hajar	2-1971		Tomb	1B	Boucharlat & Salles 1989; no. 201. On display, BNM. Not illustrated.

Table 21. Context information for vessels of Type 10.

amphoriskoi (Type 1 and especially cat. nos 1.1 and 1.2), but examples have been found in contexts dating from the first to the fourth century AD (Isings 1957: 77–78). An amphoriskos with a pointed base was found in ed-Dur (Whitehouse 1998: no. 76), which together with the find combinations from Shakhoura, Mound 1-92-93, Tomb 175 indicates that the type was present in the Gulf in the first century AD. The composition analysis conducted on a sample from cat. no. 11.1 indicates that this vessel was made of plant-ash glass, which suggests that this vessel was produced in the East (see Appendix 2).

Type 12: Aryballos

The aryballoi are also called "bath flasks" after their function in the Roman world, where they were used in baths as containers for perfumed oils, which were used instead of soap. Examples have been found with a metal chain or handle attached to the glass handles of the vessel so the bather could carry the flask (see e.g. Woolley & Randall-MacIver 1910: pl. 38, find no. 7352). Although nothing indicates the existence of Roman baths in Bahrain in the Tylos period, the bath flasks are rather common in the Bahraini tombs with twenty vessels recorded. The bath flasks have a globular body with a concave resting surface without a pontil scar, a short cylindrical neck and a broad rim, either folded out, up, in and down, or out, down, up and slightly out. The handles are attached to the shoulder, dragged up, and attached to the neck, just below the rim. Purple glass seems to have been preferred, though it is often weathered into a golden or blackish appearance. On one example, the handles were green whereas the body was purple (cat. no. 12.3).

Figure 87. Cat. no. 11.1.   *Figure 88. Cat. no. 11.1.*

Figure 89. Cat. no. 11.2.   *Figure 90. Cat. no. 11.3.*

Cat. no.	Length	Max dia.	Rim dia.	Rim	Resting surface	Colour	Remarks
11.1	12.1	4.6	2.2	Outsp. & rolled-in	Round w. ps	Green	
11.2	12.4	6	3.1	Outsp. & rolled-in	Round w. ps	Greenish	
11.3	11.3	4.6			Pointed	Clear	The colour is clear to light purple. Rim missing.

Table 22. Description of vessels of Type 11. Measurements in centimetres.

Cat. no.	BNM no.	Area	Mound	Square	Context	Number	Remarks
11.1	A9515	Shakhoura	1-92-93	I3	Tomb	175	
11.2	A9514	Shakhoura	1-92-93	I3	Tomb	175	
11.3	A9060	Hamad Town	73-85-86		Tomb	60	

Table 23. Context information for vessels of Type 11.

Dating evidence and discussion

The bath flasks belong to Isings' Form 61 (1957), with examples dating from the first century AD until probably the fourth century AD. The type is found throughout the Roman Empire and affiliated areas (Isings 1957: 78–81), e.g. Cyprus (Vessberg & Westholm 1956: Aryballos I, II), Egypt (Harden 1936: no. 773), Seleucia (Negro Ponzi 2002: fig. 8.1), Uruk (van Ess & Pedde 1992: no. 1192), Qasr-I Abu Nasr (Whitcomb 1985: fig. 58.w), ed-Dur (Whitehouse 1998: no. 79). The form features a number of vari-ations some of which may have chronological or geographical significance. The Bahraini examples do not have the so-called "dolphin" handles, where a thread is attached to the shoulder of the vessel, dragged up along the wall of the neck and looped back to the shoulder, but all have a rather plain ribbon handle. Examples with such handles and the two rim types seen on the Bahraini vessels are not well distributed and the only exact parallels come from ed-Dur (Whitehouse 1998: no. 79), Pantikapaion in eastern Crimea (Kunina 1997: no. 228) and Cyprus

Figure 91. Cat. no. 12.1.

Figure 92. Cat. no. 12.2.

Figure 93. Cat. no. 12.3.

Figure 94. Cat. no. 12.4.

Figure 95. Cat. no. 12.5.

Figure 96. Cat. no. 12.7.

Figure 97. Cat. no. 12.8.

Figure 98. Cat. no. 12.9

Figure 99. Cat. no. 12.9

Figure 100. Cat. no. 12.10.

Figure 101. Cat. no. 12.11.

Figure 102. Cat. no. 12.12.

Figure 103. Cat. no. 12.13.

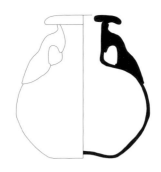

Figure 104. Cat. no. 12.13

Figure 105. Cat. no. 12.14.

Figure 106. Cat. no. 12.15.

Figure 107. Cat. no. 12.16.

Figure 108. Cat. no. 12.18.

Figure 109. Cat. no. 12.19.

Figure 110. Cat. no. 12.20.

Cat. no.	Length	Max dia.	Rim dia.	Rim	Resting surface	Colour	Remarks
12.1	6.8	6.7	4	Outsp. & rolled-in	Concave	Purple	
12.2	7.4	6.8	4	Outsp. & rolled-in	Concave	Purple	
12.3	7.4	6.9	3.2	Outwards folded	Concave	Green & purple	Green handles & purple body. Body partly restored.
12.4	7.5	7	4.1	Outsp. & rolled-in	Concave	Purple	
12.5	5.3	4.8	2.7	Outsp. & rolled-in	Concave	Clear greenish	Attempted surface restoration.
12.6			3.6	Outsp. & rolled-in	Flat	Purple	Fragments.
12.7	7.4	6.7	3.8	Outsp. & rolled-in	Concave	Purple	
12.8	7.8	6.9			Concave	Purple	
12.9	8.2	7.4	3.7	Outwards folded	Concave	Clear white	

Cat. no.	Length	Max dia.	Rim dia.	Rim	Resting surface	Colour	Remarks
12.10	6.9	6.5	3.5	Outsp. & rolled-in	Concave	Purple	
12.11	7.5	6.7	3.8	Outsp. & rolled-in	Concave	Purple	
12.12	7.3	6.6	3.4	Outsp. & rolled-in	Concave	Purple	
12.13	7.5	7.2	4	Outsp. & rolled-in	Concave	Purple	
12.14	7.6	6.9	3.8	Outwards folded	Concave	Purple	
12.15	7.4	6.9	3.5	Outsp. & rolled-in	Concave	Purple	
12.16	7.3	6.8	3.4	Outsp. & rolled-in	Concave	Pink	
12.17							No information.
12.18	6.8	6.1	3.7	Outsp. & rolled-in	Concave	Purple	
12.19	7.3	6.5	3.1	Outwards folded	Concave	Clear brownish	
12.20	8.2	7.7	3.9	Outsp. & rolled-in	Concave	Purple	Surface restored.

Table 24. Description of vessels of Type 12. Measurements in centimetres.

Cat. no.	BNM no.	Area	Mound	Square	Context	Number	Remarks
12.1	A8935	Abu Arshira	1973		Tomb	34	
12.2	A8943	Hamad Town	10-89-90	E4			
12.3							No context information.
12.4							No context information.
12.5	A9048						No context information.
12.6	A9057	Maqabah	1989	2	Tomb	1	Not illustrated.
12.7	A14383	Al-Hajar	2-1971		Tomb	1B	Boucharlat & Salles 1989: no. 219.
12.8	A14384	Hamad Town	73-85-86	1	Tomb	1	
12.9	A14399	Maqabah	1989	3	Tomb	7	
12.10	917-2-88	Abu Arshira	1973		Tomb	34	Boucharlat & Salles 1989: no. 217.
12.11	10246-2-2000						No context information.
12.12	10244-2-2000						No context information.
12.13	A9534	Hamad Town	73-85-86		Tomb	51	
12.14	A9539	Saar	5-95-96	D2	Tomb	12	
12.15	A270		1999-00				
12.16	A1486	Shakhoura	2-01-02	AD6	Tomb	95	
12.17	FM-A-985.BZ	Unplaced	T158-5		Outside tomb	1	Referred to in Jensen 2003: 143. Not illustrated.
12.18	A1053	Saar	12-95-96		Tomb	39	
12.19	A11270	Al-Hajar	2-1971		Tomb	1B	Boucharlat & Salles 1989: no. 221.
12.20	A11271	Abu Arshira	1973		Tomb	53	Boucharlat & Salles 1989: no. 216; Nenna 1999: no. 275.

Table 25. Context information for vessels of Type 12.

(Vessberg & Westholm 1956: Aryballos II), which may indicate a Syro/Palestinian origin. On the other hand, the composition analysis conducted on a sample from cat. no. 12.8 indicates that this vessel was produced in the East, as it was made of plant-ash glass (see Appendix 2). The many find combinations of the Bahraini vessels (see Appendix 1) support the broad dating suggested by Isings (1957).

Type 13: Amphoriskos
Type 13 is characterized by a globular body and compared to the bath flasks it has a long neck, accounting for nearly half of the height of the vessel. Seventeen vessels of the type were recorded.

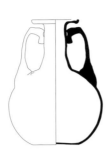

Figure 111. Cat. no. 13.1. Figure 112. Cat. no. 13.1 Figure 113. Cat. no. 13.2. Figure 114. Cat. no. 13.3.

Figure 115. Cat. no. 13.4. Figure 116. Cat. no. 13.6. Figure 117. Cat. no. 13.8. Figure 118. Cat. no. 13.9.

Figure 119. Cat. no. 13.10. Figure 120. Cat. no. 13.11. Figure 121. Cat. no. 13.12.

Dating evidence and discussion

The type may also be a variant of Isings' Form 61 (1957) (Hayes 1975: 54). Examples have been recovered in the Pantikapaion necropolis in eastern Crimea where they are believed to date to the mid- and third quarter of the first century AD of possibly eastern Mediterranean origin (Kunina 1997: cat. nos 340–344). An example with an outsplayed, sheared rim has been reported from the necropolis at ed-Dur (Whitehouse 1998: no. 78), which together with the find combinations from Bahrain (Appendix 1) supports a first-century date for Type 13.

 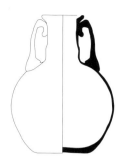  

Figure 122. Cat. no. 13.13.   *Figure 123. Cat. no. 13.13*   *Figure 124. Cat. no. 13.14.*   *Figure 125. Cat. no. 13.14.*

Figure 126. Cat. no. 13.15.   *Figure 127. Cat. no. 13.16.*   *Figure 128. Cat. no. 13.17.*   *Figure 129. Cat. no. 13.17*

Cat. no.	Length	Max dia.	Rim dia.	Rim	Resting surface	Colour	Remarks
13.1	6.8	5	2.6	Outsp. & rolled-in	Concave	Purple	
13.2	9.9	7	3.3	Outsp. & rolled-in	Round w. ps	Brownish	
13.3	7.3	5.4	2.5	Outsp. & rolled-in	Flat	Blue	
13.4	7.5	5.2	2.3	Outsp. & sheared	Concave	Blue	Handle missing.
13.5			2.3	Outsp. & rolled-in	Concave	Brownish	Fragments.
13.6	7.6	6.3	3.1	Outsp. & rolled-in	Concave	Brownish	Fragments & handle missing.
13.7			2.9	Outsp. & rolled-in		Brownish	Fragments.
13.8	7.3	5	2	Outsp. & sheared	Concave	Purple	Rim partly missing.
13.9	7.5	5.7	2.4	Outsp. & rolled-in	Concave	Brownish	
13.10	5.5	4.3	2.8	Outsp. & rolled-in	Concave w. ps	Clear brownish & green	Handles green, body clear-brownish.
13.11	8.2	6	3	Outwards folded	Flat	Brown & blue	The rim is folded out, down, up and rolled-in.
13.12	7.8	6	2.4	Outsp. & rolled-in	Concave	Blue	
13.13	7.5	5.4	2.4	Outsp. & sheared	Concave	Blue & pink	Blue handles and pink body.
13.14	8.4	6.5	2.8	Outsp. & rolled-in	Raised base	Green	Raised base.
13.15	7.5	5			Concave	Clear brownish	Upper neck and rim missing.
13.16	6.7	5.1	3	Outsp. & rolled-in	Pad	Blue/white	
13.17	7.3	5.8	3	Outsp. & sheared	Concave	Green & purple	Handles green, body brown or purple.

Table 26. Description of vessels of Type 13. Measurements in centimetres.

Cat. no.	BNM no.	Area	Mound	Square	Context	Number	Remarks
13.1	A8928	Shakhoura	1-92-93	F1	Tomb	123	
13.2	A8942	Saar	5-87-88			94	
13.3	A9046	Saar	7-95-96	C2	Tomb	137	
13.4	394	Saar	2-91-92	C2/C3	Tomb	22	
13.5	A9052	Saar	7-95-96	C5	Tomb	77	Not illustrated.
13.6	A9054	Saar	5-96-97	C6	Tomb	57	
13.7	A9053	Shakhoura	1-92-93	H3	Tomb	156	Not illustrated.
13.8	A14400	Saar	2-85-86	2	Tomb	8	
13.9	A9533	Saar	5-96-97	B5	Tomb	63	
13.10	A9532	Shakhoura	4-91		Jar	1	
13.11	A328	Hamad Town	1-94-95	C2	Tomb	2-C2	
13.12	A332	Shakhoura	1-92-93	F1	Tomb	122	
13.13	A336	Shakhoura	1-92-93	D7	Tomb	108	
13.14	A234	Saar	4-91-92	8	Tomb	36	
13.15	A2584						No context information.
13.16	A11244	Hamad Town	1-94-95	C4	Tomb	4-C4	Nenna 1999: no. 274.
13.17	A1591	Saar	10-99-01	C	Tomb	105	

Table 27. Context information for vessels of Type 13.

Mould-blown unguentaria

Forming and decorating glass vessels by inflating gathers of molten glass in a mould was probably invented in Syria and Palestine in or around the second quarter of the first century AD and the method quickly spread to most parts of the Roman Empire, although this is still disputed (Stern 1995: 65–66). Apart from a single mould-blown conical beaker (cat. no. 23.1) the mould-blown vessels from the Bahraini tombs are all small unguent bottles similar in size. The group is well discussed in recent museum catalogues (e.g. Hayes 1975; Stern 1995; Whitehouse 2000) and even though the number of mould-blown bottles from securely dated contexts is rather limited, the elaborate decorative schemes of these vessels argues for a fairly narrow dating of the individual types and a few well-dated examples are thus sufficient.

Type 14: Miniature transport amphora

Five mould-blown bottles shaped as miniature transport amphorae are recorded. Their bodies are decorated with horizontal or vertical ribs and they have a round resting surface.

Dating evidence and discussion

Imitations in glass of transport amphorae are not uncommon; examples are reported from Italy, the eastern Mediterranean, the Black Sea area and the Near East. The type was in use by AD 79, since

Figure 130. Cat. no. 14.1.   *Figure 131. Cat. no. 14.1*

Figure 132. Cat. no. 14.2.

Figure 133. Cat. no. 14.3.   Figure 134. Cat. no. 14.4.   Figure 135. Cat. no. 14.5.

Cat. no.	Length	Max dia.	Rim dia.	Rim	Resting surface	Colour	Remarks
14.1	7	3.8	2.6	Outsp. & rolled-in	Round	Purple	Partly restored.
14.2	7.7	3.7	2.8	Outsp. & sheared	Round	Purple	Body partly restored & base missing.
14.3	7.9	3.7	3	Outsp. & rolled-in	Round	Purple	Body partly restored.
14.4	6.8	4.1	2.5	Outsp. & rolled-in	Round	Purple	
14.5	7.5	3.8	2.6	Outsp. & rolled-in	Round	Clear purple	Body partly restored.

Table 28. Description of vessels of Type 14. Measurements in centimetres.

Cat. no.	BNM no.	Area	Mound	Square	Context	Number	Remarks
14.1	A281		99-00				
14.2	A11273	Al-Hajar	2-1971		Tomb	1A	Boucharlat & Salles 1989: no. 203; Nenna 1999: no. 278.
14.3	A11231	Shakhoura	1-92-93	AA2	Tomb	26	Nenna 1999: no. 277 (with incorrect context information).
14.4	A11258	Maqabah	1989	3	Tomb	7	Nenna 1999: no. 279 (with incorrect context information).
14.5							No context information.

Table 29. Context information for vessels of Type 14.

the earliest datable examples are two vessels from Pompeii (Stern 1995: 157–158). This dating is supported by the find combinations of cat. nos 14.2, 14.3 and 14.4, which have been found with vessels of Type 7, 12, 18 and 19.

Type 15: Date-flasks

The date-flasks, which imitate the ripe date fruit, are relatively common grave goods in the tombs and twenty-three flasks or diagnostic fragments have been recorded. All the Bahraini examples seem to have been brown or golden in colour, although the type has also been made in other colours (e.g. Stern 1995: no. 89 is blue).

Dating evidence and discussion

The earliest securely dated examples are from Pompeii and Herculaneum (Scatozza & Lucia 1986: 52), thus showing it was in use by AD 79. A bot-

tle that was found in a grave in Trier may be of a slightly earlier date, since this grave has been dated to the Claudian period (41–54 AD). This dating is based on the content of ceramic vessels in the grave (Goethert-Polashek 1977: 96, Form 68). I am, however, sceptical of such a precise dating being based on the typology of other vessels, which may have been used for decades before being used as funeral offerings. Further examples are reported from second-century AD contexts (Isings 1957: 94, Form 78b), though these could be heirlooms rather than reflecting a second-century production (Whitehouse 2000: 47). The date-flasks are widely distributed and examples are found in western Europe, the eastern Mediterranean and the Near East (Stern 1995: 93). Date-flasks have also been found in ed-Dur (Whitehouse 1998: nos 109–111; 2000: no. 102) and are relatively common in the Bahraini tombs. A Syro-Palestinian origin has been suggested for the date-flasks

Figure 136. Cat. no. 15.1.   *Figure 137. Cat. no. 15.2.*   *Figure 138. Cat. no. 15.2.*   *Figure 139. Cat. no. 15.4.*

Figure 140. Cat. no. 15.5.   *Figure 141. Cat. no. 15.5*   *Figure 142. Cat. no. 15.7.*   *Figure 143. Cat. no. 15.7.*

Figure 144. Cat. no. 15.9.   *Figure 145. Cat. no. 15.11*   *Figure 146. Cat. no. 15.12.*   *Figure 147. Cat. no. 15.12.*

Figure 148. Cat. no. 15.13.   *Figure 149. Cat. no. 15.14.*   *Figure 150. Cat. no. 15.15.*

Figure 151. Cat. no. 15.16.   *Figure 152. Cat. no. 15.16.*   *Figure 153. Cat. no. 15.17*   *Figure 154. Cat. no. 15.18.*

Figure 155. Cat. no. 15.19.

Cat. no.	Length	Max dia.	Rim dia.	Rim	Resting surface	Colour	Remarks
15.1	9.6	3.6	2.4	Outsp. & rolled-in	Round	Brownish	
15.2	6.6	3.1	1.6	Outsp. & rolled-in	Round	Brownish	
15.3	9.8	3.9	2.9		Round	Brownish	
15.4	6.8	3	1.8	Outsp. & rolled-in	Round	Brownish	
15.5	7.2	3.1	2	Outsp. & rolled-in	Round	Clear brownish	
15.6		3.5	2.5	Outsp. & rolled-in		Brownish	Fragments.
15.7	8.8	3.5	2.4	Outsp. & rolled-in	Round	Brownish	
15.8		3.4	2.2	Outsp. & rolled-in	Round	Brownish	Fragments.
15.9	7.1	3.1	1.9	Outsp. & rolled-in	Round	Brown	
15.10	6.8	2.9			Round	Brownish	Rim missing.
15.11	6.7	3.2	1.9	Outsp. & rolled-in	Round	Brown	
15.12	8.2	3.1	2.2	Outsp. & rolled-in	Round		
15.13	6.7	3.3	1.7	Outsp. & rolled-in	Round		
15.14	6.3	3.2			Round	Brown	Rim missing.
15.15	6.7	3.1	2	Outsp. & sheared	Round	Brown	
15.16	7	3.1	1.9	Outsp. & rolled-in	Round	Clear brownish	Tool-marks on lower neck.
15.17	6.2	3.1	2.1	Outsp. & rolled-in	Round	Clear brownish	
15.18	9.3	3.4	2.5	Outsp. & rolled-in	Round	Brownish	Rim & body partly restored.
15.19	7	3.6	1.6	Outsp. & rolled-in	Round	Decayed cream	A flat type of date-flask.
15.20							Rim fragment.
15.21							Rim fragment.
15.22							Rim fragment.
15.23							Rim fragment.

Table 30. Description of vessels of Type 15. Measurements in centimetres.

Cat. no.	BNM no.	Area	Mound	Square	Context	Number	Remarks
15.1	A8932	Shakhoura	1-92-93	I3	Tomb	175	
15.2	A11038	Shakhoura	1-92-93	D7	Tomb	75	
15.3	60	Saar	6-96	D2	Tomb	33	Vessel lost 2004. Not illustrated.
15.4	A9049	Hamad Town	83-85-86		Jar	8	
15.5	A16632	Hamad Town	1-94-95	B7	Tomb	4-B7	
15.6	A9073	Hamad Town	73-85-86		Tomb	55	Not illustrated.
15.7	A9536	Shakhoura	1-92-93	I2	Tomb	166	
15.8	A9529	Shakhoura	1-92-93	H4	Tomb	170	Not illustrated.
15.9	A294	Saar	7-95-96	C5	Tomb	77	
15.10	A1729		2000				Not illustrated.
15.11	A1095	Saar	5-96-97	C5	Tomb	59	
15.12	A12742	Shakhoura	2-91-92		Tomb	23	
15.13	A9006	Shakhoura	2-91-92		Jar	1	
15.14	A1728	Saar	10-99-01	B	Tomb	30	
15.15	A3155	Karranah	SMG1		Tomb	DIII-1	Herling 2003: abb. 150.SMG1-9.
15.16	A11230	Hamad Town	1-94-95	E2	Tomb	2-E2	Nenna 1999: no. 285 (with incorrect context information).
15.17	A11257	Saar	11-95-96		Tomb	20	Nenna 1999: no. 284.
15.18							
15.19	A12744	Saar	2-91-92	C2/C3	Tomb	22	
15.20	A11134	Shakhoura	1-92-93	I2	Tomb	166	Not illustrated.
15.21	A11134	Shakhoura	1-92-93	I2	Tomb	166	Not illustrated.
15.22	A11134	Shakhoura	1-92-93	I2	Tomb	166	Not illustrated.
15.23	A11134	Shakhoura	1-92-93	I2	Tomb	166	Not illustrated.

Table 31. Context information for vessels of Type 15.

(Stern 1995: 93), but the composition analysis con- ducted on a sample from cat. no. 15.20 indicates that this vessel was made of plant-ash glass, which suggest that the type was also produced in the East (see Appendix 2). The find combinations from the Bahraini tombs (Appendix 1) support a first- and early second-century AD dating of the type.

Type 16: Hexagonal bottle

Two hexagonal bottles are recorded from the Bahraini tombs, but their exact context information is unfor- tunately lost. They are very similar, probably from the same workshop and perhaps even from the same mould. The main scheme of the decoration is six pan- els, each illustrating fruits. The same kind of fruit is represented twice and the three fruits are pomegran- ate, a bunch of grapes and probably cedar cones.

Figure 156. Cat. no. 16.1.

Dating evidence and discussion

The hexagonal bottles are made with a wide vari- ety of motifs, e.g. birds, vessels, masks, fruits and mixed symbols in high relief. However, only a very few of these vessels and none of the fruit-type to which the Bahraini vessels belong have been found in dated contexts. The few hexagonal bottles from dated contexts seem to date from the second quarter of the first century AD, with a rather short period of use (Stern 1995: 83–84; Isings 1957: 94, Form 78b). A base fragment of a hexagonal bottle is re- ported from ed-Dur (Whitehouse 2000: no. 98).

 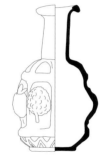

Figure 157. Cat. no. 16.2. *Figure 158a. Cat. no. 16.2*

Type 17: Lenticular bottle

Only one lenticular bottle is in the Bahraini stores and the exact context information is lost.

Dating evidence and discussion

Not a very common type. It seems to have been made and used mainly in the eastern Mediterranean in the first century AD (Stern 1995: 155).

Figure 158b. Cat. no. 16.2

Cat. no.	Length	Max dia.	Rim dia.	Rim	Resting surface	Colour	Remarks
16.1	7.8	4.5	2.3	Outsp. & rolled-in	Flat	Blue	Fragments.
16.2	8	3.7		Outsp. & rolled-in	Flat	Blue	

Table 32. Description of vessels of Type 16. Measurements in centimetres.

Cat. no.	BNM no.	Area	Mound	Square	Context	Number	Remarks
16.1							No context information.
16.2	A11267						Nenna 1999: no. 281 (with incorrect context information).

Table 33. Context information for vessels of Type 16.

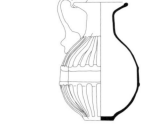

Figure 159. Cat. no. 17.1.   Figure 160. Cat. no. 17.1.   Figure 161. Cat. no. 18.1.   Figure 162. Cat. no. 18.1

Type 18: Scroll or lozenges decorated bottle

The scroll or lozenges decorated bottles often have a band of scrolls or triangles (lozenges) between vertical tongues or vertical flutes. They can be finished with either one or two handles. Eight examples have been recorded from Bahrain.

Dating evidence and discussion

Type 18 is well described in the literature. It dates probably to the second half of the first century AD and was most likely produced in the Syro-Palestinian region (Stern 1995: 150–154; Whitehouse 2001: 42–43). The dating suggested by external evidence is well supported by the find combinations (Appendix 1).

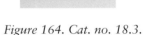

Figure 163. Cat. no. 18.2.   Figure 164. Cat. no. 18.3.

Type 19: Squat bottle with two handles

Only one complete squat bottle with two handles has been recorded together with a fragment.

Dating evidence and discussion

This type seems to be rare and only a fragment from ed-Dur may be a parallel to these vessels (Whitehouse 2000: no. 103). This very limited evidence, together with the find combinations of cat. no. 19.2 from Shakhoura, Mound 1-92-93, Tomb 166, indicate a first-century AD date for the type. Such a dating is supported by the fact that mould-blown vessels seem to be most common in the first century AD (Stern 1995: 65).

Cat. no.	Length	Max dia.	Rim dia.	Rim	Resting surface	Colour	Remarks
17.1	7.4	5.5	2.9	Outsp. & rolled-in		Irrisident	

Table 34. Description of vessel of Type 17. Measurements in centimetres.

Cat. no.	BNM no.	Area	Mound	Square	Context	Number	Remarks
17.2							No context information.

Table 35. Context information for the vessels of Type 17.

Figure 165. Cat. no. 18.4.

Figure 166. Cat. no. 18.4

Figure 167. Cat. no. 18.5.

Figure 168. Cat. no. 18.5

Figure 169. Cat. no. 18.6.

Figure 170. Cat. no. 18.6

Figure 171. Cat. no. 18.7.

Cat. no.	Length	Max dia.	Rim dia.	Rim	Resting surface	Colour	Remarks
18.1	6.9	4.4	2.5	Outsp. & rolled-in	Flat	Bluish	Half vessel.
18.2	8.1	4.3	2.6	Outsp. & rolled-in	Flat	Irrisident	Half of rim, handle and part of body missing.
18.3	7.8	4.4	2.9	Outsp. & rolled-in	Flat		Body clear white, handle blue.
18.4	7.3	4.5	2.8	Outsp. & rolled-in	Flat	Blue	
18.5	7.6	4.3	2.8	Outsp. & rolled-in	Flat	Green	Pink body and green handles.
18.6	7.5	5.4	2.7	Outsp. & rolled-in	Flat	Blue/white	
18.7	7.7		2.9	Outsp. & rolled-in			Half vessel & base missing.
18.8	7	4.2			Flat		

Table 36. Description of vessels of Type 18. Measurements in centimetres.

Cat. no.	BNM no.	Area	Mound	Square	Context	Number	Remarks
18.1	2262-2-90	Hamad Town	70A-85-86		Tomb	1	
18.2	342-2-91	Al-Hajar	2-1971		Tomb	1B	Boucharlat & Salles 1989: no. 200.
18.3	91-2-1						No context information.
18.4	A9537	Saar	7-95-96	C2	Tomb	137	
18.5	A262	Al-Hajar	2-1971		Tomb	1B	Boucharlat & Salles 1989: no. 198.
18.6	A11260	Shakhoura	1-92-93	H4	Tomb	170	Nenna 1999: no. 276 (wrongly assigned to Tomb 17).
18.7	A2058	Shakhoura	2-01-02	AC4	Tomb	61	
18.8		Al-Hajar	2-1971		Tomb	1A	Boucharlat & Salles 1989: no. 199. Vessel lost 2004. Not illustrated.

Table 37. Context information for vessels of Type 18.

Figure 172. Cat. no. 19.1.

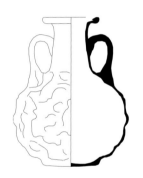

Figure 173. Cat. no. 19.1.

Type 20: Bottle, imitating a bunch of grapes

Only one complete bottle of Type 20 has been recorded.

Dating evidence and discussion

An example is known from Pompeii, documenting that the type was in use in the second half of the first century AD. Vessels imitating a bunch of grapes, but with handles, remained in use in the second and probably into the third century AD (Isings 1957: Form 91). Cat. no. 20.1 has also been found with other glass vessels most likely dating to the first century AD.

Cat. no.	Length	Max dia.	Rim dia.	Rim	Resting surface	Colour	Remarks
19.1	8.3	6.4	3	Outsp. & rolled-in	Raised base w. ps	Green	
19.2				Outsp. & rolled-in			Fragment of rim and neck.

Table 38. Description of vessels of Type 19. Measurements in centimetres.

Cat. no.	BNM no.	Area	Mound	Square	Context	Number	Remarks
19.1	A9535	Shakhoura	1-92-93	AA2	Tomb	26	
19.2	A11134	Shakhoura	1-92-93	I2	Tomb	166	Not illustrated.

Table 39. Context information for vessels of Type 19.

Free-blown beakers and bowls

Four free-blown open vessels date to this period. Two vessels are beakers and two are small bowls.

Type 21: Beaker with applied decoration

Two beakers with applied decoration have been found in Bahrain. The one is complete and made of clear colourless glass. The other vessel lacks the lower part and is weathered to look like mother-of-pearl. The outsplayed rims are cracked off; the walls are almost vertical and decorated with a continuous band of six or seven panels made of applied trails. Below these, the walls curve inwards to the tubular base.

Dating evidence and discussion

This type dates probably to the second half of the first century AD and remained in use until the mid-second century AD. It was most common in northern Italy and Switzerland with a few examples from Germany, France and Hungary (Isings 1957: Form 33). Similar vessels are said to have been manufac-

tured in the eastern Roman Empire and perhaps even outside the eastern frontier (Whitehouse 1998: 45). An example has been found in ed-Dur (*ibid.* no. 104), which together with the example from the Al-Hajar assemblage (cat. no. 21.1), supports the dating suggested above.

Type 22: Bowl with cut-out ridge

The rim is folded down and up creating a "collar", and ends in an outsplayed lip.

Dating evidence and discussion

This little bowl is common in the West and well dated to the second half of the first century AD (Isings 1957: Form 69a). A rim of a bowl with a fold below the rim has been found in Seleucia (Negro Ponzi 2002: fig. 2.19), and two complete specimens were recovered from the necropolis in ed-Dur (Whitehouse 1998: nos 63-63) together with some fragments (Whitehouse 1998: no. 62; 2000: no. 34).

Cat. no.	Length	Max dia.	Rim dia.	Rim	Resting surface	Colour	Remarks
20.1	7.5	4.3					Decayed to white.

Table 40. Description of vessel of Type 20. Measurements in centimetres.

Cat. no.	BNM no.	Area	Mound	Square	Context	Number	Remarks
20.1		Al-Hajar	2-1971		Tomb	1B	Boucharlat & Salles 1989: no. 208; Vine 1993: 68. On display BNM. Not illustrated.

Table 41. Context information for the vessel of Type 20.

Cat. no.	Length	Rim dia.	Rim	Resting surface	Colour	Remarks
21.1		8.8	Outsp. & cracked off		Clear greenish	Base missing.
21.2	12.4	10	Outsp. & cracked off	Raised base	Clear white	

Table 42. Description of vessels of Type 21. Measurements in centimetres.

Cat. no.	BNM no.	Area	Mound	Square	Context	Number	Remarks
21.1	A14377	Al-Hajar	2-1971		Tomb	1B	Boucharlat & Salles 1989: no. 204.
21.2	A787	Shakhoura	25-01		Tomb	26	

Table 43. Context information for vessels of Type 21.

Figure 174. Cat. no. 21.1.

Figure 175. Cat. no. 21.2.

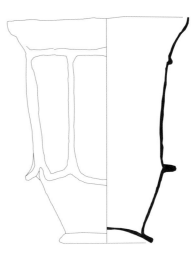

Figure 176. Cat. no. 21.2.

Figure 177. Cat. no. 22.1.

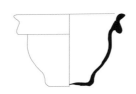

Figure 178. Cat. no. 22.2

Figure 179. Cat. no. 22.2.

Mould-blown beaker

Only one mould-blown beaker of the first to second century AD has been recorded in the Bahraini collection. It is a mould-blown conical beaker, which is a very common Roman type.

Type 23: Mould-blown conical beaker

The mould-blown conical beaker is a base fragment with a decoration of knot-shaped knobs, maybe representing the knots of Hercules' club. The vessel is blown of transparent glass with a bluish tint in a four-part mould and has three moulded concentric circles under the base.

Dating evidence and discussion

This is a common type with a wide distribution from England to Arabia and datable to the mid- and second half of the first century AD (Isings 1957: Form 31; Hayes 1975: no. 83; Price & Cottam 1998: 65–66; Stern 1995: nos 8–10). An example is also known from ed-Dur (Whitehouse 2000: no. 97).

Cat. no.	Length	Rim dia.	Rim	Resting surface	Colour	Remarks
22.1	4	6.1	Flaring	Raised base	Blue	
22.2	2.5	6	Flaring	Concave w. ps	Purple	The ps has been partly polished away.

Table 44. Description of vessels of Type 22. Measurements in centimetres.

Cat. no.	BNM no.	Area	Mound	Square	Context	Number	Remarks
22.1	A1483	Shakhoura	2-01-02	ACD4	Tomb	41	
22.2	A98	Saar	10-99-01	B	Tomb	45	

Table 45. Context information for vessels of Type 22.

Cat. no.	Length	Base dia.	Resting surface	Colour	Remarks
23.1	7.6	5.6	Flat	Clear	Made in a four-part mould. Three circles, *c.* 1 mm wide, under the base 10, 34, and 40 mm in diameter.

Table 46. Description of the vessel of Type 23. Measurements in centimetres.

Cat. no.	BNM no.	Area	Mound	Square	Context	Number	Remarks
23.1	A8937	Abu-Saybi	1985	A5			

Table 47. Context information for vessels of Type 23.

Figure 180. Cat. no. 23.1.

The late Parthian and early Sasanian assemblage (second to fifth century AD)

In this period, the glass seems to be of a poorer quality than in the previous period. The glass now contains many air bubbles, the walls of the vessels are thicker and the variety of strong colours used before is replaced with a palette containing very little apart from green or greenish/bluish tinted glass. Mould-blown vessels and other shapes with a more complex decorative scheme become rare in this period.

Free-blown unguentaria

Free-blown unguentaria is also the most common group of glass vessels of this period and twelve types have been described.

Type 24: Flask with funnel mouth

Type 24 is characterized by a relatively long, flaring neck and two of the vessels have a coil around the neck just below the vertical lip. The bases are rounded with a pontil scar. Only four vessels of this type have been recorded.

Dating evidence and discussion

Type 24 resembles very closely Isings' Form 104b (1957) and is mainly a fourth-century AD type. The coil around the neck, which is seen on two of the Bahraini vessels is not, however, seen on examples from the West, but Isings refers to similar examples from Karanis (*ibid.* 123–124). Further examples

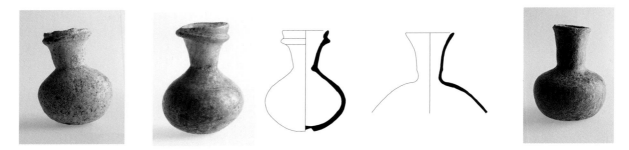

Figure 181. Cat. no. 24.1. Figure 182 and 183. Cat. no. 24.2. Figure 184. Cat. no. 24.3. Figure 185. Cat. no. 24.4.

Cat. no.	Length	Max dia.	Rim dia.	Rim	Resting surface	Colour	Remarks
24.1	5.3	4.1	2.6	Fold under lip	Round w. ps	Clear greenish	
24.2	5.7	4.1	2.7	Fold under lip	Round w. ps	Greenish	
24.3			2.7	Sheared		Decayed cream	Rim fragment.
24.4	6.1	4.8	2.5	Sheared	Concave w. ps	Blue	

Table 48. Description of vessels of Type 24. Measurements in centimetres.

Cat. no.	BNM no.	Area	Mound	Square	Context	Number	Remarks
24.1	A8924	Saar	5-87-88	C6	Mound fill		
24.2	A9074	Saar	163-91-92		Tomb	4	
24.3	A11031	Saar	5-95-96	E2	Tomb	36	
24.4	938-2-88						Boucharlat & Salles 1989: no. 213.

Table 49. Context information for vessels of Type 24.

  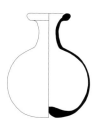

Figure 186. Cat. no. 25.1.   *Figure 187. Cat. no. 25.2.*   *Figure 188. Cat. no. 25.2*

with a coil have been found in Abu Skhair (Negro Ponzi 1972: nos 34–37), Choche (Negro Ponzi 1984: fig. 1.16–17) and Tell Mahuz (Negro Ponzi 1968–1969: no. 80). These sites support an early Sasanian date for Type 24 and indicate that the type (with the neck coil) was produced and distributed only in the East. The contextual relation of cat. nos 24.2 and 24.3 to vessels of Types 27, 28 and 34 supports the dating evidence mentioned above.

Type 25: Bulbous flask

This type is quite common in the Bahraini tombs, since twenty-two vessels have been recorded. They are characterized by a concave profile of the neck, in contrast to the cylindrical neck of Type 6, and they often have a restriction inside the neck (neck diaphragm). The rim is outsplayed with a rolled-in lip and the concave resting surface was often kicked with a pointed tool, before the pontil was applied.

Cat. no.	Length	Max dia.	Rim dia.	Rim	Resting surface	Colour	Remarks
25.1	5.9	4.2	1.6	Outsp.	Kicked	Green	
25.2	5.8	4.4	2.3	Outsp. & rolled-in	Kicked w. ps	Greenish	
25.3	7.3	4.3	2.4	Outsp. & rolled-in	Round w. ps	Clear	
25.4	5.3	4.5	2.5	Outsp. & rolled-in	Flat w. ps	Greenish	
25.5	5.8	4.5	2.7	Outsp. & rolled-in	Kicked	Greenish	Blue knobs as decoration.
25.6	4.6	5.2			Concave w. ps	Purple	Neck and rim missing.
25.7	4.7	4.1	2	Outsp. & rolled-in	Concave	Brownish	
25.8	3.8	3.3			Round	Bluish	Rim missing.
25.9	7.2	4.7	2.3	Outsp. & rolled-in	Flat	Greenish	Fragments.
25.10			2.6	Outsp. & rolled-in	Concave	Purple	Fragments.
25.11	6.4	3.7	1.7	Outsp. & rolled-in	Concave w. ps	Greenish	Partly restored.
25.12	6.7	4.6	2.5	Outsp. & rolled-in	Kicked	Greenish	
25.13	7.8	6.2	3.3	Outsp. & rolled-in	Concave w. ps	Clear bluish	
25.14	9.5	6.5	3.2	Outsp. & rolled-in	Flat w. ps	Bluish	
25.15	4	3.1	1.6	Outsp. & rolled-in	Flat	Clear bluish	
25.16	4.6	2.9	1.5	Outsp. & rolled-in	Round	Brownish	
25.17	6.5	6	2.7	Outsp. & rolled-in	Kicked	Clear greenish	
25.18	6.2	4.3	2.1	Outsp. & rolled-in	Concave	Green	
25.19	6.4	4.5	2.5	Outsp. & rolled-in	Concave w. ps	Clear greenish	Applied brownish thread as decoration.
25.20	5	2.9			Kicked w. ps	Clear greenish	Rim missing.
25.21		4.9			Concave w. ps	Clear greenish	Bluish thread applied as decoration. Neck and rim missing.
25.22	5.6	4	2.3	Outsp. & rolled-in	Kicked w. ps	Clear greenish	Applied bluish thread.

Table 50. Description of vessels of Type 25. Measurements in centimetres.

Figure 189. Cat. no. 25.3.   *Figure 190. Cat. no. 25.4.*   *Figure 191. Cat. no. 25.4*   *Figure 192. Cat. no. 25.5.*

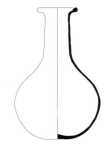

Figure 193. Cat. no. 25.6.   *Figure 194. Cat. no. 25.7.*   *Figure 195. Cat. no. 25.8.*   *Figure 196. Cat. no. 25.9.*

Figure 197. Cat. no. 25.11.   *Figure 198. Cat. no. 25.11.*   *Figure 199. Cat. no. 25.12.*

Figure 200. Cat. no. 25.13.

Figure 201. Cat. no. 25.14.   *Figure 202. Cat. no. 25.15.*   *Figure 203. Cat. no. 25.16.*

Figure 204. Cat. no. 25.17.   Figure 205. Cat. no. 25.17

Figure 206. Cat. no. 25.18.

Figure 207. Cat. no. 25.19.

Figure 208 and 209. Cat. no. 25.20

Figure 210 and 211. Cat. no. 25.21

Figure 212. Cat. no. 25.22.

Nevertheless, some of the vessels do not have any scars or tool marks under the base. The body is bulbous or pear-shaped and the glass is most often greenish or bluish, but often decayed into a crystalline brownish appearance. Type 25 is a simple form, though a few are decorated with an applied thread spiralling around the outside of the vessel (cat. nos 25.14, 25.19, 25.21 and 25.22). Another vessel is decorated with three blue blobs evenly spaced around the shoulder (cat. no. 25.5).

Dating evidence and discussion
Type 25 is closely related to Isings' Form 101 (1957), which is dated to the third and fourth cen-

turies AD and distributed over most of the Roman Empire. In the Near East similar pieces have been found in the late third to fourth century AD necropolis at Tell Mahuz (Negro Ponzi 1968–1969: nos 32-33), at Abu Skhair (Negro Ponzi 1972: nos 24-27), Uruk (van Ess & Pedde 1992: no. 1220), Seleucia (Negro Ponzi 2002: fig. 14.3), Qasr-I Abu Nasr (Whitcomb 1985: fig. 58.dd), Khārg (Steve 2003: pl. 42.8) and Kish (Moorey 1978: microfiche 3, A13, no. 1969.627e), whereas the type seems to be missing from the excavations at ed-Dur (Whitehouse 1998; 2000) and at Quseir Al-Qadim (Meyer 1992), which both declined in the second century AD. The type was thus common in the Near East from around the third century AD, and it may be a typological development of Type 6. Type 25 probably remained in use throughout the Sasanian period and into the Islamic Era.

Type 26: Unguentarium with indented body
Type 26 is very similar to Type 25, but is decorated with three to five indents around the body. Six vessels have been recorded.

Dating evidence and discussion
Close parallels have been found in Abu Skhair (Negro Ponzi 1972: no. 28) and in Karanis (Harden

Cat. no.	BNM no.	Area	Mound	Square	Context	Number	Remarks
25.1	A8910	Hamad Town	1-94-95	C4		4-C4	
25.2	A8916	Saar	5-87-88	F7		49	
25.3	A8914	Hamad Town	83-85-86			44	
25.4	A14391	Saar	5-87-88	F7	Tomb	49	
25.5	N/A						No context information.
25.6	A9068	Hamad Town	73-85-86	1	Tomb	1	
25.7	A9042	Hamad Town	1-94-95	C4		4-C4	
25.8	A14389	Hamad Town	83-85-86		Tomb	44	
25.9	A9051	Dar Kulayb	24-93-94			1	
25.10	A9058	Dar Kulayb	24-93-94		Tomb	1	Not illustrated.
25.11	A14393	Al-Maqsha	1978	4	Tomb	12	
25.12	89						No context information.
25.13	2830-2-91-3						No context information.
25.14	8007						No context information.
25.15	91-2-2						No context information.
25.16							No context information.
25.17	A9538	Saar	12-95-96		Tomb	22	
25.18	A15002	Saar	5-95-96	E4		24	
25.19	A322	Saar	5-95-96	D2	Tomb	12	
25.20	13-35	Saar	5-95-96	C5	Tomb	55	
25.21	12-35	Saar	5-95-96	C5	Tomb	55	
25.22	IMA 21	Saar	12-91		Tomb	6	Nenna 1999: no. 296.

Table 51. Context information for vessels of Type 25.

1936: nos 568–569), which could indicate a third- or fourth-century AD date. The dating is supported by the contextual relation of cat. nos 26.1, 26.4 and 26.6 with vessels of Types 25, 28 and 34, whereas the combination of cat. no. 26.5 with three vessels of Type 6 is likely to be the result of reuse of an older tomb or corrupt information. The type seems to be rare in the West, which could indicate that it was produced in the East.

Type 27: Candlestick unguentarium
Type 27 has a very long neck, a little outsplayed rim and a rolled-in lip. The body of these vessels varies slightly from rather globular with a flattened base (cat. no. 27.2) to squat with a high kicked base (i.e. cat. nos 27.5 and 27.6). The total number of this variant is six vessels.

Dating evidence and discussion
Type 27 is related to Isings' Form 82 (1957), but finds many exact parallels in the Near East, e.g. in the necropolis at Tell Mahuz (Negro Ponzi 1968–1969: nos 6–9), Seleucia (Negro Ponzi 2002: figs 3.13–3.18 and many fragments), Uruk (van Ess & Pedde 1992: nos 1200–1209), ed-Dur (Whitehouse 1998: no. 72),

Quseir al-Qadim (Meyer 1992: no. 194) and a closely related type has been found in Choche (Negro Ponzi 1984: fig. 1.20). These vessels can be dated from the second century AD until the fourth century AD and may indicate an eastern place of production of this type. In the Bahraini tombs the type is associated with Types 25, 28, 29 and 34 (cat. nos 27.1, 27.2, 27.4 and 27.6), which also support a dating from the second or third century AD to the fourth century AD.

Type 28: Bell-shaped unguentarium
Type 27 has a slightly shorter neck and a larger body than Type 26, the candlestick unguentarium. The little rim is outsplayed with a rolled-in lip. The transition between neck and shoulder is rather smooth and the base is concave with a circular pontil scar. One specimen has a mark from kicking the base with a pointed tool.

Dating evidence and discussion
Vessels of Type 28 are rare in the published literature although fairly common in Bahraini tombs, with fifteen vessels recorded. An example in the Corning Museum of Glass is said to be from Egypt and tentatively dated to the sixth century AD (Whitehouse

Cat. no.	Length	Max dia.	Rim dia.	Rim	Resting surface	Colour	Remarks
26.1	3.5	2.6			Convex	Greenish	Rim missing.
26.2	5.5	2.6	1.7	Outsp. & rolled-in	Kicked	Clear greenish	Three indents.
26.3	7.9	5.2	3.3	Outsp. & rolled-in	Concave w. ps	Clear bluish	
26.4	7.3	3.5	2.2	Outsp. & rolled-in	Kicked w. ps	Greenish	
26.5	9.5	6.9	3.3	Outsp. & rolled-in	Flat w. ps	Greenish	
26.6	6.3	3.3	2	Outsp. & rolled-in	Kicked w. ps	Clear greenish	Applied bluish thread.

Table 52. Description of vessels of Type 26. Measurements in centimetres.

Cat. no.	BNM no.	Area	Mound	Square	Context	Number	Remarks
26.1	A9070	Saar	5-95-96	E4	Tomb	24	
26.2	97-3-268						No context information.
26.3	A334	Shakhoura	A1-96-97	C3	Tomb	84	
26.4	A11236	Saar	1-96		Tomb	7	Nenna 1999: no. 297.
26.5	A11234	Saar	11-95-96		Tomb	25	
26.6	A2350	Saar	5-87-88	F7	Tomb	49	

Table 53. Context information for vessels of Type 26.

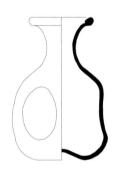

Figure 213. Cat. no. 26.1.   *Figure 214. Cat. no. 26.2.*   *Figure 215. Cat. no. 26.3.*   *Figure 216. Cat. no. 26.3*

Figure 217. Cat. no. 26.4.   *Figure 218. Cat. no. 26.5.*   *Figure 219. Cat. no. 26.6.*   *Figure 220. Cat. no. 26.6.*

Cat. no.	Length	Max dia.	Rim dia.	Rim	Resting surface	Colour	Remarks
27.1	7.6	4.1			Kicked w. ps	Greenish	Rim missing.
27.2	9.8	4	1.9	Outsp. & sheared	Flat w. ps	Greenish	
27.3	8.4	3.2	2	Outsp. & rolled-in	Kicked	Green	Thick-walled.
27.4	10.1	3.4	2.2	Outsp. & sheared	Concave w. ps	Clear greenish	
27.5	9.5	4.4	1.9		Concave	Clear greenish	
27.6	9	5	2.1	Outsp. & rolled-in	Concave w. ps	Clear greenish	

Table 54. Description of vessels of Type 27. Measurements in centimetres.

Cat. no.	BNM no.	Area	Mound	Square	Context	Number	Remarks
27.1	A11039	Saar	163-91-92		Tomb	4	
27.2	A14388	Saar	176-1988		Tomb	7	
27.3	91-2-5						No context information.
27.4	A296	Saar	163-91-92		Tomb	4	
27.5	A3160	Saar	1-1993		Tomb	C III 1	Herling 2003: 465. Vessel lost 2004. Not illustrated.
27.6	A2084	Saar	5-87-88	F7		49	

Table 55. Context information for vessels of Type 27.

Figure 221. Cat. no. 27.1.   *Figure 222. Cat. no. 27.2.*   *Figure 223. Cat. no. 27.2*   *Figure 224. Cat. no. 27.3.*

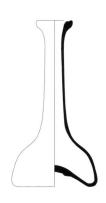

Figure 225. Cat. no. 27.4.   *Figure 226. Cat. no. 27.4.*   *Figure 227. Cat. no. 27.6.*   *Figure 228. Cat. no. 27.6.*

1997: 276). A related example (Harden 1964: fig. 13.2) was found in a tomb in Ajlun (west-northwest of Jerash in Jordan) with twenty-nine other vessels. Harden dates the group to the fourth to sixth century AD (*ibid.* 52–54). Another related specimen with a slightly shorter neck was found in a collective tomb on the Island of Khārg with a coin of the Roman emperor Honorius Flavius (AD 395–423) (Steve 2003: 70, pl. 37.3).[10] The contextual relations of cat. nos 28.1, 28.5, 28.9 and 28.10–15 with Types 25, 26, 27, 34 and 40 indicate that Type 26 should be dated to the period from the third to possibly the fifth century AD, and the find spots indicate an eastern place of production.

Type 29: Unguentarium with globular body and long neck

Only two vessels of Type 29 were recorded. They are characterized by a little globular body and a long, slightly concave neck.

Dating evidence and discussion

A vessel of Type 29 was found on top of a grave near Tell Mahuz, which contained a coin of Sapur II (AD 309–379) (Negro Ponzi 1968–1969: 316 and no. 3). A nearly complete vessel was found in the wine press tank in Jalame, also most likely dating to the second half of the fourth century AD (Weinberg 1988: 3–4 and no. 327). The contextual association

Figure 229. Cat. no. 28.1. *Figure 230. Cat. no. 28.2.* *Figure 231. Cat. no. 28.3.* *Figure 232. Cat. no. 28.4.*

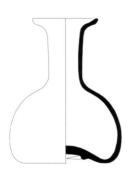

Figure 233. Cat. no. 28.5. *Figure 234. Cat. no. 28.5* *Figure 235. Cat. no. 28.6* *Figure 236. Cat. no. 28.7.*

---

[10] The dating of a tomb on the basis of single coins can be problematic, since coins can be heirlooms; or old coins may have been used as items of jewellery and thus have been in circulation for an extremely long time (Simpson 1995: 247).

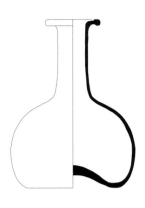

Figure 237. Cat. no. 28.8.   *Figure 238. Cat. no. 28.9.*   *Figure 239. Cat. no. 28.10.*   *Figure 240. Cat. no. 28.10*

Figure 241. Cat. no. 28.11.   *Figure 242. Cat. no. 28.12.*   *Figure 243. Cat. no. 28.12*   *Figure 244. Cat. no. 28.13.*

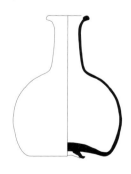

Figure 245. Cat. no. 28.14.   *Figure 246. Cat. no. 28.15.*   *Figure 247. Cat. no. 28.15*

Cat. no.	Length	Max dia.	Rim dia.	Rim	Resting surface	Colour	Remarks
28.1	8	5	2.5	Outsp. & rolled-in	Concave w. ps	Greenish	
28.2	10.3	7.4	2.8	Outsp. & rolled-in	Concave w. ps	Greenish	
28.3	7.3	5.5	1.9	Outsp. & rolled-in	Concave w. ps	Greenish	
28.4	8.2	5.8	2.3	Outsp. & rolled-in	Concave w. ps	Clear greenish	
28.5	7.6	5.9	3.1	Plain	Concave w. ps	Greenish	
28.6	7.5	5.9	2.2	Outsp. & rolled-in	Concave w. ps	Bluish	
28.7	10.2	7.2	2.6	Outsp. & rolled-in	Concave w. ps	Clear greenish	
28.8	5.9	4.3	2	Outsp. & rolled-in	Kicked		Rim partly missing.
28.9			2.3	Outsp. & rolled-in		Clear greenish	Rim fragment.
28.10	9.6	6.4	2.7	Outsp. & rolled-in	Concave w. ps	Clear greenish	
28.11	9.1	6.5	3.2	Outsp. & rolled-in	Concave w. ps	Clear greenish	
28.12	9	6.5	2.7	Outsp. & rolled-in	Concave w. ps	Clear greenish	
28.13	9.3	6.9	3.3	Outsp. & rolled-in	Concave w. ps	Clear greenish	
28.14	9.3	6.2	2.8	Outsp. & rolled-in	Concave w. ps	Clear greenish	
28.15	7.8	6.1	2.2	Outsp. & rolled-in	Concave w. ps	Clear greenish	

Table 56. Description of vessels of Type 28. Measurements in centimetres.

Cat. no.	BNM no.	Area	Mound	Square	Context	Number	Remarks
28.1	A8933	Saar	163-91-92		Tomb	4	
28.2	A8931	Saar	7-91-92	1	Tomb	2	
28.3							No context information.
28.4							No context information.
28.5	A8912	Saar	5-87-88	F7		49	
28.6	896						No context information.
28.7	A290	Saar	1995-96	C5	Tomb	55	
28.8	A12740	Saar	3-96	D4	Tomb	13	
28.9	A9056	Hamad Town	10-89-90	E4	Tomb	41-2	
28.10	5-35	Saar	5-95-96	C5	Tomb	55	
28.11	7-35	Saar	5-95-96	C5	Tomb	55	
28.12	6-35	Saar	5-95-96	C5	Tomb	55	
28.13	8-35	Saar	5-95-96	C5	Tomb	55	
28.14	9-35	Saar	5-95-96	C5	Tomb	55	
28.15	11-35	Saar	5-95-96	C5	Tomb	55	

Table 57. Context information for vessels of Type 28.

Cat. no.	Length	Max dia.	Rim dia.	Rim	Resting surface	Colour	Remarks
29.1	8.3	3.1			Round	Brownish	Rim missing.
29.2	5.3	2.1	1.5	Outsp. & rolled-in	Round	Clear greenish	

Table 58. Description of vessels of Type 29. Measurements in centimetres.

Cat. no.	BNM no.	Area	Mound	Square	Context	Number	Remarks
29.1	A8920	Saar	176-1988		Tomb	7	
29.2	A9528	Saar	6-91-92	3	Tomb	14	

Table 59. Context information for vessels of Type 29.

Cat. no.	Length	Max dia.	Rim dia.	Rim	Resting surface	Colour	Remarks
30.1	10	7.5	2.2		Round w. ps	Clear greenish	7 ribs as decoration. Partly restored.

Table 60. Description of the vessel of Type 30. Measurements in centimetres.

Cat. no.	BNM no.	Area	Mound	Square	Context	Number	Remarks
30.1	A14390	Hamad Town	83-85-86		Tomb	44	

Table 61. Context information for the vessel of Type 30.

Cat. no.	Length	Max dia.	Rim dia.	Rim	Resting surface	Colour	Remarks
31.1	9.5	4.4	2.1		Flat	Greenish	

Table 62. Description of the vessel of Type 31. Measurements in centimetres.

Cat. no.	BNM no.	Area	Mound	Square	Context	Number	Remarks
31.1	183	Dar Kulayb	24-93-94		Tomb	1	Lost 2004.

Table 63. Context information for the vessel of Type 31.

Cat. no.	Length	Max dia.	Rim dia.	Rim	Resting surface	Colour	Remarks
32.1	12.5	2.4	1.7	Outsp. & rolled-in	Round w. ps		

Table 64. Description of the vessel of Type 32. Measurements in centimetres.

Cat. no.	BNM no.	Area	Mound	Square	Context	Number	Remarks
32.1		Hamad Town	73-85-86		Tomb	44	On display BNM.

Table 65. Context information for the vessel of Type 32.

of cat. nos 29.1 and 29.2 with a vessel of Type 27 and 41 supports a dating to the third or fourth century AD.

Type 30: Unguentarium with pinched-out ribs
Type 30 is characterized by vertical pinched-out ribs around the body.

Dating evidence and discussion
No parallels have been found to this vessel, but the contextual relations to vessels of Type 25 and vessels in hard-fired ware indicate a third- to fifth-century AD date for Type 30.

Type 31: Unguentarium with conical body
Only one unguentarium of Type 31 was recorded. The upper part of the vessel is similar to the Type 28 bell-shaped unguentarium, but the lower body is conical rather than bell-shaped.

Dating evidence and discussion
No parallels have been found to this vessel, but the contextual relations to vessels of Type 25 and 41 indicate a third- to fifth-century AD date for Type 31.

Type 32: Toilet bottle
Only one toilet bottle of Type 32 was recorded (cat. no. 32.1). It is tube-shaped with the wide part in the middle.

Dating evidence and discussion
Type 32 is similar to Isings' Form 105 (1957). This type was common during the fourth century AD. The contextual relation of cat. no. 32.1 to a Type 41 bowl supports this dating well.

Type 33: Unguentarium with applied thread
Only one unguentarium of Type 33 was recorded. It is characterized by a fairly long neck and an applied thread as decoration.

Dating evidence and discussion
No parallels have been found to this vessel, but the contextual relations to vessels of Types 25, 34, 38 and 41 and vessels in hard-fired ware indicate a third- to fifth-century AD date for this unique vessel.

Type 34: Ointment jar
Small jars with a globular, onion-shaped or pear-shaped body are a well-represented group in the Bahraini tombs. They have an outsplayed rim, with a rolled-in lip and a short neck. The base is flattened or concave and in most cases with a pronounced pontil scar. Twenty-eight vessels of this type were recorded in the Main Store.

Figure 248. Cat. no. 29.1.   *Figure 249. Cat. no. 29.1.*

Figure 250. Cat. no. 29.2.   *Figure 251. Cat. no. 29.2*

 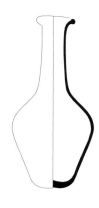

Figure 252. Cat. no. 30.1.   *Figure 253. Cat. no. 31.1.*

Dating evidence and discussion
Type 34 is related to Isings' Form 68 (1957). In the West the type was common from the Flavian period and in the second century AD (*ibid.* 88–89; Vessberg & Westholm 1956: Jar A.1), but small globular jars are reported from excavations in the Near East from a much longer period. A complete example has been found in ed-Dur (UAE) in an unrobbed collective tomb where the majority of glass vessels were dated to *c.* AD 25–75, although the exact period of use of the tomb is not clear (Whitehouse

Figure 254. Cat. no. 32.1.   Figure 255. Cat. no. 32.1.

1998: 40, 64). Further fragments from small jars were also found in ed-Dur (Whitehouse 2000: nos 35–37). Examples are reported from the necropolis at Tell Mahuz (Negro-Ponzi 1968–1969: nos 19–23), where the finds have been dated to the last quarter of the third to the beginning of the fourth century. They may, however, have been placed in the graves as late as the second half of the fourth century AD (Negro Ponzi 1968–1969: 308–309). From Abu Skhair similar jars have been published (Negro-Ponzi 1972: nos 12–19), Uruk (van Ess & Pedde 1992: nos 1225–1226). The type is not represented in the published collections from Seleucia (Negro-Ponzi 2002) and Quseir al-Qadim (Meyer 1992).

A few of the vessels from Bahrain have been found with first-century AD types, i.e. cat. nos 34.3 and 34.13, but the majority came from contexts with material dating to the late Parthian and Sasanian periods. It would appear, therefore, that the ointment jars came into fashion later in the East than in the West, but examples may have been imported to the Gulf region from the West at an earlier stage, e.g. the ed-Dur vessels and a few, possibly early vessels from the Bahraini tombs. The type was, however, most popular in the East from the second century and maybe until the fourth or fifth century AD, since it is not attested at late Sasanian sites. It is likely that the type was produced in the East at some stage.

Type 35: Miniature jug.
The miniature jugs are small bottles with one handle. It is rather unlikely that they have been used as jugs due to their small size, and the handle may only have been a decorative feature. Type 35 is closely related to Type 25, but finished with a single handle. They are made of greenish glass, which has most often decayed to brownish.

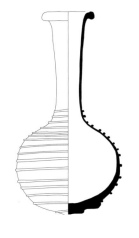

Figure 256. Cat. no. 33.1.   Figure 257. Cat. no. 33.1.

Cat. no.	Length	Max dia.	Rim dia.	Rim	Resting surface	Colour	Remarks
33.1	11.2	6.6	2.8	Outsp. & rolled-in	Round w. ps		Applied white thread as decoration.

Table 66. Description of the vessel of Type 32. Measurements in centimetres.

Cat. no.	BNM no.	Area	Mound	Square	Context	Number	Remarks
33.1	A11259	Hamad Town	73-85-86	1	Tomb	1	Nenna 1999: no 283.

Table 67. Context information for the vessel of Type 32.

Figure 258. Cat. no. 34.1.

Figure 259. Cat. no. 34.2.

Figure 260. Cat. no. 34.3.

Figure 261. Cat. no. 34.4.

Figure 262. Cat. no. 34.4

Figure 263. Cat. no. 34.5.

Figure 264. Cat. no. 34.6.

Figure 265. Cat. no. 34.8.

Figure 266. Cat. no. 34.8

Figure 267. Cat. no. 34.9.

Figure 268. Cat. no. 34.10.

Figure 269. Cat. no. 34.11.

Figure 270. Cat. no. 34.12.

Figure 271. Cat. no. 34.12

Figure 272. Cat. no. 34.15.

Figure 273. Cat. no. 34.16.   Figure 274. Cat. no. 34.17.   Figure 275. Cat. no. 34.18.

Figure 276. Cat. no. 34.19.   Figure 277. Cat. no. 34.19

Figure 278. Cat. no. 34.20.   Figure 279. Cat. no. 34.20

Figure 280. Cat. no. 34.21.   Figure 281. Cat. no. 34.21

Figure 282. Cat. no. 34.22.   Figure 283. Cat. no. 34.22

Figure 284. Cat. no. 34.23.   Figure 285. Cat. no. 34.24.   Figure 286. Cat. no. 34.25.   Figure 287. Cat. no. 34.26.

Cat. no.	Length	Max dia.	Rim dia.	Rim	Resting surface	Colour	Remarks
34.1	4.9	6.5	4.3	Outsp. & rolled-in	Concave	Clear greenish	
34.2	5.6	5.7	4	Outsp. & rolled-in	Flat	Whitish	
34.3	4.6	5.5	3.7	Outsp. & rolled-in	Concave w. ps	Greenish	
34.4	4.7	4.9	4.3	Outsp. & rolled-in	Concave w. ps	Greenish	
34.5	5.3	7.4	5.3	Outsp. & rolled-in	Concave w. ps	Clear white	
34.6	4.8	5	3.5	Outsp. & rolled-in	Concave w. ps	Greenish	
34.7	6	5.4	3.4		Concave	Brownish	
34.8	5.1	6.3	4.4	Outsp. & rolled-in	Concave w. ps	Clear greenish	
34.9	5.5	6.5	4.4	Outsp. & fp	Kicked	Blue & clear	
34.10	3.9	4	3.3	Outsp. & rolled-in	Flat	Clear	
34.11	4.5	4.8	3.7	Outsp. & rolled-in	Concave w. ps	Green	
34.12	6	7.3	4.4	Outsp. & rolled-in	Concave	Clear greenish	
34.13	10	8.8					
34.14	7.2	6.2		Outsp. & rolled-in	Concave	Purple	With two handles.
34.15	6.6	6.1	3.6	Outsp. & rolled-in	Concave w. ps	Clear greenish	
34.16	5	5.9	3.5	Outsp. & rolled-in	Concave w. ps	Clear greenish	
34.17	10.7	9.9	5.8	Outsp. & sheared	Concave w. ps	Greenish	
34.18	9	9.1	5.8	Outsp. & fp	Coil	Green	The bottom of the vessel was kicked before the pontil was applied and then the coil foot was made.
34.19	6.1	5.5	4.3	Outsp. & rolled-in	Flat	Clear greenish	Rim partly restored.
34.20	6.1	6.9	4.3	Outsp. & rolled-in	Kicked	Clear greenish	A dark green thread was applied in a spiral pattern on shoulder as decoration.
34.21	5.6	7.7	5.3	Outsp. & rolled-in	Flat w. ps	Clear greenish	The pontil scar has been partly polished away.
34.22	6.1	7.4	4.6	Outsp. & rolled-in	Concave w. ps	Clear greenish	
34.23	4.3	4	3.4	Outsp. & rolled-in	Kicked w. ps	Clear greenish	Applied bluish thread as decoration.
34.24	4	4.3	3.7	Outsp. & rolled-in	Kicked w. ps	Clear bluish	Applied thread as decoration.
34.25	6	5.6	4.5	Outsp. & rolled-in	Concave	Purple	With three handles.
34.26			4.2	Outsp. & rolled-in		Decayed cream	Rim fragment.
34.27	9	6				Green	With two handles and applied tread spiralling around the body.
34.28	9.2	6.2				Clear	

Table 68. Description of vessels of Type 34. Measurements in centimetres.

Cat. no.	BNM no.	Area	Mound	Square	Context	Number	Remarks
34.1	A8939	Hamad Town	1-94-95	C4	Tomb	4-C4	
34.2	9905-2-91						No context information.
34.3	A9043	Saar	11-95-96		Tomb	25	
34.4	A14396	Saar	2-85-86	1	Tomb	12	
34.5	91-2-27						No context information.
34.6	A14397	Saar	2-85-86	1	Tomb	12	
34.7	A14386						No context information. Boucharlat & Salles 1989: no. 193. Vessel lost 2004. Not illustrated.
34.8	A14385	Saar	5-87-88				Context information incomplete.
34.9	A9540	Saar	163-91-92		Tomb	4	
34.10	A15001	Saar	5-95-96	E4	Tomb	24	
34.11	A9526	Saar	5-95-96	E4	Tomb	24	
34.12	A14395	Saar	5-87-88	F7	Tomb	49	
34.13	FM-A-985.DC	Unplaced	T158-5		Tomb	1	Boucharlat & Salles 1989: no. 210, Jensen 2003: fig. 9.7. Vessel on display, BNM. Not illustrated.

Cat. no.	BNM no.	Area	Mound	Square	Context	Number	Remarks
34.14	FM-A-985.BX	Unplaced	T158-5		Outside tomb	1	Boucharlat & Salles 1989: no. 215, Jensen 2003: fig. 9–15. Vessel on display, BNM. Not illustrated.
34.15	A818	Saar	1-96		Tomb	7	
34.16	A15069	Hamad Town	1-94-95	C4	Tomb	4-C4	Nenna 1999: no. 292.
34.17	A11264	Saar	5-87-88	F1			
34.18	A11238	Saar	12-95-96		Tomb	22	Nenna 1999: no. 295.
34.19	A13856						No context information.
34.20	3-35	Saar	5-95-96	C5	Tomb	55	
34.21	10-35	Saar	5-95-96	C5	Tomb	55	
34.22	2-35	Saar	5-95-96	C5	Tomb	55	
34.23	IMA 22	Saar	12-91		Tomb	6	Nenna 1999: no. 300.
34.24	IMA 20	Saar	12-91		Tomb	6	Nenna 1999: no. 299.
34.25	A1575						No context information.
34.26	A11031	Saar	5-95-96	E2	Tomb	36	
34.27		Hamad Town	73-85-86	1	Tomb	1	On display, BNM. Vine 1993: 68. Not illustrated.
34.28							On display, BNM. Boucharlat & Salles 1989: 214. Not illustrated.

Table 69. Context information for vessels of Type 34.

Dating evidence and discussion

Parallels to Type 35 have been found in Kish (Moorey 1978: microfiche 3, A13, nos 116.1321, 1969.627g) and in Uruk (van Ess & Pedde 1992: no. 1220). Related vessels (although with two handles and ribbed-out or applied thread decoration) have been found at the necropolis near Tell Mahuz (Negro Ponzi 1968–1969: nos 50 and 53), whereas a specimen from Abu Skhair has a proper ring foot (Negro Ponzi 1972: no. 33). The contextual relations of cat. nos 35.3–5 to other types dating to the third to fifth century AD support the dating indicated by the external evidence. The type does not seem to have been found in the west and may thus have been produced within the Sasanian Empire.

Type 36: Globular jug

Only one globular jug of Type 36 has been recorded in the Main Stores. It is a globular vessel with an applied thread and a handle.

Cat. no.	Length	Max dia.	Rim dia.	Rim	Resting surface	Colour	Remarks
35.1	7	5.5	3.2	Outsp. & rolled-in	Flat w. ps	Brownish	Five indents as decoration.
35.2	10.2	4.8	3.4		Flat	Greenish	Restriction in neck.
35.3	9.8	6.4	3.9	Outsp. & rolled-in	Concave w. ps	Clear greenish	Restriction in bottom of the neck.
35.4	5.6	3.5	1.8	Outsp. & rolled-in	Round w. ps	Clear greenish	
35.5			3.5	Outsp. & rolled-in		Clear greenish	Rim and neck fragment. Restriction in lower part of neck.

Table 70. Description of vessels of Type 35. Measurements in centimetres.

Cat. no.	BNM no.	Area	Mound	Square	Context	Number	Remarks
35.1	A9047	Dar Kulayb	24-93-94				
35.2	250	Saar	5-96-97	B5		68	Not illustrated.
35.3	4-35	Saar	5-95-96	C5	Tomb	55	
35.4	1-35	Saar	5-95-96	C5	Tomb	55	
35.5	A11031	Saar	5-95-96	E2	Tomb	36	Cat. No. NON.8 is probably the base of this vessel.

Table 71. Context information for vessels of Type 35.

Figure 288. Cat. no. 35.1.

Figure 289. Cat. no. 35.3.

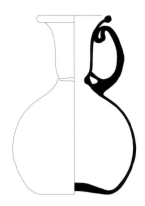

Figure 290. Cat. no. 35.3

Figure 291. Cat. no. 35.4.

Figure 292. Cat. no. 35.4

Figure 293. Cat. no. 35.5.

Cat. no.	Length	Max dia.	Rim dia.	Rim	Resting surface	Colour	Remarks
36.1	8.5	7	2.7	Outsp.	Kicked w. ps	Greenish	Applied dark green thread as decoration.

Table 72. Description of the vessel of Type 36. Measurements in centimetres.

Cat. no.	BNM no.	Area	Mound	Square	Context	Number	Remarks
36.1	A11269	Saar	5-87-88	F7	Tomb	49	Nenna 1999: no 298; Vine 1986: 44.

Table 73. Context information for the vessel of Type 36.

Dating evidence and discussion

No parallels have been found, but the contextual relation to vessels of Types 25, 26, 27, 28 and 34, indicate a dating to the third or fourth century AD.

Mould-blown unguentaria

In contrast to the rich variety of mould-blown bottles with relatively advanced decorative schemes of the first and early second century AD, the group of mould-blown vessels dating to the following centuries (see below) are much simpler and less well represented.

Figure 294. Cat. no. 36.1.

73

Cat. no.	Length	Max dia.	Rim dia.	Rim	Resting surface	Colour	Remarks
37.1	12.4	5.9	3.9	Outsp. & rolled-in	Concave w. ps	Turquoise	Rim partly missing.

Table 74. Description of the vessel of Type 37. Measurements in centimetres.

Cat. no.	BNM no.	Area	Mound	Square	Context	Number	Remarks
37.1	A264	Dar Kulayb	24-93-94		Tomb	2	

Table 75. Context information for the vessel of Type 37.

Figure 295. Cat. no. 37.1.

Figure 296. Cat. no. 37.1.

Figure 297. Cat. no. 38.1.

Type 37: "Mercury bottle"

The "mercury bottle" was blown in a square mould and takes its name from a moulded picture of Mercury often seen on the bottom of these vessels.

Dating evidence and discussion

Cat. no. 37.1 is a so-called "mercury bottle", although the Bahraini example does not have a moulded decoration underneath (Isings 1957: Form 84; Whitehouse 2000: nos 567–585). The vessel is contextually associated with vessels of Types 40 and 41 and probably dates to the third to fifth century AD.

Type 38: Mould-blown unguentarium

Type 38 is only represented by one vessel. The vessel is characterized by a rustic mould-blown decoration on the body, whereas the shoulder and neck of the vessel are free-blown and tooled.

Cat. no.	Length	Max dia.	Rim dia.	Rim	Resting surface	Colour	Remarks
38.1	10	6.3				Irrisident	Rim missing.

Table 76. Description of the vessel of Type 38. Measurements in centimetres.

Cat. no.	BNM no.	Area	Mound	Square	Context	Number	Remarks
38.1	A8941	Hamad Town	73-85-86	1	Tomb	1	

Table 77. Context information for the vessel of Type 38.

  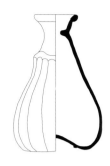 

Figure 298. Cat. no. 39.1   *Figure 299. Cat. no. 39.2.*   *Figure 300. Cat. no. 39.2.*   *Figure 301. Cat. no. 39.3.*

Dating evidence and discussion

No parallels have been found to Type 38, but the contextual relations with other vessels (i.e. Types 12, 25, 33, 34 and 41) indicate a late Parthian or Sasanian date for this type.

Type 39: Optic blown vessel

A little group of four optic blown vessels was also found in the Bahraini tombs. They were made by inflating the gather in a mould, then removing it from the mould and inflating it to its full size, leaving the pattern from the mould. These decorations are simple; the Bahraini ones have vertical ribs, whereas others were made with diagonal ribs (e.g. Negro Ponzi 1972: no. 63).

 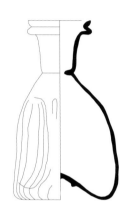

Figure 302. Cat. no. 39.4.   *Figure 303. Cat. no. 39.4.*

Cat. no.	Length	Max dia.	Rim dia.	Rim	Resting surface	Colour	Remarks
39.1	5.3	5	3.5		Kicked	Clear greenish	Rim irregularly folded.
39.2	7.5	4.8	2.3	Outsp. & rolled-in	Concave w. ps	Green	Restriction inside neck half-way down.
39.3	4.3	4.7	3.4	Outsp. & rolled-in	Kicked w. ps	Greenish	
39.4	9.8	5.9	3.2	Outsp.	Concave w. ps	Green	Restriction inside neck at transition between neck and shoulder. With indents.

Table 78. Description of the vessel of Type 39. Measurements in centimetres.

Cat. no.	BNM no.	Area	Mound	Square	Context	Number	Remarks
39.1							No context information.
39.2	160						No context information.
39.3	308						No context information.
39.4	A11232	Saar	12-95-96		Tomb	22	

Table 79. Context information for vessels of Type 39.

Dating evidence and discussion

Ribbed vessels are reported from the Sasanian layers at Tell Baruda inside Ctesiphon and believed to be a typical Sasanian production (Negro Ponzi 1987: 270, fig. C type R, S). This is supported by finds in Abu Skhair (Negro Ponzi 1972: nos 42–63), Uruk (van Ess & Pedde 1992: no. 1227; Strommenger 1967: Taf. 47–7). An optic blown vessel is, however, also reported from Al-Jawf in Yemen, indicating that the distribution may have been wider (Antonini 2000: no. 287), but the type seems not to have been found in the West. One of the Bahraini examples was found with vessels of Types 25 and 34, supporting the dating suggested by external comparison.

Free-blown cups and beakers

Cups and beakers were presumably used for drinking. They are hemispherical to cylindrical (Type 41) or conical (Type 40).

Type 40: Conical beaker

The vessels of Type 40 are all made of a greenish glass with small bubbles. The transparent greenish glass is well preserved with only very little weathering on a few specimens (cat. nos 40.1 and 40.2). The rim is often folded inwards and always fire-polished. The walls of the vessels are straight. One example (cat. no. 40.5) has a small solid base attached, hardly usable for standing, whereas the rest are rounded at the bottom. The bottoms of the vessels are rather solid and all have a pronounced pontil scar. On some it could be a scar of a base, similar to that of cat. no. 40.5, which has broken off. A function as a lamp has been suggested for these vessels because of "an oily feel and some have burnt and oily strains inside" (Harden 1936: 155). However, conical beakers seem to be depicted both as lamps and as drinking vessels, and a function as both is therefore likely (Weinberg 1988: 89–91). Since lamps are generally absent in the Bahraini tombs and conical beakers are often associated with jugs in hard-fired

Cat. no.	Length	Base dia.	Rim dia.	Rim	Resting surface	Colour	Remarks
40.1						Greenish	Base fragment.
40.2					Pointed w. ps	Greenish	Base fragment.
40.3	19.4		8.7	Straight & rolled-in	Round w. ps	Greenish	
40.4	20.3		8.9	Straight rolled-in & fp	Round w. ps	Green	The red residue is modern and from an exhibition where the vessel was filled with some red liquid.
40.5	21.5	3.5	8	Straight & fp	Moulded foot w. ps	Green	
40.6	20.5		9	Straight & rolled-in	Round w. ps	Green	
40.7	21.2		9.7	Straight & fp	Round w. ps	Clear greenish	
40.8					Flat w. ps	Clear greenish	Base fragment.
40.9					Flat w. ps		Base fragment.
40.10			11.5	Straight & fp		Clear greenish	Rim fragment.

Table 80. Description of vessels of Type 40. Measurements in centimetres.

Cat. no.	BNM no.	Area	Mound	Square	Context	Number	Remarks
40.1	A8902	Saar	5-95-96	C5	Tomb	55	
40.2	A8925	Saar	5-87-88		Tomb	19	
40.3	A9061	Saar	5-95-96	B3	Tomb	43	
40.4	A16631	Saar	7-95-96	E2	Tomb	28	
40.5	A11372	Saar	7-95-96	F5	Tomb	55	Nenna 1999: no. 288.
40.6	A870	Saar	5-95-96	E6	Tomb	83	
40.7	A11490	Dar Kulayb	24-93-94		Tomb	2	
40.8	A9056	Hamad Town	10-89-90	E4	Tomb	41-2	
40.9	A9056	Hamad Town	10-89-90	E4	Tomb	41-2	
40.10	A11031	Saar	5-95-96	E2	Tomb	36	

Table 81. Context information for vessels of Type 40.

Figure 304. Cat. no. 40.1.

Figure 305. Cat. no. 40.1.

Figure 307. Cat. no. 40.3.

Figure 308. Cat. no. 40.4.

Figure 306. Cat. no. 40.2.

Figure 309. Cat. no. 40.5.

Figure 310. Cat. no. 40.5

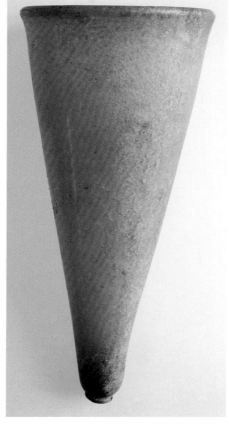

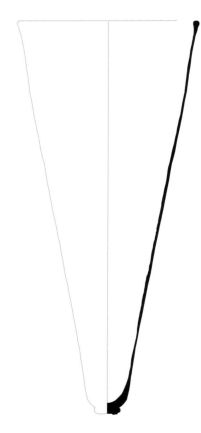

Figure 311. Cat. no. 40.6.   Figure 312. Cat. no. 40.7.   Figure 313. Cat. no. 40.7

ware and amphorae in glazed ware, a function as a drinking vessel is most likely. The Bahraini Type 40 conical beakers are thus believed to be beakers.

Dating evidence and discussion

Type 40 was quite common throughout Europe and the Middle East in the fourth and fifth centuries AD (Isings 1957: Form 106d; Hayes 1975: nos 380 and 477; Harden 1936: nos 436–463). In the East examples are reported from Seleucia (Negro Ponzi 2002: fig. 10.11), Tell Baruda in Ctesiphon (Negro Ponzi 1987: fig. B, type I) and from Uruk (van Ess & Pedde 1992: no. 1266). An example with applied threads has been reported from Choche together with a mould-blown specimen (Negro Ponzi 1984: figs 2.10 and 3.9). In Kish, conical beakers, where the lower part of the walls curves towards the bottom of the vessel, have been found (Moorey 1978: microfiche 3, A 13 nos 1969.622, 1969.618a-f). Similar bases are reported from Tell Baruda, where they are believed to be late Sasanian, whereas the ones similar to the Bahraini bases are earlier (Negro Ponzi 1987: 268), which also supports the fourth-to fifth-century AD date.

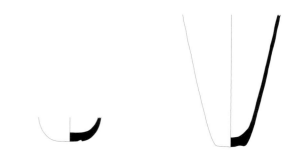

Figure 314. Cat. no. 40.8.   Figure 315. Cat. no. 40.9.

Figure 316. Cat. no. 40.10.

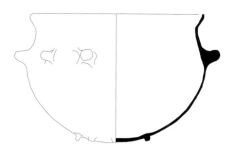

Figure 317. Cat. no. 41.1.

Figure 318. Cat. no. 41.1.

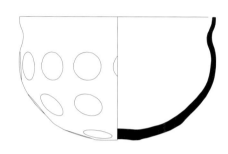

Figure 319. Cat. no. 41.2.

Figure 320. Cat. no. 41.2

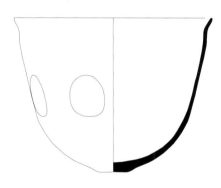

Figure 321. Cat. no. 41.3.

Figure 322. Cat. no. 41.3

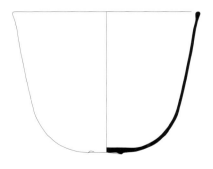

Figure 323. Cat. no. 41.4.

Figure 324. Cat. no. 41.4.

Figure 325. Cat. no. 41.5.

Figure 326. Cat. no. 41.6.

Figure 327. Cat. no. 41.7.

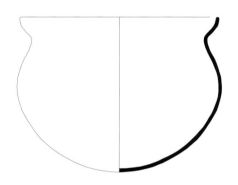

Figure 328. Cat. no. 41.7

Cat. no.	Length	Max dia.	Rim dia.	Rim	Resting surface	Colour	Remarks
41.1	7.4		9.5	Flaring & cracked off	Knobs	Brownish	Band of pinched-out knob 2.5 cm below rim as decoration. Half of the vessel is missing.
41.2	6.7	10.55	10.5	Flaring & cracked off	Round, ps polished away	Greenish	Three rows of round facets evenly spaced as decoration.
41.3	8.8		10.9	Flaring	Round, ps polished away	Greenish	One row of vertical oval facets evenly spaced in the middle of the vessel as decoration. Half of the vessel is missing.
41.4	7.9		9.5	Straight & fp	Flat w. ps	Clear greenish	Fragments.
41.5	8.1	10.7	9.4	Flaring	Knobs and ps	Bluish	Eight vertical pinched-out ribs evenly spaced on the lower part of the body as decoration. Vessel partly restored.
41.6	8.9	11.3	10.2	Outsp. & rolled-in	Concave w. ps	Greenish	Nip't diamond waies decoration.
41.7	8	11.4	10.7	Outsp. & cracked off	Round	Green	
41.8	7.5	10.5	9.9	Outsp. & rolled-in	Kicked	Green	Nip't diamond waies decoration. Partly restored.
41.9	7.9	11.4	10.7	Outsp. & cracked off	Round, ps polished away	Clear turquoise	Two rows of oval facets as decoration. Partly restored.
41.10							Vessel lost 2004.
41.11	7	10				Greenish	Pinched-out knobs on shoulder.
41.12	9.4		9.7	Flaring & polished	N/A	Clear greenish	A thin thread has been applied 2.7 cm below the rim as decoration. The body is partly restored.
41.13	7.7		8.2	Outsp. & polished.	N/A	Clear white	Surface colour decayed to brown. The vessel is decorated with two groups of nine small blobs and two larger blobs. The four elements are situated at the same height and evenly spaced.

Table 82. Description of vessels of Type 41. Measurements in centimetres.

Figure 329. Cat. no. 41.8.

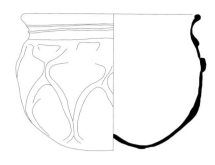

Figure 330. Cat. no. 41.8.

Figure 331. Cat. no. 41.9.

Figure 332. Cat. no. 41.12.

Type 41: Hemispherical and cylindrical bowls

These bowls are characterized by their rounded bottom, often with a pontil scar, which on three vessels (cat. nos 41.2, 41.3 and 41.9) have been polished away. The upper part of the body is either vertical creating a cylindrical appearance of the vessel, or curving slightly inwards, creating a marked transition to the flaring or outsplayed rim and a hemispherical appearance of the bowl. In the following all these bowls will be referred to as hemispherical bowls. The rim is sheared or cracked off and the lip sometimes rolled-in or fire-polished. The vessels are decorated in a vide variety of techniques, i.e. decoration of blobs (cat. no. 41.13), an applied thread under the rim (cat. no. 41.12), nip't diamond waies (cat. nos 41.8 and 41.7), facets (cat. nos 41.2, 41.3 and 41.9) and pinched-out knobs or ribs (cat. nos 41.1, 41.5 and 41.11).

Figure 333. Cat. no. 41.13.

Cat. no.	BNM no.	Area	Mound	Square	Context	Number	Remarks
41.1	A8944	Hamad Town	10-89-90	E4	Tomb	41-3	
41.2	A8945	Dar Kulayb	24-93-94		Tomb	2	
41.3	A8947	Dar Kulayb	24-93-94		Tomb	2	
41.4	A8946	Dar Kulayb	24-93-94		Tomb	2	
41.5	A14392	Hamad Town	73-85-86	1	Tomb	1	
41.6	A14030	Saar	6-91-92	3	Tomb	14	
41.7	A14394	Hamad Town	73-85-86		Tomb	44	
41.8	A548						No context information.
41.9	A283	Um Al-Hasam	1973		Outside tomb	46	Boucharlat & Salles 1989: no. 211.
41.10	IMA 37A	Dar Kulayb	24-93-94		Tomb	1	Nenna 1999: no. 287. Vessel lost 2004. Not illustrated.
41.11		Hamad Town	70A-85-86		Tomb	2	On display, BNM. Not illustrated.
41.12	929-2-88	Hamad Town	73-85-86		Tomb	1	
41.13	A261	Saar	12-91		Tomb	6	

Table 83. Context information for vessels of Type 41.

Dating evidence and discussion

Type 41 hemispherical bowls are closely related to Isings' Forms 96 and 106 (1957), which are datable to the third and fourth centuries AD. This dating corresponds very well to the contextual relations of vessels Types 25, 29, 34 and 40. Hemispherical bowls are well known in the Near East. Examples have been found in the necropolis at Tell Mahuz among which good parallels to cat. no. 41.5 (Negro Ponzi 1968–1969: no. 68), cat. nos 41.9 and 41.2 (*ibid.* no. 71) exist. Good parallels have also been found at Choche (Negro Ponzi 1984: figs 3.12 and 4.1). Cat. no. 41.13 is decorated with blobs, which together with the thin and white glass could indicate that the vessel was imported from the West.

Cast bowls

Cast vessels are relatively uncommon in the Bahraini collection and only in the pre-blowing assemblage were other cast vessels documented.

Type 42: Plain little bowl

A very simple shape made of thick green glass. One example (cat. no. 42.9) is decorated with twenty-two ribs, whereas the rest are undecorated.

Dating evidence and discussion

No parallels to this type have been found. The contextual relations of cat. no. 42.9 to vessels of Type 25 and Type 12 suggest a dating from the second to the fourth century AD, but the combinations of cat.

Cat. no.	Length	Rim dia.	Rim	Resting surface	Colour	Remarks
42.1	4.4	8	Straight & fp	Concave w. ps	Clear greenish	
42.2	5.5	9.5	Straight & fp	Concave w. ps	Clear greenish	
42.3	4.3	7.3	Straight & fp	Concave w. ps	Clear greenish	
42.4	4.1	7.2	Straight & fp	Concave w. ps	Clear greenish	
42.5	5.8	9.8	Straight & fp	Kicked w. ps	Clear greenish	
42.6	3.8	9	Flaring & fp	Concave w. ps	Clear greenish	
42.7	5	8.6	Straight & fp	Concave w. ps	Clear greenish	
42.8	4.6	7.6	Straight & fp	Concave w. ps	Clear greenish	
42.9	6.8	11.9	Straight, rolled-out & fp	Concave w. ps	Clear greenish	22 moulded ribs decorate the sides.
42.10	4.2	7.5	Straight & fp	Concave w. ps	Clear greenish	
42.11	4.5	9.1	Straight & fp	Concave w. ps	Clear greenish	

Table 84. Description of vessels of Type 42. Measurements in centimetres.

Figure 334. Cat. no. 42.1.

Figure 335. Cat. no. 42.2.

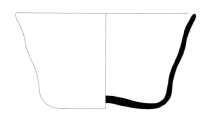

Figure 336. Cat. no. 42.2

Figure 337. Cat. no. 42.3.

Figure 338. Cat. no. 42.4.

Figure 339. Cat. no. 42.5.

Figure 340. Cat. no. 42.6.

Figure 341. Cat. no. 42.7.

Figure 342. Cat. no. 42.7

Figure 343. Cat. no. 42.8.

Figure 344. Cat. no. 42.9.

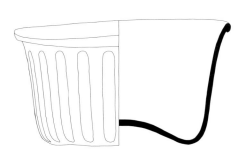

Figure 345. Cat. no. 42.9

Figure 346. Cat. no. 42.10.

Figure 347. Cat. no. 42.11.

Cat. no.	BNM no.	Area	Mound	Square	Context	Number	Remarks
42.1	A8936A	Saar	5-91-92	2	Tomb	7	
42.2	A14379	Saar	5-87-88	J5	Tomb	69	
42.3	A9063	Saar	4-91-92	7	Tomb	39	
42.4	A9063	Saar	4-91-92	7	Tomb	39	
42.5	A9064	Saar	7-95-96	D1	Tomb	119	
42.6	A9062	Saar	12-91		Tomb	15	
42.7	A291	Saar	2-91-92	C2	Tomb	29	
42.8	A292	Saar	3-90-91	1	Tomb	7	
42.9	A11389	Saar	5-95-96	D2	Tomb	12	Nenna 1999: no. 289.
42.10	A8936B	Saar	5-91-92	2	Tomb	7	
42.11	A3550	Saar	12-91		Tomb	9	

Table 85. Context information for vessels of Type 42.

nos 42.5 and 42.6 to a Type BE cup with vertical rim and a Type AL bottle with two vertical handles both in glazed ware indicate that the type may also be earlier. A dating to the second to fourth century is therefore a possibility.

Figure 348. Cat. no. 43.1.   Figure 349. Cat. no. 43.1

Type 43: Little bowl with coil base
These vessels are made of thick green glass and probably cast. Their appearance is very similar to the Type 42 plain little bowl, but this variant has a coil base.

Figure 350.
Cat. no. 43.2.

Dating evidence and discussion
No parallels to this type have been found. The contextual relation of cat. no. 43.1 to a Type CE bowl with angular profile in glazed ware indicates a second- to fifth-century AD date.

Figure 351. Cat. no. 43.3.

Cat. no.	Length	Rim dia.	Rim	Resting surface	Colour	Remarks
43.1	3.5	8.2	Outsp. & fp	Coil	Greenish	Base dia. 3.9 cm.
43.2	4.2	8.6	Straight & fp	Coil	Clear greenish	The vessel was full of beads and seashells.
43.3	4.5	9.7	Flaring, rolled-in & fp	Coil & ps	Clear greenish	

Table 86. Description of vessels of Type 43. Measurements in centimetres.

Cat. no.	BNM no.	Area	Mound	Square	Context	Number	Remarks
43.1	A9044	Hamad Town	1-94-95	B9	Tomb	1-B9	
43.2	120						No context information.
43.3	A9065	Saar	5-96-97	B2	Tomb	86	

Table 87. Context information for vessels of Type 43.

The late Sasanian assemblage (sixth to seventh century AD)

The late Sasanian assemblage forms a distinctive group among the Bahraini glass vessels. The decorative scheme does not follow the Roman tradition that is seen in the majority of the vessels of the previous periods. They are all made in a very similar glass, which decays into a greyish appearance. All types are small bottles and free-blown and most of the vessels have an applied decoration of discs, knobs or threads or a combination of these elements.

Free-blown unguentaria
Only free-blown unguentaria can be placed in this phase and four types have been defined.

Type 44: Flask with funnel mouth
The nine flasks with funnel mouth are often decorated with applied discs or threads and the glass is on most vessels decayed to greyish.

Dating evidence and discussion
Type 44 is probably a development of Type 24 (Isings 1957: Form 104b). Two very good parallels have been found in the Umm Khesham cemetery in Grave 20, Sounding 21, where they were associated with fourth- to fifth-century AD vessels (Negro Ponzi 2005: fig. 4.16 and 4.18). The zigzag pattern made by an applied thread as seen on cat. no. 44.5

Cat. no.	Length	Max dia.	Rim dia.	Rim	Resting surface	Colour	Remarks
44.1	4.6	4	1.4	Sheared	Flat	Clear brownish	Applied discs as decoration. Half of body missing.
44.2	6.4	5.3	4	Flaring & sheared	Pad	Clear greenish	Threads and bands applied as decoration.
44.3	4.3	3.9	2.9	Flaring & rolled-in	Pad	Reddish	Three discs as decoration. Rim partly restored.
44.4	4.1	4.6	2.8	Flaring & sheared	Concave w. ps	Milky white	Rim partly restored.
44.5	3.6	4.5	3	Flaring & sheared	Concave w. ps	Greyish decayed	Applied thread as decoration.
44.6	3.7	2.9	2.7	Flaring & sheared	Pad		Applied discs as decoration. Rim partly restored.
44.7	3.9	3					
44.8	3.6	2.9					
44.9	3.5	4					Applied thread as decoration.

Table 88. Description of vessels of Type 44. Measurements in centimetres.

Cat. no.	BNM no.	Area	Mound	Square	Context	Number	Remarks
44.1	A11040	Al-Hajar	1-94		Outside tomb	9	
44.2	27						No context information.
44.3	A14401	Al-Maqsha					Context information incomplete. Boucharlat & Salles 1989: no. 196.
44.4	A8315	Al-Maqsha	1978	5	Tomb	12	
44.5	A11243	Al-Hajar	1-94		Outside tomb	9	Nenna 1999: no. 306.
44.6	A15072	Al-Maqsha					Context information incomplete. Boucharlat & Salles 1989: no. 197, Nenna 1999: no. 305.
44.7		Al-Maqsha					Context information incomplete. Boucharlat & Salles 1989: no. 194. Vessel on display, BNM. Not illustrated.
44.8		Al-Maqsha					Context information incomplete. Boucharlat & Salles 1989: no. 195. Vessel on display, BNM. Not illustrated.
44.9		Al-Maqsha	1978	5	Tomb	12	On display BNM. Not illustrated.

Table 89. Context information for vessels of Type 44.

Figure 352. Cat. no. 44.1.   *Figure 353. Cat. no. 44.1.*

 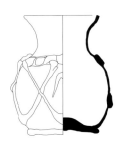

Figure 354. Cat. no. 44.2.   *Figure 355. Cat. no. 44.2.*

Figure 356. Cat. no. 44.3.   *Figure 357. Cat. no. 44.3*

Figure 358. Cat. no. 44.4.   *Figure 359. Cat. no. 44.4*

Figure 360. Cat. no. 44.5.   *Figure 361. Cat. no. 44.5.*

Figure 362. Cat. no. 44.6.

Figure 363. Cat. no. 45.1   *Figure 364. Cat. no. 45.1.*

 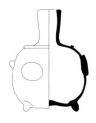

Figure 365. Cat. no. 45.2.   *Figure 366. Cat. no. 45.2.*

Figure 367. Cat. no. 45.3.   *Figure 368. Cat. no. 45.4.*   *Figure 369. Cat. no. 45.4.*

can be seen on a fragment from Qasr-I Abu Nasr (Whitcomb 1985: fig. 58.t). The type seems closely related to Types 45, 46 and 47, both stylistically and contextually, and a dating to the fifth to seventh century AD and a production within the Sasanian Empire is most likely.

Type 45: Bulbous flask
A bulbous body with a cylindrical neck characterizes Type 45. The vessels are decorated with applied discs or threads and the base is made of pinched-out knobs. The colour of the glass may have been yellowish brown, but is decayed to greyish.

Dating evidence and discussion
A characteristic type of this period is the bulbous flask. It has an almost globular body and a cylindrical neck and the vessels are decorated with applied discs, threads and pinched-out knobs. The type has good, though mainly undated, parallels published from Susa (Lamm 1931: pl. LXXVI, no. 2), Khārg (Steve 2003: pl. 45.1), Babylon (Reuther 1968: Taf. 95.233) and a long series published by Lamm (1929–1930: taf. 20, 21 and 23). In the Umm Khesham cemetery a bulbous flask of Type 45 was found in Grave 8, Sounding 24 and associated with fourth- to fifth-century AD vessels (Negro Ponzi 2005: fig. 4.12).

The characteristic form of these vessels could well derive from the bulbous flask, which came into use in the Roman Empire in the third century AD (Isings 1957: Form 103). Related examples have also been found in the Near East in, for example, the late third to mid-fourth century AD cemetery at Tell Mahuz (Negro Ponzi 1968–1969: no. 27) and Abu Skhair (Negro Ponzi 1972: no. 40).

The bulbous flask did, however, remain in fashion well into the Islamic period, since similar specimens have been reported from c. eighth-century AD layers in Seleucia (Negro Ponzi 1970–1971: nos 13–19, also with a dark-brown or greyish-brown patina), seventh- to ninth-century layers in Susa (Niveau I-III) (Kervran 1984: figs 7.10–11, with a slightly longer neck) and c. ninth- to tenth-century AD contexts in Nishapur (Kröger 1995: nos 154–159). Highly decorated examples are often depicted in Islamic art literature (see e.g. Carboni & Whitehouse 2001: nos 74, 86, 95, 99, 111), but they are most likely all of a ninth- to tenth-century AD date and characterized by a much longer neck than seen on the Bahraini examples.

The decorative scheme with applied discs, threads and knobs is not associated with Islamic glass and does not follow a Roman tradition. A globular bottle with a short cylindrical neck and two irregular rows of knobs decorating the middle of the body has been found at Abu Skhair (Negro Ponzi 1972: no. 40). It was tentatively dated to the second or third century AD, since no knobbed vessels of Sasanian date were known in 1972 to Negro Ponzi, and she generally dated the glass from the cemetery on the basis of the late Parthian pottery found there (*ibid.* 231–232). However, hemispherical bowls from Bahrain with knobs and datable to the third to fourth century AD (Type 41), indicate that the

Cat. no.	Length	Max dia.	Rim dia.	Rim	Resting surface	Colour	Remarks
45.1		4.2			Knobs and ps	Clear	Resting on 3 knobs. Rim and neck missing.
45.2	5.5	4.3	1.3	Sheared	Knobs and ps	Greyish	Resting on 3 knobs. Applied discs, thread and knobs as decoration.
45.3		4.7			Knobs and ps	Clear brownish	Resting on 3 knobs. Applied discs, thread and knobs as decoration. Upper neck and rim missing.
45.4	6	4.5		Sheared	Knobs	Greyish	

Table 90. Description of vessels of Type 45. Measurements in centimetres.

Cat. no.	BNM no.	Area	Mound	Square	Context	Number	Remarks
45.1	3777-2-91-7	Al-Maqsha	1991-92	C5	Mound fill		
45.2	A286	Al-Hajar	1-94		Outside tomb	9	
45.3	A15071	Al-Maqsha	1978	5	Tomb	12	Nenna 1999: no. 304.
45.4		Al-Maqsha	1978	5	Tomb	12	On display BNM, Vine 1993: 68.

Table 91. Context information for vessels of Type 45.

vessels from Abu Skhair could date slightly later than originally suggested. Recently Negro Ponzi has also verified the datings of the Abu Skhair cemetery, since it became apparent that the pottery belonged to a different group of graves (Negro Ponzi 2005).

Three vessels acquired in the Near East by the Corning Museum of Glass bring us much closer to a dating of the Bahraini vessels. They are also globular flasks with a cylindrical neck, but the geometric decoration, which is very similar in layout and concept to the Bahraini examples, is made by cutting down a thick blank, leaving lines and circular bosses standing out in relief, rather than applying them (von Saldern 1963: figs 10–12). This technique is well known in late Sasanian glass since fairly well dated examples of hemispherical bowls with a stylistically closely related decoration have been recovered in well-dated Far Eastern contexts. One bulbous flask very similar to one of the vessels acquired by the Corning Museum was found in a tomb where the epitaph indicates that the deceased died in AD 589 (Watt *et al.* 2004: no. 219). Possible stylistic forerunners for the examples in the Corning Museum of Glass have been found in the Chersonesos necropolis on the Crimean peninsula (Kunina 1997: cat. no. 226) and in Cologne (Doppelfeld 1966: Taf. 154), which both feature a decorative scheme of incised intersecting circles and horizontal bands, but without the deeply cut facets as seen on the Sasanian vessels.

The type seems definitely in use in the sixth century and maybe a century or so earlier, as indicated by the evidence from the Umm Khesham cemetery.

Type 46: Elongated flask

An elongated body characterizes Type 46. Two of the vessels are decorated with a "collar" around the lower neck (cat. nos 46.1 and 46.3) and one with three bands of "ribbed thread" (cat. no. 46.2). The remaining two vessels are also decorated with applied discs and threads.

Dating evidence and discussion

The elongated flask with an applied "collar" at the lower part of the neck (cat. nos 46.1 and 46.3) find a good and dated parallel in a vessel from a family tomb in Jericho, which also contained Byzantine coins of the fourth and fifth centuries. The coins were, however, quite corroded and the date they provide, due to the possibility of a long period of circulation, can only be regarded as a *terminus post quem* (Lamm 1929–1930: no. 3). The "collar" on the neck is also seen on two of the examples in cut glass from the Corning Museum of Glass mentioned above (von Saldern 1963: figs 10–11) and a remnant of this detail may be seen on a little flask with a thread around the neck found in a pit deposit in Fustat in southern Cairo. A dating of this deposit is indicated by two copper coins of Mahfuz, who was financial director of Egypt in AD 802–803 (Scanlon & Pinder-Wilson 2001: no. 32a).

Cat. no.	Length	Max dia.	Rim dia.	Rim	Resting surface	Colour	Remarks
46.1	7.3	2.9	1.1	Sheared & fp	Pad	Brownish	Applied "collar".
46.2	12	4.2	2.1	Sheared & fp	Pad	Clear brownish	Vertical bands of "ribbed threads".
46.3	5.6	2.2	1.3	Sheared & fp	Pad	Decayed brownish	Applied "collar".
46.4	9	3			Pad		Applied threads and discs.
46.5	7.9	4.6			Pad	Green	Ring-shaped vessel, with thin glass plaque closing the central part. Two discs applied to the side of the vessel.

Table 92. Description of vessels of Type 46. Measurements in centimetres.

Cat. no.	BNM no.	Area	Mound	Square	Context	Number	Remarks
46.1	22	Al-Hajar	1-94		Outside tomb	9	Vessel lost 2004.
46.2	A11262	Al-Hajar	1-94		Outside tomb	9	Nenna 1999: no. 301.
46.3	A13876	Al-Maqsha	2000	B8	Tomb	11	
46.4		Al-Maqsha	1978	5	Tomb	12	On display, BNM.
46.5							No context information. On display, BNM. Boucharlat & Salles 1989: no. 209.

Table 93. Context information for vessels of Type 46.

Figure 370. Cat. no. 46.1.   *Figure 371. Cat. no. 46.2.*   *Figure 372. Cat. no. 46.2.*

Figure 373. Cat. no. 46.3.   *Figure 374. Cat. no. 46.3.*

Figure 375. Cat. no. 46.4.   *Figure 376. Cat. no. 46.4.*   *Figure 377. Cat. no. 46.5.*

Elongated flasks without decoration, but similar in shape to the vessels of Type 46 (excluding cat. no. 46.5) have been found in Qasr-I Abu Nasr (Whitcomb 1985: fig. 58.e-f) and Khārg (Steve 2003: pls 44.1, 46.3, 48.6 and 50.2). Cat. no. 46.2 has three vertical bands of ribbed threads along the body ending in a horizontal band around the shoulder. Very similar ribbed threads can be seen on a zoomorphic vessel from Qasr-I Abu Nasr (Whitcomb 1985: Fig. 59.l), but they are also known from possibly earlier vessels in museum collections (e.g. Whitehouse 2005: no. 16, with a possible third-century AD date). A combination of applied discs as seen on cat. nos 46.4 and 46.5 and the ribbed thread can be seen on a unique anthropomorphic vessel, now in the Eretz Israel Museum, Tel Aviv (Carboni & Whitehouse 2001: no. 35; Carboni 2002), which then combine elements from some of the Bahraini vessels. A ribbed thread can also be seen on the shoulder of one of the Type 44 flasks (cat. no. 44.2), creating the upper border of a cross pattern, similar to the decoration on the miniature jug (cat. no. 47.1). Related decorative schemes find good parallels from late Sasanian sites as Qasr-I Abu Nasr (Whitcomb 1985: figs 58.j-l, 59.l), Susa (Lamm 1931: pl. LXXVI nos 1–5), but also at the cemetery on Khārg (Steve 2003: pl. 44.5).

Type 47: Miniature jug
A single miniature jug with a trefoil lip also belongs in this group (cat. no. 47.1) according to the colour of the vessel and the contextual relation to other vessels of the late Sasanian period.

Dating evidence and discussion
The miniature jug (cat. no. 47.1) has a bordered cross pattern of applied thread in the middle of the body. This kind of decoration seems to have been common on late Sasanian vessels (see above) and the contextual relation of cat. no. 47.1 to vessels of Types 44–46 suggests that these vessels, and also the rest of the group, are likely to have been produced in the late Sasanian period.

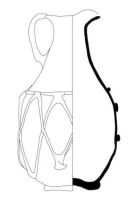

Figure 378. Cat. no. 47.1.   *Figure 379. Cat. no. 47.1.*

Cat. no.	Length	Max dia.	Rim dia.	Rim	Resting surface	Colour	Remarks
47.1	9.8	5.5	3	Trifoil & fp	Pad	Clear brownish	Applied threads.

Table 94. Description of vessels of Type 47. Measurements in centimetres.

Cat. no.	BNM no.	Area	Mound	Square	Context	Number	Remarks
47.1	A11263	Al-Hajar	1-94		Outside tomb	9	Nenna 1999: no. 302.

Table 95. Context information for vessels of Type 47.

Non-datable vessels and fragments

A few vessels cannot be dated due to a lack of dated parallels and contextual evidence, and another group is too fragmented to be assigned to one of the types described above.

Non-datable vessels

For two types no parallels have been found and no contextual relations with other vessels are documented. It is therefore not possible to suggest a dating for these vessels with an acceptable degree of certainty.

Type 48: Stemmed plate

Type 48 is made of green glass with a yellow tint. It is characterized by a high, stemmed foot.

Dating evidence and discussion

No parallels have been found and the vessel has not been recovered with any datable material.

Type 49: Low plate

Type 49 is standing on a circular trail of glass, has

Figure 380. Cat. no. 48.1, scale 1:4

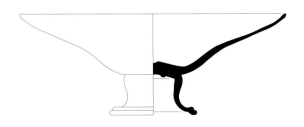

Figure 381. Cat. no. 48.1, scale 1:4

Cat. no.	Length	Rim dia.	Rim	Resting surface	Colour	Remarks
48.1	11.5	28.1	Plain	Moulded foot w. ps	Clear greenish	Pontil scars both at the bottom of the inside of the vessel and inside the stemmed foot. Base diameter 8.7 cm.

Table 96. Description of the vessel of Type 48. Measurements in centimetres.

Cat. no.	BNM no.	Area	Mound	Square	Context	Number	Remarks
48.1	A11362	Saar	5-87-88	6	Tomb	2	Nenna 1999: no 286; Vine 1993: 68.

Table 97. Context information for the vessel of Type 48.

Cat. no.	Length	Rim dia.	Rim	Resting surface	Colour	Remarks
49.1	5.2	19	Straight & fp	Ringfoot	Clear greenish	The bottom of the vessel is convex inside the ringfoot with a pontil mark, 2.7 cm in diameter. An applied thread marks the body/rim transition.

Table 98. Description of the vessel of Type 49. Measurements in centimetres.

Cat. no.	BNM no.	Area	Mound	Square	Context	Number	Remarks
49.1	A272	Saar	6-91-92	1	Tomb	1	

Table 99. Context information for the vessel of Type 49.

Figure 382. Cat. no. 49.1.

Figure 383. Cat. no. 49.1.

straight sides and a vertical rim. An applied thread marks the body/rim transition.

Dating evidence and discussion
No parallels have been found and the vessel has not been recovered with any datable material.

Diagnostic fragments
The nine diagnostic fragments are too small to assign to a specific type.

Dating evidence and discussion
Five of the fragments (cat. nos NON.3–7) were found together in a tomb where the remaining vessels date to the third to fifth century AD. Cat. no. NON.1 was found with a Type 41 vessel and cat. no. NON.8 with vessels of Types 12, 25 and 43.

Figure 384. Cat. no. NON.1.

Figure 385. Cat. no. NON.1.

Figure 386. Cat. no. NON.3.

Figure 387. Cat. no. NON.4.

Figure 388. Cat. no. NON.5.

Figure 389. Cat. no. NON.6.

Figure 390. Cat. no. NON.7.

Figure 391. Cat. no. NON.8.

Cat. no.	Base dia.	Rim dia.	Rim	Resting surface	Colour	Remarks
NON.1	7.7			Moulded foot w. ps	Bluish	Probably the base from a stemmed bowl/cup.
NON.2			Outsp. & rolled-in		Brownish	Rim fragment.
NON.3	1.8			Kicked	Clear greenish	Base fragment.
NON.4				Concave	Clear greenish	Base fragment.
NON.5		3.3	Outsp. & rolled-in		Black	Rim fragment.
NON.6						Body fragment with nip't diamond waies.
NON.7	7			Concave	Clear greenish	Base fragment. The surface very decayed.
NON.8	2.5			Kicked & ring-foot	Clear greenish	Base fragment.

Table 100. Description of the diagnostic fragments. Measurements in centimetres.

Cat. no.	BNM no.	Area	Mound	Square	Context	Number	Remarks
NON.1	A898	Hamad Town	73-85-86		Tomb	44	
NON.2	A9050	Saar	5-96-97	C3	Tomb	3	Not illustrated.
NON.3	A9056/1	Hamad Town	10-89-90	E4	Tomb	41-2	
NON.4	A9056	Hamad Town	10-89-90	E4	Tomb	41-2	
NON.5	A9056	Hamad Town	10-89-90	E4	Tomb	41-2	
NON.6	A9056	Hamad Town	10-89-90	E4	Tomb	41-2	
NON.7	A9056	Hamad Town	10-89-90	E4	Tomb	41-2	
NON.8	A11031	Saar	5-95-96	E2	Tomb	36	Cat. no. 35.5 is probably the rim of this vessel.

Table 101. Context information for the diagnostic fragments.

Conclusion

The Bahraini collection of glass vessels from the Tylos period burials covers the period from just before the invention of glass-blowing in the middle of the first century BC, followed by the production boom of blown glass in the first century AD within the Roman Empire and the development of a possible independent Parthian and Sasanian glass-making tradition. The glass vessels were presented in chronological order, as it became clear that the vessels were grouped in four chronological assemblages. It must, however, be pointed out that these groups do not reflect the chronological span of the individual types, but only the period they are most likely to date from.

A total of forty-nine types of glass vessel types have been described and the great majority of them have been dated — only two types cannot be dated at present due to the lack of dated parallels or find combinations with dated material in the Bahraini tombs

The great majority of vessels are unguentaria and a more detailed analysis of the assemblage can be found in Chapter 4 where the development of glass is viewed in relation to the pottery.

The pre-blowing assemblage and early blown types

Five types can be assigned to this assemblage, two of them are unguentaria and three are bowls.

This assemblage consists of the three core-formed bottles, four marbled unguentaria and a few cast bowls; all of these vessels are likely to date to the period from the last century BC to the first half of the first century AD. Except for cat. no. 1.3 the remainder are of well-known and well-described types. The core-formed bottles are likely to have been produced in the Syro/Palestinian region and their presence in tombs in Bahrain and in Crimea indicate that this type was well distributed and probably manufactured in large numbers, a conclusion that the vast amount of vessels in museum collections supports.

Type	Number
Type 1: Core-formed bottle	3
Type 2: Marbled unguentarium	4
Type 3: Linear incised bowl	1
Type 4: Pillar moulded bowl	2
Type 5: Unique bowl	1
Total	11

Table 103. Early types of glass vessels.

The cast bowls of which fairly large quantities have been reported from ed-Dur (Whitehouse 1998; 2000) illustrate a similar pattern. This indicates that a glass industry was well established with an international distribution before the invention of glass-blowing, and that trade relations between the production centres, probably located in the eastern Mediterranean, and the Gulf was established at this time.

Three bottles in the Bahrain National Museum and one vessel from Bahrain in the British Museum illustrate aspects of the invention of inflating glass. The four marbled vessels (Type 2) are well-known early types. They are made of a blank of multicoloured canes fused together, which was then reheated, folded around the blowpipe and inflated. The symmetrical appearance of the shape of these vessels documents a familiarity with blowing, but the use of a pre-fabricated blank illustrates a continuation of aspects of pre-blowing techniques, as this technique was used for manufacturing cast mosaic bowls, which were very popular in the Mediterranean area in the late Hellenistic period and early imperial period. In the ed-Dur assemblage the linear-cut bowl and the pillar-moulded bowl are well represented, but the contemporary core-formed and marbled unguentaria are absent.

Assemblage	No. of unguentaria	Freq. of unguentaria	No. of bowls & cups	Freq. of bowls & cups
The pre-blowing assemblage and early blown types	7	64%	4	36%
The early Roman imperial assemblage	139	97%	5	3%
The late Parthian and early Sasanian assemblage	98	73%	37	27%
The Sasanian assemblage	19	100%	0	0

Table 102. Numbers and frequencies of unguentaria and bowls in the four chronological phases counted by vessel.

The early Roman imperial assemblage

In the first half of the first century AD, the production of closed glass vessels was done solely by blowing and many open beakers and bowls were made on the blowpipe, rather than cast. However, casting of bowls remained in use, whereas core-forming of bottles went out.

Type	Number
Type 6: Plain unguentarium	43
Type 7: Plain unguentarium	5
Type 8: "Baby feeding" bottle	1
Type 9: Miniature jug	2
Type 10: Amphoriskos	6
Type 11: Amphoriskos with pointed base	3
Type 12: Aryballos	20
Type 13: Amphoriskos	17
Type 14: Miniature transport amphora	5
Type 15: Date-flask	23
Type 16: Hexagonal bottle	2
Type 17: Lenticular bottle	1
Type 18: Scroll or lozenges decorated bottle	8
Type 19: Squat bottle with two handles	2
Type 20: Bottle, imitating a bunch of grapes	1
Type 21: Beaker with applied decoration	2
Type 22: Bowl with cut-out ridge	2
Type 23: Mould-blown conical beaker	1
Total	144

Table 104. Types of the early Roman imperial assemblage.

The most common type of blown vessels in the Bahraini assemblage is the Type 6 plain unguentarium, but mould-blown vessels and amphoriskoi are also well represented. Type 6 is also the simplest form, and it is the one made of the plainest glass colours, i.e. white, or with a bluish or greenish tint, whereas the mould-blown vessels and the ones with handles are often strongly coloured, e.g. purple, blue, brown or green. Most of the vessels of this period are made of good quality glass that has been blown to rather thin-walled containers and only a few vessels have a pontil scar. The more complex types, i.e. the mould-blown vessels and the ones with handles, find good parallels from presumed Syro/Palestinian production centres and it is most likely that they are imports from that region. During the first century AD the open shapes were very rare compared to the increasing amount of small bottles placed in the graves, with a ratio of *c.* 1 in 20 (see Table 102).

By far the majority of vessels, which seem to have been imported from the Roman Empire, can be dated to the first or early second century AD, and only the bath flasks seem to have had a longer period of use. Perhaps this shape, which was used for over two centuries, was a trademark for the content, rather than just a container.

It was during the first century AD that the site of ed-Dur was flourishing, and glass vessels were rather common finds in both graves and settlements. The cast monochrome and mosaic bowls from ed-Dur indicate that some luxury vessels arrived at ed-Dur, and the absence of two distinctive types of late first to early second century AD, i.e. colourless bowls and plates with overhanging rims and facet-cut beakers, led Whitehouse to suggest that the upper date of the main occupation of the site should be around AD 75. Although such vessels are widely distributed and are found at e.g. Quseir al-Qadim and Dura Europos, their absence in the Bahraini assemblage and in Seleucia (see above and Negro Ponzi 2002), could indicate that the lack of such vessels may not be explained in terms of chronology only. Negro Ponzi suggests that the lack of high-quality tableware in the finds from Seleucia is due to the moving of the capital to Ctesiphon and the fact that the higher classes of society did not stay behind in the old capital, but followed the royal court to the new seat. Those who stayed behind in Seleucia used cheaper ceramics for serving, but small glass bottles for presumably oil and perfumes (Negro Ponzi 2002: 110). The presence of a fairly high frequency of glass tableware dating to the first three quarters of the first century AD could, according to Negro Ponzi's hypothesis, indicate that ed-Dur did have some significance during that period, but lost its importance in the second half of the first century. However, the relation between specific types of vessels and excavation context, i.e. funeral or settlement, is not addressed in the treatment of the ed-Dur material, since the material was often mixed up due to the activities of tomb robbers. This affects the comparison between the Bahraini assemblage and the glass from ed-Dur because, if the majority of the open forms relate to the settlements, the selection of glass vessels for grave goods has been quite similar to the one on Bahrain, i.e. a preference for small bottles as grave goods. On the other hand, the absence of glass vessels and fragments at Qala'at al-Bahrain is in sharp contrast to the high numbers of fragments from the settlement in ed-Dur.

No evidence for a production of glass vessels on Bahrain in the "Tylos" period has been found (slag, cullet, chunks, ingots or kilns). Neither has any proof of production facilities been found in Arabia or within the Parthian Empire. The distribution of types also suggests that most of the vessels may have been produced elsewhere, but the fact that some vessels that are likely to date to this period are produced by using plant-ash glass rather that natron-based glass, indicates that a production in the East did take place in the Parthian period (see Appendix 2). One cannot exclude the possibility of travelling glassmakers, who for a limited period set up a workshop on e.g. Bahrain and made flasks (or beads) from cullet. Since both craftsmanship and raw material is likely to have been imported then, neither stylistic nor compositional analysis could confirm such a hypothesis, but only the recovery of remnants of glass production. One should also bear in mind the possibility that the glass bottles reached eastern Arabia because of their content rather than the vessel itself.

The sudden increase in the number of glass vessels placed in the graves in this period can thus be linked to the invention of glass-blowing and the increased output of small bottles and flasks from the Syro/Palestinian production centres. But how did vessels produced in the eastern Roman Empire end up as grave goods in Bahrain? The three possible trade routes suggested by Whitehouse (1998) from the eastern Mediterranean to ed-Dur could well be applied to the Bahrain assemblage of the first and early second century AD. The implications and historical setting for this trade will be discussed further in Chapter 5.

The late Parthian and early Sasanian assemblage

The glass vessels of this period appear to differ from the previous period. The range of colours is limited, the majority of vessels are greenish in colour, and the quality of the glass seems poorer with many air bubbles and thicker walls.

As noted by Whitehouse in his treatment of the vessels from ed-Dur, some of these showed similarities with Roman vessels, but they only find exact parallels in the Near East (Whitehouse 2000: 116–117). The composition analyses conducted on vessels from this Phase indicate that the vessels were made of plant-ash glass, which also suggests that these vessels were produced in the East (see Appendix 2). Type 7 may be the earliest regionally produced vessels represented in the Bahraini collection. Relatively thick walls of plain-coloured glass and a pronounced pontil scar characterize them and the stylistic affiliation with Type 6 suggests a dating from the second half of the first century AD to the second century AD. Probably from the second century AD the great majority of glass vessels find their closest parallels in the Partho/Sasanian realm, a fact Negro Ponzi noted long ago (1972: 218). Types 24

Type	Number
Type 24: Flask with funnel mouth	4
Type 25: Bulbous flask	22
Type 26: Unguentarium with indented body	6
Type 27: Candlestick unguentarium	6
Type 28: Bell-shaped unguentarium	15
Type 29: Unguentarium with globular body and long neck	2
Type 30: Unguentarium with pinched-out ribs	1
Type 31: Unguentarium with conical body	1
Type 32: Toilet bottle	1
Type 33: Unguentarium with applied thread	1
Type 34: Ointment jar	28
Type 35: Miniature jug	5
Type 36: Globular jug	1
Type 37: "Mercury bottle"	1
Type 38: Mould-blown unguentarium	1
Type 39: Optic blown vessel	4
Type 40: Conical beaker	10
Type 41: Hemispherical bowl	13
Type 42: Plain little bowl	11
Type 43: Little bowl with coil base	3
Total	136

Table 105. Types of the late Parthian and early Sasanian period.

to 35 and 39 are all types that generally seem to be confined to the East. However, a few bottles may still originate in the West, e.g. the mercury bottle (Type 37), some of the vessels of Type 25 and cat. no. 41.13. This is similar to the glass from Nineveh, where a few Late-Roman imports were also noted (Simpson 2005). The bath flasks also appear to have remained in use well into the third century AD. During the third or fourth century AD, drinking cups and beakers also became more frequent. They are often contextually associated with jugs in hard-fired ware or glazed ware and the suggestion, initially put forward by Harden in his treatment of the Karanis material (1936), that Type 40 are lamps is thus very unlikely for those found in Bahrain. The style of the cups and beakers still relies on Roman vessels, but the vessels only find close parallels in the East. Type 42 plain little bowl and Type 43 little bowl with coil base are new types without clear relations to the Roman tradition. They are cast of thick green glass and have pronounced pontil scars and fire-polished rims. The two plates (Types 48 and 49) may also belong to the Partho/Sasanian assemblage due to the similarities of the glass and manufacturing details to Types 42 and 43, but this is only a very tentative suggestion.

Although a general dating of this assemblage to the second to fifth century AD has been suggested, it is clear when looking through the possible datings of the individual types and the find combinations that all vessels in this period can be safely dated to the fourth century AD. Furthermore typical second- and third-century AD types are absent (e.g. Isings 1957: Types 86, 91, 95, and the colourless bowls and plates with overhanging rims and the facet-cut beakers). The possibility of a hiatus in dated material in the second and third centuries must therefore be considered as a very likely possibility.

The late Sasanian assemblage

The majority of the vessels in this assemblage are from only two contexts, each containing six vessels (i.e. Al-Hajar, 1–94, outside Tomb 9 and Al-Maq-sha, 1978, Tomb 12).

Type	Number
Type 44: Flask with funnel mouth	9
Type 45: Bulbous flask	4
Type 46: Elongated flask	5
Type 47: Miniature jug	1
Total	19

Table 106. Types of the late Parthian and early Sasanian period.

Type 45 was directly influenced by what we could call the "mature Sasanian style", i.e. vessels made by cutting down a thick blank leaving lines and circular bosses standing out in relief, since this type finds close stylistic parallels in three cut vessels from the Corning Museum of Glass (von Saldern 1963: figs 10–12) and a dated vessel from China (Watt *et al.* 2004: no. 219). It is not only for the bulbous flasks that such a close stylistic relation exists between cut vessels and vessels with applied decoration. A stemmed bowl found in China with two rows of applied discs (Watt *et al.* 2004: no. 96) shows great similarity with a cut bowl from the Corning Museum of Glass (Whitehouse 2005: no. 56), and two globular bottles with two rows of applied discs and a pad base in the Nasser D. Khalili Collection of Islamic Art (Goldstein 2005: nos 16 and 17) are very similar to a vessel in cut glass from the same collection (*ibid.* no. 47). Goldstein also noted that the vessels with applied discs are imitations of vessels with cut glass (*ibid.* 39), although the vessels with applied discs are given a slightly later date (sixth–eighth century) than the cut ones (fifth–seventh century) (*ibid.* 58).

The vessels in cut glass are well-known and highly prized museum artefacts, and since most of these vessels (when the exact provenance is known) have been found at major sites and presumably belonged to the higher segments of society and were exported as far away as China and Japan, they may also have been highly prized in the past. Applying decoration is a much less time-consuming process than cutting down a thick blank and can therefore be assumed to produce much cheaper vessels. It is therefore a possibility that the smaller vessels with applied decoration were contemporary imitations of vessels in cut glass. The glass of the Bahraini examples has weathered to a greyish mass and so have some of the cut vessels. This could indicate that two lines of production were running during this period, one supplying the upper classes and their long-distance trade relations and the other supplying the masses with cheaply produced imitations. Only the cheaper versions have been found on Bahrain. The possibility of a "degeneration" or "inflation" of the production also exists and is supported by the fact that the two categories of vessels have not been found together in contemporary contexts. This is, however, an argument based on negative evidence and the number of published late Sasanian sites, which have been excavated in detail and are of a nature that could provide a significant corpus of glass, is very close to zero. The best argument so far is thus the stylistic analysis, which indicates a late Sasanian dating for this group, although a very early Islamic dating for the deposition of the vessels cannot be excluded. Nevertheless, it seems evident that a continued deposition of glass vessels in the Bahraini tombs did not take place from the previous period, since no find combinations with vessels of the two groups exist and the datings indicate a fourth-century AD date for the previous assemblage and a sixth- or seventh-century AD for this group. During this hiatus the style developed dramatically. From being rooted in the Roman tradition an independent stylistic tradition was developed, which was characterized by monochrome vessels in plain colours, but with a relatively complicated decorative schema of applied and cut decoration that created a lively expression in shades and optic effects.

The Pottery

3

In the Gulf region the study of pottery from the period of Alexander the Great's conquest of the Achaemenid Empire until Islam has over the last twenty-five years made significant progress, due to the publication of finds from old excavations and new discoveries. The main topics have been chronology and typology. However, studies of styles and influence have also been made and proved a main source for the reconstruction of the cultural history of east Arabia. The number of significant sites and detailed studies is still very limited, thus making wider discussions of the individual vessels difficult because of the lack of comparable material. In the following, I will briefly summarize the most significant works and list the most important sites that have been used for the dating of the vessels from Bahrain.

Bahrain

Only three settlement sites have produced pottery from the Tylos period in Bahrain. The largest and by far the most important is Qala'at al-Bahrain, whereas the Barbar Temple site and the Saar site have produced only few finds, and these are from the latter part of the period.

Qala'at al-Bahrain

During the first year of archaeological exploration by the Danish expedition in the 1953–1954 season, it was discovered that the so-called "Bahrain Fort" – Qala'at al-Bahrain in Arabic – which dates to the period from the fourteenth to the sixteenth century AD, was situated on top of an artificial mound, created by an accumulation of debris from human activity. During the first season, excavations had already revealed evidence of larger buildings and many stratigraphic levels, and the potential of the site became evident.

The chronology of the ancient occupation was outlined in 1958 and slightly refined in 1969 by Bibby (1958; 1996), who described six "cities" based on the typological development of the pottery. Periods I–III date to the Bronze Age, Period IV to the Iron Age, Period V is the Tylos period and Period VI the Islamic period. An independent system based on two of the Danish excavations was created

and used to discuss the long-term developments of land use (Larsen 1983). The chronological system developed by Bibby was later refined and subdivided into shorter periods in the publication of the two main areas of excavation, i.e. Excavation 520 at the northern city wall and Excavation 519 at the centre of the tell (and supplemented by studies of other excavations at the site). Period V was divided into six sub-periods and the pottery was described for each of them (Højlund & Andersen 1994; 1997; Andersen 2001; 2002).

The earliest Tylos period or Period Va1 is best attested in a pit deposit in Excavation 431 at Qala'at al-Bahrain. Here a selection of local pottery was found with seven fragments of Attic black glazed pottery dating to the late fourth and early third century BC. The assemblage of local pottery illustrates a change in fashion in the period after the Greek conquest of the Achaemenid Empire by the adoption of Greek shapes by local potters. However, the new shapes such as the fish plate and the bowl with incurving rim do not indicate any changes in habits, since small, open bowls were also very common in the Achaemenid period (Andersen 2002). For the following periods, very little evidence providing absolute dates to the sequence has been found. The periods and datings suggested by Højlund are based on the internal site stratigraphy and development of the pottery. The relative chronology is dated provisionally by parallels to other sites, especially Susa and Failaka. Period Va and Vb at Qala'at al-Bahrain are contemporary with Period I on Failaka and Period Vd with Period II (Højlund & Andersen 1994: 296-299).

Period	From	To
Va1	300 BC	275 BC
Va2	275 BC	200 BC
Vb	200 BC	100 BC
Vc	100 BC	AD 1
Vd	AD 1	AD 200
Ve	AD 200	AD 400

Table 107. Sub-periods and their suggested datings at Qala'at al-Bahrain (from Højlund & Andersen 1994; 1997).

From 1978 and until 2003 French teams have excavated next to the two main areas of the Danish excavations and recovered substantial finds from the Tylos period. However, the publication of these excavations is still in progress and only preliminary works have been published (Lombard & Kervran 1993; Lombard 1994).[11]

The Barbar Temple site

The Barbar Temple was also discovered during the first season of exploration and excavated by the Danish expedition. The temple itself dates to the centuries around 2000 BC (Andersen & Højlund 2003: 323). However, more recent pottery was recovered in all trenches from layers overlying the Bronze Age temple. A large assemblage of predominantly ninth-century AD pottery was found in the fill of a well (Frifelt 2001: 13–34) and similar material was found in other scattered contexts, together with some slightly earlier material and a few later sherds. Two groups of wares do not belong in either the Bronze Age or the ninth-century AD assemblages. The first is a group of alkaline-glazed pottery and the second consists of sherds in a very hard-fired fabric with lime grits. Based on external parallels mainly from the Oman peninsula these two classes seem to date to the period from probably the third to the ninth centuries AD (Andersen & Kennet 2003).

Saar

Near the modern village of Saar an isolated structure was excavated by the Department of Antiquities. Within a rectangular building a coin dating to the fifth century AD and a few sherds probably of hard-fired ware were recovered, but the amount of finds from this site is very limited and little-known (Crawford, Killick & Moon 1997: 20). It has, however, been suggested that the structure may have been a fire temple, since there are central niches inside the main room of the building (Lombard & Kervran 1993: 134).

North-east Arabia

A large number of sites with pottery from the Tylos period have been reported from north-east Saudi Arabia. However, very little systematic work has been carried out and although many of the sites seem to have significant potential, it has not been possible to benefit from it. Early and sporadic investigations in the region have later been supplemented by survey campaigns and some selections of pottery have been published.

Dhahran

A number of tumuli have been excavated near the modern town of Dhahran, which is the site nearest to Bahrain on the Saudi Arabian coastline. The excavation of a mound with a tomb for multiple burials revealed some fragments of pottery and a complete glass vessel dated to the fourth century AD (Potts et al. 1978: 18–19, pl. 10). A Type 41 bowl in glass datable to the third or fourth century AD has also been recovered from Tomb B-16 together with a jug with two handles in glazed ware. Further tombs have also contained pottery (Zarins, Mughannum & Kamal 1984: 41–43).

Tarut Island

Tarut Island is situated in the bay north of Dhahran off the coast from Qatif. The Island was briefly surveyed by Bibby and his team in 1968 and a tell in the middle of the island, surrounded by Tarut Town could potentially be one of the most important in eastern Arabia (Bibby 1973: 31). A little collection of pottery datable to the Tylos period was recovered from farmers, who were digging irrigations canals at Fariq al-Akhrash 1.5 km north of Tarut Town. It was mainly complete vessels and may thus be grave goods, although no tombs were encountered (Bibby 1973: 35–37).

Ain Jawan

The site is situated north of Tarut Island just inland of the sandy peninsula forming the northern barrier of Tarut Bay. The ancient site consists of both a settlement and tombs. A little selection of pottery from the surface dating to the Tylos period was published by Bowen with comments by Day and Matson (Bowen 1950: 57–68, figs 18, 21, 22 and 23). More recently a larger corpus has been published by Potts, although he was not able to refine the chronology of the site (1993a).

Thaj

The site is situated c. 90 km inland from the nearest accessible point on the coast of the Gulf and c. 160 km west-north-west of Dhahran. The main feature

---

[11] The French publication of the Coastal Fortress appeared in 2006, but after this manuscript was completed. However, the results regarding the pottery do not vary from the preliminary results published in Lombard & Kervran 1993 and references etc. are accordingly not changed.

at the site is a large fortified settlement measuring *c.* 700 x 575 m (Bibby 1973: 10). It has been suggested that Thaj is the site of Gerrha, a prosperous city in north-east Arabia in the Hellenistic period referred to by numerous ancient authors, because Thaj is by far the most significant site that has been discovered within the possible location of Gerrha.[12]

In modern times the site has been known by European scholars since the nineteenth century and in 1968 a Danish expedition made the first large survey and exploratory excavations at the site (Bibby 1973: 10–28; 1996: 222–236). A sondage measuring 2 x 2 m was laid out just within the south side of the city wall. It was taken to a depth of *c.* 5 m and produced a large amount of finds, notably pottery fragments, figurines and offering bowls. In 1983 a team from Freie Universität, Berlin in co-operation with the Saudi Arabian Department of Antiquities conducted further excavations at Thaj (Potts 1990; 1993*b*). These excavations have been followed by investigations by the Saudi Arabian Department of Antiquities (Eskoubi & al-Aila 1985).

The pottery found in the surveys and excavations in the settlement is quite coherent. Bibby noted that there were no significant differences in the material from the different layers of sondage within the city wall, and the majority of vessels could be assigned to only nine types. Potts tried in his treatment of the pottery excavated by the German expedition to present a sequence from the "deep sounding", but the chronology indicated by the archaeological layers is not reflected in the development of the pottery.

From Thaj a fairly large amount of sherds of Attic black glazed pottery has been recovered from the tomb area and the foundation trench for the city wall, which thus can be dated to the late fourth or third century BC (see Bibby 1973: fig. 6; Potts 1993*b*). Few securely datable finds from the following periods have been reported. A possible Nabataean sherd may date to the first century AD and a good handful of Nabataean, Parthian and Sasanian coins indicate some activities at the site throughout the Tylos period. Nevertheless, the majority of the pottery does probably belong to the late fourth and third century BC.

Failaka

L. Hannestad's study of the pottery finds from the Danish excavations of a Hellenistic fortress (Tell F5) on Failaka was the first exhaustive treatment of the complete pottery assemblage from a Hellenistic period site in the Gulf region. Hannestad described two assemblages of pottery representing two periods of occupation. The beginning of Period I and thus the foundation of the fortress was dated by two Attic black glazed sherds, one of which can be dated to 285–250 BC. From the occupations during Period I a coin hoard was found dating from the late third century BC, stamped Rhodian amphora handles dated to 225–200 BC and the latest finds may be a coin of Hyspaosinos, king of Characene *c.* 140–110 BC and two terracotta figurines datable to *c.* 100 BC. It was therefore suggested that Period I lasted from "around or not much before the middle of the 3ʳᵈ century BC to the very late 2ⁿᵈ or early 1ˢᵗ century BC". Although an arbitrary division of Period I in the upper and lower levels was made, no differences in the pottery assemblages could be identified (Hannestad 1983).

Period II was defined by a limited collection of pottery (the BI-ware group) found above the Period I material in front of and in the pronaos of Temple A. This assemblage was tentatively dated to the very late first century BC and the beginning of the first century AD (Hannestad 1983: 78–79). Very little of the pottery was believed to be imported from the Arabian mainland, though it was argued that a group of bowls were imitations of Nabataean pottery, whereas the majority of vessels found good parallels in Mesopotamia and Susiana (1983). Later, French excavations supplemented the sequence at the Hellenistic fortress on Failaka (Bernard, Gachet & Salles 1990).

A significant proportion of the types from Failaka illustrate Greek influence, and Hannestad supplemented her study of the pottery from Failaka with a study of Greek influence in Near Eastern pottery in the Hellenistic period. This influence was understood by Hannestad as an indicator of the degree of Hellenization in terms of colonizations after Alexander the Great. Although this hypothesis has recently been questioned (Petrie 2002), Hannestad's identification of strong Greek influence in the Near Eastern repertoire of pottery in the Seleucid period has been widely accepted.

The question of Roman influence has also been addressed in relation to the finds from Failaka, although only sporadically. Salles points out similarities between the crater with three feet (Type AE) and similar Mediterranean vessels, but suggests an eastern origin for the type, rather than it being a

---

[12] An identification first suggested by Glob (1968: 144).

western development (1990: 320–324). Potts also discusses an influence from vessels in terra sigillatae, via Nabataean bowls to the thin-walled bowls in sand-tempered ware (Potts 1993*b*). However, more recent studies (Højlund & Andersen 1994: figs 1434–1435) have documented that this type was in use in eastern Arabia before the expansion of the Romans in the East and the rise of the Nabataeans (see below for a further discussion).

South-east Arabia

Within the last twenty-five years significant investigations have been carried out in the United Arab Emirates and also partly in the Sultanate of Oman, of sites dating to the Hellenistic period. However, much of this work has not yet been published in full, but a significant corpus of published pottery is available.

Mleiha

The first excavations at the site were carried out by an Iraqi team in 1973, which resulted in the publication of a selection of pottery including a stamped handle of a Rhodian amphora (Madlhoom 1974; Taha 1974). A French team resumed work at the site in 1986 and preliminary articles presenting some of the pottery have been published (Boucharlat & Mouton 1993; 1994) and an unpublished PhD thesis by M. Mouton (1992) dealing more extensively with the pottery and other findings has been widely circulated. The pottery sequence covers the period from the late third century BC to the beginning of the second century AD.

Ed-Dur

An Iraqi team was the first to investigate the site in the early 1970s, followed by surveys by a four-nation expedition in the 1980s and 90s. Two chronological main phases have been recognized, the first is the main settlement with adjacent tombs dating to the first century AD. The second phase is a fortress dating to the third century AD and situated on a sand dune between the main settlement and the lagoon, which in ancient times gave access to the sea. From both phases some pottery has been published in a number of preliminary progress reports (Salles 1984; Haerinck, Metdepenninghen & Stevens 1991; 1992; Mouton 1992; Haerinck *et al.* 1993) and in the final publication of the tombs excavated by the Belgium team (Haerinck 2001). Studies of the finds are, however, still in progress.

Kush

The site of Kush consists of a tell measuring 120 x 100 m, which was partly excavated between 1994 and 2001. Pottery from various Islamic periods was recovered together with a significant material from possible two pre-Islamic periods. The first period has been dated to the fifth to sixth century AD due to some similarities with the pottery from the late phase at ed-Dur, but also illustrating some typological differences. The second assemblage was dated to the seventh and eighth centuries AD on basis of a single C[14] date (AD 645–710) and a coin of Kavad I (issued AD 507–519) (Kennet 2004: 12–14).

Minor sites

A small quantity of pottery comparable to the vessels from Bahrain has been recovered from tombs of the so-called "Samad culture", which is believed to be contemporary with the Tylos period. The majority is, however, of a local tradition (Yule 2001), which seems distant from the Bahraini material. The identification of pottery assemblages in the Gulf region dating to the Sasanian period has mainly been possible due to discoveries of minor sites on the Oman peninsula. The first significant assemblage to be described was found at Jazirat al-Ghanam (de Cardi 1975), which was later supplemented with assemblages from Khatt (de Cardi, Kennet & Stocks 1994; Kennet 1998). Together with the important collections dated to the Sasanian period from Kush and ed-Dur, we are now able to identify Sasanian period pottery in the Gulf region.

Mesopotamia and Iran

Over the last 100 years major sites dating to the Seleucid, Parthian and Sasanian eras have been excavated in Mesopotamia and Iran. The pottery from a number of these sites has been published in full; from others only preliminary reports exist. Added to these are a number of smaller collections and studies. However, during the study of the Bahraini material it became clear that the great majority of material from Mesopotamia and Iran did not share specific and characteristic details with the material from the Gulf, although the general inventory of shapes was in part the same. A possible significant site relating Mesopotamia with the Gulf region is Charax Spasinou, known from ancient sources to be situated at the head of the Gulf and perhaps where a now dried-up canal leads the Eulaeus River (modern-day Karkheh) into a former Tigris canal. On that location evidence of an embankment measuring *c.* 2.8 x 1.4 km has been found and a little, possibly Sasanian, pottery have been collected on the surface. However, no major excavations have been carried out and only one vessel has been illustrated (Hansman 1967; 1984).

Seleucia

The pottery from the University of Michigan excavations in Seleucia was published by Debevoise (1934) who described an assemblage, which was divided into four levels. The dating of the pottery was based on coins, but historical episodes played a significant role in the attributions of some very precise dating for the levels (*ibid*. 7–11). It is, however, questionable whether historical events, such as battles and possible sacks of the cities, are likely to have had the recognizable impact that would make them detectable in the archaeological record. Nevertheless, the datings from Seleucia correspond fairly well with the datings of most of the Bahraini types. This is probably due to the fact that coins played a significant role in the dating of the Seleucia material and most of the material belongs only to two levels (II and III) with a relatively short lifespan (Level III = 141 BC to AD 43 and Level II = AD 43 to 116). More recent Italian excavations have not yet been published in full, but some preliminary articles have been presented (Valtz 1984; 1991; 1993; 2000; 2002) and in 2002 the present author was able to study a reference collection kept in Turin. An interesting observation is that terra sigillatae served as an important source of inspiration for local potters from the second half of the second century BC, who manufactured a local red-burnished ware (Valtz 1993).

Other sites

Dura Europos was one of the larger towns en route from Palmyra to the Arabian Gulf. Yale University and the French Academy of Inscriptions and Letters conducted large-scale excavations at the site between the two world wars. From every season (except the last one) a preliminary report was published and later monographs dealt with the various find groups and architectural remains. The pottery was published in three volumes: *The Green Glazed Pottery* (Toll 1943), *The Greek and Roman Pottery* (Cox 1949) and *The Commonware Pottery. The Brittle Ware* (Dyson 1968).

A very large selection of pottery from Uruk has been published (Strommenger 1967; Finkbeiner 1991; 1992), and two sequences of pottery from Susa, excavated by the French archaeological missions, have been published by Boucharlat (1987) and Miroschedji (1987).

The pottery from the Bahraini tombs

In the following chapter, 1827 pottery vessels are presented. The typological system, in which the catalogue is organized, was created during a registration campaign conducted from January to March 2003,

when it was possible to collect all vessels of a kind from the store and sort them into coherent groups and subgroups, each defining a type or variants of types. The context information was recorded from a slip placed in the vessel during the excavation, and notes and general measurements regarding the type were made.

As with the glass vessels, the pottery is presented in chronological order. The periodization of the glass vessels has been maintained in the treatment of the pottery and the following phases are used:

Phase	From	To	Description
0	300 BC	200 BC	No finds from the tombs date to this period
I	200 BC	50 BC	No glass
II	50 BC	AD 50	Pre-blown Roman vessels
III	AD 50	AD 150	Roman blown vessels
IV	AD 150	AD 450	Near Eastern types
V	AD 450	AD 700	Imitations of late Sasanian style

Table 108. Table illustrating the phases derived from Chapter 2 and their datings.

Classes of pottery

Within each period, the material is organized in wares (classes) after the fabric and surface treatment of the vessel (see below). These classes are generally derived from Hannestad (1983) and Højlund and Andersen (1994), though slight variations exist. They are rather broad classes with distinctive characteristics, which make an attribution of a given vessel to a class easy and secure, although some variation in fabric and/or surface treatment has to be accepted, which may reflect different production centres and traditions. Within each class, the different types have been divided into forms, which may reflect function (see below).

The Glazed ware

An alkaline glaze characterizes the glazed ware, which on well-preserved examples illustrates a variety of colours in the range of white, yellowish, green and turquoise. The glaze often decays into an iridescent golden appearance, sometimes peeling off or just remaining as a white or yellowish powder on the surface. The fabric is buff to yellowish, often with a sand temper. However, since the objects that were studied are mainly complete vessels that do not offer the possibility of studying fresh breaks, fabric descriptions are omitted.

Figure 393. Cat. nos S.2 and DI.1. Grey and red ware bowls.

Figure 392. Cat. no. AI.12. Glazed ware lagynos.

Alkaline-glazed ceramic in Bahrain is commonly found at Qala'at al-Bahrain from layers dated to Period IVc/d (Højlund & Andersen 1994: 221–300) until the middle Islamic occupation (Frifelt 2001: 104). For the period in question no production facilities for glazed ceramics in Bahrain have been uncovered, but a kiln-tripod (*ibid.* 62) and a waster (Højlund & Andersen 1994: 370) might indicate a production of glazed pottery on Bahrain in some periods.

The glazed ware is the most common class of pottery from the tombs and accounts for 76 % of the pottery assemblage. Glazed-ware vessels were made in a wide range of shapes and in the following morphologic treatment, seventy-five different types will be described and discussed.

The Grey Ware

The grey ware is an easily identifiable ware with a coherent fabric. A reduced firing has given the fine fabric a grey colour, which characterizes this class of pottery. In most of the open shapes, a fine slip has been applied internally, and due to the reduced firing and denser surface, it has become a darker grey than the fabric itself. Burnishing is also common.

The grey ware was introduced in Period IVc at Qala'at al-Bahrain and remained in use until Period Vd, although the ware is rare in Period Vb levels. Fish plates and bowls are the most common shape and closed vessels seem to be very rare (Højlund & Andersen 1994), although a couple of well-preserved Mesopotamian amphorae have been found (Andersen 2001: nos 96, 98).

On Failaka around twenty fragments of grey ware "Arabian black-washed ware" were found in the Danish excavation in both upper and lower levels (Hannestad 1983: 49). Minor investigations in north-east Arabia have also produced grey ware (Bibby 1973; Bowen 1950; Potts 1993*a*; 1993*b*), but according to Daniel Potts the grey ware was rather rare, whereas the red ware was more common (pers. comm. in Hannestad 1983: 49). Related grey wares are found in Ai-Khanoun, Merv and Seleucia (Bernard 1973; Herrmann *et al.* 1999; Valtz 1991), but the shapes are slightly different. The grey ware does not seem to have been identified in ed-Dur and in other sites on the Oman peninsula.

The grey ware vessels are rather rare in the tombs as the fifty-one vessels recorded only account for *c.* 2.5 % of the total pottery assemblage from the tombs. Grey ware vessels are found in tombs throughout the island, but with a concentration in the Saar area where thirty-six of the fifty-one vessels recorded originate. Only eight types in grey ware have been defined of which five are open and three are closed shapes.

The Red Ware

An oxidizing firing has given the fine fabric a red colour, which characterizes this class of pottery. In most of the open shapes, a very fine slip has been applied internally, and due to the oxidizing firing, it has become dark red. The red ware is quite varied in fabric from fine clay to a more sandy texture close to the sand-tempered ware. The colour of the fabric varies from cream to reddish and many vessels are burnished.

The red ware is well distributed in the Gulf region and the Near East. At Qala'at al-Bahrain the class is attested in most sub-periods from the Achaemenid period until Period Vd (Højlund & Andersen 1994). The class is attested on Failaka, but it is not very common and believed to be imported (Hannestad 1983: 49–50). The red ware is also found along the north-east coast of Saudi Arabia e.g. Farig al-Akhrash (Bibby 1973: figs 32d and e), Thaj[13] (*ibid.* 24) and Ayn Jawan, where it seems to be rather common (Potts 1993*a*). In Mleiha the class is characterized as a rare ware (Boucharlat & Mouton 1993: 227). A few sherds of fabric and surface treatment very similar to some of the vessels from the tombs on Bahrain also exist in the Stein Collection, a survey collection from Iran, now in the British Museum and made available to the present author.[14]

The red ware is quite rare in the tombs and a total of only sixty-five vessels of this class have been recorded. The variety of shapes is quite limited and only eight types have been defined, of which six are open shapes and two are closed.

The Sand-tempered Ware
A well-fired fabric with much sand temper characterizes the sand tempered ware. The fabric is, however, rather varied and some vessels have a reddish slip applied, which makes a clear separation from the red ware difficult.

The sand-tempered ware is well known from Qala'at al-Bahrain. In the Danish excavations it has been named "red sand- and lime-tempered ware" and it is common from pre-Hellenistic times (Højlund & Andersen 1994: 247). The ware seems to be well distributed in eastern Arabia. In Thaj in Saudi Arabia, sand-tempered ware is very common (Bibby 1973: 20–25). On Failaka the so-called "Nabataean ware", which is very similar to the sand-tempered ware, was believed to be imitating Nabataean pottery (Hannestad 1983: 51–52). On the Oman peninsula cooking pots in sand-tempered ware have been reported from ed-Dur (Haerinck *et al.* 1993: 187).

Only open shapes are recorded in the sand-tempered ware. Twelve complete cooking pots are included in the group. They were recovered during

excavations of the Tylos mounds, but most of them were not found in the tombs but in the mound fill, and may thus be of later or earlier date. Only four types have been defined.

The Plain Ware
This class is defined as vessels without distinctive surface treatment as glaze or slip or vessels made in characteristic wares as sand-tempered ware or the hard-fired ware. One could thus expect a very broad class, but it is a rather coherent group. The colour is buff or yellowish and the fabric rather fine with some sand temper. The execution of the vessels is most often rather crude, with marks from string-cutting under the base, when the vessel was lifted from the wheel, and sometimes scraping marks on the lower body.

Plain ware vessels are found throughout the island. They are also very common in the excavations at Qala'at al-Bahrain and most types found in the tombs are reported from the settlement. On Failaka the echinus bowl, the saucer with flaring sides and the fish plate are well attested (Hannestad 1983: nos 436–450, 453–458, 464–473). These shapes are also common in numerous Mesopotamian sites (1983: 57–58), but due to their simplicity and practicality for daily use they are likely to be of local production, perhaps influenced by prototypes in glazed wares. No parallels have been found for the incense burners and the one lamp.

The plain ware is the second largest class of pottery after the glazed ware with a total of 229 vessels recorded (12.6 %). The fabric is generally yellowish, sometimes very fine, which is characteristic for the bowl with flaring sides and vertical rim, or with a more sandy texture. Most common are the open shapes with six types recorded, and only one closed type has been defined. A few incense burners and a single lamp add to the assemblage together with some unique bowls.

The Hard-fired Ware
A very hard-fired fabric with lime grits characterizes the hard-fired ware. The colour of the fabric is dark grey, brown or reddish. The shapes are bowls, beakers, jars and most commonly, jugs. They all have a plain resting surface and marks of scraping on the lower body. Of this easy identifiable class, forty-six vessels have been recorded.

Hard-fired ware has been identified in small quantities at Qala'at al-Bahrain (Andersen 2001) and in layers overlaying the Bronze Age Temple at Barbar (Andersen & Kennet 2003). The identification of this specific class of pottery can be assigned to recent excavations of sites in the UAE e.g.

---

[13] Bibby mentions that only six sherds painted terracotta red were found.

[14] I am most grateful to Assistant Keeper Dr. St John Simpson for granting me access and providing the background information to the Stein Collection.

Figure 394. Cat. nos CI.3 and CN.10. Vessels in hard-fired ware.

Kush, Khatt, Mleiha and ed-Dur, where fabrics illustrating the same characteristics as described for the hard-fired ware were found in a layer datable from the late Parthian period to the early Islamic period. There are variations in fabric from the different sites, indicating different production series or chronological variations.

The majority of the hard-fired ware vessels found in Bahrain are jugs, although a few open shapes have been recovered too. A total of ten types have been defined and in addition to these are two fragmentary jugs that cannot be placed in one of the other groups.

The Fine Ware
The fine ware class is very small. Two vessels appear to have been imported from the Mediterranean region (Type CA) and one vessel is very unusual, probably made as an imitation of a core-formed glass flask (Type AM).

Forms
Within each class of pottery the catalogue is organized in general forms. These are believed to reflect function to some degree. The allocation is based on the terminology of forms commonly used in publications of pottery from the Gulf and the Classical world. Functions of specific vessels are often well understood in the Classical world from written evidence and figurative art and during the analysis of the material from Bahrain, it became clear that Mediterranean influence had a significant impact on the choice of shapes, partly in Phase I, but more

pronounced in Phases II and III. It is therefore assumed that it was both the form and the function of the prototypes that were copied by local potters. The contextual evidence from Bahrain does not at present provide the possibilities for further analysis, and the allocations and analysis in Chapter 4 should be regarded as tentative.

Bowls
The bowls were probably utility vessels, used in everyday life to serve and store food. They are simple shapes that lack the characteristic features that can be associated with drinking vessels, but some types could well have been used for both drinking and eating (e.g. the hemispherical bowls). Bowls are very common.

Crater
Only one possible type of crater has been defined, due to similarities with Mediterranean prototypes (Type AE). The crater was used in the Mediterranean region as a mixing bowl for wine, and could thus have had a function – in relation to wine drinking – similar to that of a jug.

Cups
The cups have a stylistic inspiration from the Mediterranean prototypes. The similarities with drinking cups from the Mediterranean world indicate that the cups were used for drinking. In funerary contexts in Bahrain, they are often found upside down and filled with ash on the capstone of the chamber, thus indicating a more specialized function during the funeral ceremony.

Plates
The plates are not very common grave goods. They are shallow and have flaring sides. They were most likely used to serve food.

Jars and jugs
The jars and jugs were most likely used to store and serve liquids for consumption.

Bottles
The bottles are smaller than the jars and jugs and were probably used as containers for unguents for personal adornment.

Methodology
The glass was dated primarily on external evidence, but only a few of the pottery types presented in the following find exact and good parallels in the published literature. The contextual information is therefore important, but as it was stated in the in-

troduction, the dataset is not ideal. A total of 1827 complete vessels were recorded in the Main Store in the Bahrain National Museum. Of these 1607 could be dated (see below), whereas the remaining 220 vessels could not because of inconsistent or missing dating evidence. Some 1299 vessels have a fully recorded context and seventeen of these vessels have been found in burial jars, whereas the remaining 1282 were found in or in relation to a tomb. Eight hundred and ninety-six tombs contained pottery vessels and of these 825 contained datable pottery. However, since it is quite impossible to find out the total number of tombs, and the count of tombs presented above may also contain errors (see Chapter 1) these figures only serve to give an idea of the size of the collection and the complexity of the information. More interesting are the 300 tombs (listed in Appendix 1), which contained more than one type of glass or pottery vessel. Forty-nine of these tombs have been omitted from further analysis. Two of the tombs contained only Phase V material and have thus been excluded, since that group of glass vessels was limited and very coherent, but other tombs have obvious problematic evidence. These are often tombs that has been reused or where the context information appears to be corrupt. Some tombs contained a vessel of a type that is poorly defined or has had a long period of use and is thus unsuitable for chronological purposes. The omitted tombs have not been assigned a tomb number in Appendix 1. Nevertheless, 251 tombs combine different types of glass and pottery vessels and an initial overview of the chronological development of the pottery was gained by seriating these tombs.

The WINBASP program version 5.2 was used with standard settings. The resulting sequence, which is illustrated in Figure 395, has been used as the framework for the discussion of the dating of the individual pottery types. When a type has been found in a reasonable number of contexts together with other types, the individual combinations are not discussed, but only a general reference to the seriation is made. Less well represented types may have been found only with a few other types and sometimes the combinations give a blurred picture, often due to the reuse of a tomb or possibly corrupted information. In these cases, the contextual evidence is discussed in more detail. The dating for a type suggested by the Bahraini material is compared with external dating when good and well-dated parallels have been found to verify the datings. Since the glass has also been included in the seriation, the sequence has been supplied with some absolute dated material, which furthermore serves the purpose

of verifying the seriation results. However, it is in the discussion of each type that the final dating has been settled and the seriation only serves to provide an initial overview. The high proportion of glass vessels in Phases III and IV has made the allocation of pottery types to these Phases easy, whereas Phases I and II are more difficult to define. However, from these periods, extensive and relatively well-dated material from Failaka and also partly from Qala'at al-Bahrain has been published, and that material is therefore important for the definition of these phases. It must also be pointed out that an allocation of a type to a phase is not conclusive, since most types are likely to have a lifespan independent of the artificial phases that I have defined, and the types are thus likely to appear in more than one phase. The allocations to phases should therefore be regarded as the most probable dating of the types, but not the only possible one.

The discussions also include distribution patterns and style. Since very little scientific work has been done to relate fabrics to specific clay sources and hardly any production facilities from the Tylos period have been found in the region, distribution patterns are so far the only sources we can use to indicate places of production of specific types. The resolution of these patterns is broadly given in the above list of sites from which pottery has been published, and will often be marginal. The allocation of the production of specific types to specific areas is thus problematic and could very well be affected by the trade patterns of specific classes or types. This is demonstrated with Islamic pottery where monochrome sgraffiato, which is likely to have been produced in Iran, but is found in much higher quantities in Shanga in East Africa than in Kush, which is situated much closer to the place of production (Kennet 2004: 78).

The style of the pottery can, as Hannestad demonstrated in her study of the pottery from the Danish excavations on Failaka (1983) be a significant indicator for cultural influence. It will therefore form the second level of the analysis after the chronological foundation has been established. Indeed, by emphasizing style, when we can safely identify convincing prototypes, rather than places of production and trade networks, we may obtain better results. This implies an assumption that a deliberate choice has been made by the consumers for specific styles and that choice expressed a knowledge of broader cultural values embedded in the style.

All illustrations of pottery vessels are in scale 1:4 (25%) unless otherwise stated.

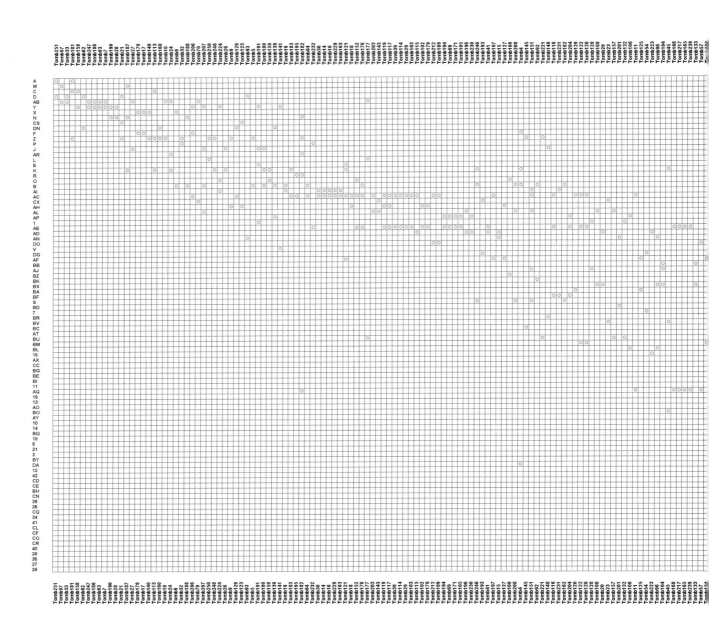

Figure 395. Seriation plot of glass and pottery types versus tombs

Phase I. The early tombs (*c.* 200 BC to 50 BC)

The pottery assemblage of Phase I offers a varied impression. Glazed ware, red and grey ware, sand-tempered ware and plain ware are all well represented and many types find good parallels in Period Va–c at Qala'at al-Bahrain and in Period I in the Hellenistic settlement at Failaka.

Glazed ware bowls

Type A: Hemispheric bowl

Type A hemispheric bowls are characterized by a vertical rim and an almost flat resting surface. They form a coherent group. One example has a green glazed rim on a white body preserved, whereas the glaze on the rest is decayed to white or golden.

Dating evidence and discussion

Two of these hemispheric bowls were found with Phase I material (cat. nos A.6 and A.8) whereas cat. no. A.7 was found with an amphora in hard-fired ware, which is characteristic of Phase IV, but this last context is assumed to be mixed. No external parallels have been found.

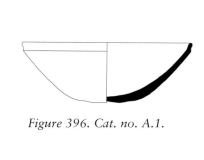

Figure 396. Cat. no. A.1.

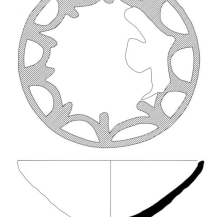

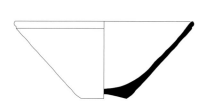

Figure 397. Cat. no. B.27.   *Figure 398. Cat. no. B.30.*   *Figure 399. Cat. no. B.31.*

Number	Height, min.	Height, max.	Rim dia., min.	Rim dia., max.
8	6	7	18	19

Table 109. Description of vessels of Type A. Measurements in centimetres.

Cat. no.	BNM no.	Area	Mound	Square	Context	Number	Remarks
A.1	18	Saar	4-87		Tomb	2	Figure 396.
A.2	4788-2-90-29						
A.3	9999-2-91	Karranah	1986				
A.4	97-7-5	Saar	1997	B3	Tomb	20	
A.5	5159-2-91-3	Saar	2-91		Tomb	26	
A.6	3874-2-91-3	Saar	1-91		Tomb	30	
A.7	A4837	Hamad Town	83-85-86		Tomb	31	
A.8	FM-A-985.CV	Unplaced	T158-4		Tomb	2	

Table 110. Context information for vessels of Type A.

Number	Height, min.	Height, max.	Rim dia., min.	Rim dia., max.
40	6.5	8.5	18	24

Table 111. Description of vessels of Type B. Measurements in centimetres.

Cat. no.	BNM no.	Area	Mound	Square	Context	Number	Remarks
B.1	172	Al-Hajar	2-92-93		Tomb	41	
B.2	5154-2-91-3	Saar	5-91-92	7	Tomb	27	
B.3	2040-2-90	Ali	1988		Tomb	6	
B.4	91-2-35	Saar	10-91	3	Tomb	5	
B.5	304	Saar	4-91-92	8	Tomb	48	
B.6	3819-2-91	Saar	4-91-92	12	Tomb	22	
B.7	2145-2-90	Ali	60-88-89		Tomb	17	
B.8	186	Al-Hajar	2-92-93		Tomb	35	
B.9	23	Saar	3-96	D4	Tomb	4	
B.10	191	Saar	10-91	1	Tomb	1	
B.11	3796-2-91-3	Saar	5-91-92	3	Tomb	4	
B.12	1936-2-89	Maqabah	1989	2	Tomb	1	
B.13	18	Saar	1-96		Tomb	2	
B.14	93	Al-Hajar	1-92-93		Tomb	4	
B.15	202	Al-Hajar	6-92-93	C6	Tomb	35	
B.16	5160-2-91	Saar	5-91-92	7			
B.17	91-2-50	Saar	1-91		Tomb	3	
B.18	5	Barbar	1996	C3	Tomb	4	
B.19	172	Saar	5-95-96	D3	Tomb	46	
B.20	3859-2-91-3	Saar	1-91		Tomb	18	
B.21	206	Al-Hajar	6-92-93	D2	Tomb	10	
B.22	405-2-88	Saar	5-87-88	D6	Jar	8	
B.23	3725-2-91-3	Saar	4-91-92	13	Tomb	32	
B.24	98	Al-Hajar	1-92-93		Tomb	1	
B.25	4279-2-91	Karranah	4-86		Tomb	69	
B.26	5209-2-91-3	Saar	12-91		Tomb	7	
B.27	3728-2-91-3	Saar	4-91-92	2	Tomb	25	Figure 397.
B.28	3786-2-91-6	Shakhoura	1-91		Tomb	6	
B.29	5153-2-91-3						No context information.
B.30	5155-2-91-3	Saar	5-91-92	2	Tomb	8	W. bichrome decoration. Figure 398.
B.31	201	Al-Hajar	6-92-93	C6	Tomb	33	Figure 399.
B.32	76	Al-Hajar	1-92-93		Tomb	5	
B.33	91-2-36	Saar	9-91	4	Tomb	1	
B.34	7193-2-91	Al-Hajar					
B.35	2012-2-90	Ali	60-88-89		Tomb	28	
B.36	A797	Saar	8-97	36	Tomb	8	
B.37	A778	Shakhoura	29-00-01		Tomb	17	
B.38	A639	Shakhoura	29-00-01		Tomb	5	
B.39	IMA105						No context information.
B.40	IMA530						No context information.

Table 112. Context information for vessels of Type B.

Type B: Hollow-based bowl

This is a slightly varied group of larger bowls. A hollow base and flaring sides characterize them. The rim is plain, often with an external groove and in a few cases with an internal thickening. The glaze is most often preserved as whitish and sometimes with a green rim. One example (cat. no. B.30) has an internal decoration preserved.

Dating evidence and discussion

The Type B hollow-based bowl is a common type in the tombs and has been combined with a good number of other types. The seriation suggests a dating to Phase I and early Phase II. The type seems to be rare at Qala'at al-Bahrain with only one published example (Lombard & Kervran 1993: fig. 19.13). In Mesopotamia four examples were reported from Seleucia from levels II–III (AD 43–165) (Debevoise 1934: no. 197), which seems to be slightly later than the Bahraini dating. The dating of the Seleucid material is, as pointed out in the introduction, based on the assumption that "destruction" layers reflect known historic events and thus provide absolute dates to the stratigraphical sequence. This method should be regarded with suspicion and does not take into account that most destruction was probably caused by common fires rather than wars.

It has not been possible to trace the origin of the hollow-based bowls to any specific type or location. Similar shapes have been made in metal in the Near East and may have influenced potters in Athens to make hemispherical cups, sometimes with a hollow base (Rotroff 1997: 110–117).

Type C: Bowl with flaring sides and offset lip

Flaring sides and a vertical rim with a small external thickening creating an offset lip characterizes these bowls. They have a false ring-foot and the glaze is green or whitish.

Figure 400. Cat. no. C.1.

Figure 401. Cat. no. C.8.

Figure 402. Cat. no. C.10.

Number	Height, min.	Height, max.	Rim dia., min.	Rim dia., max.
14	3.5	7.5	11	16.5

Table 113. Description of vessels of Type C. Measurements in centimetres.

Cat. no.	BNM no.	Area	Mound	Square	Context	Number	Remarks
C.1	71	Shakhoura	4-92-93	C5	Tomb	5	Figure 400.
C.2	3858-2-91-3	Saar	1-91		Tomb	30	
C.3	1139-2-88	Jannussan					
C.4	A3375	Hamad Town	10-89-90		Tomb	16	
C.5	9951-2-91	Karranah	4-86				
C.6	A793	Shakhoura	29-00-01		Outside tomb		
C.7	7222-2-91						
C.8	298	Saar	5-96-97	D4	Tomb	33	Figure 401.
C.9	3	Saar	1-96				
C.10	1019-2-88	Al-Hajar	1-71		Tomb	A2	Figure 402.
C.11	A4825	Hamad Town					
C.12	A3436		89				
C.13		Karranah	1-1992		Tomb	D-III-5	
C.14	FM-A-961.A	Saar	1-1960		Outside tomb	1	

Table 114. Context information for vessels of Type C.

Dating evidence and discussion

The bowls with flaring sides and offset lip are found at Qala'at al-Bahrain in Period Vb contexts (Højlund & Andersen 1994: figs 1409–1411). The type is very common on Failaka in the lower and upper levels, but rare in BI-ware and has been divided into three variants (Hannestad 1983: 23). The Bahraini examples are all of variant 2. A few vessels of variant 2 from Failaka belong, however, in the BI-group (Hannestad 1983: nos 125–126), but as they have an internal notch on the lip, which is not seen on the Bahraini examples, they are likely to be a late development of the type. Related pieces have been reported from Uruk, Seleucia and Susa (Strommenger 1967: Taf. 9.15–16; Debevoise 1934: no. 191; Boucharlat 1987: fig. 59.14–15). However, the distribution of the bowls with flaring sides and offset lip in the Bahraini version seems to be confined

Number	Height, min.	Height, max.	Rim dia., min.	Rim dia., max.
32	3.5	5.5	11	15

Table 115. Description of vessels of Type D. Measurements in centimetres.

Cat. no.	BNM no.	Area	Mound	Square	Context	Number	Remarks
D.1	195	Al-Hajar	2-93		Outside tomb	36	
D.2	219	Saar	7-95-96	E5	Tomb	6	
D.3	91-1-55	Shakhoura	1991-92		Outside tomb	52	
D.4	A630	Shakhoura	29-00-01		Outside tomb	18	
D.5	192	Al-Hajar	2-93		Outside tomb	48	Figure 403.
D.6	A559	Shakhoura	29-00-01		Outside tomb	20	
D.7	3720-2-91-3	Saar	4-91-92	2			
D.8	97-3-217	Shakhoura	A1-96-97	D5	Tomb	76	
D.9	4286-2-91-15	Ali	1984				
D.10	97-3-96	Shakhoura	A1-96-97	F5	Outside tomb	19	Figure 404.
D.11	91-2-98	Saar	2-91-92	F4			
D.12	A205	Shakhoura	30-98-99	B4	Outside tomb	11	
D.13							No context information.
D.14	71	Al-Hajar	2-92	9			
D.15	125	Hamad Town	1-94-95	D4	Tomb	4-D4	
D.16	128	Al-Hajar	2-92	B6			
D.17	209	Al-Hajar	7-92-93	G4	Tomb	15	
D.18	96	Al-Hajar	1-92-93		Tomb	2	
D.19	A562	Saar	8-97	E2	Tomb	4	
D.20	3784-2-91-3	Saar	5-91-92	8	Outside tomb	17	
D.21	10052-2-91	Karranah	1986				
D.22	210	Al-Hajar	7-92-93		Outside tomb	8	
D.23	3825-2-91-3	Saar	2-91		Tomb	28	
D.24	13	Barbar	1996		Tomb	8	Figure 405.
D.25	68	Al-Hajar	1-92-93		Tomb	2	
D.26	1045-2-88	Isa Town	1972-73				
D.27	10042-2-91						No context information.
D.28	4293-2-91-15						No context information.
D.29	2382-2-90-15	Ali	61-88-89		Tomb	3	
D.30	A693	Hamad Town	100-00-01		Tomb	S.1	
D.31		Karranah	1-1992		Tomb	C-IV-2	
D.32	FM-A-985.CY	Unplaced	T158-4		Tomb	2	

Table 116. Context information for vessels of Type D.

Figure 403. Cat. no. D.5.

Figure 404. Cat. no. D.10.

Figure 405. Cat. no. D.24.

Figure 406. Cat. no. E.1.

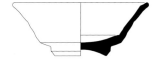

Figure 407. Cat. no. F.4.

Figure 408. Cat. no. F.6.

Number	Height, min.	Height, max.	Rim dia., min.	Rim dia., max.
4	2.5	2.5	6.5	8.5

Table 117. Description of vessels of Type E. Measurements in centimetres.

Cat. no.	BNM no.	Area	Mound	Square	Context	Number	Remarks
E.1	29	Shakhoura	7-93	D2	Tomb	61	Figure 406.
E.2	91-2-10	Saar	4-91-92	11	Tomb	14	
E.3							No context information.
E.4	A4808	Hamad Town	73-85-86		Tomb	65	

Table 118. Context information for vessels of Type E.

Number	Height, min.	Height, max.	Rim dia., min.	Rim dia., max.
8	4.5	7	13	17.5

Table 119. Description of vessels of Type F. Measurements in centimetres.

Cat. no.	BNM no.	Area	Mound	Square	Context	Number	Remarks
F.1	80-2-4803	Al-Hajar					
F.2	74	Al-Hajar	1-92-93		Outside tomb	1	
F.3	292	Saar	10-91	1	Tomb	11	
F.4	173	Al-Hajar	6-92-93	B8	Tomb	36	Figure 407.
F.5	3847-2-91-3	Saar	1-91		Outside tomb	2	
F.6	3817-2-91-3	Saar	5-91-92	8	Outside tomb	16	Figure 408.
F.7	9895-2-91	Karranah	4-86				
F.8	219	Al-Hajar	2-92-93		Outside tomb	46	

Table 120. Context information for vessels of Type F.

to the upper Gulf region. The seriation supports the external dating and indicates that Type C dates to Phase 1. The bowl with flaring sides and offset lip is probably a development of the Assyrian carinated bowls (Hannestad 1983: 25).

Type D: Echinus bowl
The echinus bowl is a rather varied group, but all vessels have the characteristic incurving rim. The base is a ring-foot, a false ring-foot or a raised base. A few examples have internal incised rings and some an internal central depression. The glaze is green, a few may have been white, or it has decayed to whitish or golden.

Dating evidence and discussion
Echinus bowls are found at Qala'at al-Bahrain in Period Va and Vb contexts (Højlund & Andersen 1994: figs 1213, 1220, 1407, 1408). On Failaka, it is one of the most common shapes from the Hellenistic settlement in both the upper and lower levels, but the type is not attested in the BI-Ware (Hannestad 1983: 15). In glazed ware the type seems to be absent in Mesopotamia and Persia. The shape is, however, very common in other wares, where a red-painted version of the echinus bowl is the most common painted bowl in Nippur (Oates & Oates 1958: 141), and plain ware bowls are for example common in Uruk (Finkbeiner 1991: nos 136, 148, 174, 202–203 etc.) and Susa (Boucharlat 1987: tab. 18). To the south on the Oman peninsula, the type seems to be absent.

The seriation indicates that the echinus bowl dates to Phase I, which corresponds well with the dating evidence from Qala'at al-Bahrain and Failaka.

The echinus bowl is a very simple shape and vessels in plain ware are known from Period III contexts at Qala'at al-Bahrain (Højlund & Andersen 1994: figs 727–728), but they are also well known in Attic black glazed ware and popular in the fourth century BC (Rotroff 1997: 161). Their presence in early Hellenistic contexts in the Gulf region suggests therefore that they may have been reintroduced in the Near East just after Alexander the Great's conquest of the Achaemenid Empire. It is therefore likely that the Attic vessels served as prototypes for the Near Eastern echinus bowl of the Hellenistic period.

Type E: Miniature echinus bowl
A little group of miniature bowls with incurving rim.

Dating evidence and discussion
Two miniatures of echinus bowls (cat. nos E.1 and E.2) have been found with other pottery datable to Phase I, which supports the morphologic relation to Type D. No external parallels have been found.

Type F: Bowl with angular profile and out-turned rim
The bowls with angular profile and out-turned rim are characterized by a carination between the lower and upper body, giving the type an angular profile. The foot is a false ring-foot and the rim is out-turned and on most examples with an internal notch. The glaze is white or yellowish, probably due to weathering.

Dating evidence and discussion
The Type F bowl with angular profile and out-turned rim was found at Qala'at al-Bahrain in Period Va, Vb and Vd contexts by the Danish excavations (Højlund & Andersen 1994: figs 1226–1227, 1414, 1536) and in the "niveau hellénistique supérieur" by the French excavations (Lombard & Kervran 1993: fig. 20.17). The one example from Period Vd (Højlund & Andersen 1994: fig. 1536) has incised lines under the rim which is a feature not seen on any of the examples from the tombs.

On Failaka it is a common type, which is found in both upper and lower level, with only one example in the BI-group (Hannestad 1983: 18) and further to the north in Mesopotamia it is also attested (Debevoise 1934: no. 209; Toll 1943: no. I-23). The type is also well represented in Susa from Apadana Est, Niveaux 5e–5c (Boucharlat 1987: tab. 18).

The seriation indicates that the bowl with angular profile and out-turned rim was used in Phase I, which corresponds well with most of the external parallels mentioned above.

Type F is most likely a Near Eastern imitation of the Attic bowl with out-turned rim (as suggested by Hannestad 1983: 18). That type is known from the fifth century BC and very popular in the third and second century BC in Athens (Rotroff 1997: 156-157). Fragments of the Attic bowl with out-turned rim were also found in early Hellenistic contexts at Qala'at al-Bahrain (Andersen 2002: fig. 21) and in Thaj (Bibby 1973: fig. 6) so the Attic type must have been well known in the Near East. However, carinated bowls with an out-turned rim were common in the late Achaemenid period in Qala'at al-Bahrain and one cannot exclude the possibility that Type F is a development of that type.

Glazed ware plates

Type G: Plate with internal thickened rim

Type G comprises small plates with an internally thickened rim. The glaze is green or turquoise or decayed to brown, white or golden.

Dating evidence and discussion

On Failaka, the plate with internally thickened rim is the most common shape in glazed ware in all levels (Hannestad 1983: 32). At Qala'at al-Bahrain, the type is attested in Period Va–Vc contexts (Højlund & Andersen 1994: figs 1221–1223, 1402–1404, 1473) and it is found in Susa (Boucharlat 1987: tab. 19). The type is not as well represented in glazed ware as the fish plate and seems to be absent from the published material from the UAE. The single combination of a plate with internally thickened rim and a Type Y bowl in plain ware supports the external dating evidence.

The plate with internally thickened rim may have been influenced by Greek prototypes, since the form is not known in pre-Hellenistic contexts in Bahrain, but is said to be a popular form at sites on the eastern shores of the Mediterranean in the Hellenistic period (Hannestad 1983: 32).

Glazed ware jugs

Two lagynoi dating to Phase I have been recorded.

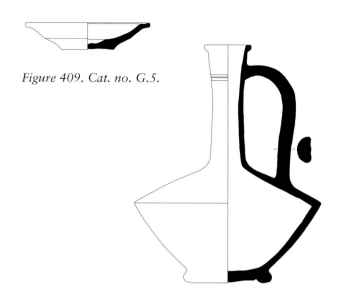

Figure 409. Cat. no. G.5.

Figure 410. Cat. no. H.1.

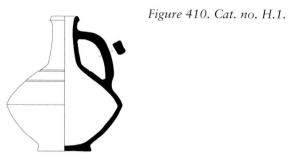

Figure 411. Cat. no. H.2.

Number	Height, min.	Height, max.	Rim dia., min.	Rim dia., max.
11	2.5	3.5	11.5	15

Table 121. Description of vessels of Type G. Measurements in centimetres.

Cat. no.	BNM no.	Area	Mound	Square	Context	Number	Remarks
G.1	740	Saar	12-95-96		Tomb	8	
G.2	7240-2-91	Um Al-Hasam	1973		Tomb	17	
G.3	10059-2-91	Al-Hajar					
G.4	97-3-279	Shakhoura	A1-96-97	D4	Tomb	75	
G.5	3743-2-91-3	Saar	4-91-92	12			Figure 409.
G.6	45	Shakhoura	6-92-93	E4	Tomb	9	
G.7	1369-2-90						
G.8	2535-2-90	Saar	4-87	B5	Outside tomb	5	
G.9	A1674		01-02				
G.10	A2333		97-98				
G.11	A4878	Hamad Town	69-85-86		Tomb	4	

Table 122. Context information for vessels of Type G.

Type H: Lagynos

The lagynos is characterized by a long cylindrical neck, a handle attached to the shoulder and upper neck and a squat body. Type H has a strap-handle with a rectangular cross-section and an angular shoulder profile.

Dating evidence and discussion

The lagynos takes its name from ancient Greek sources where it has been applied to a wine jug with a single handle and a long neck, giving a gurgling sound when the wine is poured. It was used at the Greek symposia, where the participant brought it along as his contribution to the feast. The type is well attested in the whole of the Mediterranean region in a tableware version and as a large household-ware jug. As tableware the lagynos was most popular between 150–50 BC, but it is attested in late third-century BC contexts as well (Rotroff 1997: 226–228).

At Qala'at al-Bahrain a few fragments of lagynoi with an angular profile have been recovered. From the French excavations a shoulder sherd from the lower Hellenistic levels has been published (Lombard & Kervran 1993: fig. 19.5) with a suggested dating of 300–100 BC (1993: 136) and Excavation 421 from the Danish Archaeological Expeditions

produced some fragments of lagynoi (Andersen 2001: no. 44). One lagynos of Type H (cat. no. H.2) was found with Phase I vessels, which corresponds well with the possible influence from Mediterranean prototypes.

Glazed ware bottles

Type I: Handleless bottle

Type I is characterized by a false ring-foot, piriform body and out-turned rim. The glaze is green but decayed to brown and white.

Dating evidence and discussion

Cat. no. I.2 was found with Phase I material and since handleless bottles are quite common in the pre-Hellenistic periods in Mesopotamia, it is most likely that the examples from Bahrain follow that tradition and date to the relatively early Tylos period.

Type J: Bottle with two shoulder-attached loop-handles

This is a small and slightly varied group of bottles with a projecting or out-turned rim, often with an external thickening. The type has two shoulder-attached pierced loop-handles, and a globular or pear-shaped body with a low ring-foot or false ring-foot. The defining criterion is only the shoulder-attached loop-handles, which are made as a horizontally

Number	Height, min.	Height, max.	Rim dia., min.	Rim dia., max.
2	15	26.5	3	5

Table 123. Description of vessels of Type H. Measurements in centimetres.

Cat. no.	BNM no.	Area	Mound	Square	Context	Number	Remarks
H.1	3776-2-91	Saar	1-91-92	2	Tomb	7	Figure 410.
H.2	2039-2-90	Ali	60-88-89		Tomb	17	Figure 411.

Table 124. Context information for vessels of Type H.

Number	Height, min.	Height, max.	Rim dia., min.	Rim dia., max.
2	8	11	2.5	2.5

Table 125. Description of vessels of Type I. Measurements in centimetres.

Cat. no.	BNM no.	Area	Mound	Square	Context	Number	Remarks
I.1	254	Saar	7-95-96	B2	Mound fill		Figure 412.
I.2	6	Saar	3-96	D4	Tomb	12	

Table 126. Context information for vessels of Type I.

Figure 412. Cat. no. I.1.   Figure 413. Cat. no. J.1.   Figure 414. Cat. no. J.7.   Figure 415. Cat. no. J.11.

 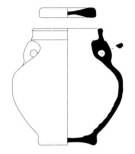

Figure 418. Cat. no. K.17.   Figure 416. Cat. no. K.1.   Figure 417. Cat. no. K.2.

Number	Height, min.	Height, max.	Rim dia., min.	Rim dia., max.
15	8	15.5	2.5	3

Table 127. Description of vessels of Type J. Measurements in centimetres.

Cat. no.	BNM no.	Area	Mound	Square	Context	Number	Remarks
J.1	3761-2-91-3	Saar	1-91		Tomb	3	Figure 413.
J.2	1938-2-89	Ali	60-88-89		Tomb	36	
J.3	832-2-88	Hamad Town	30-84-85		Tomb	21	
J.4	219	Al-Hajar	6-92-93	C6	Tomb	32	
J.5	184	Al-Hajar	2-92-93		Tomb	34	
J.6	9497-2-91	Karranah	2-86				
J.7	9408-2-91	Hamad Town	106-84-85		Tomb	1	Figure 414.
J.8	9817-2-91						
J.9	1147-2-88						
J.10	67	Saar	5-91-92	3	Tomb	4	
J.11	3752-2-91-3	Saar	4-91-92	11	Tomb	14	Figure 415.
J.12		Barbar	1996				
J.13	9517-2-91	Ali	60-88-89		Tomb	29	
J.14	A549						
J.15	A93	Saar	10-99-01	B	Tomb	43	

Table 128. Context information for vessels of Type J.

pierced lug. The glaze is green or decayed to white, yellowish or golden.

Dating evidence and discussion

The bottles with two shoulder-attached loop-handles are rare among the findings from the settlement at Qala'at al-Bahrain with only a few pieces published. Two fragments of loop-handles, which may or may not be remnants of Type J vessels, have been recovered from a period Va context (Højlund & Andersen 1994: figs 1325 and 1365). Adding to these fragments is one almost complete bottle found in Danish Excavation 421 (Andersen 2001: 41).

The bottles with two shoulder-attached loop-handles seem to be widely distributed in the region. The type is found in northern Mesopotamia in Nimrud, where one example was found in a grave with a coin of Alexander I Balas (150–146 BC) (Oates & Oates 1958: 149 and pl. XXVI.3 and 5), although the incised decoration and the proper ring-foot on one of

the illustrated specimens (XXVI.3) is not repeated on the Bahraini examples. The type is, however, rare at Nimrud and it is likely that the examples are imports from southern Mesopotamia (Hannestad 1983: 38). A related piece was found in Nippur, but with a hollow base instead of the low ring-foot or false ring-foot commonly associated with the type (McCown, Haines & Biggs 1978: pl. 54.6). From Uruk-Warka in southern Mesopotamia (Strommenger 1967: Taf. 27.6–8 and 40.3; Finkbeiner 1991: figs 115, 137, 160 and 186), and Masjid-i Suleiman in south-western Persia (Ghirshman 1976: pl. 50, nos GMIS 361, 360 and 362), close parallels to the Bahraini examples have been found. To the north in the Gulf the majority of bottles recovered in the Danish excavations of the Seleucid fortress on Failaka were bottles with two shoulder-attached loop-handles found in Period I layers (Hannestad 1983: 38–40). A similar picture is seen in the findings from the French excavations at Failaka (Bernard, Gachet & Salles 1990). To the south, a few examples

Number	Height, min.	Height, max.	Rim dia., min.	Rim dia., max.
20	7	17	3.5	8

Table 129. Description of vessels of Type K. Measurements in centimetres.

Cat. no.	BNM no.	Area	Mound	Square	Context	Number	Remarks
K.1	91-2-105	Saar	1-91		Tomb	3	Figure 416.
K.2	72	Shakhoura	4-92-93	C3	Tomb	5	Figure 417.
K.3	193	Ali	60-88-89		Tomb	10	
K.4	2534-2-90	Saar	4-87	D2	Tomb	6	
K.5	7	Saar	3-96	D4	Tomb	12	
K.6	1143-2-88	Jannussan	1-69				
K.7	27	Shakhoura	7-93	D8	Tomb	61	
K.8	220						
K.9	61-2-10	Saar	9-91		Tomb	3	
K.10	1837-2-89	Ali	61-88-89		Tomb	4	
K.11	2184-2-90	Ali	60-88-89		Tomb	29	
K.12	84	Al-Hajar	1-92-93		Tomb	1	
K.13	248	Saar	9-91	1	Tomb	1	
K.14	236	Saar	5-96-97	C3	Mound fill		
K.15	163	Hamad Town	1-94-95	E4	Tomb	3-E4	
K.16	274	Saar	5-96-97	D2	Tomb	17	
K.17	262	Saar	1-91-92	3	Tomb	5	With lid. Figure 418.
K.18	A263	Saar	4-91-92		Tomb	11	With lid.
K.19	IMA747						Salles & Lombard 1999: no. 233.
K.20	FM-A-963.E	Saar	1-1960		Tomb	3	

Table 130. Context information for vessels of Type K.

have been reported from the Oman peninsula, i.e. the Samad graves (Yule 2001: Taf. 205.6) and Mleiha (Boucharlat & Mouton 1993: fig. 14.6), but none from the graves at ed-Dur (Haerinck 2001).

The seriation of combined finds from the Bahraini tombs indicates that the bottle with two shoulder-attached loop-handles belongs in Phase I, which corresponds well with the external dating.

The origin of Type J is most likely to be found in Mesopotamia. In Babylon in pre-Hellenistic contexts bottles of similar body shape, but without handles have been found together with vessels with shoulder-attached loop-handles (Reuther 1968: Taf. 73.125. a and c). Core-made glass vessels may also have influenced the bottles with two handles with shoulder-attached loop-handles in glazed ware, since some similarities in the position and shape of the handles can be noted. See for example the core-formed glass bottle (cat. no. 1.3), which also dates to Phase I.

Type K: Mesopotamian amphora

A vertical offset rim, often creating a stepped rim, characterizes the Type K Mesopotamian amphora. It has two loop-handles attached either to the short neck and upper shoulder or on the shoulder. The body is globular and the base is a false ring-foot. Sometimes a lid made of a base fragment that fits the stepped rim has been found together with the amphora. The glaze is turquoise or decayed to brown or white.

Dating evidence and discussion

A well-preserved example of a Type K Mesopotamian amphora is published from Qala'at al-Bahrain (Højlund & Andersen 1994: fig. 1530), but the type does not seem to be common at the settlement. Related vessels have been found in Dura Europos (Toll 1943: gr. I-A, I-D) and Mesopotamian amphorae have been reported from Nippur (McCown, Haines

& Biggs 1978: pl. 54.2), Uruk (Finkbeiner 1991: nos 142, 156, 165), Failaka (Bernard, Gachet & Salles 1990: no. 135; Hannestad 1983: nos 288–289), Susa (Haerinck 1983: fig. 6.6), and Masjid-i Suleiman (Ghirshman 1976: pl. 53). Tombs containing Type K cluster in Phase I and into Phase II according to the seriation. This dating corresponds very well with most of the external evidence, since the examples from Failaka, Masjid-i Suleiman and Susa are believed to date to the third or second century BC (Hannestad 1983: 75–78; Haerinck 1983: 12-17). The example from Qala'at al-Bahrain was found in a Period Vd context (Højlund & Andersen 1994: 276), which seems to be slightly late if the dates suggested by Højlund are followed (1994: 296–299). The Mesopotamian amphora is most likely a Near Eastern type (Hannestad 1983: 37).

Red ware bowls
Type L: Bowl with three feet

Three feet with a rectangular cross-section characterize these bowls. But the overall size of the vessels and the shape of the rims vary. All three vessels of the type have an internal red slip.

Dating evidence and discussion

Bowls with three feet in red ware are common at Qala'at al-Bahrain in Period Va to Vd (Højlund & Andersen 1994: 262, 270, figs 1262, 1491, 1564, 1568; Andersen 2002: fig. 6). They are also known from Failaka (Hannestad 1983: cat. no. 405) and the bottom of a bowl with three feet in red or grey ware has been reported from Ain Jawan (Bowen 1950: fig. 22.H).

Two of the three bowls of Type L were found with other material. Cat. no. L.1 was from a mixed context and cat. no. L.3 was found with a Phase I bowl. Together with the external evidence this suggests that a Phase I dating of Type L is most likely.

Number	Height, min.	Height, max.	Rim dia., min.	Rim dia., max.
3	8.5	10.5	15.5	18.5

Table 131. Description of vessels of Type L. Measurements in centimetres.

Cat. no.	BNM no.	Area	Mound	Square	Context	Number	Remarks
L.1	111	Saar	1-91		Tomb	19	
L.2	282	Saar	7-95-96		Tomb	85	Figure 419.
L.3	FM-A-985.BE	Unplaced	T158-2		Tomb	2	

Table 132. Context information for vessels of Type L.

Number	Height, min.	Height, max.	Rim dia., min.	Rim dia., max.
14	9.5	13	13	16

Table 133. Description of vessels of Type M. Measurements in centimetres.

Cat. no.	BNM no.	Area	Mound	Square	Context	Number	Remarks
M.1	5164-2-91-3	Saar	1991-92				
M.2	637	Shakhoura	2-91-92		Tomb	14	
M.3	353	Saar	4-91-92	2	Tomb	26	
M.4	275	Saar	7-95-96	G4	Tomb	88	Figure 420.
M.5	10	Saar	3-96	D4	Tomb	12	
M.6	296	Saar	4-91-92	3	Tomb	6	
M.7	4267-2-91-7	Al-Maqsha	1990-91		Tomb	18	
M.8	2063-2-90-15	Ali	60-88-89	8	Outside tomb		
M.9	2194-2-90-15	Ali	1988		Tomb	41	
M.10	A547						No context information.
M.11	A282	Shakhoura	2-91-92		Tomb	15	
M.12	A683	Shakhoura	25-01		Tomb	5	
M.13	A763	Al-Hajar	7-92-93		Mound fill		
M.14	IMA118						Salles & Lombard 1999: no. 226.

Table 134. Context information for vessels of Type M.

Number	Height, min.	Height, max.	Rim dia., min.	Rim dia., max.
15	4.5	6.5	11	15.5

Table 135. Description of vessels of Type N. Measurements in centimetres.

Cat. no.	BNM no.	Area	Mound	Square	Context	Number	Remarks
N.1	9869-2-91	Karranah	4-86				
N.2	9826-2-91	Saar	5-87-88		Tomb	77	Figure 421.
N.3	16	Saar	1-96				
N.4	24	Saar	3-96	D4	Tomb	4	
N.5	3783-2-91-3	Saar	6-91-92	1			
N.6	2802-2-91-3						No context information.
N.7	3720-2-91-3	Saar	4-91-92	2			
N.8	2	Saar	3-96	D4	Tomb	6	
N.9	3806-2-91-3	Saar	1-91		Tomb	4	
N.10	1	Saar	3-96	D4	Tomb	12	
N.11	54	Shakhoura	3-92-93	3	Tomb	4	
N.12	2237-2-90-15	Ali	60-88-89		Tomb	5	
N.13	4794-2-90-15	Ali			Tomb	41	
N.14	A557	Shakhoura	23-00-01		Tomb	7	
N.15	A2886		93				

Table 136. Context information for vessels of Type N.

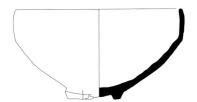
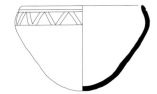

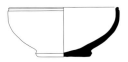

Figure 419. Cat. no. L.2.   *Figure 420. Cat. no. M.4.*   *Figure 421. Cat. no. N.2.*   *Figure 422. Cat. no. O.7.*

Type M: Hemispheric bowl
The rounded bottom characterizes this varied group. The sides are flaring or almost vertical, which gives the vessel a baggy look. The rims are either vertical or incurving. The hemispheric bowls are often decorated. Some have an internal red slip with radial streak burnishing; others are completely covered in red slip or have geometric patterns externally below the rim.

Dating evidence and discussion
No parallels have been found, but I have been informed that the Archaeological Museum in Riyadh, Saudi Arabia exhibits many similar vessels (pers. communication, Mohammed Rider, Bahrain, 2006). Four of the Bahraini vessels (cat. nos M.2, M.5, M.9 and M.11) have been found with other vessels dating to Phase I.

Type N: Carinated bowl
A carination between the body and rim characterize these bowls. They have an internal red slip often with radial streak burnishing and sometimes an external white or cream slip.

Dating evidence and discussion
The carinated bowl is not a common type among the published material. An example is reported from "The Palace of Uperi" at Qala'at al-Bahrain (Lombard & Kervran 1993: fig. 20.8) and an exact parallel has been found in Farig al-Akhrash (Bibby 1973: fig. 32d). Five carinated bowls in red ware have been found with other material, four of them with Phase I material (cat. nos N.4, N.8, N.10 and N.12). Cat. no. N.9 was contextually related to Phase III material, which is likely to be due to the reuse of a tomb or corrupted information.

The shape recalls the Achaemenid "snake bowls" in plain ware found in abundance at Qala'at al-Bahrain in Period IVd contexts (Højlund & Andersen 1994: figs 1154–1158), but also red ware bowls with a groove below the rim (Højlund & Andersen 1994: figs 1107–1109). It is therefore most likely that the shape is a Near Eastern, pre-Hellenistic type that continued into the Tylos Period.

Type O: Echinus bowl
Curved sides with an incurving rim characterize these bowls. Below the rim there are often external incised lines. Internally a red slip has been applied, which also covers *c.* 1 cm of the outside. The interior is often decorated with radial streak burnishing.

Dating evidence and discussion
Type O is closely related to Type D. The shape is believed to have been inspired by the Attic echinus bowl in black glazed ware (see the discussion of Type D). Type O bowls are fairly common at Qala'at al-Bahrain from Period Va to Vc (Højlund & Andersen 1994: figs 1252, 1256, 1257, 1422, 1423, 1485) and attested on Failaka (Hannestad 1983: cat. no. 400).

The vessels from the Bahraini tombs are mainly found with Phase I material, which supports the external dating evidence.

Grey ware bowls
Type P: Bowl with three feet
Three feet with a rectangular cross-section characterize Type P. All examples also have a rounded body, a small shoulder and an almost vertical rim. The shoulder and lip are marked with incised lines and the vessels have an internal grey slip with streak burnishing.

Dating evidence and discussion
A bowl with three feet in grey ware was found at Qala'at al-Bahrain in a Period Va context (Højlund & Andersen 1994: fig. 1278) and another from a probably late Period Va or Vb context (Andersen 2001: no. 94), but the examples from Qala'at al-Bahrain are coarser than the ones from the tombs. The bottom of a bowl with three feet in either red or grey ware has been reported from Ain Jawan (Bowen 1950: fig. 22.H). The bowls with three feet in both red and grey ware seem to have been introduced in the earliest Tylos period where the feet had a triangular cross-section. During Period Va the cross-section became more quadrangular (Andersen 2002: 242–243 and fig. 6). Two of the vessels from the tombs

have been found with other vessels, cat. no. P.4 with a Phase I vessel and cat. no. P.2 with Phase II vessels.

Type Q: Carinated bowl

The flaring sides and the carination to the out-turned rim characterize this small group.

Dating evidence and discussion

One of the two carinated bowls in grey ware (cat. no. Q.2) was found in a Phase I context. Stylistically the type is related to the bowls with flaring sides and offset lip, commonly found on Failaka and believed to be a development of Assyrian types (Hannestad 1983: 24).

Type R: Echinus bowl

The Type R Echinus bowl is formed by a varied group of bowls with curved sides and a raised base. The rim is incurved or vertical and often with external incised lines.

Dating evidence and discussion

The Type R bowls resemble Type D and O and could thus be an imitation of the Attic echinus bowl (see above). The type is found at Qala'at al-Bahrain in grey ware in a Period Va context (Højlund & Andersen 1994: figs 1268) and probably on Failaka (Hannestad 1983: figs. 412–414). Two of the vessels from the tombs have been found with other vessels, the one (cat. no. R.2) from a mixed context containing Phase I and III material and the other (cat. no. R.9) with a Phase II bowl. However, the well-dated examples from Qala'at al-Bahrain and also partly from Failaka suggest, together with the morphologic relation to the echinus bowls in red and glazed ware, that the type is likely to belong in Phase I.

Type S: Bowl with angular profile

A sharp carination between the lower body and sides characterizes these bowls. They have a raised base and are often decorated with incised lines. Internally most of the bowls with angular profile have radial burnishing.

Dating evidence and discussion

Type S bowls with angular profile are closely related to Type F, which was most likely inspired by the Attic bowl with out-turned rim (Rotroff 1997: fig. 59–61; Hannestad 1983: 18). Seven grey ware bowls with angular profile have been found with

Number	Height, min.	Height, max.	Rim dia., min.	Rim dia., max.
18	5	6.5	12	15.5

Table 137. Description of vessels of Type O. Measurements in centimetres.

Cat. no.	BNM no.	Area	Mound	Square	Context	Number	Remarks
O.1							No context information.
O.2	A6111	Hamad Town	1-94-95	E3	Tomb	4-E3	
O.3	9793-2-91	Karranah	3-86				
O.4	22	Saar	3-96	C2	Tomb	9	
O.5	686	Shakhoura	2-91-92		Outside tomb	26	
O.6	10058-2-91	Hamad Town		6			
O.7	10	Saar	6-91-92	2	Tomb	3	Figure 422.
O.8	183	Saar	11-95-96		Outside tomb	18	
O.9	9	Saar		B2	Tomb	24	
O.10	11	Shakhoura	2-92	I5	Mound fill		
O.11	10050-2-91	Karranah	1986				
O.12	2573-2-90						No context information.
O.13	A566	Shakhoura	23-00-01		Outside tomb	5	
O.14	A3438	Hamad Town	10-89-90	E4	Tomb	41A	
O.15	A623	Karzakan	3-78		Tomb	2	
O.16	181	Saar	7-91		Tomb	1	
O.17	IMA451						No context information.
O.18	FM-A-963.D	Saar	1-1960		Tomb	3	

Table 138. Context information for vessels of Type O.

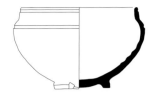

Figure 423. Cat. no. P.1. *Figure 424. Cat. no. Q.1.* *Figure 425. Cat. no. R.1.*

Figure 426. Cat. no. R.5. *Figure 427. Cat. no. R.15.* *Figure 428. Cat. no. S.6.* *Figure 429. Cat. no. S.9.*

Figure 430. Cat. no. T.1. *Figure 431. Cat. no. U.1.* *Figure 432. Cat. no. U.2.* *Figure 433. Cat. no. V.1.*

Number	Height, min.	Height, max.	Rim dia., min.	Rim dia., max.
4	7.5	10	11	14

Table 139. Description of vessels of Type P. Measurements in centimetres.

Cat. no.	BNM no.	Area	Mound	Square	Context	Number	Remarks
P.1	156	Al-Hajar	6-92-93	D4	Outside tomb	24	Figure 423.
P.2	43	Saar	7-95-96	F3	Tomb	22	
P.3	24	Saar	4-94-95	B2	Outside tomb		
P.4	183	Al-Maqsha	1992-93	C15	Tomb	4	
P.5	A3433		89-90				

Table 140. Context information for vessels of Type P.

Number	Height, min.	Height, max.	Rim dia., min.	Rim dia., max.
2	6	6	17	17

Table 141. Description of vessels of Type Q. Measurements in centimetres.

Cat. no.	BNM no.	Area	Mound	Square	Context	Number	Remarks
Q.1	17	Saar	7-95-96	C3			Figure 424.
Q.2	2045-2-90	Ali	60-88-89		Tomb	17	

Table 142. Context information for vessels of Type Q.

Number	Height, min.	Height, max.	Rim dia., min.	Rim dia., max.
18	4	8.5	10.5	19

Table 143. Description of vessels of Type R. Measurements in centimetres.

Cat. no.	BNM no.	Area	Mound	Square	Context	Number	Remarks
R.1	12	Saar	1995		Tomb	5	Figure 425.
R.2	3875-2-91-3	Saar	1-91		Tomb	4	
R.3	9994-2-91	Hamad Town	30-84-85				
R.4	138	Saar	5-95-96	E4	Tomb	42	
R.5	28	Hamad Town	1-94-95	D1	Tomb	5-D1	Figure 426.
R.6	186	Saar	11-95-96		Tomb	16	
R.7	107	Saar	7-95-96	G6	Tomb	86	
R.8	57	Saar	12-95-96	A3	Tomb	31	
R.9	10040-2-91	Saar	5-87-88	C4	Tomb	13	
R.10	1956-2-89	Saar	5-87-88	E3	Tomb	31	
R.11	73	Al-Hajar	2-92	6			
R.12	2408-2-90	Saar	5-87-88	E3	Tomb	31	
R.13	117	Shakhoura	1-92-93	C4	Tomb	30	
R.14	1939-2-89	Saar	5-87-88	6	Tomb	5?	
R.15	9996-2-91	Hamad Town	106-84-85				Figure 427.
R.16	1844-2-89	Ali	111-88-89		Tomb	16	
R.17	A3128		93				No context information.
R.18	A3407		94-95				No context information.

Table 144. Context information for vessels of Type R.

Number	Height, min.	Height, max.	Rim dia., min.	Rim dia., max.
14	5.5	7	13.5	17

Table 145. Description of vessels of Type S. Measurements in centimetres.

Cat. no.	BNM no.	Area	Mound	Square	Context	Number	Remarks
S.1	3870-2-91-3	Saar	10-91	3	Outside tomb	6	
S.2	A6584	Saar	5-95-96	D4	Mound fill		
S.3	3805-2-91-3	Saar	5-91-92	2			
S.4	16	Saar	7-95-96	D4	Tomb	13	
S.5	91-2-34	Saar	9-91	4	Tomb	1	
S.6	182	Saar	11-95-96		Outside tomb	10	Figure 428.
S.7	3865-2-91-3	Saar	12-91		Outside tomb	7	
S.8	185	Saar	11-95-96		Outside tomb	1	
S.9	3925-2-91-3	Saar	4-91-92	8			Figure 429.
S.10	3881-2-91-3	Saar	12-91		Outside tomb	6	
S.11	3724-2-91-3	Saar	5-91-92	2	Tomb	8	
S.12	184	Saar	11-95-96		Mound fill	12	From the mound fill close to the tomb.
S.13	126	Hamad Town	1-94-95	E6			
S.14	11	Saar	3-96	B4	Outside tomb	17	
S.15	A478	Saar	1-95	B2	Outside tomb	12	
S.16	FM-A-962.C	Saar	1-1960		Outside tomb	2	

Table 146. Context information for vessels of Type S.

Number	Height, min.	Height, max.	Rim dia., min.	Rim dia., max.
2	8.5	8.5	14	14

Table 147. Description of vessels of Type T. Measurements in centimetres.

Cat. no.	BNM no.	Area	Mound	Square	Context	Number	Remarks
T.1	91-2-37	Saar	9-91	1	Tomb	7	Figure 430.
T.2	FM-A-985.J	Unplaced	T158-2		Tomb	1	

Table 148. Context information for vessels of Type T.

Number	Height, min.	Height, max.	Rim dia., min.	Rim dia., max.
4	9.5	14.5	6	8

Table 149. Description of vessels of Type U. Measurements in centimetres.

Cat. no.	BNM no.	Area	Mound	Square	Context	Number	Remarks
U.1	A3372	Al-Maqsha	1992-93	C15	Tomb	3	Figure 431.
U.2	3727-2-91-3	Saar	4-91-92	I3	Tomb	31	Figure 432.
U.3	2182-2-90-15	Ali	1988		Tomb	41	
U.4	A274	Saar	9-91	1	Tomb	8	

Table 150. Context information for vessels of Type U.

Number	Height, min.	Height, max.	Rim dia., min.	Rim dia., max.
4	8	10.5	2.5	3

Table 151. Description of vessels of Type V. Measurements in centimetres.

Cat. no.	BNM no.	Area	Mound	Square	Context	Number	Remarks
V.1	400	Saar	2-91-92	2/3	Tomb	22	Figure 433.
V.2	3773-2-91-3	Saar	10-91	5	Tomb	3	
V.3	5617-2-91	Isa Town	1972				
V.4	2631-2-90	Saar	4-87	C4	Mound fill		

Table 152. Context information for vessels of Type V.

other vessels in the Bahraini tombs, five of them with datable material. Three of them were found with Type B bowls, one vessel (cat. no. S.6) with Phase II material and one (cat. no. S.10) with Phase IV glass vessels. The types are thus most likely to be dated to Phase I but may have continued into Phase II, whereas the vessel found with Phase IV material is probably from a reused tomb or the context information is corrupt.

Type T: Rounded bowl
The rounded shape and flat resting surface characterize this small group.

Dating evidence and discussion
One of the two rounded bowls in grey ware was found with a Phase I vessel (cat. no. T.2). No parallels to the type have been found.

Grey ware bottles

Type U: Amphora with strap-handles

Two strap-handles with an oval to rectangular cross-section attached from the upper neck to the shoulder characterize this group. The angular profile of the body is also a characteristic feature. The rim is out-turned and externally thickened.

Dating evidence and discussion

No parallels have been found, but the contextual relation of cat. no. U.3 to a Type M hemispheric bowl indicates that the type was in use in Phase I. The type illustrates some similarities with the Attic amphorae (Rotroff 1997: figs 24–33), which supports the dating to Phase I.

Type V: Bottle with two shoulder-attached loop-handles

A small group of bottles characterized by two shoulder-attached loop-handles, a globular body and a narrow neck with an out-turned rim.

Dating evidence and discussion

The bottles with two shoulder-attached loop handles in grey ware are closely related to Type J. The type is most likely of Mesopotamian/Babylonian origin and developed in the early Hellenistic period (see Type J). Two of the grey ware vessels were found with other vessels. One (cat. no. V.2) with a Phase I vessel, which corresponds well with the dating of the glazed ware bottles, but the other (cat. no. V.1) appears to be from a mixed context containing both Phase I and Phase III material.

Sand-tempered ware bowls

Type X: Thin-walled bowl

These bowls are characterized by their thin walls, flaring sides and vertical or curved rims. The walls were thinned down by scraping at the lower part. The vessels often have an internal red slip and a white rim.

Dating evidence and discussion

At Qala'at al-Bahrain thin-walled bowls have been found in Period Vb and Vc contexts, where the vessels from Period Vb seems to have a shorter and straighter rim than the ones from Period Vc (Højlund & Andersen 1994: figs 1434–1435, 1497–1500). In Thaj in Saudi Arabia Bibby's Type 3 was a very common type in the Danish sounding accounting for 24 % (Bibby 1973: 21–24) and well attested in the small excavations undertaken by Freie Universität, Berlin (Potts 1993b: Type 4). Examples from Failaka are similar in shape to the ones from Period Vb at Qala'at al-Bahrain, but have an

Figure 434. Cat. no. X.2.

Figure 435. Cat. no. X.12.

external rouletting, which is not seen on the examples from Qala'at al-Bahrain or the Bahraini tombs (Hannestad 1983: figs 419–422).

The seriation indicates a date for the thin-walled bowls to Phase I, which supports the dating of the vessels from Qala'at al-Bahrain and Failaka.

An inspiration from Nabataean prototypes has been suggested for the origin of the examples from Thaj and Failaka due to the similarities between Nabataean bowls and the vessels from eastern Arabia (Lapp 1963; Hannestad 1983: 51–52). A significant part of the argument has been a dating of the vessels from eastern Arabia to a period after *c.* 100 BC where influence from the Nabataeans could be expected. This also included a lowering of the dating of the majority of finds from Thaj from the original Hellenistic dating (Bibby 1973: 25) to after *c.* 100 BC (Hannestad 1983: 51–52). However, since thin-walled bowls in sand-tempered ware can now safely be dated to before *c.* 100 BC, the type pre-dates the rise of the Nabataeans and their possible influence in the region. It is thus unlikely that Nabataeans vessels would have inspired north-east Arabian potters. It is more likely that the thin-walled bowls are an inland Arabian tradition, which explains the high frequency of the type at Thaj. Another possible explanation for the similarities between the Nabataean and north-east Arabian vessels is, as suggested by Vickers, that both groups relied on prototypes in silver or gold (1994: 240–241).

Plain ware bowls

Type Y: Bowl with flaring sides and vertical rim

Type Y is formed by a coherent group of bowls with flaring sides and vertical rim. The fabric is light buff

and sometimes with patches in bright orange, and
the walls of the vessels are relatively thin.

Dating evidence and discussion

Type Y is well known from Period Vb at Qala'at-
al-Bahrain (Højlund & Andersen 1994: figs 1448-
1450), but the type was not found on Failaka or
further north. A possible development of the type
was found in a Period Vc context at Qala'at al-Bahrain (Højlund & Andersen 1994: fig. 1523).
Type Y bowls have mainly been found with Phase

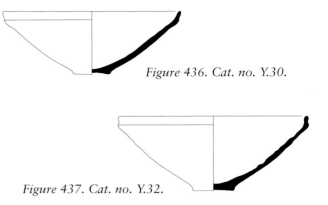

Figure 436. Cat. no. Y.30.

Figure 437. Cat. no. Y.32.

Number	Height, min.	Height, max.	Rim dia., min.	Rim dia., max.
30	5	8	13	17

Table 153. Description of vessels of Type X. Measurements in centimetres.

Cat. no.	BNM no.	Area	Mound	Square	Context	Number	Remarks
X.1	164	Saar	5-95-96	E4	Tomb	47	
X.2	94	Al-Hajar	1-92-93	7	Mound fill		Figure 434.
X.3	5	Shakhoura	1-92-93	C5	Outside tomb	40	
X.4	10044-1-11	Karranah	4-86				
X.5	10085-2-91	Hamad Town		5			
X.6	3995-2-91	Al-Maqsha	1991-92		Tomb	1	
X.7	41	Al-Maqsha	1991-92		Tomb	1	
X.8	91-2-58	Saar	4-91-92	14	Tomb	51	
X.9	A6187	Saar	5-91-92	8	Tomb	18	
X.10	419-2-88	Karranah	4-86				
X.11	3818-2-91	Saar	5-91-92	3	Tomb	3	
X.12	80	Saar	5-95-96	E3	Tomb	10	Figure 435.
X.13	3818-2-91-3						No context information.
X.14	91-1-40	Shakhoura	1-91	C4	Mound fill		
X.15	10086-2-91	Al-Hajar					
X.16	107	Al-Hajar	2-92		Jar	1	
X.17	134	Saar	5-95-96	4	Tomb	34	
X.18	113	Saar	5-91-92	7	Tomb	24	
X.19	200	Al-Hajar	2-92-93		Tomb	39	
X.20	3872-2-91-3	Saar	10-91		Outside tomb	2	
X.21	66	Al-Hajar	1-92-93		Tomb	5	
X.22	217	Al-Hajar	2-92-93		Tomb	46	
X.23	91-2-39	Saar	4-91-92	2	Tomb	28	
X.24	10072-2-91	Ali	60-88-89		Tomb	21	
X.25	819-2-88	Um Al-Hasam	1973		Tomb	2	
X.26	3794-2-91-3	Saar	1-91		Tomb	2	
X.27	A635	Shakhoura	29-00-01		Tomb	7	
X.28	A232	Al-Hajar	6-92-93		Tomb	19	
X.29	IMA114	Karranah	4				
X.30	IMA115	Karranah	2				

Table 154. Context information for vessels of Type X.

Number	Height, min.	Height, max.	Rim dia., min.	Rim dia., max.
45	4	8.5	17	23

Table 155. Description of vessels of Type Y. Measurements in centimetres.

Cat. no.	BNM no.	Area	Mound	Square	Context	Number	Remarks
Y.1		Al-Hajar	7-92-93	F2	Tomb	6	
Y.2	9906-2-91	Jannussan	1980				
Y.3	9943-2-91	Al-Hajar			Tomb	1	
Y.4	91-2-33	Saar	11-91		Outside tomb	8	
Y.5	21	Saar	1-96				
Y.6	91-2-83	Saar	3-90-91		Tomb	2	
Y.7	180	Saar	7-91		Tomb	1	
Y.8	3722-2-91	Saar	10-91	5	Tomb	3	
Y.9	3839-2-91-3	Saar	10-91	6	Mound fill		
Y.10	3781-2-91-6	Shakhoura	2-91-92	E2	Mound fill		
Y.11	3723-2-91-3	Saar	4-91-92		Tomb	21	
Y.12	9755-2-91	Karranah	1986				
Y.13	9965-2-91	Saar	4-85-86				
Y.14	4277-2-91-6	Shakhoura			Tomb		
Y.15	9813-2-91	Karranah	1986				
Y.16	10167-2-91			C	Tomb	2	
Y.17	46		7-95-96	D5	Mound fill		
Y.18	987-2-88	Al-Hajar	1973		Tomb	110	
Y.19			2-95-96			1	
Y.20	3844-2-91-3	Saar	5-91-92		Outside tomb	4	
Y.21	5067-2-91-3	Saar	2-90	25	Tomb	3	
Y.22	3	Saar	3-96	D4	Tomb	6	
Y.23	211	Al-Hajar	7-92-93	F2	Outside tomb	7	
Y.24	359	Saar	5-96-97	D4	Tomb	90	
Y.25	45	Shakhoura	6-92-93	E4	Tomb	9	
Y.26	274	Saar	4-91-92	11	Tomb	14	
Y.27	4410-2-91	Karranah	2-85				
Y.28	719-2-91-3	Saar	5-91-92	8	Tomb	16	
Y.29	69	Al-Hajar	1-92-93		Tomb	8	
Y.30	3822-2-91-3	Saar	5-91-92	3	Tomb	4	Figure 436.
Y.31	9447-2-91	Jabal al Dok	1970				
Y.32	A6172	Saar	9-91	4	Tomb	2	Figure 437.
Y.33	91-2-8	Saar	10-91-92		Tomb	7	
Y.34	4789-2-9016		1994				
Y.35	3836-2-91-3	Saar	2-91		Tomb	29	
Y.36	10013-2-91	Jannussan	1980				
Y.37	5066-2-91-3	Saar	1990	B1	Tomb	1	
Y.38	2025-2-90	Ali	60-88-89	4			
Y.39	1964-2-89	Ali	60-88-89		Tomb	20	
Y.40	2090-2-90	Ali	60-88-89		Tomb	5	
Y.41	A235	Al-Hajar	1979	2			
Y.42	A3120		1993				
Y.43	A553	Shakhoura	23-00-01				
Y.44		Karranah	1-1992		Tomb	C-V-2	
Y.45	FM-A-961.B	Saar	1-1960		Outside tomb	1	

Table 156. Context information for vessels of Type Y.

Number	Height, min.	Height, max.	Rim dia., min.	Rim dia., max.
67	3	7	10	16

Table 157. Description of vessels of Type Z. Measurements in centimetres.

Cat. no.	BNM no.	Area	Mound	Square	Context	Number	Remarks
Z.1		Al-Maqsha	1992-93	C15	Tomb	4	
Z.2		Al-Maqsha	1992-93	G6	Tomb	1	
Z.3	73	Al-Hajar	1-92-93	6	Outside tomb	13	
Z.4	65	Al-Hajar	1-92-93		Outside tomb	4	
Z.5	1083-2-88						No context information.
Z.6	2371-2-90	Saar	5	E5	Tomb	58	
Z.7	91-1-20	Shakhoura	3-91		Outside tomb	2	
Z.8	70	Shakhoura	4-92-93	C3	Tomb	5	
Z.9	7161-2-91	Al-Hajar	1981	1	Tomb	2	
Z.10	2	Saar	1995	C2	Tomb	26	
Z.11	4435-2-91-2	Hamad Town	157-84-85	D			
Z.12	3793-2-91-3	Saar	5-91-92	9	Outside tomb	22	
Z.13	5615-2-91	Al-Hajar	1979		Tomb	2	
Z.14	4437-2-91-3	Saar	1-90	B2	Outside tomb	2	
Z.15	9753-2-91	Karranah	4-86				
Z.16	3792-2-91-3	Saar	6-91-92	3	Tomb	15	
Z.17	2627-2-90	Saar	3-87	5	Tomb	1	
Z.18	7821-2-91	Karranah	1986				
Z.19	4383-2-91-3	Saar	1-90	22	Outside tomb	6	
Z.20	3879-2-91-3	Saar	12-91		Outside tomb	16	
Z.21	7171-2-91	Al-Hajar	1979		Tomb	1	
Z.22	10010-2-91	Karranah	1986				
Z.23	207	Saar	7-95-96	A3			
Z.24	251	Saar	7-95-96	B2	Outside tomb	110	
Z.25	7156-2-91	Al-Hajar	1979		Tomb	2	
Z.26	9772-2-91	Al-Hajar	1979		Tomb	3	
Z.27	1081-2-88						
Z.28	222	Al-Hajar	7-92-93		Outside tomb	8	
Z.29	3820-2-91-3	Saar	6-91-92	3	Outside tomb	12	
Z.30	7168-2-91	Hamad Town	153-85		Tomb	27	
Z.31	7239-2-91	Um Al-Hasam	1973		Tomb	47	
Z.32	14	Saar	7-95-96	A3	Outside tomb		
Z.33	111	Saar	5-91-92	9	Tomb	22	
Z.34	91-2-49	Saar	10-91	5	Outside tomb	2	
Z.35	3876-2-91-3	Saar	1-91	3	Tomb	30	
Z.36	5465-2-91	Al-Hajar		K			
Z.37	87	Saar	1-91		Tomb	4	
Z.38	7169-2-91	Hamad Town	153-85		Tomb	33	
Z.39	4906-2-90-2	Hamad Town	84-85	B2			
Z.40	7160-2-91	Hamad Town	84-85	C2	Tomb	97	
Z.41	96-4-8	Saar	13-96	A2	Tomb	3	Figure 438.
Z.42	7188-2-91	Al-Hajar					
Z.43	7167-2-91	Al-Hajar	1979		Tomb	1	
Z.44	7183-2-91	Al-Hajar			Tomb	3	

Cat. no.	BNM no.	Area	Mound	Square	Context	Number	Remarks
Z.45	55	Saar	6-96	C3			Figure 439.
Z.46	233	Saar	9-91	3	Tomb	3	Figure 440.
Z.47	5611-2-91	Al-Hajar	1979		Tomb	1	
Z.48	7172-2-91	Al-Hajar	1979		Tomb	2	
Z.49	91-2-13	Saar	8-90-91	2	Outside tomb	8	
Z.50	2021-2-90-15	Ali	60-88-89		Tomb	45	
Z.51	2220-2-90-15	Ali	60-88-89		OUT	8	
Z.52	A888	Al-Maqsha	1999-00	B7	Tomb	12	
Z.53	A5839	Hamad Town	1984-85	B2			
Z.54	A5846	Hamad Town	153-85		Tomb	27	
Z.55	A5845	Hamad Town	153-85	B	Tomb	27	
Z.56	A5735	Hamad Town	153-85	C	Tomb	27	
Z.57	A5737	Hamad Town	1984-85	B3			
Z.58	A5734	Hamad Town	1984-85	C2	Tomb	E47	
Z.59	A5602	Hamad Town	1985		Tomb	2-100	
Z.60	A4782	Hamad Town	1986-87	D6	Tomb	2	
Z.61	A4811	Hamad Town	88-85-86		Tomb	4	
Z.62	A151	Shakhoura	30-98-99	C4	Tomb	9	
Z.63	A48	Saar	10-99-01	B	Tomb	33	
Z.64	FM-A-985.Z	Unplaced	T158-1		Tomb	1	
Z.65	FM-A-985.L	Unplaced	T158-2		Tomb	1	
Z.66	FM-A-985.BC	Unplaced	T158-2		Tomb	2	
Z.67	FM-A-985.T	Unplaced	T158-3		Tomb	1	

Table 158. Context information for vessels of Type Z.

Figure 438. Cat. no. Z.41.

Figure 439. Cat. no. Z.45.

Figure 440. Cat. no. Z.46.

I materials, which corresponds well with the dating of the vessels from Qala'at. The lack of parallels outside Bahrain could indicate that the production was local. The type could well have been inspired by eggshell bowls commonly found on Failaka (i.e. Hannestad 1983: nos 354–360) as pointed out by Højlund (Højlund & Andersen 1994: 265).

Type Z: Echinus bowl

Curved sides with an incurving rim characterize Type Z. Most of them also have a rough string-cut surface under the raised foot. Few of the vessels have incised lines below the rim.

Dating evidence and discussion

Type Z is related to Types D, O and R and the shape is likely to have been inspired by the Attic echinus bowl (see the discussion of type D). The type is known from Period Vb contexts at Qala'at al-Bahrain (Højlund & Andersen 1994: figs 1444–1445) and is well attested from the lower layers at the Danish excavations at Failaka (Hannestad 1983: nos 464–473).

The seriation indicates that the type belongs in Phase I, which corresponds well with the evidence from Qala'at al-Bahrain and Failaka.

Number	Height, min.	Height, max.	Rim dia., min.	Rim dia., max.
3	6	8	14	15.5

Table 159. Description of vessels of Type AA. Measurements in centimetres.

Cat. no.	BNM no.	Area	Mound	Square	Context	Number	Remarks
AA.1	4795-2-90-3	Saar	3-85-86	2	Tomb	4	
AA.2	5310-2-91-6	Shakhoura	2-91-92		Tomb	15	Figure 441.
AA.3	10084-2-91	Jannussan	1981				

Table 160. Context information for vessels of Type AA.

Type AA: Saucer with vertical rim
A little group of rather small bowls with flaring sides and a vertical rim.

Dating evidence and discussion
No parallels have been found, but the form of these vessels is closely related to the echinus bowl, and the contextual relation of cat. no. AA.2 with a Type M hemispheric bowl in red ware supports a dating in Phase I.

Type AB: Saucer with flaring sides
This is a little shallow saucer with straight flaring sides. Many of them also have the rough string-cut surface under the raised foot.

Dating evidence and discussion
Type AB is attested at Qala'at al Bahrain in Period Vb contexts (Højlund & Andersen 1994: figs 1446–1447), and on Failaka in the lower levels (Hannestad 1983: nos 436–452), which corresponds well with the seriation that indicates a Phase I dating for Type AB.

Figure 441. Cat. no. AA.2.

Figure 442. Cat. no. AB.24.

Figure 443. Cat. no. AB.25.

Number	Height, min.	Height, max.	Rim dia., min.	Rim dia., max.
35	2.5	4.5	11.5	17

Table 161. Description of vessels of Type AB. Measurements in centimetres.

Cat. no.	BNM no.	Area	Mound	Square	Context	Number	Remarks
AB.1	149	Saar	3-90-91		Tomb	2	
AB.2	633	Shakhoura	2-91-92		Tomb	14	
AB.3	9505-2-91	Jannussan	1980				
AB.4	4715-2-90-3	Saar	1-87		Tomb	1	
AB.5	3791-2-91-6	Shakhoura	1-91		Tomb	4	
AB.6	4275-2-91-4	Al-Hajar	1979	C	Tomb	2	
AB.7	215	Al-Hajar	7-92-93	G3	Tomb	13	
AB.8	10141-2-91	Karranah	4-86				
AB.9	204	Al-Hajar	6-92-93	B5	Tomb	A21	
AB.10	9867-2-91	Karranah	4-86				
AB.11	3864-2-91-3	Saar	11-91		Outside tomb	9	
AB.12	7246-2-91	Abu-Saybi	1983	80(2)			
AB.13	269	Saar	10-91	2	Outside tomb	9	
AB.14	173	Saar	5-95-96	E4	Outside tomb	27	
AB.15							No context information.
AB.16	140	Al-Hajar	1993	D7			
AB.17	7143-2-91	Jannussan	1-69				
AB.18	12	Barbar	1996		Tomb	8	
AB.19	7238-2-91	Shakhoura	1972				
AB.20	4793-2-90-4	Al-Hajar					
AB.21	236	Saar	9-91	4	Outside tomb	2	
AB.22	3842-2-91-3	Saar	1-91		Tomb	19	
AB.23	10148-2-91						
AB.24	60	Al-Hajar	1-92-93		Tomb	8	Figure 442.
AB.25	62	Saar	6-96	C3	Tomb	9	Figure 443.
AB.26	403	Saar	2-91-92	E6			
AB.27	5161-2-91	Saar	4-91-92	12			
AB.28	2060-2-90	Ali	60-88-89		Tomb	10	
AB.29	2204-2-90-15	Ali	39-88-89		Tomb	3	
AB.30	2224-2-90-15	Ali	60-88-89		OUT	36	
AB.31	4904-2-90-15	Ali	25-88		Tomb	2	
AB.32	2201-2-90-15	Ali	60-88-89		Tomb	30	
AB.33	A3476	Al-Maqsha	1991-92		Tomb	2	
AB.34	A2889						No context information.
AB.35		Karranah	1-1992		Tomb	C-V-2	

Table 162. Context information for vessels of Type AB.

Phase II. The "BI-ware period" (*c.* 50 BC to AD 50)

The Phase is defined as the late "pre-glass-blowing" and the period of early glass-blowing. The material from this Phase is also contemporary with the so-called BI-ware from Failaka.

Glazed ware bowls

Type AC: Shallow hollow-based bowl
This is a coherent group of shallow bowls with a flat or slightly concave resting surface. The sides of the bowls are flaring and the rim is most often plain or with an external thickening or marked lip.
The glaze is green or preserved as whitish, where some examples appear to have had a green rim. Two vessels have internal bi-chrome decoration.

Dating evidence and discussion
A large fragment of a Type AC bowl from Qala'at al-Bahrain was found in a Period Vd context (Højlund & Andersen 1994: fig. 1538) and on Failaka the type is quite common in BI-ware (Hannestad 1983: 23). In the seriation of the finds from the Bahraini tombs Type AC dates to Phase II. The type seems to follow Type B and may have been replaced by Type AQ.

A typological and thus functional relation to the Greek *phiale*, which were used for libations in religious contexts, has been suggested for the Type AC bowls from the area of Temple A on Failaka (Hannestad 1983: 23). However, the high numbers found in the Bahraini tombs and their morphological relation to other hollow-based bowls, indicates that such a highly specialized function may be exaggerated to apply to the vessels found in Bahrain. Assuming that the type is not a typological development of Type B, shallow bowls or plates without a proper base became popular in the Mediterranean region from the second century BC and were widely exported in Augustan times (Hayes 1997: 78–79) and is well attested in Hama in Syria (Christensen & Johansen 1972: Forme 10). These bowls could well have served as prototypes for Type AC, and so could shallow cast glass bowls, which became common in this period in the Roman Empire and were evidently exported to eastern Arabia (e.g. Type 4).

Type AD: Saucer with vertical rim
The little bowl with vertical rim is related to the echinus bowls. They have a ring-foot, a false ring-foot or a raised base and a few examples have internal incised rings.

Figure 444. Cat. no. AC.8.

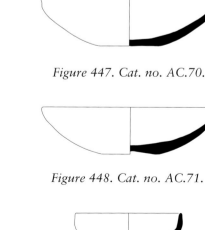

Figure 447. Cat. no. AC.70.

Figure 448. Cat. no. AC.71.

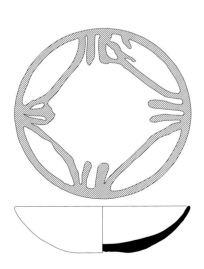

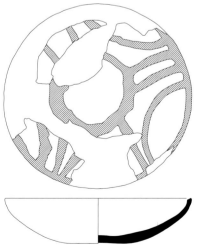

Figure 445. Cat. no. AC.47.

Figure 446. Cat. no. AC.57.

Figure 449. Cat. no. AD.8.

Number	Height, min.	Height, max.	Rim dia., min.	Rim dia., max.
81	4.5	6	18	22

Table 163. Description of vessels of Type AC. Measurements in centimetres.

Cat. no.	BNM no.	Area	Mound	Square	Context	Number	Remarks
AC.1		Shakhoura	A1-96-97	F2/F3	Tomb	27	
AC.2	116	Saar	12-95-96		Tomb	12	
AC.3	133	Al-Hajar	6-92-93	E3	Tomb	2	
AC.4	75	Saar	7-95-96	D4	Tomb	15	
AC.5	1969-2-89	Saar	5-87-88	D5	Tomb	24	
AC.6							No context information.
AC.7	3719-2-91	Saar	5-91-92	8	Tomb	16	
AC.8	3785-2-91-3	Saar	5-91-92	3	Tomb	2	Figure 444.
AC.9	3807-2-91-3	Saar	7-91-92	1	Tomb	1	
AC.10	243	Al-Hajar	2-92-93		Tomb	37	
AC.11	174	Al-Hajar	6-92-93	C6	Tomb	27	
AC.12	167	Al-Hajar	2-92-93		Tomb	33	
AC.13	77	Al-Hajar	1-92-93		Tomb	15	
AC.14		Shakhoura	7-93	C6	Tomb	25	
AC.15							No context information.
AC.16	2441-2-90	Maqabah	1989	2	Tomb	1	
AC.17	31	Shakhoura	7-93	D6	Tomb	46	
AC.18	3734-2-91-3	Saar	5-91-92	9	Tomb	23	
AC.19	153	Shakhoura	7-93	D8	Tomb	59	
AC.20	5	Shakhoura	7-93	B7	Tomb	30	
AC.21	21	Shakhoura	7-93	B6	Tomb	9	
AC.22	281	Al-Hajar	3-93		Tomb	8	
AC.23	4432-2-91-19	Um Al-Hasam	1973				
AC.24	97-3-51	Shakhoura	A1-96-97	F6	Tomb	12	
AC.25	9916-2-91	Abu-Saybi	1986				
AC.26	129	Saar	12-95-96		Tomb	23	
AC.27	156	Shakhoura	7-93	F6	Tomb	114	
AC.28	2013-2-90	Ali	53-88-89		Tomb	2	
AC.29	2527-2-90	Shakhoura					
AC.30	2417-2-90	Saar	5-87-88	C5	Tomb	7	
AC.31	176	Saar	5-95-96	D3	Tomb	44	
AC.32	91-2-41	Saar	1-91		Tomb	1	
AC.33	2380-2-90	Al-Hajar	1-89		Tomb	11	
AC.34	1	Shakhoura	1991		Tomb	1	
AC.35	904-2-88	Hamad Town	1984-85		Tomb	3	
AC.36	212						No context information.
AC.37	197	Al-Maqsha	1992-93	C5	Tomb	1	
AC.38	1839-2-89	Al-Manama Suq Magasis	1989		Tomb	2	
AC.39	81	Al-Maqsha	1992-93	E6	Tomb	3	
AC.40	136	Al-Hajar	1-92-93		Tomb	14	
AC.41	9717-2-91	Hawar	1983		Tomb	2	
AC.42	85	Al-Hajar	2-92		Tomb	11	
AC.43	7814-2-91	Um Al-Hasam			Tomb	4	

Cat. no.	BNM no.	Area	Mound	Square	Context	Number	Remarks
AC.44	218	Saar	5-96-97	C4	Tomb	32	
AC.45	115	Saar	7-95-96	E3	Tomb	27	
AC.46	3921-2-91-3	Saar	163-91-92		Tomb	22	
AC.47	91-2-22	Saar	1-91		Tomb	18	W. bichrome decoration. Figure 445.
AC.48	2398-2-90	Saar	5-87-88		Tomb	13	
AC.49	287	Saar	1995-96		Tomb	9	
AC.50	227	Saar	5-96-97	D4	Tomb	35	
AC.51	7149-2-91	Saar	5-87-88	E4	Tomb	34	
AC.52	99	Al-Hajar	2-92		Tomb	9	
AC.53	145	Hamad Town	1-94-95	D4	Tomb	1-D4	
AC.54	1937-2-89	Saar	5-87-88	E6	Tomb	51	
AC.55	352	Saar	11-95-96		Tomb	15	
AC.56	91-1-8	Shakhoura	2-92		Tomb	56	
AC.57	9432-2-91	Um Al-Hasam	1973				W. bichrome decoration. Figure 446.
AC.58	122	Shakhoura	7-93	E6	Tomb	62	
AC.59	2317-2-90	Buri	2-84				
AC.60	91-2-21	Saar	1-91		Tomb	12	
AC.61	6076-2-90						No context information.
AC.62	320	Saar	11-95-96		Tomb	11	
AC.63	28	Shakhoura	7-93	D8	Tomb	61	
AC.64	219	Saar	5-96-97	D5	Tomb	73	
AC.65	1	Abu-Saybi	5-97	B2			
AC.66	325	Saar	11-95-96		Tomb	18	
AC.67	5224-2-91-3	Saar	1-91-92	3	Tomb	5	
AC.68	47	Shakhoura	7-93	C8	Tomb	32	
AC.69	139	Hamad Town	1-94-95	D3	Tomb	1-D3	
AC.70	258	Saar	11-95-96		Tomb	10	Figure 447.
AC.71	25	Shakhoura	7-93	D8	Tomb	58	Figure 448.
AC.72	9774-2-91	Al-Hajar					
AC.73	796-2-88						No context information.
AC.74	10186-2-91	Al-Hajar	1981	B	Tomb	1	
AC.75	91-2-61	Saar	11-91		Tomb	3	
AC.76	A3117		1993				
AC.77	A633	Shakhoura	29-00-01		Tomb	22	
AC.78	A572	Al-Maqsha	1978	14			
AC.79	A3394		96-97				
AC.80	A277	Saar	3-96	D4	Tomb	5	
AC.81	A665	Shakhoura	29-00-01			19	

Table 164. Context information for vessels of Type AC.

Number	Height, min.	Height, max.	Rim dia., min.	Rim dia., max.
18	4	5	9.5	12

Table 165. Description of vessels of Type AD. Measurements in centimetres.

136

Cat. no.	BNM no.	Area	Mound	Square	Context	Number	Remarks
AD.1	142	Hamad Town	1-94-95	E4	Tomb	1-E4	
AD.2							No context information.
AD.3	9841-2-91	Hamad Town	30-84-85		Outside tomb	33	
AD.4	1	Shakhoura	2-91-92		Outside tomb	50	
AD.5	77	Al-Hajar	2-92		Outside tomb	6	
AD.6	31	Hamad Town	1-94-95	C4			
AD.7	10137-2-91	Karranah	1986				
AD.8	277	Saar	7-95-96	C4	Tomb	20	Figure 449.
AD.9	2383-2-90	Saar	5-97-98	D6	Tomb	22	
AD.10	1	Shakhoura	7-93	C6	Outside tomb	25	
AD.11	194	Al-Hajar	2-93		Outside tomb	38	
AD.12	5666-2-91	Saar	5-87-88		Outside tomb	6	
AD.13	3827-2-91-6	Shakhoura	1991	2			
AD.14	59	Saar	6-96	D2	Tomb	33	
AD.15							No context information.
AD.16	2412-2-90	Saar	5-87-88	D6	Tomb	22	
AD.17	130	Al-Hajar	2-92	E6			
AD.18	221	Al-Hajar	7-92-93	E2	Tomb	2	

Table 166. Context information for vessels of Type AD.

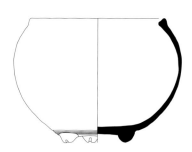

Figure 450. Cat. no. AE.1.

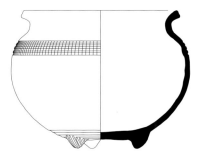

Figure 451. Cat. no. AE.13.

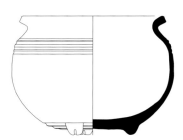

Figure 452. Cat. no. AE.31.

Dating evidence and discussion

Type AD has been found with Phase II and III material. This dating suggests that Type AD may be a typological development of Type D. No external parallels have been found.

Glazed ware craters

Type AE: Crater with three feet

Three small feet characterize this type. The feet are probably moulded and shaped like seashells or astragals. The rim is externally thickened or outturned. There is often incised decoration just below the shoulder. The glaze is green or turquoise and thick, often with drops from the rim.

Dating evidence and discussion

At Qala'at al-Bahrain a few craters with three feet in glazed ware have been recovered. From the French excavations, a complete profile has been recovered from the "niveau hellénistique supérieur" at the "Palais d'Oupéri" (Lombard & Kervran 1993: 20.19) and Excavation 520 from the Danish Archaeological Expeditions has produced a fragment from a Period Vd context (Højlund & Andersen 1994: fig. 1548). Type AE is well distributed throughout the Gulf region and examples are reported from ed-Dur (Haerinck, Metdepenninghen & Stevens 1992: fig. 1.10) and Mleiha (Boucharlat & Mouton 1993: fig. 13.12). On Failaka the type is attested in BI-ware (Hannestad 1983: nos 175–

Number	Height, min.	Height, max.	Rim dia., min.	Rim dia., max.
43	12	15	14	20

Table 167. Description of vessels of Type AE. Measurements in centimetres.

Cat. no.	BNM no.	Area	Mound	Square	Context	Number	Remarks
AE.1	91-2-64	Saar	1-91		Tomb	18	Figure 450.
AE.2	31	Shakhoura	2-94		Tomb	4	
AE.3	7252-2-91	Saar	5-87-88	F3	Tomb	55	
AE.4	296	Shakhoura	1-87	D3	Tomb	9	
AE.5	29	Shakhoura	2-94		Tomb	8	
AE.6	96-1-56	Shakhoura	2-92		Outside tomb	55	
AE.7	91-2-94	Saar	1-91		Tomb	21	
AE.8	91-1-31	Shakhoura	2-91-92		Outside tomb	37	
AE.9	37	Shakhoura	2-92		Tomb	65	
AE.10	444	Saar	7-95-96	E2	Tomb	22	
AE.11	32	Shakhoura	7-93	D6	Tomb	46	
AE.12	91	Saar	12-95-96		Tomb	34	
AE.13	A8403	Shakhoura	A1-96-97	F6	Tomb	12	Figure 451.
AE.14	3938-2-92	Saar	163-91-92		Tomb	28	
AE.15	805-2-88						
AE.16	5177-2-91-3						
AE.17	231	Saar	7-95-96	F5	Tomb	57	
AE.18	7251-2-91	Al-Manama Suq Magasis	1989		Tomb	2	
AE.19	7249-2-91	Saar	5-87-88	C4	Tomb	11	
AE.20	157	Shakhoura	7-93	F6	Tomb	114	
AE.21	2360	Saar	5-87-88	H5	Tomb	78	
AE.22	91-2-77	Saar	5-91-92	3	Tomb	5	
AE.23	7250-2-91	Saar	5-87-88	G4	Tomb	83	
AE.24	404-2-88	Jannussan	1-69				
AE.25	804-2-88						
AE.26	60	Shakhoura	2-92		Tomb	56	
AE.27	5197-2-91-3	Saar	163-91-92		Tomb	8	
AE.28	7	Shakhoura	7-93	B7	Tomb	30	
AE.29	24	Shakhoura	7-93	D8	Tomb	58	
AE.30	1845-2-89	Al-Manama Suq Magasis	1989		Tomb	1	
AE.31	324	Saar	11-95-96		Tomb	18	Figure 452.
AE.32	240	Saar	5-96-97	C1	Tomb	39	
AE.33	474	Saar	7-95-96	C2	Tomb	114	
AE.34	A231	Saar	12-95-96		Tomb	5	
AE.35	A228	Shakhoura	7-93	E6	Tomb	62	
AE.36	A3278	Hamad Town	1-94-95	D4	Tomb	1-D4	
AE.37	A590	Saar	8-97	E4	Tomb	38	
AE.38	A3396		94-95				
AE.39	A491	Hamad Town	1-94-95	E4	Tomb	1-E4	
AE.40	IMA95						
AE.41	IMA22	Shakhoura	7-94	B6	Tomb	8	
AE.42	IMA67						
AE.43	IMA69						

Table 168. Context information for vessels of Type AE.

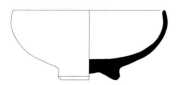

Figure 453. Cat. no. AF.1.

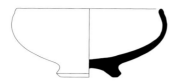

Figure 454. Cat. no. AF.15.

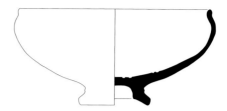

Figure 455. Cat. no. AF.17.

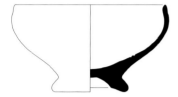

Figure 456. Cat. no. AF.21.

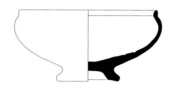

Figure 457. Cat. no. AF.27.

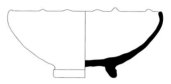

Figure 458. Cat. no. AF.31.

176). The seriation indicates a dating for the pots with three feet to Phase II and into Phase III, since some vessels have been found with both Type AP and Type AQ. This corresponds well with the external dating evidence mentioned above.

The characteristic shape of the pot with three feet has convincingly been linked with examples in Cypriot sigillata ware (Salles 1990: 320–324), which also corresponds well with the dating of the Bahraini vessels.

Glazed ware cups

Type AF: Cup with incurving rim
An incurving rim, sometimes with a little out-turned lip and a fairly high foot, characterizes Type AF. The foot can be a false ring-foot or a ring-foot. A few of the vessels also have two pairs of internal incised lines.

The glaze is turquoise or green and often decayed to golden. Others have a white body with a green rim. A few of the vessels also have drops of glaze on the rim.

Dating evidence and discussion
Two rim fragments of footed bowls with incurving rim have been reported from ed-Dur (Mouton 1992: fig. 62.7–8), but none seems to have been found at Qala'at al-Bahrain and on Failaka. The seriation indicates that Type AF may be the earliest of the cups, since it is mainly found with Phase II material.

The cups with incurving rim find convincing prototypes in eastern sigillata, with a good parallel in Form 16 from Hama (Christensen & Johansen 1972).

Type AG: Cup with angular profile
Type AG differs from Type AH by having a higher foot.

Dating evidence and discussion
Three cups were found in Seleucia in level II (AD 43–116) (Debevoise 1934: no. 222), which illustrate some similarity with type AG. The contextual relation of cat. no. AG.4 to a Type AE crater indicates that the type may have been used in Phase II and/or Phase III.

Type AH: Cup with angular profile
Type AH is characterized by a carination between the base and lower body and straight flaring sides. The low position of the carination and the straight sides separates them from Type F. The base is most often a false ring-foot with a few ring-feet as the exceptions. The rim is plain or with a little out-turned lip and the glaze is green, whitish or decayed to golden.

Dating evidence and discussion
Type AH is attested at Qala'at al-Bahrain from Period Vd contexts (Højlund & Andersen 1994: figs 1535, 1537), but not on Failaka where all the published examples have an out-turned rim and are thus similar to Type F from the Bahraini tombs (Hannestad

139

Number	Height, min.	Height, max.	Rim dia., min.	Rim dia., max.
35	7	11	15.5	21

Table 169. Description of vessels of Type AF. Measurements in centimetres.

Cat. no.	BNM no.	Area	Mound	Square	Context	Number	Remarks
AF.1	8		7-93	A5	Outside tomb	3	Figure 453.
AF.2	9341-2-91	Abu-Saybi	1986				
AF.3	167	Shakhoura	7-93	H5	Outside tomb	116	
AF.4	91-1-17	Shakhoura	2-91-92		Outside tomb	49	
AF.5	33	Shakhoura	7-93	C4	Outside tomb	21	
AF.6	141	Saar		C3	Outside tomb	3	
AF.7	119	Shakhoura	7-93	F5	Outside tomb	79	
AF.8	40	Shakhoura	7-93	J5	Outside tomb	90	
AF.9	1046-2-88				No context information.		
AF.10	10	Shakhoura	7-93	B6	Outside tomb	8	
AF.11	76	Al-Hajar	2-92		Tomb	17	
AF.12	91-1-7	Shakhoura	1-91-92		Tomb	4	
AF.13	2388-2-90	Saar	5-87-88				
AF.14	7231-2-91	Saar	5-87-88	G	Tomb	66	
AF.15	125	Shakhoura	6-91-92		Outside tomb	6	Figure 454.
AF.16	79	Shakhoura	7-93	D7	Outside tomb	61	
AF.17	96-3-2	Shakhoura	A1-96-97	F8	Outside tomb	1	Figure 455.
AF.18	A867	Shakhoura	13-00-01	2	Outside tomb	24	
AF.19	7235-2-91	Saar	5-87-88	E2	Outside tomb	28	
AF.20	4799-2-90-8	Abu-Saybi	1986				
AF.21	9345-2-91	Abu-Saybi	1986				Figure 456.
AF.22	3735-2-91-3	Saar	6-91-92	4	Outside tomb	11	
AF.23	75	Shakhoura		C7	Tomb	29	
AF.24	97-3-44	Shakhoura	A1-96-97	F6	Outside tomb	15	
AF.25	113	Shakhoura	1-92-93	E4	Outside tomb	91	
AF.26	239	Saar	7-95-96	D1			
AF.27	A271	Shakhoura	30-98-99	D2	Outside tomb	27	Figure 457.
AF.28	51	Saar	7-95-96	C6			
AF.29	126	Shakhoura	6-91-92		Jar	1	
AF.30	34	Shakhoura	7-93	F7	Outside tomb	74	
AF.31	2413-2-90	Maqabah	1989	2	Outside tomb	2	Figure 458.
AF.32	191	Al-Hajar	6-92-93	E4	Outside tomb	4	
AF.33	4845-2-90-3	Saar	5-87-88	D5	Outside tomb	24	
AF.34	A4803	Hamad Town	81-85-86		Tomb	14	
AF.35	IMA58				No context information.		

Table 170. Context information for vessels of Type AF.

1983: nos 24–34; Bernard, Gachet & Salles 1990: nos 81–85). A very close parallel is illustrated from Seleucia, where three vessels are found in levels III–IV (c. 300 BC to AD 43) (Debevoise 1934: 7–10 and no. 221), but the type does not appear to be common in glazed ware in Mesopotamia or Persia.

Type AH follows Type F in the seriation. The type is often found in combination with Type AC and AE, and Type AH therefore belongs in Phase II.

Type AH could be a typological development of Type F, but the dimensions with the low position

Number	Height, min.	Height, max.	Rim dia., min.	Rim dia., max.
6	8	9.5	14	19.5

Table 171. Description of vessels of Type AG. Measurements in centimetres.

Cat. no.	BNM no.	Area	Mound	Square	Context	Number	Remarks
AG.1	108	Saar	5-95-96	B3			Figure 459.
AG.2	2450-2-90	Saar	2-85-86	2			
AG.3	242	Saar	7-95-96	B2	Mound fill		Figure 460.
AG.4	3842-2-91-3	Saar	163-91-92		Tomb	8	
AG.5	138	Saar	6-96	E2	Outside tomb	37	
AG.6	7253-2-91	Saar	5-87-88	G4	Outside tomb	5	Figure 461.

Table 172. Context information for vessels of Type AG.

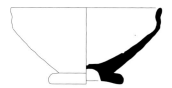

Figure 459. Cat. no. AG.1.

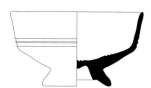

Figure 460. Cat. no. AG.3.

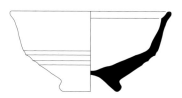

Figure 461. Cat. no. AG.6.

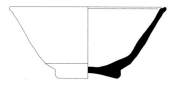

Figure 462. Cat. no. AH.10.

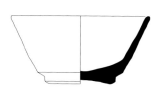

Figure 463. Cat. no. AH.25.

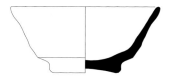

Figure 464. Cat. no. AH.37.

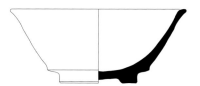

Figure 465. Cat. no. AH.44.

Number	Height, min.	Height, max.	Rim dia., min.	Rim dia., max.
50	6.5	9.5	15	21

Table 173. Description of vessels of Type AH. Measurements in centimetres.

Cat. no.	BNM no.	Area	Mound	Square	Context	Number	Remarks
AH.1		Shakhoura	A1-96-97	F5	Jar	2	
AH.2	36	Shakhoura	2-92		Tomb	61	
AH.3	20	Shakhoura	7-93	D6	Outside tomb	46	
AH.4	164	Shakhoura	1-92-93	G4	Outside tomb	135	
AH.5	4	Shakhoura	2-92		Outside tomb	55	
AH.6	2410-2-90	Saar	5-87-88	F3	Tomb	43	
AH.7	91-1-12	Shakhoura	2-91-92		Outside tomb	30	
AH.8	213	Saar	1-91-92	4	Tomb	2	
AH.9	97-3-57	Shakhoura	A1-96-97	F6	Tomb	15	
AH.10	97-3-238	Shakhoura	A1-96-97	D4	Outside tomb		Figure 462.
AH.11	136	Shakhoura	7-93	F6	Outside tomb	113	
AH.12	78	Al-Hajar	2-92	4			
AH.13	35	Shakhoura	2-92		Outside tomb	71	
AH.14	682	Shakhoura	2-91-92		Outside tomb	31	
AH.15	35	Hamad Town	1-94-95	D7	Outside tomb	3-D7	
AH.16	35	Shakhoura	7-93	F7	Outside tomb	77	
AH.17	1	Saar	1-96		Outside tomb	6	
AH.18	74	Al-Hajar	2-92		Tomb	16	
AH.19	5170-2-91-3	Saar	1-91		Tomb	5	
AH.20	9381-2-91	Shakhoura	1-89		Outside tomb	12	
AH.21	91-1-35	Shakhoura	1-91-92		Tomb	2	
AH.22	37	Shakhoura	7-93	D5	Tomb	37	
AH.23	5671-2-91	Buri					
AH.24	169	Shakhoura	7-93	J2	Tomb	110	
AH.25	15	Shakhoura	7-93	C8	Tomb	33	Figure 463.
AH.26	17	Shakhoura	7-93	D8	Tomb	58	
AH.27	279	Al-Hajar	3-93		Outside tomb	8	
AH.28	21	Saar	1-91		Outside tomb	21	
AH.29	6	Saar	1999	C2	Outside tomb	22	
AH.30	70	Shakhoura	7-93	E9			
AH.31	36	Shakhoura	7-93	E9	Outside tomb	75	
AH.32	97-3-239	Shakhoura	A1-96-97	D4			
AH.33	91-1-43	Shakhoura	2-92	G4			
AH.34	2530-2-90	Buri					
AH.35	91-1-11	Shakhoura	2-92		Outside tomb	71	
AH.36	5670-2-91	Shakhoura	1-87	E3			
AH.37	18	Shakhoura	7-93	C6	Outside tomb	24	Figure 464.
AH.38	9450-2-91	Al-Hajar	1979		Outside tomb	1	
AH.39	830-2-88						No context information.
AH.40	171	Al-Hajar	6-92-93	C8	Tomb	38	
AH.41		Shakhoura	7-93	F6	Tomb	114	
AH.42	134	Shakhoura	1-92-93	C5	Tomb	134	
AH.43	6	Shakhoura	2-92	J4			
AH.44	38	Shakhoura	7-93	E8	Outside tomb	72	Figure 465.
AH.45	2803-2-91-3						No context information.
AH.46	91-4-72	Saar	1-91		Outside tomb	5	
AH.47	A2378	Shakhoura	30-98-99	C6	Mound fill		Figure 618.
AH.48	A793	Shakhoura	29-00-01		Mound fill		
AH.49	A629	Saar	8-97	C5	Tomb	48	
AH.50	A3315		96-97				

Table 174. Context information for vessels of Type AH.

142

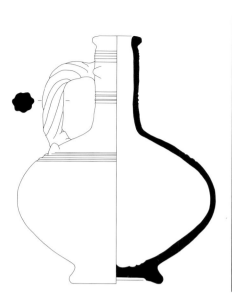

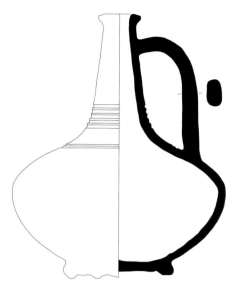

Figure 466. Cat. no. AI.6.   Figure 467. Cat. no. AI.11.   Figure 468. Cat. no. AI.14.

Number	Height, min.	Height, max.	Rim dia., min.	Rim dia., max.
23	27	34	3	5.5

Table 175. Description of vessels of Type AI. Measurements in centimetres.

Cat. no.	BNM no.	Area	Mound	Square	Context	Number	Remarks
AI.1	198	Al-Maqsha	1992-93	C5	Tomb	1	
AI.2	351	Saar	11-95-96				
AI.3	84	Al-Hajar	2-92		Tomb	11	
AI.4	98	Al-Hajar	2-92		Tomb	9	
AI.5	115	Saar	12-95-96		Tomb	12	
AI.6	259	Saar	7-95-96	G4	Tomb	21	Figure 466.
AI.7							No context information.
AI.8	32	Shakhoura	1-91		Tomb	10	
AI.9		Al-Hajar	1				
AI.10	91-2-53	Saar	12-91	4	Mound fill		
AI.11	10208-8-2-91						W. repair. Figure 467.
AI.12	A6825	Saar	7-95-96	D4	Tomb	15	
AI.13	259	Saar	11-95-96		Tomb	10	
AI.14	193	Al-Hajar	6-92-93	D2	Tomb	10	Figure 468.
AI.15							No context information.
AI.16							No context information.
AI.17	216	Al-Hajar	6-92-93		Tomb	3	
AI.18	9384-2-91						No context information.
AI.19	287	Saar	5-87-88	E5	Tomb	36	
AI.20	A276	Saar	4-91-92	13	Tomb	30	
AI.21	A329	Saar	10-99-01	C	Tomb	113	
AI.22	IMA76	Saar	7-91		Cist grave	1	Salles & Lombard 1999: no. 245.
AI.23	IMA544	Al-Hajar	1-70		Cist grave	13	

Table 176. Context information for vessels of Type AI.

of the carination and the conical appearances of the walls, represents the "cup with sloping wall and plain rim" in Italic sigillatae (Conspectus form 7) far better.[15] This type was common from the beginning of our era and well distributed within the Roman Empire and beyond, which corresponds well with the suggested dating of Type AH.

Glazed ware jugs

Type AI: Lagynos

Type AI is a coherent group of vessels defined by a long cylindrical neck, a handle attached to the shoulder and upper neck and a squat body. The lagynoi have a strap-handle with a rectangular cross-section, or a rope-handle often with bosses on each side where the handle is attached to the shoulder and upper neck. The body has a rounded shape and stands on a ring-foot. The glaze is green or decayed to brown/golden. On one specimen the remnant of the glaze is white, which may be an underglaze. That example has also been repaired (cat. no. AI.11).

Dating evidence and discussion

The lagynos is a well-known type in the Mediterranean region and was most popular between 150–50 BC (See Type H for further information). At Qala'at al-Bahrain a few fragments of lagynoi have been recovered, but only one is of Type AI, whereas the rest is of Type H. In Excavation 432 a nearly complete vessel with a rounded shoulder was found (Bibby 1967: 83). A Type AI lagynos was reportedly found in Fariq al-Akhrash on the island of Tarut (Bibby 1973: 35–37) and a characteristic neck was found in Ain Jawan (Bowen 1950: fig. 19.15). On Failaka the lower part of a small lagynos was found (Hannestad 1983: 42–43) and an example is reported from Uruk (Strommenger 1967: Taf. 26.11), although the size and spirals at the base of the handle differ from the Bahraini examples. Also slightly different is an example from Susa dated to the "Phase Moyenne", i.e. 150 BC–1 (Haerinck 1983: 12–17, fig. 11.10).

Type AI vessels are often found with Type AC shallow hollow-based bowls, which is a very typical type for Phase II, but the suggested dating for Phase II (50 BC–AD 50), which is based on the glass, seems slightly late for the lagynoi of the Hellenistic period to have served as prototypes for Type AI. However, the lagynoi remained popular in the Mediterranean region in Roman times (Hayes 1997: 75–76) and the "Roman" vessels illustrate a great similarity with the Bahraini ones, as they have a rounded body and a narrower foot, compared with the Greek examples. It is thus likely that the relative popularity of lagynoi in the Bahraini tombs in Phase II was a result of Mediterranean relations, rather than the rediscovery or local continuation of a Greek type that was never very common in the Gulf region. One cannot exclude the possibility that glass jugs were imitated in glazed ware, since examples with the exact same form as the Bahraini vessels are known (e.g. British Museum no. GR 1868.5–1.85).

---

[15] Ettlinger *et al.* (1990) referred to as *Conspectus*.

Number	Height, min.	Height, max.	Rim dia., min.	Rim dia., max.
8	7.5	9	4	6.5

Table 177. Description of vessels of Type AJ. Measurements in centimetres.

Cat. no.	BNM no.	Area	Mound	Square	Context	Number	Remarks
AJ.1	148	Hamad Town	1-94-95	D3	Tomb	3-D3	Figure 469.
AJ.2	1136-2-88						No context information.
AJ.3	96-3-21	Shakhoura	A1-96-97	E10	Tomb	2	
AJ.4	2807-2-91						No context information.
AJ.5	1137-2-88						No context information.
AJ.6	22	Shakhoura	2-92		Tomb	57	
AJ.7	256	Saar	11-95-96		Tomb	10	
AJ.8	38	Shakhoura	1-92-93	D5	Mound fill		

Table 178. Context information for vessels of Type AJ.

Glazed ware bottles

Type AJ: Cosmetic pot

Type AJ is formed by a varied group of small pots. They are characterized by a fairly tall neck with a little projecting rim and have a false ring-foot and a globular/squat body. The glaze is green or decayed to brown or golden.

Dating evidence and discussion

No exact parallels to Type AJ have been found. Two of the vessels from Bahrain were found with Phase II material (cat. nos AJ.3 and AJ.7) and two with Phase III vessels (cat. nos AJ.1 and AJ.6). Cosmetic pots in glazed ware are known from pre-Hellenistic contexts in Bahrain, since an example has been found in a bathtub coffin with an Achaemenid stamp seal in the French excavations at Qala'at al-Bahrain (Lombard 1999: 144). Related vessels have also been found in pre-Hellenistic burial contexts in Babylon (Reuther 1968: Taf. 74) and it is therefore most likely that the form represented in the Bahraini tombs is a continuation of a Near Eastern

Number	Height, min.	Height, max.	Rim dia., min.	Rim dia., max.
2	6.5	6.5	2	2

Table 179. Description of vessels of Type AK. Measurements in centimetres.

Cat. no.	BNM no.	Area	Mound	Square	Context	Number	Remarks
AK.1	159	Al-Hajar	2-92-93		Tomb	33	Figure 470.
AK.2	159	Hamad Town	1-94-95	E3	Tomb	2-E3	

Table 180. Context information for vessels of Type AK.

Number	Height, min.	Height, max.	Rim dia., min.	Rim dia., max.
18	7	13.5	2	3

Table 181. Description of vessels of Type AL. Measurements in centimetres.

Cat. no.	BNM no.	Area	Mound	Square	Context	Number	Remarks
AL.1	A6684	Saar	5-87-88	5	Tomb	7	Figure 471
AL.2	2502-2-91	Saar	5-87-88	D6	Tomb	22	
AL.3							No context information.
AL.4	7813-2-91	Um Al-Hasam					
AL.5	A6661	Saar					Figures 471 and 472.
AL.6	3855-2-91-3	Saar	12-91		Tomb	15	
AL.7	151	Saar	12-95-96		Tomb	47	
AL.8	A6677	Saar	5-91-92	3	Tomb	4	Figures 471 and 473.
AL.9	7802-2-91						
AL.10	2579-2-90	Saar	5-91-92	2	Tomb	8	
AL.11	257	Saar	11-95-96		Tomb	10	
AL.12	A3132		1993				
AL.13	2200-2-90						No context information.
AL.14	A326						No context information.
AL.15	A295	Saar	11-95-96		Tomb	9	
AL.16	A259	Shakhoura	30-98-99		Tomb	3	
AL.17	A180	Saar	10-99-01	2	Tomb	110	
AL.18	IMA87	Saar					Salles & Lombard 1999: no. 240.

Table 182. Context information for vessels of Type AL.

Figure 469. Cat. no. AJ.1.

Figure 470. Cat. no. AK.1.

Figure 471. Cat. nos AL.5, AL.1 and AL.8.

Figure 472. Cat. no. AL.5.

Figure 473. Cat. no. AL.8.

shape. No cosmetic pots have been found in Period V contexts at Qala'at al-Bahrain.

Type AK: Handleless bottle

Type AK is formed by only two vessels. They have a raised base, which is separated from the globular body by a carination. The transition from the shoulder to the narrow neck is sharp and the rim is outturned. The glaze is decayed to brown and white.

Dating evidence and discussion

One of the two handleless bottles (cat. no. AK.1) was found with a Type AC bowl, indicating that Type AK should be dated to Phase II. Handleless bottles are quite common in the pre-Hellenistic periods in Mesopotamia and it is most likely that this type also follows that tradition.

Type AL: Bottle with two vertical handles

Type AL is a coherent group of vessels. The base is a false ring-foot and the rim is projecting. The type has two strap-handles with a round cross-section attached from the upper neck and down to the shoulder, and the vessels are often with incised decoration on the shoulder. The glaze is green, often decayed to brown or golden.

Dating evidence and discussion

Type AL has close parallels from Susa (Miroschedji 1987: fig. 26.3; Haerinck 1983: fig. 8.14–16). A dating of *c.* 0–AD 230 has been suggested for the type by Haerinck (1983: 53). Type AL vessels have mainly been found with Phase II material indicating a slightly earlier dating than the one suggested by Haerinck, but his periodization has, however, been criticized, since only a very few finds provide absolute dates between the Achaemenid floors and Islamic layers in Susa (Boucharlat 1993: 44–46).

Number	Height, min.	Height, max.	Rim dia., min.	Rim dia., max.
1	7	13.5	2	3

Table 183. Description of vessels of Type AM. Measurements in centimetres.

Cat. no.	BNM no.	Area	Mound	Square	Context	Number	Remarks
AM.1	A11044	Shakhoura	A1-96-97	D9	Tomb	35	Figure 474 to 476.

Table 184. Context information for vessels of Type AM.

The bottles with two vertical handles illustrate great similarities with Greek and Roman amphorae and it is most likely that the type imitates Mediterranean vessels.

Fine ware unguentaria

Type AM: Vessel imitating core-formed glass unguentaria

One very unique vessel was discovered in Tomb 35 in Shakhoura, A1-96-97. It is made of clay, but imitates both the manufacturing techniques and decoration of core-formed glass unguentaria.

Dating evidence and discussion

Tomb 35 in Shakhoura, Mound A1 was situated betwen two tombs that contained wooden coffins dated to the time around the beginning of our era (Andersen *et al.* 2004). It is therefor most likely that cat. no. AM. 1 should be dated to Phase II.

Figure 474 and 475. Cat. no. AM.1.

Figure 476. Detail of surface of cat. no. AM.1.

Phase III. The Roman period (*c.* AD 50 to 150)

In the previous period, we saw influence from the Roman Empire in the repertoire. In this period, this tendency continues, but we also see an increased number of vessels being placed in the tombs. The glass vessels indicate a dating of this period from *c.* AD 25–50 to the beginning of the second century. All vessels can be dated to the second half of the century, but some may have continued for longer.

Glazed ware bowls

Type AN: Hemispheric bowl
A hemispheric body with a sharp carination and an out-turned rim characterizes Type AN. Some examples have an elaborate incised decoration whereas others are without decoration. The size is rather varied but the group is too small to determine whether some are miniatures. The glaze is greenish, whitish, or decayed to golden or brown.

Dating evidence and discussion
A complete example was found during the Danish excavations at Qala'at al-Bahrain in a Period Vd context (Højlund & Andersen 1994: fig. 1545) and the type is represented on Failaka in the BI-ware (Hannestad 1983: no. 35). From Seleucia a glazed bowl relating to the hemispheric bowls with out-turned rim was reported from levels II–III with a suggested dating of 141 BC–AD 116 (Debevoise 1934: no. 211). The seriation indicates a dating for Type AN to Phase III, but the type may start earlier since two of the five vessels combined with other types have been found with earlier material (cat. nos AN.8 and AN.10) and the parallels from Failaka and Qala'at al-Bahrain are probably also slightly earlier than Phase III (See below).

In the Greek world the Megarian bowls became popular as drinking cups in the late third century BC and are believed to be inspired by Alexandrian metal works (Rotroff 1982: 6–9). In the following centuries, the type continued in terra sigillata. Type AN is likely to be an imitation of the terra sigillata bowls (Hannestad 1983: 21–22).

Type AO: Shallow hemispheric bowl
Type AO is characterized by being shallower than the other hemispheric bowls. They have a plain rim. On some vessels the glaze has peeled off, but the rest illustrates a well-preserved surface. The possible colours have faded or decayed to brown, golden or whitish.

Dating evidence and discussion
Very few parallels have been found. From Seleucia a glazed bowl, relating closely to the shallow hemispheric bowl has been reported from level II (AD 43–116) (Debevoise 1934: no. 220). A similar vessel was found in Dura Europos (Toll 1943: no. 1938.4862). The seriation indicates a dating to Phase III, which is emphasized by the contextual relations of two Type AO bowls to glass vessels datable to the first century AD (cat. nos AO.4 and AO.14).

Type AP: Hollow-based bowl
A rounded transition between the outside of the body and the hollow base characterizes these bowls. They have slightly curving sides and a plain rim. The glaze is most often preserved as whitish and sometimes with a green rim. Type AP is very closely related to Type AQ, which has a sharp transition between the outside of the body and the concavity underneath.

Dating evidence and discussion
Type AP does not find any parallels in the published literature. The seriation indicates that the type dates early in Phase III and may have started in Phase II, due to combinations with Type AE. Type AQ follows Type AP in the seriation and must be regarded as a typological development. Type AP could be a development of the Type AC shallow hollow-based bowl.

Type AQ: Hollow-based bowl
Type AQ is very similar in design and size to Type AP, but with a sharp transition between the body and the hollow base. Type AQ is the most common type of pottery found in the Bahraini tombs with 155 vessels recorded.

Dating evidence and discussion
Although Type AQ is by far the most common type of pottery in the Bahraini tombs with 155 vessels recorded, no exact parallels have been found outside Bahrain. This could indicate that the type may have been manufactured on Bahrain or in the vicinity and was not widely distributed. No complete profiles have been reported from Qala'at al-Bahrain,

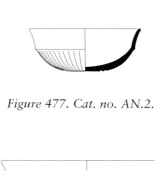

Figure 477. Cat. no. AN.2.

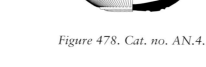

Figure 478. Cat. no. AN.4.

Figure 479. Cat. no. AN.6.

Figure 480. Cat. no. AO.1.

Figure 481. Cat. no. AP.14.

Figure 482. Cat. no. AP.17.

Figure 483. Cat. no. AQ.25.

Figure 484. Cat. no. AQ.28.

Figure 485. Cat. no. AQ.29.

Figure 486. Cat. no. AR.1.

though a few bases may be remnants of the type (Lombard & Kervran 1993: fig. 18.17; Andersen 2001: no. 49).[16]

The Type AQ hollow-based bowl appears to be a typological development of Type AP and the seriation places the type in Phase III. The many contextual relations with glass vessels indicate that this type was popular from the first century AD, since the type has been found with typical glass types of the second half of the first century AD. Three Type AQ vessels are associated with glass vessels of the late Parthian and early Sasanian assemblage (i.e. cat. nos AQ.26, AQ.44 and AQ.104), which indi-

cated that Type AQ remained in use until the third or fourth century AD.

The very large numbers in the Bahraini tombs and the lack of parallels from elsewhere suggest that the type was produced on Bahrain or in an area closely connected to Bahrain.

Type AR: Miniature of hollow-based bowl
Type AR comprises miniatures of the Types AP and AQ hollow-based bowls. The glaze is often very decayed, but a few examples appear to have traces of a white body with a green rim.

Dating evidence and discussion
No parallels to Type AR have been found and the few find combinations with other types (cat. nos AR.2, AR.3 and AR.7) do not give a clear indication of their dating. However, the close stylistic relation to Types AP and AQ suggest a dating to Phase III.

---

[16] The possible absence of Types AP and AQ at Qala'at al-Bahrain may indicate that there are some problems comparing the inventories of Period Vd and Phase III. This problem may by chronological and will be discussed at the end of this chapter.

Number	Height, min.	Height, max.	Rim dia., min.	Rim dia., max.
11	3.5	8.5	11.5	17

Table 185. Description of vessels of Type AN. Measurements in centimetres.

Cat. no.	BNM no.	Area	Mound	Square	Context	Number	Remarks
AN.1	273	Saar	11-95-96		Tomb	34	
AN.2	91-2-40	Saar	12-91		Tomb	11	Figure 477.
AN.3	91-1-26	Shakhoura	2-91-92		Tomb	11	
AN.4	480-2-88	Karranah	2-86				Figure 478.
AN.5	401-2-88	Hamad Town	30-84-85				
AN.6	7150-2-91	Saar	5-87-88	F2	Tomb	42	Figure 479.
AN.7	5162-2-91-3	Saar	4-91-92	4	Tomb	2	
AN.8	94	Al-Hajar	2-92		Tomb	6	
AN.9	A712		1978				
AN.10	A802	Shakhoura	29-00-01		Tomb	20	
AN.11	A477	Saar	10-99-01	C	Tomb	114	

Table 186. Context information for vessels of Type AN.

Number	Height, min.	Height, max.	Rim dia., min.	Rim dia., max.
16	5	6	16	19

Table 187. Description of vessels of Type AO. Measurements in centimetres.

Cat. no.	BNM no.	Area	Mound	Square	Context	Number	Remarks
AO.1	1993-2-90	Maqabah	1989	3	Tomb	2	Figure 480.
AO.2	4805-2-90-8	Abu-Saybi	1983		Tomb	90	
AO.3	2000-1-36	Saar	10-99-01	B	Tomb	39	
AO.4	97	Saar	12-95-96		Tomb	39	
AO.5	2435-2-90	Maqabah	1989	3	Tomb	6	
AO.6	841-2-88	Hamad Town	73-85-86	9	Tomb	1	
AO.7	151	Shakhoura	1-92-93	F5	Tomb	111	
AO.8	4282-2-91-6	Shakhoura	1971				
AO.9	333-2-88	Al-Hajar	1971		Tomb	1	
AO.10	4791-2-90-6	Shakhoura	3-1969	4	Tomb	1	
AO.11	9446-2-91	Al-Hajar	1971				
AO.12	A1630	Shakhoura	2-01-02	AE6	Tomb	82	
AO.13	A807	Shakhoura	25-01		Tomb	3	
AO.14	A4816	Hamad Town	73-85-86		Tomb	54	
AO.15	A4937	Hamad Town	107-83-84		Tomb	1	
AO.16	A38	Saar	15-00	2			

Table 188. Context information for vessels of Type AO.

Number	Height, min.	Height, max.	Rim dia., min.	Rim dia., max.
23	5.5	6	15.5	16.5

Table 189. Description of vessels of Type AP. Measurements in centimetres.

Cat. no.	BNM no.	Area	Mound	Square	Context	Number	Remarks
AP.1	203	Karranah	1-1992		Tomb	A-IV-2	
AP.2	3864-2-91-3	Saar	10-91	1	Tomb	1	
AP.3	3937-2-92-3						No context information.
AP.4	6	Saar	4-94-95	C2	Tomb	9	
AP.5	1586-2-91-3	Saar	163-91-92		Tomb	28	
AP.6	2158-2-90	Shakhoura	1-87	B4			
AP.7	91-2-20	Saar	10-91-92		Tomb		Main grave.
AP.8	40	Shakhoura	2-94		Tomb	13	
AP.9	91-1-10	Shakhoura	2-92		Tomb	65	
AP.10	241	Saar	7-95-96	G4	Tomb	20	
AP.11	4265-2-91-6	Shakhoura	1-87	D9	Tomb	9	
AP.12	4434-2-91-7		1972				
AP.13	7808-2-92						No context information.
AP.14	97-3-78	Shakhoura	A1-96-97	F3	Outside tomb	28	Figure 481.
AP.15	2577-2-90	Saar	5-87-88	C4	Tomb	11	
AP.16	10005-2-91	Abu Arshira					
AP.17	4274-2-91-3	Saar	5-87-88	G4	Tomb	83	Figure 482.
AP.18	1149-2-88	Jannussan	1-71				
AP.19	138	Hamad Town	1-94-95	C5	Tomb	6-C5	
AP.20	9792-2-91	Saar	5-87-88	F1	Tomb	40	
AP.21	1846-2-89	Al-Manama Suq Magasis	1989				
AP.22	A3319		99				
AP.23	A4832	Hamad Town	88-85-86		Tomb	4	

Table 190. Context information for vessels of Type AP.

Number	Height, min.	Height, max.	Rim dia., min.	Rim dia., max.
155	5.5	7	15	17.5

Table 191. Description of vessels of Type AQ. Measurements in centimetres.

Cat. no.	BNM no.	Area	Mound	Square	Context	Number	Remarks
AQ.1	BM 1999 10-30,34	Unplaced	Higham		Tomb	45	During-Caspers 1980: 8b.
AQ.2	199	Karranah	1-1992		Tomb	B-III-4	
AQ.3	128	Karranah	1-1992		Tomb	C-III-3	
AQ.4		Shakhoura	A1-96-97	F5	Moundfill		
AQ.5	9859-2-91	Um Al-Hasam					
AQ.6	5675-2-91	Um Al-Hasam					
AQ.7	9896-2-91	Shakhoura					
AQ.8	9924-2-91	Abu Arshira					
AQ.9	234	Hamad Town	1-94-95	E3	Tomb	3-E3	
AQ.10	73	Shakhoura	7-93	E4	Tomb	56	
AQ.11	3834-2-91-3	Saar	1-91		Tomb	4	
AQ.12	2258-2-90	Buri					
AQ.13	9434-2-91	Abu Arshira	1973				
AQ.14	232	Saar	7-95-96	F5	Tomb	57	
AQ.15	9920-2-91	Karranah	2-87				
AQ.16	170	Shakhoura	1-92-93	G5	Tomb	136	

Cat. no.	BNM no.	Area	Mound	Square	Context	Number	Remarks
AQ.17	97-7-29	Saar	8-97	C2	Tomb	17	
AQ.18	136	Shakhoura	1-92-93	D6	Tomb	108	
AQ.19	116	Shakhoura	1-92-93	C4	Tomb	29	
AQ.20	155	Shakhoura	1-92-93	F1	Tomb	124	
AQ.21	9860-2-91	Al-Hajar					
AQ.22	108	Shakhoura	7-93	E10	Tomb	105	Figure 619.
AQ.23	83	Saar	12-95-96		Tomb	5	
AQ.24	47	Shakhoura	1-92-93	C3	Tomb	13	
AQ.25	136	Saar	5-95-96	D6	Tomb	78	Figure 483.
AQ.26	172	Saar	12-95-96		Tomb	22	
AQ.27	3996-2-91-3	Saar	163-91-92		Tomb	6	
AQ.28	97-3-276	Shakhoura	A1-96-97	C4	Tomb	74	Figure 484.
AQ.29	143	Hamad Town	1-94-95	B4	Tomb	1-B4	Figure 485.
AQ.30	10015-2-91	Al-Hajar					
AQ.31	7146-2-91	Jannussan	1-69				
AQ.32	97-3-194	Shakhoura	A1-96-97	B8	Tomb	36	
AQ.33	92	Saar	12-95-96		Tomb	34	
AQ.34	43	Shakhoura	1-92-93	A1	Tomb	1	
AQ.35	87	Saar	6-96	D2	Tomb	31	
AQ.36	1047-2-88	Abu Arshira	1973		Tomb	6	
AQ.37	12	Saar	7-95-96		Tomb	4	
AQ.38	237	Shakhoura	1-92-93	H3	Tomb	156	
AQ.39	415	Saar	7-95-96		Tomb	130	
AQ.40	2781	Saar	5-96-97	C2	Tomb	28	
AQ.41	97-3-157	Shakhoura	A1-96-97	C7	Tomb	45	
AQ.42	2526-2-90	Buri	2-84	16	Tomb	17	
AQ.43	4377-2-91-30	Abu Arshira			Tomb	16	
AQ.44	97-3-222	Shakhoura	A1-96-97	C3	Tomb	84	
AQ.45	7144-2-91	Shakhoura	1-69				
AQ.46	280	Saar	5-96-97	B2	Tomb	85	
AQ.47	240	Saar	7-95-96	B2			
AQ.48	4	Abu-Saybi	5-97	C2	Tomb	6	
AQ.49	216	Saar	5-96-97	C2	Tomb	26	
AQ.50	2	Shakhoura	1-92-93	A7	Tomb	57	
AQ.51	23	Maqabah	1989	3	Tomb	7	
AQ.52	215	Shakhoura	1-92-93	H3	Tomb	169	
AQ.53	4417-2-91-19		1973				
AQ.54	172	Shakhoura	1-92-93	G5	Tomb	136	
AQ.55	239	Shakhoura	1-92-93	H6	Tomb	185	
AQ.56	249	Saar	7-95-96	H5			
AQ.57	445	Saar	7-95-96	E2	Tomb	122	
AQ.58	38	Saar	7-95-96	B3	Tomb	40	
AQ.59	108	Saar	12-95-96		Tomb	37	
AQ.60	133	Shakhoura	1-92-93	F1	Tomb	123	
AQ.61	A237	Shakhoura	1-92-93	H4	Tomb	156	
AQ.62	479	Saar	5-97-98	H5	Tomb	28	
AQ.63	503	Saar	5-97-98	G4	Tomb	16	
AQ.64	2400-2-90	Saar	5-87-88		Tomb	15	
AQ.65	2430-2-90	Saar	5-87-88	H6			

Cat. no.	BNM no.	Area	Mound	Square	Context	Number	Remarks
AQ.66	2397-2-90	Saar	5-87-88	I4	Tomb	94	
AQ.67	1975-2-89	Saar	5-87-88		Tomb	63	
AQ.68	9805-2-91	Saar	5-87-88	G3	Tomb	63	
AQ.69	2370-2-90	Saar	5-87-88	G4	Tomb	102	
AQ.70	10172-2-91	Saar	5-87-88	F6	Tomb	59	
AQ.71	9922-2-91	Karranah	2-87		Tomb	53	
AQ.72	3600-2-91-6	Shakhoura	2-87		Tomb	1	
AQ.73	10103-2-91	Saar	8-87	3	Tomb	2	
AQ.74	9764-2-91	Karranah	3-86		Tomb	45	
AQ.75	10070-2-91	Karranah	1987				
AQ.76	2250-2-90	Karranah	2-87	B4	Tomb	31	
AQ.77	32-5114	Hamad Town	1-94-95				
AQ.78	3833-2-91-6	Shakhoura	5-91-92		Tomb	2	
AQ.79	9449-2-91-1282	Abu Arshira					
AQ.80	219	Al-Maqsha	1992-93	G3	Tomb	3	
AQ.81	166	Shakhoura	1-92-93	H4	Tomb	170	
AQ.82	4266-2-91-8-35	Abu-Saybi	1983	96			
AQ.83	3920-2-91-3	Saar	163-91-92		Tomb	20	
AQ.84	4272-2-91-8	Abu-Saybi	1983	99			
AQ.85	217	Shakhoura	1-92-93	I3	Tomb	174	
AQ.86	239	Saar	5-96-97	C1	Tomb	39	
AQ.87	9978-2-91	Abu Arshira					
AQ.88	217	Saar	5-96-97	C3	Tomb	7	
AQ.89	141	Shakhoura	1-92-93	E5	Tomb	94	
AQ.90	122-5588	Saar	12-95-96		Tomb	4	
AQ.91	127-1768	Shakhoura	1-92-93	C4	Tomb	28	
AQ.92	9909-2-91	Abu Arshira					
AQ.93	203	Shakhoura	1-92-93	I3	Tomb	181	
AQ.94	91-5592	Saar	1995-96	C3	Tomb	7	
AQ.95	9775-2-91	Abu-Saybi		79-I			
AQ.96	3943-2-91-3	Saar	163-91-92		Tomb	19	
AQ.97	75-1854	Shakhoura	4-92-93	C6	Tomb	21	
AQ.98	238	Shakhoura	1-92-93	H3	Tomb	156	
AQ.99	478-6049	Saar	7-95-96	G2	Tomb	140	
AQ.100	97-3-2-1/8025	Shakhoura	A1-96-97	B5	Tomb	59	
AQ.101	5107-153	Hamad Town	1-94-95	D2	Tomb	1-D2	
AQ.102	10	Shakhoura	1-92-93	AA2	Tomb	26	
AQ.103	739/91-1-44	Shakhoura	2-91-92		Tomb	47	
AQ.104	339/5639	Saar	11-95-96		Tomb	25	
AQ.105	254/5096	Hamad Town	1-94-95	C8	Tomb	1-C8	
AQ.106	79/5692	Saar	12-95-96		Tomb	35	
AQ.107	197/5363	Saar	7-95-96	D5	Tomb	67	
AQ.108		Saar	1995	B3	Tomb	7	
AQ.109	180/5085	Hamad Town	5-94-95	C6	Tomb	2	
AQ.110	218	Shakhoura	1-92-93	I2	Tomb	166	
AQ.111	145	Shakhoura	1-92-93	G6	Tomb	147	
AQ.112	304/5736	Saar	5-95-96	C3	Tomb	8	
AQ.113	10000-2-91	Abu-Saybi	1987				
AQ.114	48	Shakhoura	1-92-93	C3	Tomb	14	

Cat. no.	BNM no.	Area	Mound	Square	Context	Number	Remarks
AQ.115	70/5736	Saar	7-95-96	C5			
AQ.116	4385-2-91	Karranah	1986				
AQ.117	9997-2-91	Abu-Saybi	1986				
AQ.118	9998-2-91	Abu-Saybi	1986				
AQ.119	9698-2-91	Saar	1985-86	2	Tomb	5	
AQ.120	2242-2-90	Saar	1985-86	2	Tomb	4	
AQ.121	4905-2-90	Shakhoura	3-1969	4	Tomb	1	
AQ.122	9980-2-91	Al-Hajar	2				
AQ.123	10006-2-91	Al-Hajar	1981	8? G?	Tomb	1	
AQ.124	4792-2-90-4	Al-Hajar					
AQ.125	9490-2-91	Abu-Saybi	1970				
AQ.126	4389-2-91-8	Abu-Saybi	1970				
AQ.127	A3440		1991				
AQ.128	A2314		01-02				
AQ.129	A1493		01-02				
AQ.130	A2881		92				
AQ.131	A3113		93				
AQ.132	A3069	Karranah	1-1992	D4	Tomb	D-IV-3	
AQ.133	A2319		01-02				
AQ.134	A3111		1993				
AQ.135	A1632		01-02				
AQ.136	A3153		1993				
AQ.137	A3126		1993				
AQ.138	A941		99-00				
AQ.139	A1105	Saar	1996-97	E4	Tomb	38	
AQ.140	A1112	Shakhoura	13-00-01	1	Tomb	15	
AQ.141	A718	Shakhoura	13-00-01	1	Tomb	17	
AQ.142	A576	Shakhoura	25-01		Tomb	15	
AQ.143	A636	Shakhoura	29-00-01		Tomb	16	
AQ.144	A724	Karzakan	3-78		Tomb	36	
AQ.145	A54	Saar	10-99-01	2	Tomb	87	
AQ.146	A4806	Hamad Town	73-85-86				
AQ.147	A4814	Hamad Town	73-85-86	2	Tomb	4	
AQ.148	A4443	Hamad Town	254-82-83				
AQ.149	A4809	Hamad Town	81-85-86		Tomb	11	
AQ.150	A4807	Hamad Town	73-85-86	1	Tomb	1	
AQ.151	A4848	Hamad Town	73-85-86		Tomb	41	
AQ.152	A611	Shakhoura	25-01		Tomb	13	
AQ.153	A4839	Hamad Town	73-85-86		Tomb	52	
AQ.154	A1745	Shakhoura	2-01-02	AC3			
AQ.155	163	Al-Maqsha	1992-93	D9	Tomb	4	

Table 192. Context information for vessels of Type AQ.

Number	Height, min.	Height, max.	Rim dia., min.	Rim dia., max.
13	3.5	5	11	12

Table 193. Description of vessels of Type AR. Measurements in centimetres.

Cat. no.	BNM no.	Area	Mound	Square	Context	Number	Remarks
AR.1	97-3-107	Shakhoura	A1-96-97	F4	Tomb	21	Figure 486.
AR.2	191	Ali	60-88-89		Tomb	10	
AR.3	90	Saar	1-91		Tomb	4	
AR.4	177	Dar Kulayb	24-93-94				
AR.5	362	Saar	2-91-92	F2	Tomb	11	
AR.6	97-3-362	Shakhoura	A1-96-97	C6	Tomb	94	
AR.7	83	Saar	1-91		Tomb	4	
AR.8	91-2-5621	Shakhoura					
AR.9	91-2-3809	Saar	1-91		Tomb	24	
AR.10	3887-2-91						No context information.
AR.11	A3439		96-97				
AR.12	A49	Saar	10-99-01	2	Tomb	9	
AR.13	A1	Shakhoura	30-98-99	D3	Tomb	24	

Table 194. Context information for vessels of Type AR.

Number	Height, min.	Height, max.	Rim dia., min.	Rim dia., max.
2	5	5.5	12	12.5

Table 195. Description of vessels of Type AS. Measurements in centimetres.

Cat. no.	BNM no.	Area	Mound	Square	Context	Number	Remarks
AS.1	144	Al-Hajar	1-92-93		Outside tomb	16	Figure 487.
AS.2	282	Al-Hajar	3-93		Outside tomb	10	

Table 196. Context information for vessels of Type AS.

Number	Height, min.	Height, max.	Rim dia., min.	Rim dia., max.
12	3	4	10	11

Table 197. Description of vessels of Type AT. Measurements in centimetres.

Cat. no.	BNM no.	Area	Mound	Square	Context	Number	Remarks
AT.1	293	Saar	5-96-97	C3	Tomb	5	
AT.2	84	Shakhoura	1-92-93	D5	Tomb	72	
AT.3	44	Shakhoura	1992-93	E4	Tomb	9	
AT.4	168	Shakhoura	7-93	D3	Tomb	44	
AT.5	191	Shakhoura	1-92-93	C5	Tomb	84	
AT.6	10049-2-91	Abu-Saybi	1986				
AT.7	161	Shakhoura	7-93	J9	Tomb	101	
AT.8	624	Shakhoura	1-91-92		Tomb	12	
AT.9	108	Saar	6-96	D3	Tomb	27	
AT.10		Abu-Saybi	1986				
AT.11	27	Saar	7-95-96	D4	Tomb	12	
AT.12	279	Saar	5-96-97	D5	Jar	12	Figure 488.
AT.13	A3437		96-97				
AT.14	A2360		96-97				
AT.15	A2067	Shakhoura	A1-96-97	C5	Tomb	65	

Table 198. Context information for vessels of Type AT.

Number	Height, min.	Height, max.	Rim dia., min.	Rim dia., max.
4	6.5	8.5	15.5	17

Table 199. Description of vessels of Type AU. Measurements in centimetres.

Cat. no.	BNM no.	Area	Mound	Square	Context	Number	Remarks
AU.1	69	Al-Hajar	2-92		Outside tomb	18	Figure 489.
AU.2	37	Hamad Town	1-94-95	D6	Tomb	1-D6	
AU.3	91-2-5668	Al-Maqsha	1988	20	Tomb	9	
AU.4	157	Al-Hajar	2-93		Outside tomb	57	

Table 200. Context information for vessels of Type AU.

Number	Height, min.	Height, max.	Rim dia., min.	Rim dia., max.
5	4.5	5.5	10.5	12.5

Table 201. Description of vessels of Type AV. Measurements in centimetres.

Cat. no.	BNM no.	Area	Mound	Square	Context	Number	Remarks
AV.1	85	Saar	5-95-96	B3	Tomb	43	
AV.2	2384-2-90	Saar	5-87-88				
AV.3	274	Saar	11-95-96		Tomb	34	Figure 490.
AV.4	2439-2-90	Saar	5-87-88	F4	Tomb	56	
AV.5	A3092		92-93				

Table 202. Context information for vessels of Type AV.

Number	Height, min.	Height, max.	Rim dia., min.	Rim dia., max.
8	4.5	5.5	11	12

Table 203. Description of vessels of Type AX. Measurements in centimetres.

Cat. no.	BNM no.	Area	Mound	Square	Context	Number	Remarks
AX.1	A392	Saar	10-99-01	B	Tomb	27	Figure 491.
AX.2	91-1-2	Shakhoura	4-91		Tomb	4	
AX.3	9816-2-91						No context information
AX.4	A555	Shakhoura	25-01		Tomb	3	
AX.5	2374-2-90	Saar	5-87-88	A3	Tomb	32	
AX.6		Saar	10-99-01	2	Tomb	4	
AX.7	154	Shakhoura	1-92-93	I4			
AX.8	15	Saar	7-95-96	B3	Outside tomb	28	

Table 204. Context information for vessels of Type AX.

Figure 487. Cat. no. AS.1.

Figure 488. Cat. no. AT.12.

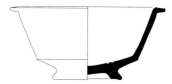

Figure 489. Cat. no. AU.1.

Figure 490. Cat. no. AV.3.

Figure 491. Cat. no. AX.1.

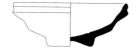

Figure 492. Cat. no. AY.3.

Type AS: Bowl with rounded body and out-turned lip

A rounded body with a little out-turned lip characterizes Type AS. The glaze is green or decayed to whitish or golden.

Dating evidence and discussion

Vessels related to the bowl with rounded body and out-turned lip have been found in Dura Europos (Toll 1943: no. 1931.470i) and Seleucia level II (AD 43–116) (Debevoise 1934: no. 229) indicating a Phase III dating. The few Bahraini examples have not been found with other glass or ceramic vessels.

Type AT: Bowl with angular profile

Type AT is very similar to Type AU, since they both have an angular transition between the lower body and the sides of the vessels. Type AT is, however, significantly lower and has more sloping walls. Most of the bowls have internal incised rings. The green or turquoise glaze is often partly decayed to golden.

Dating evidence and discussion

Type AT does not find any exact parallels, but the contextual relations of cat. nos AT.1, AT.8, AT.11 and AT.15 with other types indicate a dating to Phase III.

Type AU: Bowl with angular profile

An angular profile and a well-marked projecting rim characterize Type AU. They have the same sharpness and thin walls as Type BH. The glaze is green or decayed to light green.

Dating evidence and discussion

Type AU vessels have not been found with other types of glass or pottery vessels, nor have any exact parallels been found. However, the deep bowl with

angular profile and out-turned rim published by Hannestad has the same proportions, thin walls and sharp carination (1983: no. 31), but the rim is out-turning, ending in a lip rather than the projecting rim seen on the examples from the Bahraini tombs. Similarities with Type BH should also be noted. The shape of the carinated cylindrical cup with flat rim in Italic sigillatae (Conspectus form 27) is very close to Type AU and Type AU may thus be an imitation of the sigillatae vessels. A dating to Phase III is therefore likely.

Type AV: Miniature of bowl with angular profile

Type AV is a miniature of Type AU. They have the same sharpness in the execution as their bigger sisters. The glaze is decayed to golden.

Dating evidence and discussion

Type AV does not find any exact parallels and the contextual relations with other vessels only indicate a Phase III or Phase IV dating. The similarities with Type AU and thus a possible relation with Italic sigillatae types of the first century AD point, however, towards a Phase III dating.

Type AX: Saucer with flaring rim

The Type AX vessels have a low ring-foot and a plain, flaring rim, with an internal notch on some examples. Most of them also have internal incised rings and some an internal central depression. The glaze is dark green and often partly decayed to golden.

Dating evidence and discussion

Type AX seems only to have been found on Bahrain. Cat. nos AX.4 and AX.6 have been found with Phase III material and cat. no. AX.8 with Phase IV vessels.

Type AY: Saucer with moulded rim

A moulded, vertical rim characterizes these bowls.

Number	Height, min.	Height, max.	Rim dia., min.	Rim dia., max.
3	4.5	4.5	11.5	12

Table 205. Description of vessels of Type AY. Measurements in centimetres.

Cat. no.	BNM no.	Area	Mound	Square	Context	Number	Remarks
AY.1	470	Saar	7-95-96	2	Tomb	137	
AY.2	A3154	Hamad Town	612A-93		Tomb	1	
AY.3	139	Shakhoura	1-92-93	D6	Tomb	108	Figure 492.

Table 206. Context information for vessels of Type AY.

Number	Height, min.	Height, max.	Rim dia., min.	Rim dia., max.
2	11	N/A	13 excl. handles	N/A

Table 207. Description of vessels of Type AZ. Measurements in centimetres.

Cat. no.	BNM no.	Area	Mound	Square	Context	Number	Remarks
AZ.1	97-3-221	Shakhoura	A1-96-97	D3	Mound fill		Figure 493.
AZ.2	IMA659	Shakhoura	A1-96-97	D3	Tomb	81	

Table 208. Context information for vessels of Type AZ.

The sides of the vessels have a carination and internally there are incised rings. The glaze is green or turquoise and well preserved.

Dating evidence and discussion
Two of the three bowls with moulded rim were found with Phase III vessels (cat. nos AY.1 and AY.3). No external parallels have been found.

Glazed ware cups
Type AZ: Kantharos
A very small group of kantharoi, which is characterized by the vertical strap-handles with thumb rests and a stemmed foot. They have a very elaborate incised decoration and the glaze is green or decayed to whitish.

Dating evidence and discussion
The kantharos is well known in the Greek world in the Classical and Hellenistic periods as a drinking cup. The two kantharoi found in the Bahraini tombs were not combined with other types, although Tomb 81, in the Shakhoura Mound A1-96-97 is situated among Phase III tombs (see Salman & Andersen, forthcoming). Two feet, which most likely are remnants of kantharoi and a handle fragment, have been published from Period Va and Vb

contexts at Qala-at al-Bahrain (Højlund & Andersen 1994: figs 1239, 1462, 1344), and added to these fragments is a single, nearly complete example from Excavation 421 (Andersen 2001: no. 40). The above parallels date most likely to the third or second century BC and are likely to be imitations of Greek types, similar to the ones in west slope ware found at the Athenian Agora and datable to the early third century BC (Rotroff 1997: nos 141–146). However, cast and polished examples made of glass are also well known from the Hellenistic period and could also have served as prototypes for the vessels in glazed ware (see Harden 1968: no. 9) as well as lead-glazed early Roman imperial examples (see Hochuli-Gysel 1977: Taf. 11.S45).

A kantharos, probably in BI-ware very similar to the two examples from the Bahraini tombs, was found during the Danish excavations on Failaka (Hannestad 1983: no. 190) together with some fragments of kantharoi (*ibid.* nos 189, 191–197). In the excavations at ed-Dur a fragment from a kantharos was recovered (Mouton 1992: fig. 71.13). The overall dating of this site to the first century AD suggests, together with the BI-ware kantharos from Failaka and the contextual information regarding cat. no. AZ.2, that the examples from the tombs could date

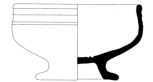

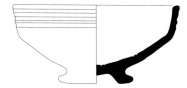

Figure 493. Cat. no. AZ.1   Figure 494. Cat. no. BA.1.   Figure 495. Cat. no. BA.3.

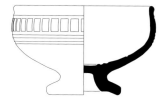

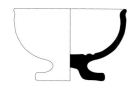

Figure 496. Cat. no. BA.20.   Figure 497. Cat. no. BA.21.   Figure 498. Cat. no. BB.4.   Figure 499. Cat. no. BB.7.

to Phase II or III. It is therefore possible to suggest two periods of Mediterranean influence, one in which the vessels from Qala'at al-Bahrain were influenced by Greek prototypes of the third century BC, and the other reflecting continued or resumed contacts around the beginning of our era.

Type BA: Stemmed cup with projecting foot

These cups are characterized by a high base with a projecting foot. They have in most cases a fluted and almost vertical rim. Most of the vessels also have internally incised lines. The glaze is turquoise or dark green and often decayed golden or resembling mother-of-pearl.

Dating evidence and discussion

In the excavations at the settlement at the first-century AD site at ed-Dur, a fragment of a projecting foot was found (Mouton 1992: fig. 63.13). This corresponds well with the seriation of combined finds from the Bahraini tombs, since the tombs containing stemmed cups with projecting foot cluster in Phase III. One vessel (cat. no. BA.12) has, however, been found with a shallow hollow-based bowl, which is a typical Phase II type, and another (cat. no. BA.10) with a cup with incurving rim. This could indicate that the type came in use during Phase II and was used into Phase III.

Type BB: Miniature of stemmed cup with projecting foot

These vessels are miniatures of Type BA and as their close relatives they have a fluted and almost ver-

tical rim and incised lines internally. The glaze is turquoise or green and often decayed to golden or resembling mother-of-pearl.

Dating evidence and discussion

The contextual relations of cat. nos BB.2 and BB.4 to pilgrim flasks indicate, together with the similarities with Type BA, that Type BB should be dated to Phase III. No external parallels have been found.

Type BC: Plain stemmed cup

A total of fifteen plain stemmed cups have been recorded. They are quite large and have flaring sides and a vertical rim with an out-turned lip. A few examples are decorated with internal incised circles. The glaze is dark green or often decayed to brown.

Dating evidence and discussion

The seriation indicates that Type BC dates to Phase III. No external parallels have been found.

Type BD: Stemmed cup with handles

Type BD is characterized by two appliqué "handles". A few examples also have internal incised circles. The glaze is green, white or decayed to brown or whitish.

Dating evidence and discussion

The seriation indicates that Type BD dates to Phase III. No good external parallels have been found, but a rim fragment from Ain Jawan may be from a Type BB cup (Bowen 1950: fig. 22.I).

Number	Height, min.	Height, max.	Rim dia., min.	Rim dia., max.
23	7.5	8.5	15	17

Table 209. Description of vessels of Type BA. Measurements in centimetres.

Cat. no.	BNM no.	Area	Mound	Square	Context	Number	Remarks
BA.1		Hamad Town	1-94-95	D3	Tomb	3-D3	Figure 494.
BA.2	96-3-26	Shakhoura	A1-96-97	F11			
BA.3	A889	Shakhoura	13-00-01	2	Outside tomb	11	Figure 495.
BA.4	2235-2-90	Shakhoura	1-87	E3	Tomb	8	
BA.5	96-3-29	Shakhoura	A1-96-97	G13	Outside tomb	7	
BA.6	34	Shakhoura	1994		Tomb	5	
BA.7	97-3-83	Shakhoura	A1-96-97	E3	Outside tomb	30	
BA.8	3811-2-91	Shakhoura	1-92-93		Tomb	4	
BA.9	2286-2-90	Shakhoura	1-87	D4			
BA.10	96-3-5	Shakhoura	A1-96-97	F8	Outside tomb	1	
BA.11	96-3-38	Shakhoura	A1-96-97	G7	Outside tomb	14	
BA.12	31	Shakhoura	7-93	E8	Outside tomb	59	
BA.13	5196-2-91-6	Shakhoura	1-92-93		Tomb	11	
BA.14	91-1-38	Shakhoura	1-92-93		Outside tomb	29	
BA.15	A3314		-94-95				
BA.16	100	Al-Hajar	2-92	1			
BA.17	76	Shakhoura	7-93	D5	Outside tomb	38	
BA.18	115	Shakhoura	7-93	E5	Tomb	67	
BA.19	19	Shakhoura	7-93	C3	Outside tomb	17	
BA.20	13	Shakhoura	7-93	A6	Tomb	5	Figure 496.
BA.21	91-2-59	Saar	1-91	3			Figure 497.
BA.22	IMA534						
BA.23	IMA60						

Table 210. Context information for vessels of Type BA.

Number	Height, min.	Height, max.	Rim dia., min.	Rim dia., max.
9	4.5	6	75	105

Table 211. Description of vessels of Type BB. Measurements in centimetres.

Cat. no.	BNM no.	Area	Mound	Square	Context	Number	Remarks
BB.1	2376-2-90	Saar	5-87-88	F5	Tomb	46	
BB.2	91-1-23	Shakhoura	2-92		Tomb	57	
BB.3	91-1-1	Shakhoura	2-91-92		Tomb	4	
BB.4	97-3-114	Shakhoura	A1-96-97	F3	Jar	6	Figure 498.
BB.5	986-2-88	Isa Town	1972				
BB.6	10244-2-2000	Shakhoura					
BB.7	129	Hamad Town	1-94-95	C5	Tomb	3-C5	Figure 499.
BB.8	9894-2-91	Ali					
BB.9	A4824	Hamad Town	70A-85-86		Tomb	3	

Table 212. Context information for vessels of Type BB.

Number	Height, min.	Height, max.	Rim dia., min.	Rim dia., max.
15	10.5	12	18.5	21

Table 213. Description of vessels of Type BC. Measurements in centimetres.

Cat. no.	BNM no.	Area	Mound	Square	Context	Number	Remarks
BC.1	104	Saar	1-91		Outside tomb	15	
BC.2	A574	Saar	10-99-01	B	Outside tomb	33	
BC.3	A781	Saar	10-99-01	B	Outside tomb	35	
BC.4	153	Shakhoura	1-92-93	I3	Outside tomb	175	Figure 500.
BC.5	A1471	Shakhoura	2-01-02	AD1	Outside tomb	26	
BC.6	10225-2-91						No context information.
BC.7	157	Shakhoura	1-92-93	G5	Outside tomb	176	
BC.8	161	Shakhoura	1-92-93	I2	Outside tomb	166	
BC.9	181	Shakhoura	1-92-93	I4			
BC.10	A732	Hamad Town	119-98		Outside tomb	4	
BC.11	A755	Saar	8-97		Outside tomb	38	
BC.12	97-7-33	Saar	8-97	D4			
BC.13	411	Saar	7-95-96	D1	Outside tomb	130	
BC.14	5667-2-91	Al-Hajar	1971				
BC.15							No context information.

Table 214. Context information for vessels of Type BC.

Number	Height, min.	Height, max.	Rim dia., min.	Rim dia., max.
7	9.5	11.5	14.5	16.5

Table 215. Description of vessels of Type BD. Measurements in centimetres.

Cat. no.	BNM no.	Area	Mound	Square	Context	Number	Remarks
BD.1	11	Saar	7-95-96		Tomb	4	Figure 501.
BD.2	A275	Saar	10-99-01	B	Outside tomb	39	
BD.3	247	Saar	7-95-96		Outside tomb	44	
BD.4	2393-2-90	Saar	5-87-88	F2	Outside tomb	42	
BD.5	3110-2-91-6	Shakhoura	1-91-92		Tomb	12	Figure 502.
BD.6	33	Shakhoura	1994	F6	Mound fill		
BD.7	IMA62						

Table 216. Context information for vessels of Type BD.

Number	Height, min.	Height, max.	Rim dia., min.	Rim dia., max.
82	7	10.5	15	21

Table 217. Description of vessels of Type BE. Measurements in centimetres.

Cat. no.	BNM no.	Area	Mound	Square	Context	Number	Remarks
BE.1	235	Karranah	1-1992		Tomb	A-V-1	Fragment.
BE.2	74	Karranah	1-1992		Tomb	C-III-1	
BE.3	2217-2-90	Abu-Saybi	1986				
BE.4	5674-2-91	Saar	5-87-88				
BE.5	4433-2-91-3	Saar	5-87-88	D4	Outside tomb	25	
BE.6	106	Saar	7-95-96	H5	Outside tomb	51	
BE.7	424	Saar	7-95-96	D1	Tomb	119	
BE.8	250	Saar	7-95-96	A1/A2			
BE.9	130	Saar	7-95-96	I4	Outside tomb	53	Figure 503.
BE.10	4419-2-91-4	Al-Hajar	1974		Tomb	137	
BE.11	163	Shakhoura	1-92-93	H4	Outside tomb	170	
BE.12	127	Al-Hajar	2-92	C6			
BE.13	432	Saar	7-95-96	H2	Outside tomb	138	
BE.14	4386-2-91	Karranah	2-86				
BE.15	33	Hamad Town	1-94-95	F2			
BE.16	9352-2-91	Abu-Saybi	1986				
BE.17	359	Saar	2-92-93	I3	Outside tomb	3	
BE.18	137	Saar	5-95-96	C4	Outside tomb	3	
BE.19	10	Saar	7-95-96	G4			
BE.20	38	Hamad Town	1-94-95	C6	Outside tomb	4-C6	
BE.21	53	Shakhoura	1-92-93	E1	Outside tomb	102	
BE.22	97-3-335	Shakhoura	A1-96-97	C5	Outside tomb	65	
BE.23	7233-2-91	Abu-Saybi	1983	81			
BE.24	97-7-6	Saar	8-97	A3	Outside tomb	13	
BE.25	97-7-24	Saar	8-97	B4	Outside tomb	52	Figure 504.
BE.26	9353-2-91	Abu-Saybi	1986				
BE.27	111	Shakhoura	1-92-93	D1	Outside tomb	83	
BE.28	2551-2-90	Hamad Town	83-85-86		Outside tomb	42	
BE.29	139	Saar	5-95-96	C5	Outside tomb	56	
BE.30	110	Saar	7-95-96	H5			
BE.31	255	Saar	7-95-96	B2	Outside tomb	108	
BE.32	255	Hamad Town	1-94-95	C8	Outside tomb	4-C8	
BE.33	130	Shakhoura	1-92-93	D6	Outside tomb	105	
BE.34	118	Saar	7-95-96		Outside tomb	72	
BE.35	5	Saar	1995	D3	Outside tomb	8	
BE.36	79-2440-2-90	Saar	5-96-97	6	Outside tomb	2	
BE.37	1966-2-89	Saar	5-97-98	H2	Outside tomb	73	
BE.38	2253-2-90	Saar	5-97-98	G5	Outside tomb	69	
BE.39	A1495	Shakhoura	2-01-02	AD1	Outside tomb	26	
BE.40	248	Saar	7-95-96	C3	Outside tomb	102	
BE.41	234	Hamad Town	1-94-95	B7	Outside tomb	6-B7	
BE.42	13	Saar	7-95-96	C3			
BE.43	170	Saar	8-90-91	3	Outside tomb	7	
BE.44	4800-2-90-8	Abu-Saybi	1986				
BE.45	4719-2-90-8	Abu-Saybi	1986				
BE.46	8676-2-91	Abu-Saybi	1986				
BE.47	3867-2-91-3	Saar	8-97		Outside tomb	5	
BE.48	243	Saar	7-95-96	C2			
BE.49	10142-2-91	Abu-Saybi	1986				

Cat. no.	BNM no.	Area	Mound	Square	Context	Number	Remarks
BE.50	12	Al-Hajar	1-94		Outside tomb	5	
BE.51	A1488		01-02				
BE.52	797-2-88	Shakhoura	1-69				
BE.53	134	Shakhoura	1-92-93	F1	Outside tomb	123	
BE.54	97-3-224	Shakhoura	A1-96-97	C4			
BE.55	135	Saar	6-96	E2	Outside tomb	39	
BE.56	26	Shakhoura	7-93	E2	Outside tomb	70	
BE.57	27	Hamad Town	1-94-95	5	Outside tomb	5	Figure 505.
BE.58	95	Saar	6-96	C2	Outside tomb	30	
BE.59	227	Saar	5-87-88	D2	Outside tomb	29	
BE.60	5	Saar	4-94-95	B2	Outside tomb	4	
BE.61	36	Hamad Town	1-94-95	C4	Outside tomb	4-C4	
BE.62	97-3-225	Shakhoura	A1-96-97	4			
BE.63	126	Saar	7-95-96	H4	Outside tomb	46	
BE.64	10074-3-91	Abu-Saybi	1986				
BE.65	4	Saar	4-94-95	D2			
BE.66	245	Saar	7-95-96	C2			
BE.67	6024	Saar	1996	F4	Outside tomb	17	
BE.68	A561	Saar	8-97	D5	Outside tomb	38	
BE.69	308	Saar	5-87-88	F1	Outside tomb	39	
BE.70	160	Shakhoura	1-92-93	F7	Outside tomb	120	
BE.71	109	Shakhoura	7-93	J9	Outside tomb	100	
BE.72	7236-2-91	Hamad Town	30-84-85		Tomb	40	
BE.73	15	Saar	5-95-96	F2			
BE.74	140	Saar	5-95-96	C6	Outside tomb	57	
BE.75	5678-2-91	Shakhoura	1-87	F3			
BE.76	A870						Context information corrupt.
BE.77	A658	Shakhoura	25-01		Outside tomb	4	
BE.78	A3408	Hamad Town	1-94-95	D3	Outside tomb	2-D3	
BE.79	A3125		93				
BE.80	A2579		96				
BE.81	A4818	Hamad Town	73-85-86	5	Tomb	33	
BE.82	FM-A-985.CJ	Unplaced	T158-5		Outside tomb	2	

Table 218. Context information for vessels of Type BE.

Type BE: Cup with vertical rim

A fairly high false ring-foot and a vertical rim characterize these vessels. The rim has an external groove or incision marking the lip. The transition between the flaring walls of the body and the vertical rim is slightly rounded. The glaze is in most cases badly preserved and pealing off, but in the cases where it has been preserved the body seems to have been white and the rim green. Sometimes a decayed golden glaze has been preserved.

Dating evidence and discussion

The seriation of combined types indicates a dating to Phase III for Type BE. Only a possible Type BE rim fragment found in ed-Dur indicates that the type was distributed outside Bahrain. The shape of Type BE could very well be inspired by prototypes in eastern sigillata, due to close similarities with Forme 23 from Hama (Christensen & Johansen 1972).

Type BF: Cup with vertical rim

Type BF is formed by a large and coherent group of bowls on a relatively high ring-foot. They are characterized by a vertical rim, often fluted or with incised lines. Most of the vessels also have two pairs of internally incised circles, some only with

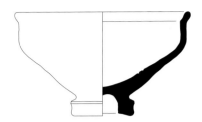

Figure 500. Cat. no. BC.4.

Figure 501. Cat. no. BD.1.

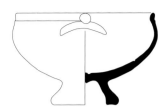

Figure 502. Cat. no. BD.5.

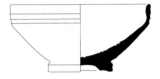

Figure 503. Cat. no. BE.9.

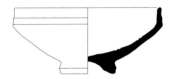

Figure 504. Cat. no. BE.25.

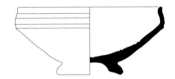

Figure 505. Cat. no. BE.57.

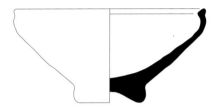

Figure 506. Cat. no. BF.1.

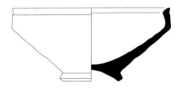

Figure 507. Cat. no. BF.15.

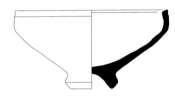

Figure 508. Cat. no. BF.47.

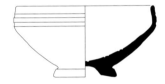

Figure 509. Cat. no. BF.55.

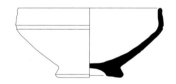

Figure 510. Cat. no. BF.67.

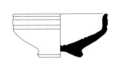

Figure 511. Cat. no. BG.4.

Figure 512. Cat. no. BG.5.

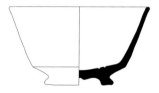

Figure 513. Cat. no. BH.2.

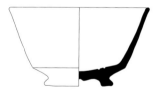

Figure 514. Cat. no. BI.6.

Number	Height, min.	Height, max.	Rim dia., min.	Rim dia., max.
78	7.5	8.5	15	17

Table 219. Description of vessels of Type BF. Measurements in centimetres.

Cat. no.	BNM no.	Area	Mound	Square	Context	Number	Remarks
BF.1	97-3-223	Shakhoura	A1-96-97	C3	Outside tomb	86	Figure 506.
BF.2	7	Shakhoura	1-92-93	C5	Outside tomb	39	

Cat. no.	BNM no.	Area	Mound	Square	Context	Number	Remarks
BF.3	329	Saar	7-95-96	C2	Outside tomb	159	
BF.4	47	Saar	7-95-96	5			
BF.5	162	Shakhoura	1-92-93	5	Outside tomb	136	
BF.6	7237-2-91						No context information.
BF.7	A1494	Shakhoura	2-01-02	AA3	Outside tomb	15	
BF.8	25	Hamad Town	1-94-95	C3			
BF.9	361	Saar	2-92-93	F3			
BF.10	97-3-191-8042	Shakhoura	A1-96-97	B7	Outside tomb	52	
BF.11	A467	Saar	10-99-01	13	Outside tomb	30	
BF.12	216	Shakhoura	1-92-93	H4	Outside tomb	169	
BF.13	291	Saar	7-95-96	G3	Jar	21	
BF.14	40	Shakhoura	1-92-93	E5			
BF.15	3835-2-91-3	Saar	5	3	Outside tomb	3	Figure 507.
BF.16	3	Shakhoura	7-93	P5	Outside tomb	26	
BF.17	6	Shakhoura	1-92-93	C4	Outside tomb	29	
BF.18	2548-2-90	Saar	2	2			
BF.19	3828-2-91-3	Saar	5	3	Outside tomb	1	
BF.20	1068-2-88	Um Al-Hasam	1973				
BF.21	9881-2-91	Saar	7-79		Tomb	1	
BF.22	187	Saar	11-95-96		Outside tomb	22	
BF.23	12	Shakhoura	7-93	6	Tomb	5	
BF.24	10183-2-91	Abu-Saybi	1986				
BF.25	7243-2-91-345	Saar	5-87-88	F2	Outside tomb	41	
BF.26	39	Hamad Town	1-94-95	C7	Tomb	2-C7	
BF.27	3857-2-91-3-217	Saar	6-91-92	4			
BF.28	55-5-3	Saar	5-95-96	C3			
BF.29	3924-2-91-6-1640-377	Shakhoura	1-92-93		Tomb	13	
BF.30	2008-50	Saar	7-95-96	D6			
BF.31	91-2-82-335	Saar	4-91-92	7	Outside tomb	42	
BF.32	A1615	Shakhoura	2001-02				
BF.33	10017-2-91	Shakhoura					
BF.34	97-3-3-04	Shakhoura	A1-96-97	C5	Outside tomb	65	
BF.35	2411-2-90	Abu-Saybi					
BF.36	97-3-109	Shakhoura	A1-96-97	D8			
BF.37	38-5058	Shakhoura	2-94		Outside tomb	6	
BF.38	477	Saar	7-95-96	E1			
BF.39	29	Hamad Town	1-94-95	C4	Outside tomb	1-C4	
BF.40	A1473	Shakhoura	2-01-02	AA3	Outside tomb	14	
BF.41	403	Saar	5-87-88	G5	Outside tomb	9	
BF.42	106	Shakhoura	7-93	J7	Outside tomb	91	
BF.43	120	Shakhoura	1-92-93	D5	Outside tomb	42	
BF.44	4	Shakhoura	7-93	D3	Outside tomb	42	
BF.45	356	Saar	2-91-92	G2	Outside tomb	6	
BF.46	1997-3-217	Shakhoura	A1-96-97	C4	Outside tomb	74	
BF.47	165	Shakhoura	1-92-93	E5	Outside tomb	112	Figure 508.
BF.48	889	Saar	163-91-92		Outside tomb	16	
BF.49	118	Saar	6-91-92	4			
BF.50	A2322	Shakhoura	2-01-02	AA1	Out of Tomb	11	
BF.51	97-3-148	Shakhoura	A1-96-97	D14			

Cat. no.	BNM no.	Area	Mound	Square	Context	Number	Remarks
BF.52	121	Shakhoura	1-92-93	D3	Outside tomb	16	
BF.53	9354-2-91	Abu-Saybi					
BF.54	41	Shakhoura	7-93	F4	Outside tomb	80	
BF.55	114	Shakhoura	1-92-93	E4	Outside tomb	89	Figure 509.
BF.56	162	Shakhoura	7-93	K5	Outside tomb	131	
BF.57	7232-2-91	Shakhoura	1-87	C5			
BF.58	27	Shakhoura	2-94		Outside tomb	2	
BF.59	16	Shakhoura	7-93	D4	Outside tomb	35	
BF.60	6	Shakhoura	7-93	B7	Tomb	30	
BF.61	32	Shakhoura	1994		Outside tomb	4	
BF.62	9356-2-91	Abu-Saybi	1986				
BF.63	244	Saar	7-95-96	D2			
BF.64	2386-2-90-3	Saar	5-87-88	G6	Tomb	70	
BF.65	3957-2-91-6	Shakhoura	1-91-92		Outside tomb	7	
BF.66	4	Shakhoura	1-92-93	D2			
BF.67	97-3-70	Shakhoura	A1-96-97	F4	Outside tomb	20	Figure 510.
BF.68	7234-2-91	Saar	5-87-88		Outside tomb	83	
BF.69	7241-2-91						No context information.
BF.70	2436-2-90	Saar	5-87-88	F5	Outside tomb	44	
BF.71	107	Saar	5-95-96	B4			
BF.72	97-3-153	Shakhoura	A1-96-97	D6			
BF.73	11	Shakhoura	7-93	D4	Outside tomb	34	
BF.74	A1487	Shakhoura	2-01-02	AA3	Outside tomb	16	
BF.75	710	Shakhoura	2-92-93		Tomb	42	
BF.76	3	Shakhoura	1-94		Tomb	9	
BF.77	4804-2-90-6	Shakhoura	3-1971		Tomb	1	
BF.78	A3698		1995				

Table 220. Context information for vessels of Type BF.

Number	Height, min.	Height, max.	Rim dia., min.	Rim dia., max.
10	4.5	6	10	11

Table 221. Description of vessels of Type BG. Measurements in centimetres.

Cat. no.	BNM no.	Area	Mound	Square	Context	Number	Remarks
BG.1	9503-2-91	Abu Saybi					
BG.2	A458		01-02				
BG.3	9463-2-91	Karranah	2-88		Tomb	136	
BG.4	97-3-194	Shakhoura	A1-96-97	B8	Tomb	36	Figure 511.
BG.5	3851-2-91-3	Saar	5-91-92	6	Tomb	36	Figure 512.
BG.6	108	Saar	7-95-96	A5	Tomb	82	
BG.7	74	Saar	7-95-96	D5	Tomb	68	
BG.8	72	Shakhoura	7-93	D4	Outside tomb	36	
BG.9	211	Shakhoura	7-93	K7	Jar	4	
BG.10	10053-2-91	Abu Arshira					

Table 222. Context information for vessels of Type BG.

one pair and a few without this feature. The glaze is turquoise or green and often decayed golden or resembling mother-of-pearl.

Dating evidence and discussion
A complete profile of a Type BF cup has been published from ed-Dur (Mouton 1992: fig. 71.22) and from Seleucia a cup relating to the type has been reported from level II (AD 43–116) (Debevoise 1934: no. 223). This corresponds well with the contextual relations mainly to Phase III material, though a few vessels are found with Phase II vessels (i.e. cat. nos BF.68, BF.60 and BF.13).

Type BF closely resembles the shape of terra sigillata cups found in Hama (Christensen & Johansen 1972: Formes 23, 24), which corresponds well with a dating to Phase III.

Type BG: Miniature of cup with vertical rim
Type BG is formed by a group of miniature cups relating to Type BF. They are characterized by a vertical rim, often fluted or with incised lines. The base is a ring-foot, a false ring-foot or just a raised base. Most of the vessels also have two pairs of internally incised lines, some only one pair and a few without this feature. The glaze is green and often decayed to golden, whitish or brown.

Dating evidence and discussion
From Uruk a Type BG cup has been published (Finkbeiner 1991: fig. 117). The two vessels found with other pottery in Bahrain (cat. nos BG.4 and BG.7) indicate that the type also dates to Phase III.

Type BH: Cup with angular profile
Type BH is characterized by a sharp carination between the lower body and the straight flaring sides. The base is a ring-foot and the rim is plain. The walls of the vessels in this group are thinner than Type BI and they have internal incised rings. The glaze is green or decayed to light green.

Dating evidence and discussion
Two of the five cups with angular profile have been found with other vessels. Cat. no. BH.2 was found with Phase IV glass and pottery and no. BH.5 with a Type BU Mesopotamian amphora, which dates to Phase III. The thin walls, the sharp carination between the lower body and bottom of the vessel, the straight flaring sides, the ring-foot and the internal incised circles are characteristics shared with the cup or bowl with sloping wall and plain rim in Italic sigillatae (Conspectus form 7). This type was common from the beginning of our era and well distributed within the Roman Empire and beyond. The dating indicated by cat. no. BH.2 may be rather late, but this vessel could be from a reused tomb or an heirloom and a tentative dating of the type to the Phase III seems more likely.

Type BI: Cup with angular profile
Type BI is closely related to Type BH, but has a lower height to rim-diameter ratio (c. 0.36 versus 0.44 on average) and a more rounded false ring-foot. The glaze is green or decayed to golden.

Dating evidence and discussion
The contextual relation between Type BI (cat. nos BI.1, BI.2 and BI.6) and vessels of Type BC, Type BL and Type AQ indicates that Type BI belongs in Phase III, which is supported by the similarities with Type BH and thus cups in terra sigillatae. No external parallels have been found.

Glazed ware plates
Type BJ: Fish plate
A concave base characterizes Type BJ. The vessels often have internally incised rings and the rim is thickened underneath or downturned. The glaze is green or decayed to brown or golden.

Dating evidence and discussion
Type BJ seems not to be widely distributed, but since both the rim and the base are required to identify this type, the picture may be affected by preservation. Examples are reported from ed-Dur (Haerinck et al. 1993: figs 1.5, 1.7) indicating that the type dates to Phase III and could be a late development of the fish plate commonly found at Qala'at al-Bahrain (see Type CY).

Type BK: Miniature fish plate

Dating evidence and discussion
Four of the miniature fish plates have been found with other vessels. Three of these were found with Phase III material (cat. nos BK.4, BK.5 and BK.6) and one with a Phase I vessel (cat. no. BK.7). This evidence suggests a Phase III dating, since the one combination indicating a Phase I dating is likely to be corrupted by the reuse of a tomb or inconsistency of the documentation. No external parallels have been found.

Glazed ware jars and jugs
Type BL: Jar
Type BL is formed by a fairly coherent group of globular jars. They have a low ring-foot or a false ring-foot, a globular body, a rather sharp transition to the short and slightly out-turned neck and a lit-

Figure 515. Cat. no. BJ.2.

Figure 516. Cat. no. BK.4.

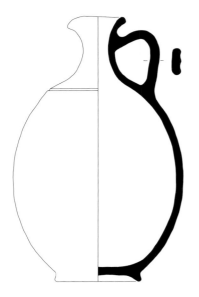

Figure 517. Cat. no. BL.17.

Figure 518. Cat. no. BL.26.

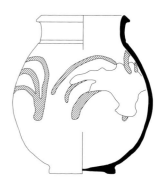

Figure 519. Cat. no. BL.27.

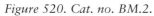

Figure 520. Cat. no. BM.2.

Figure 521. Cat. no. BN.4.

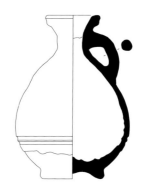

Figure 522. Cat. no. BN.8.

Number	Height, min.	Height, max.	Rim dia., min.	Rim dia., max.
5	7.5	9	15	15

Table 223. Description of vessels of Type BH. Measurements in centimetres.

Cat. no.	BNM no.	Area	Mound	Square	Context	Number	Remarks
BH.1	883	Saar	163-91-92		Tomb	29	
BH.2	9	Saar	1-96		Tomb	7	Figure 513.
BH.3	72	Al-Hajar	2-92	8			
BH.4	2	Shakhoura	7-93	B5	Outside tomb	27	
BH.5	3795-2-91-3	Saar	5-87-88	E3	Outside tomb	35	

Table 224. Context information for vessels of Type BH.

Number	Height, min.	Height, max.	Rim dia., min.	Rim dia., max.
9	6.5	7.5	16	17

Table 225. Description of vessels of Type BI. Measurements in centimetres.

Cat. no.	BNM no.	Area	Mound	Square	Context	Number	Remarks
BI.1	3871-2-91-3	Saar	1-91		Outside tomb	15	
BI.2	122	Hamad Town	1-94-95	B7	Tomb	3-B7	
BI.3	5206-2-91-6	Shakhoura	2-91-92		Tomb	43	
BI.4	188	Saar	1995-96	A2	Outside tomb	6	
BI.5	3946-2-91-6	Shakhoura	1-91-92		Outside tomb	1	
BI.6	131	Saar	7-95-96	C4	Outside tomb	67	Figure 514.
BI.7	26	Hamad Town	1-94-95	F2	Outside tomb	1-F2	
BI.8	1067-2-88	Shakhoura	1-69				
BI.9	A715	Al-Maqsha		15	Tomb	13	

Table 226. Context information for vessels of Type BI.

Number	Height, min.	Height, max.	Rim dia., min.	Rim dia., max.
8	6	7	21.5	21.5

Table 227. Description of vessels of Type BJ. Measurements in centimetres.

Cat. no.	BNM no.	Area	Mound	Square	Context	Number	Remarks
BJ.1	9917-2-91	Al-Hajar					
BJ.2	10046-2-91	Abu-Saybi	1983	SS1			Figure 515.
BJ.3	4285-2-91-9	Karranah	3-86				
BJ.4	10230-2-91						
BJ.5	A2877	Karranah	1-1992	B4	Tomb	B-VI-6	
BJ.6	A3110		93				
BJ.7	A1677		01-02				
BJ.8		Karranah	1-1992		Tomb	C-VI-3	

Table 228. Context information for vessels of Type BJ.

Number	Height, min.	Height, max.	Rim dia., min.	Rim dia., max.
7	2	3	10	13

Table 229. Description of vessels of Type BK. Measurements in centimetres.

Cat. no.	BNM no.	Area	Mound	Square	Context	Number	Remarks
BK.1	1034-2-91	Al-Hajar	3				
BK.2	3264-29-91		1978				
BK.3	6016-2-72	Al-Hajar	1972		Tomb	39	
BK.4	91-1-27	Shakhoura	1-91-92		Tomb	12	Figure 516.
BK.5	265	Saar	11-95-96		Tomb	40	
BK.6	91-1-25	Shakhoura	2-91-92		Jar	1	
BK.7	A663	Shakhoura	29-00-01		Tomb	17	

Table 230. Context information for vessels of Type BK.

Number	Height, min.	Height, max.	Rim dia., min.	Rim dia., max.
44	14.5	19	8	10.5

Table 231. Description of vessels of Type BL. Measurements in centimetres.

Cat. no.	BNM no.	Area	Mound	Square	Context	Number	Remarks
BL.1	BM 1999 10-30,25	Unplaced	Higham		Tomb	39	During-Caspers 1980: fig. 8a.
BL.2	115	Shakhoura	1-92-93	C4	Tomb	29	
BL.3	30	Shakhoura	2-94	D4	Mound fill		
BL.4	390	Shakhoura	2-91-92		Tomb	11	
BL.5	2404-2-90	Abu-Saybi	1986	WF3	Tomb	39	
BL.6	174	Shakhoura	1-92-93	F2	Tomb	121	
BL.7	39	Shakhoura	2-94		Tomb	13	
BL.8	5215-2-91-3	Saar	163-91-92		Tomb	6	
BL.9	2244-2-90	Hamad Town	83-85-86		Tomb	42	
BL.10	97-3-158	Shakhoura	A1-96-97		Tomb	45	
BL.11	10195-2-91	Shakhoura					
BL.12	3939-2-92-3	Saar	163-91-92		Tomb	19	
BL.13	96-1-46	Shakhoura	4-91		Tomb	1	
BL.14	97-3-274	Shakhoura	A1-96-97	C4	Tomb	74	
BL.15	97-3-193	Shakhoura	A1-96-97	B8	Tomb	36	
BL.16	53	Hamad Town	1-94-95	C8	Tomb	4-C8	
BL.17	A6081	Hamad Town	1-94-95	D2	Tomb	1-D2	Figure 517.
BL.18	373	Hamad Town	30-84-85		Tomb	41	
BL.19	23	Shakhoura	2-94		Tomb	7	
BL.20	107	Shakhoura	7-93	F5	Tomb	78	
BL.21	6	Abu-Saybi	5-97	C2	Tomb	6	
BL.22	9490-1-91						
BL.23	91-2-60	Saar	163-91-92		Tomb	20	
BL.24	401	Saar	7-95-96	D1	Tomb	118	
BL.25	278	Saar	7-95-96	H5	Tomb	95	
BL.26	80	Saar	12-95-96		Tomb	35	Figure 518.
BL.27	152	Saar	6-96	D3	Tomb	25	W. bichrome decoration. Figure 519.
BL.28	52	Saar	7-95-96	D6	Mound fill		
BL.29	197	Saar	7-95-96	D5	Tomb	67	
BL.30	A3371	Hamad Town	1-94-95	B7	Tomb	6-B7	
BL.31	A227	Shakhoura	1-92-93	C3	Tomb	13	
BL.32	A2327		01-02				
BL.33	A3156		1993				
BL.34	A1059	Shakhoura	A1-96-97	C5	Tomb	65	
BL.35	A851	Saar	7-95-96	C3	Tomb	37	
BL.36	A750	Shakhoura	13-00-01	1	Tomb	15	
BL.37	A389	Saar	5-96-97	C3	Tomb	7	
BL.38	A4731	Hamad Town	73-85-86	5	Tomb	28	
BL.39	A310	Saar	1995-96				
BL.40	A39	Saar	10-99-01	B	Tomb	45	
BL.41	A94	Saar	10-99-01	2	Tomb	100	
BL.42	A40	Saar	10-99-01	2	Tomb	4	
BL.43	IMA92						
BL.44	IMA90						

Table 232. Context information for vessels of Type BL.

tle projecting rim. The glaze is green, turquoise or white with a simple green or turquoise decoration as seen on cat. no. BL.27.

Dating evidence and discussion

The jars are found in tombs throughout the island and are one of the most common closed shapes from the tombs. They seem, however, to be rare in the region. An example has been reported from Dastova in south-western Iran (Haerinck 1983: fig. 11.11) and from Baghuz in Mesopotamia, though the rim is slightly different (Toll 1943: 59). The seriation of the pottery indicates a date in Phase III. Unglazed jars are common in the Near East from pre-Hellenistic times and onwards and it is therefore likely that the glazed jars originate in that tradition.

Type BM: Jug

The Type BM jugs are coherent in shape but the size is quite varied. A narrow neck and an out-turned rim with a pouring spout characterize these vessels. The edged shoulder transition is a special feature. The single strap-handle with a rectangular cross-section

is decorated with two or three vertical grooves and the glaze is green or decayed to golden.

Dating evidence and discussion

No external parallels have been found to Type BM, but in Bahrain ten of the seventeen large jugs were found with other material, which provides good dating evidence for the type. A single vessel (cat. no. BM.4) was found with Phase IV material, which could indicate that the tomb was reused, but the majority of large jugs have been found with Phase III vessels. Two jugs (cat. nos BM.3 and BM.2) were, however, found with possible Phase II vessels, indicating that the type may have been introduced in Phase II.

Type BN: Jug

Type BN is characterized by a slim globular or slightly pear-shaped body. A single strap-handle is attached from the middle of the neck to the shoulder. The glaze is green or turquoise but often decayed to brown, golden or white. A few of the bottles do not have glaze on the base.

Number	Height, min.	Height, max.	Rim dia., min.	Rim dia., max.
17	17.5	30	3.5	6.5

Table 233. Description of vessels of Type BM. Measurements in centimetres.

Cat. no.	BNM no.	Area	Mound	Square	Context	Number	Remarks
BM.1	71	Abu-Saybi	5-97	C2	Tomb	6	
BM.2	97-3-52	Shakhoura	A1-96-97	F6	Tomb	12	Figure 520.
BM.3	23	Shakhoura	7-93	B6	Tomb	8	
BM.4	185	Dar Kulayb	24-93-94		Tomb	1	
BM.5	123	Shakhoura	7-93	E6	Tomb	62	
BM.6	97-3-275	Shakhoura	A1-96-97	C4	Tomb	74	
BM.7	2361-2-90-29						
BM.8	126	Shakhoura	1-92-93	C4	Tomb	28	
BM.9	22	Shakhoura	2-94		Tomb	12	
BM.10	169	Shakhoura	1-92-93	G3	Tomb	138	
BM.11	2000-1-170	Saar	10-99-01	2	Tomb	100	
BM.12	A872	Shakhoura	13-00-01	1	Tomb	19	
BM.13	A271	Shakhoura	30-98-99	D2	Tomb	27	
BM.14	A2325		01-02				
BM.15	A487	Shakhoura	A1-96-97	C5	Tomb	63	Without spout.
BM.16	IMA80						Salles & Lombard 1999: no. 246 (with corrupt context information).

Table 234. Context information for vessels of Type BM.

Number	Height, min.	Height, max.	Rim dia., min.	Rim dia., max.
8	17	20	2.5	3.5

Table 235. Description of vessels of Type BN. Measurements in centimetres.

Cat. no.	BNM no.	Area	Mound	Square	Context	Number	Remarks
BN.1	3739-2-91-3	Saar	4-91-92	4	Tomb	4	
BN.2	91-2-29	Saar	12-91		Tomb	8	
BN.3	91-1-36	Shakhoura	1-91-92		Tomb	9	
BN.4	97	Shakhoura	1-92-93	C3	Tomb	15	Figure 521.
BN.5	A2367	Shakhoura	2-01-02	AA3	Tomb	16	
BN.6	A1628		01-02				
BN.7	A4525	Hamad Town	1986				
BN.8	163	Al-Maqsha	1992-93	D9	Tomb	4	Figure 522.

Table 236. Context information for vessels of Type BN.

Dating evidence and discussion

Type BN does not find any parallels and only one vessel (cat. no. BN.5) is contextually associated with Phase III material.

Glazed ware bottles

Type BO: Cosmetic pot

The Type BO cosmetic pots are a coherent group. A very low neck with a projecting rim characterizes them and they have a false ring-foot and a globular body. The glaze is green, turquoise or decayed to brown, golden or white.

Dating evidence and discussion

Type BO finds dated parallels in group X-A-1 from Dura Europos, which is dated to 50 BC to AD 100 (Toll 1943: 70). Eleven tombs in Bahrain combined Type BM with other types and the seriation suggests

Number	Height, min.	Height, max.	Rim dia., min.	Rim dia., max.
23	5	7.5	2.5	5

Table 237. Description of vessels of Type BO. Measurements in centimetres.

Cat. no.	BNM no.	Area	Mound	Square	Context	Number	Remarks
BO.1	BM 1999 10-30,4	Unplaced	Higham		Tomb	36	During-Caspers 1980: fig. 7a.
BO.2	97-3-240	Shakhoura	A1-96-97	C3	Tomb	87	Figure 523.
BO.3	2389-2-90	Saar	5-87-88	D4	Tomb	25	
BO.4	175	Saar	7-95-96	D5	Tomb	65	
BO.5	91-1-13	Shakhoura	2-91		Tomb	3	
BO.6	91-1-14	Shakhoura	2-91-92		Tomb	23	
BO.7	212	Hamad Town	1-94-95	E2	Tomb	2-E2	Figure 524.
BO.8	157	Hamad Town	1-94-95	E4	Tomb	3-E4	
BO.9	980-2-88	Abu Arshira	1973		Tomb	130	
BO.10	946-2-88	Abu Arshira	1973		Tomb	89	
BO.11	97-7-36	Saar	1997	D2	Tomb	26	
BO.12	2399-2-90	Saar	5-87-88	D2	Tomb	27	
BO.13	91-1-33	Shakhoura	3-91		Tomb	3	
BO.14	346	Saar	7-95-96	C3	Tomb	39	

Figure 523. Cat. no. BO.2.

Figure 524. Cat. no. BO.7.

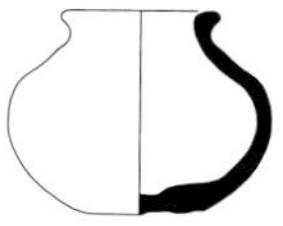

Figure 525. Cat. no. BP.3.

Figure 526. Cat. no. BQ.27.

Figure 527. Cat. no. BQ.28.

Figure 528. Cat. no. BR.1.

Figure 529. Cat. no. BR.8.

Figure 530. Cat. no. BS.2.

Figure 531. Cat. no. BT.1.

Figure 532. Cat. no. BU.3.

Figure 533. Cat. no. BU.7.

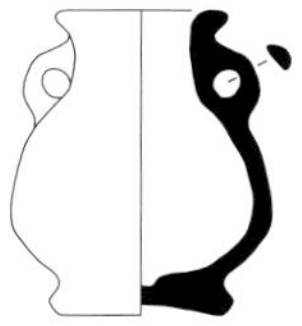

Figure 534. Cat. no. BU.25.

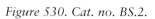

Figure 535. Cat. no. BU.26.

BO.15	229	Shakhoura	1-92-93	G3	Jar	5	
BO.16	91-1-4/387	Shakhoura	7-91-92		Tomb	9	
BO.17	1838-2-89	Ali	101-88-89		Tomb	16	
BO.18	170	Saar	7-95-96	D6	Tomb	70	
BO.19	12	Shakhoura	1-92-93	A2	Tomb	5	
BO.20	9906-2-91						No context information.
BO.21							No context information.
BO.22	A230	Saar	10-99-01	C	Jar	21	
BO.23	A5644	Hamad Town	70A-85-86		Tomb	21	

Table 238. Context information for vessels of Type BO.

a Phase III dating of the type. This date correspond with the dating suggested for the vessels from Dura Europos.

Type BP: Cosmetic pot
A small coherent group which is very similar to Type BO, but without a proper base. The glaze is decayed to white.

Dating evidence and discussion
The similarity with and contextual relation of cat. nos BP.1 and BP.3 to Type BO indicate that Type BP may be contemporary with Type BO and thus is likely to have been used during Phase III.

Type BQ: Bottle with one handle
The Type BQ bottles are a coherent group characterized by a piriform body, and sometimes with a carination just above the base. The base is a false ring-foot and the neck is very short with an out-turned rim. The strap-handle with an oval or rectangular cross-

section is attached to the shoulder. The glaze is green or greyish often decayed to white or golden.

Dating evidence and discussion
Type BQ is well represented in the Bahraini tombs. They account for nearly 20 % of the bottles in ceramic, but seem not to be well documented elsewhere. Only one fragmented example from the Oman peninsula has been reported (Yule 2001: taf. 464.3). Related vessels are, however, reported from Susa (Haerinck 1983: fig. 3.8), Uruk (Finkbeiner 1992: no. 444), Seleucia (Debevoise 1934: no. 267) and a first-century tomb in Dura Europos (Toll 1943: gr. VII-A-2). In Bahrain, the Type BQ bottles have been found with both glass and pottery vessels typical of Phase III, although a single vessel has been contextually associated with Phase IV material (cat. no. BQ.40).

Type BR: Bottle with one handle
Type BR is a fairly coherent group of bottles with

Number	Height, min.	Height, max.	Rim dia., min.	Rim dia., max.
3	5	6	4.5	5.5

Table 239. Description of vessels of Type BP. Measurements in centimetres.

Cat. no.	BNM no.	Area	Mound	Square	Context	Number	Remarks
BP.1	2193-2-90	Ali	101-88-89		Tomb	16	
BP.2	493-2-88						No context information.
BP.3	2168-2-90	Ali	101-88-89		Tomb	16	Figure 525.

Table 240. Context information for vessels of Type BP.

Number	Height, min.	Height, max.	Rim dia., min.	Rim dia., max.
45	8.5	10.5	1.5	2.5

Table 241. Description of vessels of Type BQ. Measurements in centimetres.

Cat. no.	BNM no.	Area	Mound	Square	Context	Number	Remarks
BQ.1	BM 1999 10-30,26	Unplaced	Higham		Tomb	37	During-Caspers 1980: fig. 8d.
BQ.2	1134-2-88						No context information.
BQ.3	173	Shakhoura	1-92-93	F2	Tomb	121	
BQ.4	9537-2-91	Abu Arshira	8		Tomb	19	
BQ.5	62	Shakhoura	6-92-93	B3	Tomb	26	
BQ.6	186	Shakhoura	7-93	F4	Tomb	95	
BQ.7	206	Hamad Town	1-94-95	B6	Tomb	5-B6	

Cat. no.	BNM no.	Area	Mound	Square	Context	Number	Remarks
BQ.8	200	Saar	7-95-96	C4	Tomb	11	
BQ.9	97-3-206	Shakhoura	A1-96-97	B6	Tomb	53	
BQ.10	30	Shakhoura	7-93	C3	Tomb	18	
BQ.11	408	Saar	7-95-96	H4	Tomb	50	
BQ.12	253	Saar	7-95-96	H5	Tomb	91	
BQ.13	199	Saar	7-95-96	C4	Tomb	11	
BQ.14	86	Saar	12-95-96		Tomb	7	
BQ.15	103	Saar	1-91		Tomb	15	
BQ.16	7801-2-91	Buri	2-84	9	Tomb	1	
BQ.17	3861-2-91-3	Saar	4-91-92	8	Tomb	36	
BQ.18	266	Hamad Town	1-94-95	D2	Tomb	1-D2	
BQ.19	924-2-88						No context information.
BQ.20	934-2-88		1983				
BQ.21		Al-Hajar	1-94		Tomb	5	
BQ.22	3748-2-91-3	Saar	4-91-92	7	Tomb	40	
BQ.23	2355-2-90	Saar	5-87-88	C7	Tomb	1	
BQ.24	161	Hamad Town	1-94-95	C4	Tomb	3-C4	
BQ.25	1135-2-88						No context information.
BQ.26	242	Al-Hajar	7-92-93	F2			
BQ.27	97-3-310	Shakhoura	A1-96-97	C5	Tomb	63	Figure 526.
BQ.28	260	Hamad Town	1-94-95	E6	Jar	P2	Figure 527.
BQ.29	3815-2-91-6	Shakhoura	2-91		Tomb	2	
BQ.30	7810-2-91	Abu Arshira					
BQ.31	9937-2-91	Hamad Town	A70-95-96		Tomb	21	
BQ.32	97-3-340	Shakhoura	A1-96-97	C5	Tomb	65	
BQ.33	A1474	Shakhoura	2-01-02	AB1	Tomb	4	
BQ.34	A2405	Shakhoura	2-01-02	AA3	Tomb	16	
BQ.35	A2330		01-02				
BQ.36	A897	Shakhoura	13-00-01	1	Tomb	16	
BQ.37	A772	Shakhoura	25-01		Tomb	24	
BQ.38	A565	Shakhoura	25-01		Tomb	26	
BQ.39	A3441		94-95				
BQ.40	A5631	Hamad Town	70A-85-86		Tomb	6	
BQ.41	A5629	Hamad Town	82-85-86		Tomb	12	
BQ.42	A5630	Hamad Town	70A-85-86		Tomb	26	
BQ.43	A5633	Hamad Town	70A-85-86		Tomb	26	
BQ.44	A5632	Hamad Town	83-85-86				
BQ.45	IMA656						Salles & Lombard 1999: no. 242.

Table 242. Context information for vessels of Type BQ.

Number	Height, min.	Height, max.	Rim dia., min.	Rim dia., max.
11	10	12	2.5	3

Table 243. Description of vessels of Type BR. Measurements in centimetres.

Cat. no.	BNM no.	Area	Mound	Square	Context	Number	Remarks
BR.1	119	Saar	7-95-96	B5	Mound fill		Figure 528.
BR.2	186	Saar	7-95-96	B4	Tomb	3	
BR.3	160	Shakhoura	7-93	K3	Tomb	143	
BR.4	211	Shakhoura	1-92-93	H4	Tomb	169	
BR.5	7816-2-91	Abu-Saybi	1983	79	Tomb	1	
BR.6	9394-2-91	Abu-Saybi	1983		Tomb	118	
BR.7	787-2-91						No context information.
BR.8	73	Shakhoura	4-92-93	C6	Tomb	21	Figure 529.
BR.9	A2057	Shakhoura	2-01-02		Jar	1	
BR.10	A550	Saar	10-99-01	B	Tomb	43	
BR.11	A26	Saar	10-99-01	A	Tomb	46	

Table 244. Context information for vessels of Type BR.

one handle. They are characterized by the lack of a base, i.e. they have a plain resting surface. They have an out-turned rim, which sometimes has a wavy profile. The strap-handle has a round or oval cross-section and the glaze is green and often decayed to white or brown.

Dating evidence and discussion

Vessels related to Type BR were found in a first-century AD tomb in Dura Europos (Toll 1943: gr. VII-C-2), in level I and II in Seleucia (AD 43–200) (Debevoise 1934: no. 257) and in Oman (Yule 2001: taf. 426.8), but no exact parallels have been found. The seriation indicates a Phase III dating of the type, which corresponds well with the dating indicated by the external evidence.

Number	Height, min.	Height, max.	Rim dia., min.	Rim dia., max.
4	9	17	1.5	3

Table 245. Description of vessels of Type BS. Measurements in centimetres.

Cat. no.	BNM no.	Area	Mound	Square	Context	Number	Remarks
BS.1	101	Al-Hajar	2-92	3	Mound fill		
BS.2	393	Saar	2	C2/C3	Tomb	22	Figure 530.
BS.3	810-2-88						No context information.
BS.4	2190-2-90						No context information.

Table 246. Context information for vessels of Type BS.

Number	Height, min.	Height, max.	Rim dia., min.	Rim dia., max.
2	13	14	2.5	2.5

Table 247. Description of vessels of Type BT. Measurements in centimetres.

Cat. no.	BNM no.	Area	Mound	Square	Context	Number	Remarks
BT.1	249						No context information. Figure 531.
BT.2	4932-2-91-7	Al-Maqsha	1991		Tomb	6	

Table 248. Context information for vessels of Type BT.

Number	Height, min.	Height, max.	Rim dia., min.	Rim dia., max.
42	7	21	4	7

Table 249. Description of vessels of Type BU. Measurements in centimetres.

Cat. no.	BNM no.	Area	Mound	Square	Context	Number	Remarks
BU.1	BM 1999 10-30,26	Unplaced	Higham		Tomb	40	During-Caspers 1980: fig. 7b.
BU.2	BM 1999 10-30,32	Unplaced	Higham		Tomb	42	During-Caspers 1980: fig. 8c.
BU.3	297	Saar	5-96-97	C3	Tomb	5	Figure 532.
BU.4	9504-2-91	Abu-Saybi	1986				
BU.5	320	Saar	5-95-96	C6	Tomb	57	
BU.6	299	Saar	11-95-96		Tomb	7	
BU.7	44	Saar	6-91-92	3	Tomb	15	Figure 533.
BU.8	9829-2-91	Saar	5-87-88	E7	Tomb	35	
BU.9	298	Saar	11-95-96		Tomb	7	
BU.10	285	Saar	11-95-96		Tomb	9	
BU.11	309	Saar	5-96-97	C3	Tomb	4	
BU.12	14	Saar	6-91-92	2	Tomb	4	
BU.13	124	Hamad Town	1-94-95	D4	Tomb	4-D4	
BU.14	29	Al-Hajar	1-94		Tomb	17	
BU.15	69	Shakhoura	7-93	C4	Tomb	22	
BU.16	9866-2-91	Shakhoura	1-87	9	Tomb	3	
BU.17	89	Saar	6-96	C2	Tomb	10	
BU.18	3832-2-91-3	Saar	1-91		Tomb	19	
BU.19	91-2-89	Saar	54-91-92		Tomb	1	
BU.20	30	Al-Hajar	1-94		Tomb	17	
BU.21	3767-2-91-7	Al-Maqsha	1991-92	B5	Tomb	79	
BU.22	885-2-88						
BU.23	406-2-88						
BU.24	341	Saar	7-95-96	C3	Tomb	38	
BU.25	294	Saar	5-96-97	C3	Tomb	5	Figure 534.
BU.26	97-3-184	Shakhoura	A1-96-97	D13	Tomb	47	Figure 535.
BU.27	A2326	Shakhoura	2-01-02	AA3	Tomb	14	With lid.
BU.28	A596	Shakhoura	25-01		Tomb	3	
BU.29	A391	Saar	10-99-01	2	Tomb	99	
BU.30	A899	Shakhoura	13-00-01	1	Tomb	12	
BU.31	A1060	Saar	8-97		Tomb	38	
BU.32	A803	Saar	8-97	D1	Tomb	19	
BU.33	A297	Saar	7-95-96	C3	Tomb	34	
BU.34	A338	Saar	6-96	C4	Tomb	19	
BU.35	A28	Shakhoura	A1-96-97	C5	Tomb	65	
BU.36	A99	Saar	10-99-01	B	Tomb	45	
BU.37		Hamad Town	1-94-95	B4	Tomb	1-B4	
BU.38	IMA84						With lid. Salles & Lombard 1999: no. 232.
BU.39	IMA83	Saar	1-90				Salles & Lombard 1999: no. 234.
BU.40	IMA85	Hamad Town	1-94-95		Tomb	4	Salles & Lombard 1999: no. 235.
BU.41	IMA89	Saar	5-96-97	B4	Tomb	62	Salles & Lombard 1999: no. 231.
BU.42	IMA88	Saar	5-95-96	E5	Tomb	49	

Table 250. Context information for vessels of Type BU.

Type BS: Bottle with one handle

The Type BS bottles are rather varied in size. They have false ring-foot and a projecting rim. The strap-handle has a round cross-section. Two of the four vessels have an incised spiral line on the neck as decoration. The glaze is decayed to brown or mustard yellow.

Dating evidence and discussion

One Type BS bottle has been found in Seleucia in level I (AD 116–200) (Debevoise 1934: no. 258). This vessel also features the incised spiral on the neck, similar to two of the Bahraini vessels. One vessel from Bahrain has been found in a Phase III context (cat. no. BS.2).

Type BT: Bottle with one handle

Type BT is characterized by the edged transition from neck to shoulder. The glaze is decayed to white or mustard yellow.

Dating evidence and discussion

The two vessels from Bahrain have not been found with other vessels in glass or ceramic, but the type finds very good parallels in northern Mesopotamia and is common in Dura Europos. Here exact parallels were found in first-century contexts (Toll 1943: 70, gr. VII-A-1). It is thus likely that the examples from Bahrain have been imported from northern Mesopotamia and datable to Phase III.

Type BU: Mesopotamian amphora

A little horizontal projecting rim characterizes the Mesopotamian amphora of Type BU. It has two loop-handles attached to the neck and upper shoulder or on the shoulder. The body is globular, sometimes with a carination on the lower part. The base is a false ring-foot or a low ring-foot. The vessels often have incised decoration on the shoulder or neck. The glaze is green, turquoise or decayed to brown or white.

Dating evidence and discussion

The Type BU Mesopotamian amphora is known from Failaka in "BI-ware" (Hannestad 1983: nos 290–291) and ed-Dur (Haerinck 1993: fig. 2.4). These datings corresponds well with the seriation, which places most vessels of Type BU in Phase III, but the type has also been found with Phase II vessels. It is thus likely that Type BU is a typological development of Type K.

Type BV: Bottle with two neck-attached loop-handles

This is a fairly coherent type of small bottle, with two loop-handles attached to the neck, from the rim or just below, and down to the shoulder. The rim is externally thickened and slightly out-turned. The body is pear-shaped, sometimes with a carination just above the false ring-foot. This carination is similar to the one seen on many of the Type BQ bottles. The glaze is turquoise or decayed to brown or iridescent golden.

Dating evidence and discussion

The bottles of Type BV seem not to be as well distributed in the region as the typologically related bottles of Type J. A related vessel with a ring-foot was found in Nimrud (Oates & Oates 1958: pl. XXVI.4). Related pieces were also reported from Susa (Haerinck 1983: fig. 6.13) and Uruk-Warka (Finkbeiner 1991: figs 198, 343).

According to the seriation, Type BV belongs in Phase III. However, as with Type BU a few examples are found with earlier types indicating that the type may also have been in use earlier than Phase III. It is therefore likely that Type BU is a typological development of Type J.

Type BX: Pilgrim flask

The pilgrim flasks are characterized by a circular body. They have strap-handles or loop-handles attached to the shoulder. The rim is vertical or in a very few cases projecting. Four of the pilgrim flasks are slightly different from the illustrated example, as they are flatter or with a kind of double handle. The glaze is green, turquoise or decayed to brown or white.

Dating evidence and discussion

The pilgrim flask was known in Palestine and Jordan from the late Bronze Age (Dornemann 1983: 32), but in eastern Arabia the type only became popular after Alexander the Great. In glazed ware, pilgrim flasks are known throughout the Near East. A pilgrim flask with moulded decoration was found at Qala'at al-Bahrain (Højlund & Andersen 1997: 215, fig. 897). Examples are reported from Period I on Failaka (Hannestad 1983: nos 311–322), Uruk (Strommenger 1967: taf. 10.10–14), Seleucia, mainly from levels II and III, (Debevoise 1934: nos 298–306). From Dura Europos an example was found in a grave with four coins of Orodes II (51–37 BC) (Toll 1943: 53–54), and examples are known from Susa (Miroschedji 1987: figs 26.6–8), Masjid-i Soleiman and Bard-e Nechandeh (Ghirshman 1976: pls 6.59, 16.66–67, 67.386), Kangevar (Haerinck 1983: fig. 17.6) and Mleiha (Boucharlat & Mouton 1993: fig. 11.5, dated to the second half of the second century to the first century BC).

Figure 536. Cat. no. BV.3.

Figure 537. Cat. no. BV.7.

Figure 538. Cat. no. BX.2.

Figure 539. Cat. no. BY.7.

Figure 540. Cat. no. BZ.2.

The seriation places most of the pilgrim flasks in Phase III contexts, but a specimen has been found in Tomb 6 in Shakhoura Mound A1-1996-97 (cat. no. BX.14). This tomb belongs to the first phase of the necropolis, which dates to Phase II. The pilgrim flasks found throughout the region are only in one case of the exact type as the majority of the Bahraini vessels (i.e. Boucharlat & Mouton 1993: fig. 11.5 from Mleiha). However, a few vessels from Bahrain are slightly different (see for example Boucharlat & Salles 1989: nos 171–172) and so are most of the comparable examples from the other sites mentioned above. This indicates that the pilgrim flask became popular in glazed ware in the region in the Seleucid period and remained in use probably until the end of the Parthian period. During this long period the type experienced some changes and developments, but only the examples from the Bahraini tombs seem to provide a large and coherent collection, which defines a subtype with a Phase III dating.

Type BY: Bottle with two handles

The size of the vessels of this type is rather varied but they are all characterized by a globular body on a raised base with two strap-handles attached from the neck to the shoulder. The rim is projecting and slightly out-turned. The glaze is green, decayed to brown or white. Some examples were not glazed on the base.

Dating evidence and discussion

Type BY is fairly well distributed, since it is found in Susa (Boucharlat 1987: fig. 65.3), Khurha (Haerinck 1983: fig. 17.7) and Dura Europos (Toll 1943: 45 group VI-C-3). The lack of glaze on the base of some of the Bahraini vessels indicates a Mesopotamian origin for some of the vessels, since that is a common feature in Seleucia (Elisabetta Valtz, pers. communication, Dec. 2002; see also Valtz 2002: figs 1.7–8).

Two of the bottles of Type BY have been found with Phase III material (cat. nos BY.1 and BY.7). The Dura Europos material indicates a similar date (Toll 1943: 70).

Type BZ: Bottle with two vertical handles

Type BZ is a varied group, but closely related to Type AL; it does not, however, have the elegance and sharpness of Type AL, and it is characterized by a rather "baggy" body. The base is a low ring-foot or a false ring-foot and the rim is out-turned or projecting. The vessels have two strap-handles attached from the upper neck down to the shoulder. The glaze is green, often decayed to brown or golden.

Dating evidence and discussion

Type BZ does not find any close parallels, and the three vessels with contextual relations to other types provide only an indication of a dating to Phase III (cat. nos BZ.2, BZ.3 and BZ.6). It is likely that Type BZ is a typological development of Type AL.

Number	Height, min.	Height, max.	Rim dia., min.	Rim dia., max.
30	6.5	13	2	2

Table 251. Description of vessels of Type BV. Measurements in centimetres.

Cat. no.	BNM no.	Area	Mound	Square	Context	Number	Remarks
BV.1	129	Karranah	1-1992		Tomb	C-III-3	
BV.2	132	Saar	5-95-96	D6	Tomb	78	
BV.3	3862-2-91-3	Saar	2-91-92	C2/C3	Tomb	22	Figure 536.
BV.4	351	Saar	7-95-96	C3	Tomb	39	
BV.5	297	Saar	11-95-96		Tomb	7	
BV.6	91-2-62	Saar	11-91		Tomb	1	
BV.7	97-7-37	Saar	8-97	D2	Tomb	5	Figure 537.
BV.8	2467-2-90	Ali	105-89-90		Tomb	1	
BV.9	1032-2-88	Abu Arshira	1973		Tomb	36	
BV.10	2575-2-90	Saar	2-85-86	2	Tomb	5	
BV.11	3775-2-91	Saar	2-91-92	C2/C3	Tomb	22	
BV.12	91-1-50	Shakhoura	2-91-92		Tomb	47	
BV.13	1050-2-88	Abu Arshira	1973		Tomb	89	
BV.14	3849-2-91-3	Saar	1-91		Jar	11	
BV.15	3	Al-Hajar	1-94		Tomb	7	
BV.16	458	Saar	7-95-96	D3	Tomb	118	
BV.17	156	Hamad Town	1-94-95	E4	Tomb	3-E4	
BV.18	252	Hamad Town	1-94-95	D9	Tomb	7-D9	
BV.19	9851-2-91	Abu Arshira					
BV.20	211	Hamad Town	1-94-95	D2	Tomb	5-D2	
BV.21	7803-2-91	Um Al-Hasam					
BV.22	808-2-88	Hamad Town	30-84-85		Tomb	21	
BV.23	A865	Shakhoura	13-00-01	1	Tomb	23	
BV.24	A1054	Saar	5-96-97	D3	Tomb	45	
BV.25	A670	Shakhoura	25-01		Tomb	16	
BV.26	A4579	Hamad Town	68-86-87		Tomb	1	
BV.27	A5647	Hamad Town	73-85-86	5	Tomb	34	
BV.28	A16	Shakhoura	30-98-99	D3	Tomb	6	
BV.29	A14						No context information.
BV.30	A110	Saar	10-99-01	A	Tomb	1	

Table 252. Context information for vessels of Type BV.

Number	Height, min.	Height, max.	Rim dia., min.	Rim dia., max.
22	8.5	14.5	2	4.5

Table 253. Description of vessels of Type BX. Measurements in centimetres.

Cat. no.	BNM no.	Area	Mound	Square	Context	Number	Remarks
BX.1	BM 1999 10-30,32	Unplaced	Higham		Tomb	36	During-Caspers 1980: figs 7c-d.
BX.2	97-3-290	Shakhoura	A1-96-97	D4	Tomb	78	Figure 538.
BX.3	97-3-298	Shakhoura	A1-96-97	C5	Tomb	66	
BX.4	91-1-48	Shakhoura	2-92		Tomb	57	
BX.5	4796-2-90	Um Al-Hasam			Tomb	9	
BX.6	404	Shakhoura	2-91-92		Tomb	11	
BX.7	19	Al-Hajar	1-94		Tomb	5	
BX.8	1	Shakhoura	1-94-95	C1	Mound fill		
BX.9	218	Al-Hajar	7-92-93	E2	Tomb	2	
BX.10	171	Saar	5-95-96	D2	Tomb	20	
BX.11	447	Saar	7-95-96	F3	Tomb	24	
BX.12	277	Saar	5-96-97	C2	Tomb	24	
BX.13	1226	Saar	5-96-97	D6	Tomb	80	
BX.14	A1825	Shakhoura	A1-96-97	F3	Tomb	6	
BX.15	A892	Shakhoura	13-00-01	1	Tomb	23	
BX.16	A490	Shakhoura	30-98-99	C3	Tomb	5	Large with double handles.
BX.17	A320	Shakhoura	30-98-99		Tomb	3	
BX.18	A5300	Hamad Town	30-84-85				Flat.
BX.19	A327						Flat with impressed decoration. No context information.
BX.20	A29	Shakhoura	30-98-99				
BX.21							No context information.
BX.22	IMA						With double handles. Salles & Lombard 1999: no. 243.

Table 254. Context information for vessels of Type BX.

Number	Height, min.	Height, max.	Rim dia., min.	Rim dia., max.
11	8	15	1.5	3

Table 255. Description of vessels of Type BY. Measurements in centimetres.

Cat. no.	BNM no.	Area	Mound	Square	Context	Number	Remarks
BY.1	152	Shakhoura	1-92-93	E5	Tomb	111	
BY.2	9899-2-91	Abu Arshira					
BY.3	164	Hamad Town	1-94-95	A7	Tomb	3-A7	
BY.4	9480-2-91	Abu Arshira	1973		Tomb	61	
BY.5	7809-2-91						No context information.
BY.6	45	Hamad Town	1-94-95	E1	Tomb	2-E1	
BY.7	2536-2-90	Hamad Town	73-85-86		Tomb	51	Figure 539.
BY.8	46	Hamad Town	1-94-95	E1	Tomb	2-E1	
BY.9	3941-2-91-3	Saar	163-91-92		Tomb	17	
BY.10	A1625	Shakhoura	2-01-02	AC2			
BY.11	IMA86						Salles & Lombard 1999: no. 242.

Table 256. Context information for vessels of Type BY.

Fine ware bottles

Type CA: Unguentarium
A piriform body and a long black glazed neck characterize Type CA.

Dating evidence and discussion
Very good parallels exist from Dura-Europos and the type is believed to be of Roman origin. It is well distributed and dates to the first two centuries AD (Dyson 1968: 9–11), which is supported by the contextual relation of cat. no. CA.1 to a Phase III pilgrim flask.

Figure 541. Cat. no. CA.1.   *Figure 542. Cat. no. CA.2.*

Number	Height, min.	Height, max.	Rim dia., min.	Rim dia., max.
7	7.5	13	2	3

Table 257. Description of vessels of Type BZ. Measurements in centimetres.

Cat. no.	BNM no.	Area	Mound	Square	Context	Number	Remarks
BZ.1	BM 1999 10-30,33	Unplaced	Higham		Tomb	44	During-Caspers 1980: fig. 8e.
BZ.2	97-3-331	Shakhoura	A1-96-97	C5	Tomb	65	Figure 540.
BZ.3	91-1-6	Shakhoura	2-91-92		Tomb	26	
BZ.4	32	Saar	7-95-96	C4	Tomb	10	
BZ.5	205	Shakhoura	1-92-93	F4	Tomb	152	
BZ.6	15	Saar	6-91-92	2	Tomb	4	
BZ.7	218	Hamad Town	1-94-95	E4	Tomb	2-E4	

Table 258. Context information for vessels of Type BZ.

Number	Height, min.	Height, max.	Rim dia., min.	Rim dia., max.
2	13.5	13.5	3	3

Table 259. Description of vessels of Type CA. Measurements in centimetres.

Cat. no.	BNM no.	Area	Mound	Square	Context	Number	Remarks
CA.1	97-3-297	Shakhoura	A1-96-97	C5	Tomb	66	Most of neck missing. Figure 541.
CA.2	A3539	Al-Maqsha	1991-92	C5	Tomb	88	Figure 542.

Table 260. Context information for vessels of Type CA.

Number	Height, min.	Height, max.	Rim dia., min.	Rim dia., max.
6	5	6	11	14.5

Table 261. Description of vessels of Type CB. Measurements in centimetres.

Cat. no.	BNM no.	Area	Mound	Square	Context	Number	Remarks
CB.1	9940-2-91	Karranah	4-86				
CB.2	16	Shakhoura	2-92		Tomb	57	
CB.3	3782-2-91-6	Shakhoura	3-91	3	Tomb	3	Figure 543.
CB.4	2058-2-90-15	Ali	101-88-89		Tomb	16	
CB.5	A2572	Saar					
CB.6							No context information.

Table 262. Context information for vessels of Type CB.

Number	Height, min.	Height, max.	Rim dia., min.	Rim dia., max.
31	9	19	2.5	7

Table 263. Description of vessels of Type CC. Measurements in centimetres.

Cat. no.	BNM no.	Area	Mound	Square	Context	Number	Remarks
CC.1	225	Saar	5-96-97	D6	Tomb	8	
CC.2	2638-2-90	Hamad Town	70A-85-86		Tomb	1	
CC.3	843-2-88						No context information.
CC.4	183	Saar	5-91-92	8	Jar	3	
CC.5	813-2-88	Abu-Saybi	1983		Tomb	85	
CC.6	9398-2-91	Hamad Town	73-85-86	6	Tomb	38	
CC.7	91-2-115	Saar	2-91-92	C5	Tomb	13	Figure 544.
CC.8	9960-2-91	Hamad Town	83-85-86		Tomb	43	
CC.9	9914-2-91	Hamad Town	73-85-86		Tomb	12	
CC.10	9952-2-91	Hamad Town	73-85-86		Tomb	54	
CC.11	271	Saar	11-95-96		Tomb	40	Figure 545.
CC.12	71	Saar	7-95-96	D5	Tomb	68	
CC.13	97-3-334	Shakhoura	A1-96-97	C3	Tomb	65	
CC.14	2137-2-90	Hamad Town	C83		Tomb	41	
CC.15	7287-2-91	Hamad Town	71-85-86		Tomb	4	
CC.16	97-3-333	Shakhoura	A1-96-97	C5	Tomb	65	Figure 546.
CC.17	9403-2-91	Hamad Town	81-85-86		Tomb	2	
CC.18	84	Saar	7-95-96	C4	Tomb	7	
CC.19	91-1-22	Shakhoura	1-91-92		Tomb	12	
CC.20	97	Saar	7-95-96	C3	Tomb	35	
CC.21	327	Saar	4-91-92				
CC.22	9835-2-91	Saar	5-85-86		Tomb	1	
CC.23	9946-1-91	Karranah	4-86				
CC.24	91-2-79	Saar	4-91-92	10	Tomb	17	Figure 547.
CC.25	2538-2-9-3	Saar	2-87		Tomb	2	
CC.26	4835-2-90-3	Saar	1-87				
CC.27	A583	Saar	8-97	D4	Tomb	32	
CC.28	A3218						No context information.
CC.29	A2887		1993				
CC.30	A1651		01-02				
CC.31	A27	Saar	10-99-01	B	Tomb	10	
CC.32	A10975	Shakhoura	A1-96-97	B4	Tomb	71	

Table 264. Context information for vessels of Type CC.

Sand-tempered ware bowls
Type CB: Hemispheric bowl
The rounded bottom characterizes this type.

Dating evidence and discussion
Two of the hemispheric bowls in sand-tempered ware (cat. nos CB.2 and CB.4) were found with other vessels that are most likely to belong in Phase III.

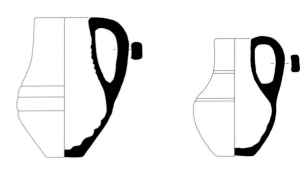

Figure 544. Cat. no. CC.7. *Figure 545. Cat. no. CC.11.*

Figure 543. Cat. no. CB.3.

Plain ware bottles
Type CC: Little jug with one handle
The strap-handle with a rectangular cross-section attached to the rim and down to the shoulder characterizes Type CC. The shape is without much variation but the size varies with heights between *c.* 9 and 19 cm, without any grouping within this interval.

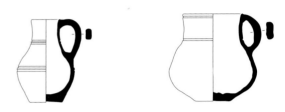

Figure 546. Cat. no. CC.16. Figure 547. Cat. no. CC.24.

Dating evidence and discussion
Type CC is known from the excavations at Qala'at al Bahrain with one published example (Højlund & Andersen 1994: fig. 1609), and no close parallels have been found outside Bahrain. This could indicate that the type was produced locally. The seriation indicates a Phase III dating with few possibly earlier vessels. The single example from Qala'at al-Bahrain was found in a Period Vd context (Højlund & Andersen 1994: fig. 1609).

Phase IV. The late Parthian and early Sasanian assemblage (*c.* AD 150 to 450)

Glazed ware bowls

Type CD: Hollow-based bowl

An internal notch below the rim and a concave base characterize this group. Some of the vessels have internally incised concentric circles at the bottom. The turquoise glaze is quite well preserved, but in some places decayed to brown or golden.

Dating evidence and discussion

A fairly large group of Type CD, hollow-based bowls was found in ed-Dur at the coastal fortress site, where the finds are dated to the third century AD (Lecomte 1993: fig. 3.1–6). This dating corresponds well with the Bahraini evidence, where cat. nos CD.1, CD.2, CD.5 and CD.6 are contextually associated with both glass and pottery datable to Phase IV. The type may be a typological development of Type AQ, the hollow-based bowl.

Type CE: Bowl with angular profile

Type CE has a raised base, an angular profile and flaring sides ending in a plain rim. The glaze is turquoise.

Dating evidence and discussion

Two of the four Type CE vessels have been found with glass vessels of Phase IV (cat. nos CE.1 and CE.2). This indicates that the type is a late development of the bowls and cups with angular profile. No external parallels have been found.

Figure 548. Cat. no. CD.4.

Figure 549. Cat. no. CD.5.

Figure 550. Cat. no. CE.2.

Number	Height, min.	Height, max.	Rim dia., min.	Rim dia., max.
6	5	7	16.5	20

Table 265. Description of vessels of Type CD. Measurements in centimetres.

Cat. no.	BNM no.	Area	Mound	Square	Context	Number	Remarks
CD.1	176	Dar Kulayb	24-93-94		Tomb	1	
CD.2	205	Dar Kulayb	24-93-94		Tomb	1	
CD.3	227	Saar	4-91-92	13	Tomb	33	
CD.4		Dar Kulayb	24-93-94		Mound fill		Figure 548.
CD.5	135	Hamad Town	1-94-95	D3	Tomb	3-D3	Figure 549.
CD.6	A4815	Hamad Town	73-85-86		Tomb	44	

Table 266. Context information for vessels of Type CD.

Number	Height, min.	Height, max.	Rim dia., min.	Rim dia., max.
4	3	3	9.5	10

Table 267. Description of vessels of Type CE. Measurements in centimetres.

Cat. no.	BNM no.	Area	Mound	Square	Context	Number	Remarks
CE.1	155	Hamad Town	1-94-95	B9	Tomb	1-B9	
CE.2	178	Dar Kulayb	24-93-94		Tomb	1	Figure 550.
CE.3	180	Dar Kulayb	24-93-94		Tomb	1	
CE.4	A3445		89-90				

Table 268. Context information for vessels of Type CE.

Number	Height, min.	Height, max.	Rim dia., min.	Rim dia., max.
9	21	31	5	9

Table 269. Description of vessels of Type CF. Measurements in centimetres.

Cat. no.	BNM no.	Area	Mound	Square	Context	Number	Remarks
CF.1	115	Saar	5-95-96	E6	Tomb	83	Figure 551.
CF.2	5364	Saar	1-96		Tomb	7	
CF.3	193	Saar	7-91-92	2	Tomb	3	
CF.4	234	Saar	7-95-96	F5	Tomb	55	Figure 552.
CF.5	90	Saar	5-95-96	E3	Tomb	11	
CF.6	486	Saar	7-95-96	E2	Tomb	28	
CF.7	2000-1-1	Saar	10-99-01	A	Tomb	8	
CF.8	A493	Saar	7-95-96	203	Tomb	38	
CF.9	IMA73	Saar	3-96		Tomb	43	W. three handles, Salles & Lombard 1999: no. 250.

Table 270. Context information for vessels of Type CF.

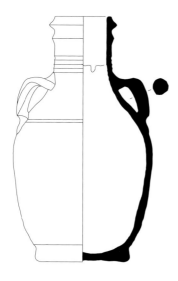

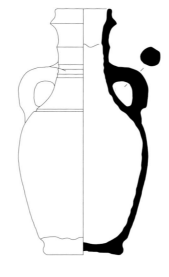

Figure 551. Cat. no. CF.1.   Figure 552. Cat. no. CF.4.   Figure 553. Cat. no. CG.1.

Glazed ware amphorae
Type CF: Amphora
Type CF is formed by a coherent group of larger jugs with two strap-handles attached to the shoulder. Sometimes the handles are twisted. The base is a raised base and the rim moulded. The very well preserved glaze is turquoise and does not cover the base or occasionally the lower part of the body.

Dating evidence and discussion
The amphorae with shoulder-attached handles are all found in the Saar cemetery. The lack of glaze on the base is seen on all of them, which is a common detail in the glazed pottery from Seleucia (Debevoise 1934: no. 281; Valtz, pers. communication, Turin, Dec. 2002). However, no proper parallels to the type have been found. Four of the amphorae with shoulder-attached handles were found with other pottery and three of them with a glass conical beaker datable to Phase IV, and probably to the later half of this rather long period. The last amphora with shoulder-attached handles (cat. no. CF.2) was also in a tomb containing Phase IV material.

The amphora with shoulder-attached handles looks very much like an enlarged and elongated Mesopotamian amphora and with the suggested dating it could very well be a late development of that type.

Glazed ware bottles
Type CG: Bottle with two handles
Only two bottles of Type CG have been recorded in the Bahraini stores. They have two strap-handles attached to the neck. The rim is flaring and the body elongated and pear-shaped with a carination just above the false ring-foot. The glaze is decayed to mustard yellow.

Dating evidence and discussion
Type CG may be of Mesopotamian origin, since very similar vessels have been found at the Sasanian levels at Tell Mahuz (Ricciardi 1970–1971: fig. 92.49–55) and in Choche (1967: fig. 160). Bottles with two handles and elongated body have also been found in Susa (Haerinck 1983: fig. 8.12–13) and Qaryat al-Fau (al-Ansary 1982: 64, nos 3–4).

The two bottles of Type CG from Bahrain were found in the same tomb (Hamad Town, Mound A70 1995-96, Tomb 6) but without other datable material. The vessels from Tell Mahuz date, however, to the Sasanian period (Ricciardi 1967: 427) and the Bahraini vessels can thus be placed in Phase IV or perhaps in Phase V.

Figure 554. Cat. no. CH.1.

Hard-fired ware bowls
Type CH: Bowl
One bowl with flaring sides was recorded in hard-fired ware.

Dating evidence and discussion
No parallels have been found to this bowl and it was not found with other material. However, hard-fired ware is only known in Phase IV (and later) and the vessel can thus be dated on the basis of the characteristic fabric alone.

Number	Height, min.	Height, max.	Rim dia., min.	Rim dia., max.
2	16	18	3	3

Table 271. Description of vessels of Type CG. Measurements in centimetres.

Cat. no.	BNM no.	Area	Mound	Square	Context	Number	Remarks
CG.1	945-2-88	Hamad Town	A70-95-96		Tomb	6	Figure 553.
CG.2	799-2-88	Hamad Town	A70-95-96		Tomb	6	

Table 272. Context information for vessels of Type CG.

Figure 555. Cat. no. CI.1.

Hard-fired ware beakers

Type CI: Beaker

The flaring sides from the base of the vessel to the rim characterize these beakers.

Dating evidence and discussion

Type CI has not been found with other datable vessels, but the shape is very similar to the beakers in fine orange painted ware found at Qala'at al-Bahrain and dating to the third and fourth century AD (Højlund & Andersen 1997: 213–215; Lamberg-Karlovsky 1970: fig. 4; Lecomte 1993: fig. 12.1–4). It is therefore most likely that the beakers in hard-fired ware are local imitations of the painted ones and are contemporary. A similar beaker in a coarse ware, but with a handle has been reported from the Sasanian fortress at Qasr-I Abu Nasr (Whitcomb 1985: fig. 54.K).

Hard-fired ware jars and jugs

Type CJ: Jar

An out-turned rim characterizes these vessels.

Dating evidence and discussion

Out-turned rims in hard-fired ware have been found at Qala'at al-Bahrain (Andersen 2001: nos 138–140), at the Barbar Temple site (Andersen & Kennet 2003: fig. 796). The type also find a good parallel in the thin grey ware from ed-Dur (Lecomte 1993: fig. 8.11), but is also well attested at various other Sasanian sites on the Oman peninsula, i.e. Jazirat al-Ghanam (de Cardi 1975: fig. 8.28–29), Kush (Kennet 2004: fig. 35, type 81) and Khatt (Kennet 1998: fig. 5.11–12). However, these examples are in a brown or reddish fabric, which might reflect a different place of production. One of the jars (cat. no. CJ.1) was found with other vessels in hard-fired ware.

Type CK: Jar

One unique jar defines Type CK.

Dating evidence and discussion

The Type CK jar has not been found with any other vessels, nor have any parallels been found, but the characteristic fabric dates this vessel to Phase IV.

Type CL: Jug with trefoil rim

The trefoil rim characterizes this type. The handles often feature a knot at the attachment to the rim, and most of the vessels have incised lines as decoration on the shoulder and neck.

Dating evidence and discussion

One rim fragment of a jug with trefoil rim in hard-fired ware is known from "chantier F" at ed-Dur (Lecomte 1993: fig. 9.10) and from Khatt two almost complete vessels very similar to the ones from the Bahraini tombs were recovered from Pit 7 in the "Step Trench". From the same pit a dipper of possible Mesopotamian origin, and probably dating to the fourth or fifth century AD, was found (Kennet 1998). Two of the Bahraini vessels (cat. nos CL.7 and CL.10) were found in contexts that contained glass-vessels mainly datable to the third to fourth century AD and thus Phase IV.

Type CM: Jug with vertical rim

One jug with a vertical rim has been found.

Number	Height, min.	Height, max.	Rim dia., min.	Rim dia., max.
1	8	N/A	17.5	N/A

Table 273. Description of vessels of Type CH. Measurements in centimetres.

Cat. no.	BNM no.	Area	Mound	Square	Context	Number	Remarks
CH.1	2438-2-90	Maqabah	1989		Tomb	4	Figure 554.

Table 274. Context information for vessels of Type CH.

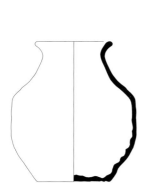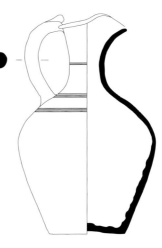

Figure 556. Cat. no. CJ.1.   *Figure 557. Cat. no. CK.1.*   *Figure 558. Cat. no. CL.1.*

Number	Height, min.	Height, max.	Rim dia., min.	Rim dia., max.
3	17	17	13	14

Table 275. Description of vessels of Type CI. Measurements in centimetres.

Cat. no.	BNM no.	Area	Mound	Square	Context	Number	Remarks
CI.1	A551	Shakhoura	13-00-01		Tomb	1	Figure 555.
CI.2	A1442		92-93				
CI.3	A11583	Ali	1989				

Table 276. Context information for vessels of Type CI.

Number	Height, min.	Height, max.	Rim dia., min.	Rim dia., max.
2	16	16	8	8

Table 277. Description of vessels of Type CJ. Measurements in centimetres.

Cat. no.	BNM no.	Area	Mound	Square	Context	Number	Remarks
CJ.1	A3407	Hamad Town	1-94-95	C3	Tomb	3-C3	Figure 556.
CJ.2	A1401		01-02				

Table 278. Context information for vessels of Type CJ.

Number	Height, min.	Height, max.	Rim dia., min.	Rim dia., max.
1	20	N/A	9.5	N/A

Table 279. Description of vessels of Type CK. Measurements in centimetres.

Cat. no.	BNM no.	Area	Mound	Square	Context	Number	Remarks
CK.1	7310-2-91	Maqabah	1989	3	Tomb	3	Figure 557.

Table 280. Context information for vessels of Type CK.

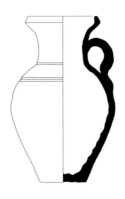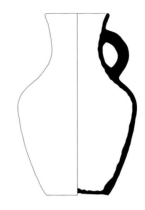

Figure 559. Cat. no. CM.1.   Figure 560. Cat. no. CN.1.   Figure 561. Cat. no. CN.9.

Number	Height, min.	Height, max.	Rim dia., min.	Rim dia., max.
11	17	23	N/A	N/A

Table 281. Description of vessels of Type CL. Measurements in centimetres.

Cat. no.	BNM no.	Area	Mound	Square	Context	Number	Remarks
CL.1		Hamad Town	1-94-95	C3	Tomb	3-C3	Figure 558.
CL.2	172	Saar	8-90-91	1			
CL.3	42	Hamad Town	1-94-95	E1	Tomb	1-E1	
CL.4	476-2-88						No context information.
CL.5	A6117	Hamad Town	70A-85-86		Tomb	6	
CL.6	332	Saar	12-91				
CL.7	88-2-747	Hamad Town	73-85-86	1	Tomb	1	
CL.8	A4512	Hamad Town	1986-87	C18	Tomb	2	
CL.9	A4511	Hamad Town	88-85-86		Tomb	4	
CL.10	A4736	Hamad Town	10-89-90	E4	Tomb	41	
CL.11	A3423		94-95				

Table 282. Context information for vessels of Type CL.

Number	Height, min.	Height, max.	Rim dia., min.	Rim dia., max.
1	18.5	N/A	7.5	N/A

Table 283. Description of vessels of Type CM. Measurements in centimetres.

Cat. no.	BNM no.	Area	Mound	Square	Context	Number	Remarks
CM.1	41	Saar	6-96	B3	Tomb	7	Figure 559.

Table 284. Context information for vessels of Type CM.

Number	Height, min.	Height, max.	Rim dia., min.	Rim dia., max.
10	14	21	4	8.5

Table 285. Description of vessels of Type CN. Measurements in centimetres.

Cat. no.	BNM no.	Area	Mound	Square	Context	Number	Remarks
CN.1		Hamad Town	1-94-95	A8	Tomb	1-A8	With incised decoration. Figure 560.
CN.2	85-2-6191	Saar	1984-85	D5			
CN.3	1074	Hamad Town	73-85-86	1	Tomb	1	
CN.4	49	Hamad Town	83-85-86		Tomb	25	
CN.5	91-2-7354	Saar	5-87-88	D2	Tomb	27	
CN.6	43	Hamad Town	1-94-95	D2	Tomb	6-D2	
CN.7	311	Hamad Town	73-85-86	1	Tomb	1	
CN.8	88-2-1004	Al-Hajar	1-70		Tomb	14	
CN.9	355	Hamad Town	70A-85-86		Tomb	6	Figure 561.
CN.10	A6083	Hamad Town	73-85-86	1	Tomb	1	

Table 286. Context information for vessels of Type CN.

Number	Height, min.	Height, max.	Rim dia., min.	Rim dia., max.
9	18	23	8	9.5

Table 287. Description of vessels of Type CO. Measurements in centimetres.

Cat. no.	BNM no.	Area	Mound	Square	Context	Number	Remarks
CO.1		Hamad Town	1-94-95	C3	Tomb	3-C3	Figure 562.
CO.2	41	Hamad Town	1-94-95	E1	Tomb	1-E1	
CO.3	90-2-2215	Hamad Town	70A-85-86		Tomb	11	
CO.4	310	Hamad Town	73-85-86	1	Tomb	1	
CO.5	310	Hamad Town	1-94-95	F5	Tomb	1-F5	
CO.6	68	Hamad Town	83-85-86		Tomb	26	
CO.7	A3406		94-95				
CO.8	A3312		94-95				
CO.9	A196	Hamad Town	10-89-90	E4	Tomb	41	

Table 288. Context information for vessels of Type CO.

Number	Height, min.	Height, max.	Rim dia., min.	Rim dia., max.
1	10	N/A	3.5	N/A

Table 289. Description of vessels of Type CP. Measurements in centimetres.

Cat. no.	BNM no.	Area	Mound	Square	Context	Number	Remarks
CP.1		Hamad Town	1-94-95	B7	Tomb	3-B7	Part of the rim is missing. Figure 563.

Table 290. Context information for vessels of Type CP.

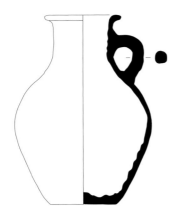

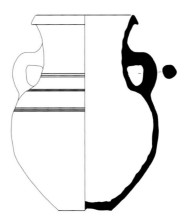

Figure 562. Cat. no. CO.1.   Figure 563. Cat. no. CP.1.   Figure 564. Cat. no. CQ.1.

Dating evidence and discussion
The jug with vertical rim has not been found with any datable vessels and no parallels have been found. However, the characteristic fabric dates this vessel to Phase IV.

Type CN: Jug with flaring rim
The flaring rim characterizes this type. The handles have a rectangular or round cross-section.

Dating evidence and discussion
No parallels have been found to this type, but one tomb (Hamad Town, Mound 73-85-86, Tomb 1) contained three jugs with flaring rim and various glass vessels dating to the third to fourth century AD, thus supporting a Phase IV dating of Type CN.

Type CO: Jug with horizontal rim
Similar to the jug with flaring rim, but with a horizontal rim.

Dating evidence and discussion
Two of the jugs with a horizontal rim (cat. nos CO.4 and CO.9) were found with Phase IV glass vessels. No external parallels have been found.

Type CP: Globular jug
One jug with globular body was recorded. Part of the rim and the handle are missing.

Dating evidence and discussion
No parallels have been found and only the contextual relations of cat. no. CP.1 to vessels in glazed

Number	Height, min.	Height, max.	Rim dia., min.	Rim dia., max.
5	22	25	10	10.5

Table 291. Description of vessels of Type CQ. Measurements in centimetres.

Cat. no.	BNM no.	Area	Mound	Square	Context	Number	Remarks
CQ.1	198	Hamad Town	83-85-86		Tomb	44	Figure 564.
CQ.2	91-2-7201	Hamad Town	83-85-86		Tomb	44	
CQ.3	2478-2-90-15	Ali	103-88-89	C2	Tomb	1	
CQ.4	A4537	Hamad Town	83-85-86		Tomb	31	
CQ.5	A197	Ali	103-88-89	C2			

Table 292. Context information for vessels of Type CQ.

ware (Type BI) provide a supplementary dating to the fabric. Type BI has, however, been dated to Phase III, which could indicate that the hard-fired ware may have been introduced in small quantities in Phase III. This is also likely, since a similar class is reported from the first-century AD site at ed-Dur (Haerinck *et al.* 1993: 187). At present the single vessel of Type CP has been tentatively placed in Phase IV due to the fabric.

Type CQ: Amphora
The two handles characterize this type.

Dating evidence and discussion
No complete parallels to the amphora have been found. One context containing vessels of Type CQ (Hamad Town, Mound 83-85-86, Tomb 44) also contained two amphorae in hard-fired ware and Phase IV glass vessels.

Type CR: Non-diagnostic jugs
Two jugs are missing the rims and it has thus been impossible to determine to which exact type they belong, but since these two jugs can be dated by their fabric they have been assigned a type code.

Dating evidence and discussion
The non-diagnostic jugs have been found with other vessels in hard-fired ware and a Phase IV glass-vessel.

Cat. no.	BNM no.	Area	Mound	Square	Context	Number	Fig. no.	Remarks
CR.1	2645-2-90-15	Ali	103-88-89	C2	Tomb	1		Rim missing.
CR.2	A4742	Hamad Town	10-89-90	E4	Tomb	41		Rim missing.

Table 293. Context information for vessels of Type CR.

Non-datable vessels

As with the glass, where two types and nine fragments could not be dated, some of the pottery cannot be dated either. The information on some of the following types of pottery may indicate that the types have been used over a long period of time and thus can be dated, but it would be meaningless to attempt to place these types in one of the Phases. Other types have been poorly defined, mainly due to the lack of diagnostic features and/or the relatively small number of vessels in the group. Within some of the categories an assemblage called "Unique vessels" is presented. They are types where only one vessel has been identified and for which no proper parallels have been found. Therefore possible contextual combinations with other types cannot be verified and indicated datings are thus problematic. Such unique vessels do not provide much useful information to the Bahraini collection, but as many as possible have been illustrated to enable future dating.

Glazed ware bowls

Type CS: Hemispherical bowl
A varied group of hemispherical bowls without clear diagnostic features.

Dating evidence and discussion
Type CS is a varied and poorly defined group and no specific dating or distribution pattern can be defined. The hemispherical bowls are found in tombs throughout the main island of Bahrain and a few have been reported from Qala'at al-Bahrain (Højlund & Andersen 1994: figs 1479, 1545; Lombard & Kervran 1993: fig. 19.11), documenting that the type has been used both in settlements and as grave goods. From Failaka a mixed collection of hemispherical bowls has been published (Hannestad 1983: nos 35–49). The heterogeneous impression of that assemblage seems very similar to that of Type CS from the Bahraini tombs. Glazed hemispherical bowls seem to be lacking in the published material from eastern Iran and southern Mesopotamia, though plain ware examples are quite common in Susa (Boucharlat 1987: tableau 17). The scattered dating evidence indicates that the hemispherical bowls have been used from Phase I to III or IV.

Type CT: Hollow-based bowl
Type CT is a little bowl with a concave base. The glaze is green, white with a green rim or decayed to golden. The relatively low numbers of this type and the simple shape makes it a poorly defined type.

Dating evidence and discussion
No parallel to this type has been found. Type CT could be a miniature of Type B or Type AP, but only two vessels of Type CT have been found with other types. Cat. nos CT.3 and CT.6 were found with a glass date-flask, a Type K Mesopotamian amphora and a Type J bottle, which does not provide sufficient evidence to clarify whether the type is a contemporary miniature of Type B or Type AP.

Type CU: Shallow hollow-based bowl
The overall shape of this type is similar to Type AC, but the vessels in this group have grooved walls giving the profile a wavy look. It also features an internal central depression and the rim is plain. The glaze is preserved as whitish and often pealing off.

Dating evidence and discussion
No parallels have been found and the three Type CU bowls found in one tomb seem to be from a mixed assemblage, probably due to reuse of the tomb (Jensen 2003: 138).

Type CV: Bowl
A low and small ring-foot and a hemispherical body characterize these bowls. They have internal incised rings. The glaze is green or turquoise but often decayed to whitish.

Dating evidence and discussion
No parallels have been found and the single Type CV Bowl (cat. no. CV.9) that was found with other material is from a mixed context (Jensen 2003: 138).

Unique bowls
Three unique glazed ware bowls have been recorded.

Dating evidence and discussion
Cat. no. NON.12 has been found with possible Phase I material and cat. no. NON.11 with material indicating a Phase III dating for this vessel.

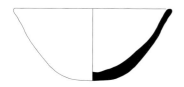 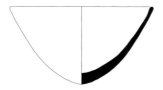  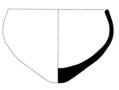

Figure 565. Cat. no. CS.2.   *Figure 566. Cat. no. CS.5.*   *Figure 567. Cat. no. CS.8.*   *Figure 568. Cat. no. CS.9.*

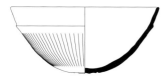 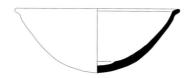 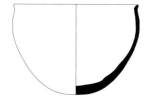

Figure 569. Cat. no. CS.10.   *Figure 570. Cat. no. CS.11.*   *Figure 571. Cat. no. CS.14.*

Number	Height, min.	Height, max.	Rim dia., min.	Rim dia., max.
28	6	9.5	10.5	18

Table 294. Description of vessels of Type CS. Measurements in centimetres.

Cat. no.	BNM no.	Area	Mound	Square	Context	Number	Remarks
CS.1	6	Barbar	1996	C3	Tomb	5	
CS.2	168	Saar	12-91		Tomb	4	Figure 565.
CS.3	315	Saar	12-91		Tomb	8	
CS.4	2407-2-90	Saar	5-87-88	F4	Tomb	56	
CS.5	49	Saar	7-95-96	C6	Outside tomb		Figure 566.
CS.6	327	Saar	11-95-96		Outside tomb	12	
CS.7	212	Al-Hajar	6-92-93	D7	Tomb	30	
CS.8	9893-2-91	Saar	5-87-88	E6	Tomb	51	Figure 567.
CS.9	5	Abu-Saybi	5-97	B2	Tomb	3	Figure 568.
CS.10	129	Al-Hajar	2-92		Tomb	12	Figure 569.
CS.11	4806-2-9-9	Karranah	2-86				Figure 570.
CS.12	133	Shakhoura	7-93	E9	Tomb	75	
CS.13	205	Al-Hajar	7-92-93	F3	Outside tomb	8	
CS.14	5001-2-91-6	Shakhoura	2-91-92		Outside tomb	21	Figure 571.
CS.15	15	Saar	1-96				
CS.16	2106-2-90	Ali	60-88-89	5			
CS.17	97-3-39	Shakhoura	A1-96-97	G7	Outside tomb	14	
CS.18	241	Al-Hajar	2-92-93		Tomb	31	
CS.19	4790-2-90-21						No context information.
CS.20	2362-2-90	Saar	5-85-86		Tomb	1	
CS.21	2038-2-90-15	Ali	101-88-89		Tomb	16	
CS.22	A337		99-00				
CS.23	A3112		1993				
CS.24	A30	Saar	10-99-01	A	Tomb	1	
CS.25	A333						No context information.
CS.26	IMA111						No context information.
CS.27	FM-A-985.CX	Unplaced	T158-4		Tomb	2	
CS.28	FM-A-962.D	Saar	1-1960		Tomb	2	

Table 295. Context information for vessels of Type CS.

Figure 572. Cat. no. CT.1.

Figure 573. Cat. no. CT.5.

Figure 574. Cat. no. CU.4.

Figure 575. Cat. no. CV.4.

Number	Height, min.	Height, max.	Rim dia., min.	Rim dia., max.
7	4	7	11	12

Table 296. Description of vessels of Type CT. Measurements in centimetres.

Cat. no.	BNM no.	Area	Mound	Square	Context	Number	Remarks
CT.1	97-3-101	Shakhoura	A1-96-97	E4	Tomb	22	Figure 572.
CT.2	91-2-9343	Hamad Town	30-84-85		Tomb	6	
CT.3	653	Shakhoura	2-91-92		Tomb	23	
CT.4	116	Al-Hajar	2-92		Tomb	10	
CT.5	222	Al-Hajar	2-92-93		Tomb	42	Figure 573.
CT.6	285	Ali	60-88-89		Tomb	29	
CT.7	A4482	Hamad Town	1989		Tomb	36	

Table 297. Context information for vessels of Type CT.

Number	Height, min.	Height, max.	Rim dia., min.	Rim dia., max.
9	5	5.5	18	20

Table 298. Description of vessels of Type CU. Measurements in centimetres.

Cat. no.	BNM no.	Area	Mound	Square	Context	Number	Remarks
CU.1	4801-2-90-8	Abu-Saybi					
CU.2	24	Hamad Town	1-94-95	B6			
CU.3	9981-2-91	Saar	7-79				
CU.4	3922-2-91-3	Saar	2-91-92	21	Tomb	25	Figure 574.
CU.5	9464-2-91	Karranah	2-86				
CU.6	A1621	Shakhoura	2-01-02	AC3	Tomb	53	
CU.7	FM-A-985.DA	Unplaced	T158-5		Tomb	1	Jensen 2003: fig. 9.4.
CU.8	FM-A-985.DE	Unplaced	T158-5		Tomb	1	Jensen 2003: fig. 9.5.
CU.9	FM-A-985.DD	Unplaced	T158-5		Tomb	1	Jensen 2003: fig. 9.6.

Table 299. Context information for vessels of Type CU.

Number	Height, min.	Height, max.	Rim dia., min.	Rim dia., max.
9	6	7.5	16	21.5

Table 300. Description of vessels of Type CV. Measurements in centimetres.

Cat. no.	BNM no.	Area	Mound	Square	Context	Number	Remarks
CV.1	9875-2-91	Al-Maqsha	1982				
CV.2	10164	Diraz	1972				
CV.3	149	Shakhoura	1-92-93	G6	Tomb	146	
CV.4	110	Saar	5-95-96	A3	Outside tomb	88	Figure 575.
CV.5	9456-2-91	Abu-Saybi	1982-83		Outside tomb	89	
CV.6	A1634		00-01				
CV.7	A2337		00-01				
CV.8	A1472	Shakhoura	2-01-02	AD2			
CV.9	FM-A-985.BY	Unplaced	T158-5		Outside tomb	1	

Table 301. Context information for vessels of Type CV.

Figure 576. Cat. no. NON.10.

Figure 577. Cat. no. NON.11.

Figure 578. Cat. no. NON.12.

Cat. no.	BNM no.	Area	Mound	Square	Context	Number	Remarks
NON.10	106	Shakhoura	7-93	J8	Tomb	151	Green to golden glaze. Figure 576.
NON.11	119	Hamad Town	1-94-95	C5	Tomb	3-C5	Green to brown glaze. Figure 577.
NON.12	A637	Shakhoura	29-00-01		Tomb	17	Green to white glaze. Figure 578.

Table 302. Context information for the unique bowls.

Glazed ware cups

Type CX: Cup with angular profile

The small cups with angular profile and flaring sides are characterized by a carination between the base and lower body and straight flaring sides. The base is a false ring-foot and the rim is plain or with a little out-turned lip. The glaze is green, turquoise, or decayed to golden.

Dating evidence and discussion

The contextual relations of cat. nos CX.4, CX.6, CX.8, CX.9 and CX.10 with other types indicate that the Type CX cup is a long-lived type or poorly defined, since it has been found with material dating to Phases I to III. No external parallels have been found.

Unique cups

Three unique cups were recorded. One example (cat. no. NON.14) was much decorated externally and had an incised star internally. This could be the only noted example of a potter's mark.

Dating evidence and discussion

None of the unique cups has been found with other vessels.

Glazed ware plates

Type CY: Fish plate

Type CY has a raised base or a low false ring-foot and an internal depression. The rim is thickened underneath or down turned. The glaze is white.

Figure 579. Cat. no. CX.2.

Figure 580. Cat. no. CX.7.

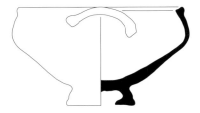

Figure 581. Cat. no. NON.13.

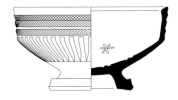

Figure 582. Cat. no. NON.14.

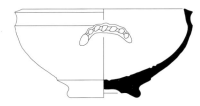

Figure 583. Cat. no. NON.15.

Figure 584. Cat. no. CY.1.

Figure 585. Cat. no. CY.3.

Figure 586. Cat. no. CY.4.

Number	Height, min.	Height, max.	Rim dia., min.	Rim dia., max.
11	4	5.5	11	13.5

Table 303. Description of vessels of Type CX. Measurements in centimetres.

Cat. no.	BNM no.	Area	Mound	Square	Context	Number	Remarks
CX.1	1	Saar	1995	B2	Outside tomb	23	
CX.2	97-3-103	Shakhoura	A1-96-97	E4	Tomb	24	Figure 579.
CX.3	220	Al-Maqsha	1992-93	I7	Tomb	1	
CX.4	29	Shakhoura	1-91		Tomb	4	
CX.5	4	Saar	1995	B3	Tomb	9	
CX.6	342	Hamad Town	30-84-85		Outside tomb	41	
CX.7	314	Shakhoura	7-93	C7	Tomb	29	Figure 580.
CX.8	300	Saar	4-91-92	9	Tomb	46	
CX.9	146	Ali	105-89-90		Tomb	1	
CX.10	A390	Saar	10-99-01	2	Tomb	110	
CX.11	A677	Shakhoura	29-00-01		Tomb	19	

Table 304. Context information for vessels of Type CX.

198

Cat. no.	BNM no.	Area	Mound	Square	Context	Number	Remarks
NON.13	9828-2-91	Shakhoura					Figure 581.
NON.14	127	Al-Maqsha	1992-93	D14	Outside tomb	1	Figure 582.
NON.15	34	Al-Hajar	1-94				Figure 583.

Table 305. Context information for the unique cups.

Number	Height, min.	Height, max.	Rim dia., min.	Rim dia., max.
8	5.5	9	18	35

Table 306. Description of vessels of Type CY. Measurements in centimetres.

Cat. no.	BNM no.	Area	Mound	Square	Context	Number	Remarks
CY.1	289	Saar	4-91-92	13	Tomb	30	Figure 584.
CY.2	4428-2-91	Saar	5-87-88		Outside tomb	14	
CY.3	3	Shakhoura	1-92-93	B3	Outside tomb	7	Figure 585.
CY.4	4283-2-91-4	Al-Hajar					Figure 586.
CY.5	7185-2-91	Um Al-Hasam	1973				
CY.6	9454-2-91	Al-Hajar	1970-71				
CY.7	IMA96						Large. Context information corrupt.
CY.8	IMA97						Large. Context information corrupt.

Table 307. Context information for vessels of Type CY.

Cat. no.	BNM no.	Area	Mound	Square	Context	Number	Remarks
NON.16	9880-2-91	Al-Hajar					Figure 587.

Table 308. Context information for the unique plate.

Dating evidence and discussion

The fish plate is well known in the Greek world in the late Classical and Hellenistic periods, and only seen on Bahrain after Alexander the Great's conquest of the Achaemenid Empire. However, early versions of the fish plates from Qala'at al-Bahrain illustrate features that may be rooted in an Achaemenid tradition, indicating that the adoption of the Greek shapes by local potters was not instant (Andersen 2002: 242). Type CY fish plates have not been found with other datable material in the tombs. They are, however, very common at Qala'at al-Bahrain in Periods Va to Vd contexts, where the plates from Period Vd contexts seem to be larger. At Qala'at al-Bahrain the Type CY fish plate may even be the most common type of tableware in Period V (Højlund & Andersen 1994: 240–277). It is therefore surprising that the type is rather rare

Figure 587. Cat. no. NON.16.

in the tombs. On Failaka Type CY is a common type (Hannestad 1983: nos 199–212). Throughout the Near East the fish plate became a popular shape in the Hellenistic period and is reported from most excavations (Hannestad 1983: 28–32). More recent excavations in the UAE have also revealed an abundance of fish plates from Mleiha and ed-Dur (Mouton 1992: figs 34.1–2, 62.1–3, 71.1–7, 107.1–6). The limited numbers of fish plates in the Bahraini tombs have not been found with any other glass or ceramic vessels and the established typology does not enable a more precise dating than indicated above.

Number	Height, min.	Height, max.	Rim dia., min.	Rim dia., max.
3	18	21	9	9

Table 309. Description of vessels of Type CZ. Measurements in centimetres.

Cat. no.	BNM no.	Area	Mound	Square	Context	Number	Remarks
CZ.1	10202-2-91	Hamad Town	30-84-85		Tomb	39	
CZ.2	66	Saar	5-95-96	D1	Tomb	21	Figure 588.
CZ.3	A2478	Abu-Saybi	1973				With incised decoration.

Table 310. Context information for vessels of Type CZ.

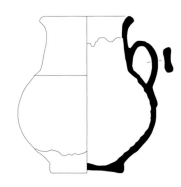

Figure 588. Cat. no. CZ.2.

Unique plate
A single unique plate related to the plate with internally thickened rim was recorded.

Dating evidence and discussion
No close parallels have been found.

Glazed ware jugs
Type CZ: Jug
A wide neck and an out-turned, thickened rim characterize the three jugs of Type CZ. The one straphandle is elegantly attached to the upper body like a bird tail. The glaze is green, but decayed to golden or white and does not cover the base and lower body.

Dating evidence and discussion
Type CZ does not find any parallels, but the shape of the handle and its attachment to the upper body are seen on vessels from Seleucia (Debevoise 1934: no. 281), as is the lack of glaze on the base (Valtz, pers. communication, Turin, Dec. 2002). Since these features are very rare in the Bahraini assemblage, it is likely that the plain jugs are imported from the middle Mesopotamian area. No dating evidence has been found.

Unique jugs
Fifteen unique jugs and amphorae were recorded.

Dating evidence and discussion
Five of the unique jugs were found with other datable material. Cat. no. NON.18 was found with Phase IV material, as was cat. no. NON.30. Cat. nos NON.31 and NON.27 were found with Phase III vessels, and cat. no. NON.28 was from a mixed context (Jensen 2003: 138). No external parallels have been found which can verify these datings.

Glazed ware bottles
Type DA: Cosmetic pot
Type DA is also a rather varied group characterized by a raised base and a low out-turned rim. The glaze is green, turquoise or decayed to brown, golden or white.

Dating evidence and discussion
Type DA has been found with Phase I material (cat. nos DA.6 and DA.9), Phase II (cat. no. DA.1) and Phase IV (cat. nos DA.3 and DA.10). No exact parallels have been found.

Type DB: Handleless bottle
Type DB is a varied group of bottles without handles characterized by an elongated shape of the body. The glaze is green or decayed to brown, white or golden.

Dating evidence and discussion
Type DB vessels have been found with both Phase I and Phase III material. Only a very few related vessels have been published. Two glazed bottles have been reported from Masdjid-i Soleiman (Haerinck 1983: fig. 3.6–7) and in Dura Europos a large group of cylindrical jars was found (Toll 1943: 55–58). It is thus not possible to suggest a dating. Handleless bottles are quite common in the pre-Hellenistic periods in Mesopotamia and it is most likely that Type DB follows that tradition.

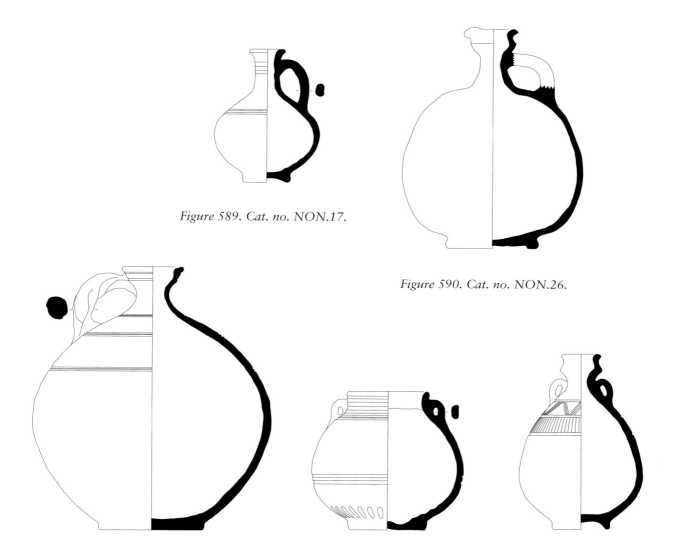

Figure 589. Cat. no. NON.17.

Figure 590. Cat. no. NON.26.

Figure 591. Cat. no. NON.27.

Figure 592. Cat. no. NON.30.

Figure 593. Cat. no. NON.31.

Cat. no.	BNM no.	Area	Mound	Square	Context	Number	Remarks
NON.17	A479	Hamad Town	10-89-90	E4	Tomb	41A	Figure 589.
NON.18	A4732	Hamad Town	83-85-86		Tomb	44	
NON.19	IMA70	Dar Kulayb	24-93-94		Cist grave	2	Salles & Lombard 1999: no. 249.
NON.20	IMA72	Dar Kulayb	24-93-94				Salles & Lombard 1999: no. 251.
NON.21	IMA71	Hamad Town	10-89-90		Cist grave	41-1	Salles & Lombard 1999: no. 252.
NON.22	IMA81						Salles & Lombard 1999: no. 247.
NON.23	196	Al-Hajar	2-93		Outside tomb	48	
NON.24	4363-2-91-2	Hamad Town	73-85-86		Tomb	12	
NON.26	97-3-250	Shakhoura	A1-96-97	D3	Tomb	81	Figure 590.
NON.27	97-2-192	Shakhoura	A1-96-97	B8	Tomb	36	Figure 591.
NON.28	FM-A-985.CC	Unplaced	T158-5		Outside tomb	1	Jensen 2003: fig. 9.18.
NON.29	IMA652	Saar					Salles & Lombard 1999: no. 253.
NON.30	168	Dar Kulayb	24-93-94		Tomb	1	Figure 592.
NON.31	5180-2-91-3	Saar	2-91-92	C2/C3	Tomb	22	Figure 593.

Table 311. Context information for the unique jugs.

Figure 594. Cat. no. DA.1.

Figure 595. Cat. no. DB.1.

Figure 596. Cat. no. DC.2.

Figure 597. Cat. no. DD.1.

Figure 598. Cat. no. DE.1.

Number	Height, min.	Height, max.	Rim dia., min.	Rim dia., max.
10	4.5	7	3	5

Table 312. Description of vessels of Type DA. Measurements in centimetres.

Cat. no.	BNM no.	Area	Mound	Square	Context	Number	Remarks
DA.1	91-1-19	Shakhoura	1-91-92		Tomb	2	Figure 594.
DA.2	166	Dar Kulayb	24-93-94		Tomb	1	
DA.3	214	Dar Kulayb	24-93-94		Tomb	1	
DA.4	10054-2-91						No context information.
DA.5	982-2-88	Al-Hajar	1-71		Tomb	23	
DA.6	86	Al-Hajar	1-92-93		Tomb	1	
DA.7	9871-2-91	Abu Arshira					
DA.8	2555-2-90	Hamad Town	65-85-86		Outside tomb	1	
DA.9	A5850	Hamad Town	1984-85		Tomb	E47	
DA.10	A5649	Hamad Town	83-85-86		Tomb	44	

Table 313. Context information for vessels of Type DA.

Type DC: Bottle with one handle
Type DC has a false ring-foot, a globular body and an out-turned rim with a spout. The handle is a strap-handle and the glaze is decayed to white or brown.

Dating evidence and discussion
A bottle with one handle and a pouring spout is reported from Uruk (Finkbeiner 1992: no. 1058). The Bahraini examples have not been found with other vessels.

Type DD: Bottle with one handle
Type DD has a relatively long and wide neck. It has a raised base and a projecting rim. The strap-handle is attached to the shoulder and the rim, and the handle is much wider at the top. The glaze is greenish and decayed to brown.

Dating evidence and discussion
One Type DD bottle (cat. no. DD.2) was found with a Phase I thin-walled bowl in sand-tempered ware. The type does not find any parallels.

Type DE: Squat bottle
Only one vessel of Type DE was recorded. It has two handles and a squat body. The handles are attached at the transition between the shoulder and neck and they are not pierced, which is a unique feature.

Number	Height, min.	Height, max.	Rim dia., min.	Rim dia., max.
17	9	24	1.5	3

Table 314. Description of vessels of Type DB. Measurements in centimetres.

Cat. no.	BNM no.	Area	Mound	Square	Context	Number	Remarks
DB.1	91-2-78	Saar	4-91-92	11	Tomb	14	Figure 595.
DB.2	1970-2-89	Ali	60-88-89		Tomb	16	
DB.3	1954-2-89	Ali	60-88-89		Tomb	16	
DB.4	1968-2-89	Ali	60-88-89		Tomb	16	
DB.5	1941-2-89	Ali	60-88-89		Tomb	16	
DB.6	920-2-88	Jeed Hafs School					
DB.7	238	Al-Hajar	2-92-93		Tomb	31	
DB.8	91-2-112	Saar	11-91		Tomb	11	
DB.9	223	Al-Hajar	6-92-93		Tomb	35	
DB.10	4933-2-91-3	Saar	1-90		Tomb	1	
DB.11	4931-2-91-7	Al-Maqsha	1991		Tomb	8	
DB.12	118	Shakhoura	7-93	F4	Tomb	82	
DB.13	A1349		00-01				
DB.14	A52	Shakhoura	30-98-99	D3	Tomb	6	
DB.15	IMA649	Saar	4-91-92		Tomb	14	Salles & Lombard 1999: no. 254.
DB.16	IMA644	Saar	4-91-92		Tomb	33	Salles & Lombard 1999: no. 255.
DB.17	IMA657	Saar	4-91-92		Tomb	14	Salles & Lombard 1999: no. 257.

Table 315. Context information for vessels of Type DB.

Number	Height, min.	Height, max.	Rim dia., min.	Rim dia., max.
2	9.5	10	2.5	2.5

Table 316. Description of vessels of Type DC. Measurements in centimetres.

Cat. no.	BNM no.	Area	Mound	Square	Context	Number	Remarks
DC.1	1049-2-88						
DC.2	91-1-32	Shakhoura	1-91-92		Tomb	8	Figure 596.

Table 317. Context information for vessels of Type DC.

Number	Height, min.	Height, max.	Rim dia., min.	Rim dia., max.
2	7.5	7.5	3	3

Table 318. Description of vessels of Type DD. Measurements in centimetres.

Cat. no.	BNM no.	Area	Mound	Square	Context	Number	Remarks
DD.1	96-4-2	Saar	13-96	A2	Mound fill		Figure 597.
DD.2	2042-2-90	Ali	60-88-89		Tomb	21	

Table 319. Context information for vessels of Type DD.

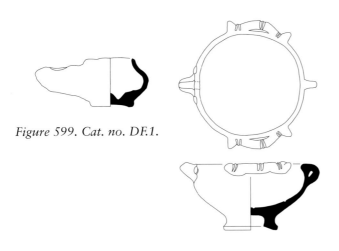

Figure 599. Cat. no. DF.1.

Figure 600. Cat. no. NON.32.

Glazed ware lamps
Type DF: Oil lamp
Five lamps in glazed ware have been found. Three of them have a handle at the back.

Dating evidence and discussion
Lamps are quite rare at Qala'at al-Bahrain with only examples in glazed ware found in Period Va contexts, and without a handle (Højlund & Andersen 1994: fig. 1233). They seem to be much more common on Failaka, from where a larger selection of lamps with and without handles have been published (Hannestad 1983: cat. nos 690-706). Cat. nos DF1 and DF.3 have been found with Phase III material, whereas the examples from the settlements at Qala'at al-Bahrain and Failaka are earlier.

Unique vessel
A unique vessel with a pouring spout and handles has been found. The function of this vessel is unknown to the author.

Dating evidence and discussion
No parallels have been found and the context information is lost.

Dating evidence and discussion
The single bottle of Type DE was found with Phase III or IV material. Since no parallels have been found which could confirm such a dating, it should be regarded as rather preliminary.

Cat. no.	BNM no.	Area	Mound	Square	Context	Number	Remarks
DE.1	162	Hamad Town	1-94-95	B7	Tomb	3-B7	Figure 598.

Table 320. Context information for vessels of Type DE.

Number	Height, min.	Height, max.	Rim dia., min.	Rim dia., max.
5	5	6	4	6

Table 321. Description of vessels of Type DF. Measurements in centimetres.

Cat. no.	BNM no.	Area	Mound	Square	Context	Number	Remarks
DF.1	28	Saar	7-95-96	D4	Tomb	12	Figure 599.
DF.2	A280		99-00				W. Handle.
DF.3	A3400	Hamad Town	1-94-95	E2	Tomb	2-E2	W. Handle.
DF.4	IMA123						W. Handle.
DF.5	IMA554						

Table 322. Context information for vessels of Type DF.

Cat. no.	BNM no.	Area	Mound	Square	Context	Number	Remarks
NON.32	A330						Green to white glaze. No context information. Figure 600.

Table 323. Context information for the unique vessel.

Number	Height, min.	Height, max.	Rim dia., min.	Rim dia., max.
3	5.5	8.5	4	5

Table 324. Description of vessels of Type DG. Measurements in centimetres.

Cat. no.	BNM no.	Area	Mound	Square	Context	Number	Remarks
DG.1	154	Saar	12-95-96		Tomb	46	
DG.2	3851-2-91-3	Saar	4-91-92	9	Tomb	46	Figure 601.
DG.3	4693-2-90-2	Hamad Town	73-85-86		Tomb	27	

Table 325. Context information for vessels of Type DG.

Figure 601. Cat. no. DG.2.

Grey ware bottles

Type DG: Mesopotamian amphora
Type DG has two shoulder-attached loop-handles, a wide neck and a vertical or flaring rim.

Dating evidence and discussion
The Mesopotamian amphorae in grey ware are related to the Mesopotamian amphorae in glazed ware (Types K and BU). The glazed ware examples date to Phases I to III and are likely to be a development of a Neo-Babylonian jar with loop-handles (Hannestad 1983: 37). Two almost complete vessels in grey ware were found at Qala'at al-Bahrain in Period Vb-Vd contexts (Andersen 2001: nos 96, 98). One of the Mesopotamian amphorae in grey ware (cat. no. DG.3) was found with a Phase III glass

vessel and another (cat. no. DG.2) was found with a Type CX cup, for which no date can be provided. A grey ware Mesopotamian amphora is also reported from Qasr-I Abu Nasr (Whitcomb 1985: fig. 48.b).

Red ware bowls

Type DH: Baskets
Vessels imitating a basket with an external decoration in red slip.

Dating evidence and discussion
No parallels have been found and none of the three vessels was found with other vessels.

Type DI: Bowl with angular profile
A sharp carination between the lower and upper body characterizes these two vessels.

Dating evidence and discussion
The bowls with angular profile in red ware are related to Type F bowls with angular profile and out-turned rim dating to Phase I. No parallels have been found and neither of the two vessels from the Bahraini tombs was found with other vessels.

Unique bowls
Six unique bowls were recorded. Three of them are illustrated.

Dating evidence and discussion
Cat. no. NON.33 was found with a little jug in plain ware, indicating a Phase III dating.

Figure 602. Cat. no. DH.1. Figure 603. Cat. no. DI.1.

Number	Height, min.	Height, max.	Rim dia., min.	Rim dia., max.
3	N/A	9 (inc. handle)	N/A	12

Table 326. Description of vessels of Type DH. Measurements in centimetres.

Cat. no.	BNM no.	Area	Mound	Square	Context	Number	Remarks
DH.1	A598	Shakhoura	29-00-01		Tomb	12	Figure 602.
DH.2	A541	Shakhoura	1-92-93	G3	Tomb	138	
DH.3	IMA110	Shakhoura	2-91-92		Tomb	57	Lombard 1999: no. 230.

Table 327. Context information for vessels of Type DH.

Number	Height, min.	Height, max.	Rim dia., min.	Rim dia., max.
2	5.5	6	13	14

Table 328. Description of vessels of Type DI. Measurements in centimetres.

Cat. no.	BNM no.	Area	Mound	Square	Context	Number	Remarks
DI.1	A6697	Saar	12-91		Outside tomb	24	Figure 603.
DI.2	3866-2-91-3	Saar	9-91	3	Outside tomb	5	

Table 329. Context information for vessels of Type DI.

Cat. no.	BNM no.	Area	Mound	Square	Context	Number	Remarks
NON.33	2461-2-90	Saar	5-85-86		Tomb	1	Figure 604.
NON.34	91-2-84	Saar	10-91	3	Tomb	5	Figure 605.
NON.35	147	Saar	3-90-91		Tomb	1	Figure 606.
NON.36	A597	Al-Maqsha	1978	8	Tomb	1	
NON.37	A586	Shakhoura	23-00-01		Tomb	12	
NON.38	IMA577	Saar	11-96		Tomb	43	Salles & Lombard 1999: no. 229.

Table 330. Context information for the unique bowls.

Figure 604. Cat. no. NON.33.

Figure 605. Cat. no. NON.34.

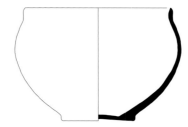

Figure 606. Cat. no. NON.35.

Red ware bottles

Type DJ: Mesopotamian amphora

Three Mesopotamian amphorae in red ware were recorded.

Dating evidence and discussion

The Mesopotamian amphorae in red ware are typologically closely related to the Type K Mesopotamian amphora in glazed ware. The glazed ware version dates to Phase I, which does not correspond with the contextual relation between cat. no. DJ.3 and a Type CC bottle. This vessel most likely dates

Figure 607. Cat. no. DJ.1.

Number	Height, min.	Height, max.	Rim dia., min.	Rim dia., max.
3	9	14	7	8

Table 331. Description of vessels of Type DJ. Measurements in centimetres.

Cat. no.	BNM no.	Area	Mound	Square	Context	Number	Remarks
DJ.1	69	Shakhoura	4-92-93	D3/D4	Tomb	14	Figure 607.
DJ.2	IMA126	Hamad Town	73-85-86		Tomb	39	Salles & Lombard 1999: no. 224.
DJ.3	IMA125	Saar	4-91-92		Tomb	17	Salles & Lombard 1999: no. 225.

Table 332. Context information for vessels of Type DJ.

Cat. no.	BNM no.	Area	Mound	Square	Context	Number	Remarks
DK.1	431	Al-Maqsha	1991-92	A4	Tomb	66B	

Table 333. Context information for vessels of Type DK.

Number	Height, min.	Height, max.	Rim dia., min.	Rim dia., max.
7	3	6	11.5	16.5

Table 334. Description of vessels of Type DL. Measurements in centimetres.

Cat. no.	BNM no.	Area	Mound	Square	Context	Number	Remarks
DL.1	5156-2-91-3	Saar	4-91-92	13	Mound fill		Figure 608.
DL.2	246	Saar	5-95-96	E3	Outside tomb	10	
DL.3	139	Al-Hajar	1993	B4			
DL.4	150	Hamad Town	1-94-95	A9	Tomb	1-A9	
DL.5	320	Saar	7-95-96	F3	Mound fill		
DL.6	3955-91-3						No context information.
DL.7	A3140		99-00				

Table 335. Context information for vessels of Type DL.

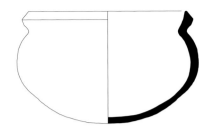

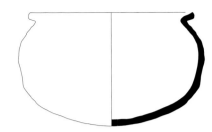

Figure 608. Cat. no. DL.1.   *Figure 609. Cat. no. DM.1.*   *Figure 610. Cat. no. DM.10.*

Number	Height, min.	Height, max.	Rim dia., min.	Rim dia., max.
12	12	17	17	19

Table 336. Description of vessels of Type DM. Measurements in centimetres.

Cat. no.	BNM no.	Area	Mound	Square	Context	Number	Remarks
DM.1	7	Al-Maqsha	1994-95	B1	Mound fill		Figure 609.
DM.2							No context information.
DM.3	6228-2-78	Al-Maqsha	1978	4	Mound fill		
DM.4	106	Al-Maqsha	1988	12	Mound fill		
DM.5	91-1-45	Shakhoura	2-92	D1	Mound fill		
DM.6	5481	Shakhoura	1991	9	Mound fill		
DM.7	6223-2-81	Saar		B2?	Mound fill		
DM.8	123	Al-Maqsha	1992-93	F13	Mound fill		
DM.9	2	Jablet Habashe	1995		Tomb	2	
DM.10	91-1-54	Shakhoura	2-91	D1	Mound fill		Figure 610.
DM.11	70	Shakhoura	2-91	D1	Mound fill		
DM.12	A726	Shakhoura	1990-91		Tomb	9	

Table 337. Context information for vessels of Type DM

to Phase III. No external parallels have been found which can verify the dating.

Type DK: Squat bottle
One squat bottle with two handles in red ware was recorded. It is similar to Type DE in glazed ware.

Dating evidence and discussion
No parallels have been found and the vessel was not found with other material.

Sand-tempered ware bowls
Type DL: Carinated bowl
A sharp carination between the sides and flaring rim characterizes these vessels. As for the Type X bowls, the carinated bowls also have facets left from scraping on the lower part of the body.

Dating evidence and discussion
No good parallels have been found to Type DL and none of the vessels from the tombs was found with other types. The shape is, however, close to Bibby's Type 4 from Thaj, but he describes the fabric as "red or grey straw-tempered clay", which cannot be applied to the vessels from Bahrain (Bibby 1973: 23–24). The shape is also attested at Thaj by Potts, but he lacks a description of the fabric (Potts 1993b: Type 1).

Type DM: Cooking pot
A varied group of cooking pots in a reddish and poorly fired fabric.

Dating evidence and discussion
Most of the cooking pots are found in the mound fill and do not find any exact parallels among the

Figure 611. Cat. no. NON.39.

Figure 612. Cat. no. NON.40.

Table 338. Context information for the unique vessels.

Cat. no.	BNM no.	Area	Mound	Square	Context	Number	Remarks
NON.39	91-1-18	Shakhoura	1991		Tomb	2	Figure 611.
NON.40	10071-2-91	Saar	5-87-88	D6	Outside tomb	23	Figure 612.

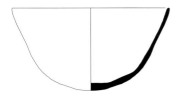

Figure 613. Cat. no. DN.4.

Figure 614. Cat. no. DN.12.

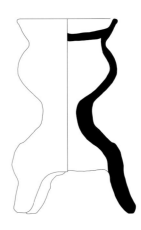

Figure 617. Cat. no. NON.49.

Figure 615. Cat. no. DO.2.

Figure 616. Cat. no. DO.6.

published material from Qala'at al-Bahrain. This could indicate that they are of a later date than the vessels from Qala'at, e.g. after the possible abandonment of the settlement, and may belong to settlements connected with the cemeteries, rather than being grave goods.

Unique bowls

A unique plate and a bowl add to the assemblage.

Dating evidence and discussion

Bibby's Type 5 from Thaj is equivalent to cat. no. NON.40 (Bibby 1973: 20–25).

Plain ware bowls

Type DN: Hemispherical bowl

A slightly varied group of hemispherical bowls. For most of the vessels the fabrics are light yellowish with some sand temper, but a few of the vessels are in a greenish eggshell ware.

Dating evidence and discussion

A hemispherical bowl in plain ware was found at Qala'at al-Bahrain in a Period Vd context (Højlund & Andersen 1994: fig. 1624). On Failaka the shape is common in eggshell ware, but seems to be absent in plain ware (Hannestad 1983: nos 340-–353). Plain ware hemispherical bowls are very common in Seleucia (Debevoise 1934: nos 1–6; Valtz, pers. communication, Turin, Dec. 2002).

The hemispherical bowl in plain ware has been found with Phase I material (cat. nos DN.19 and DN.3), Phase II material (cat. no. DN.1) and pos-

Number	Height, min.	Height, max.	Rim dia., min.	Rim dia., max.
20	6.5	9.5	13	21

Table 339. Description of vessels of Type DN. Measurements in centimetres.

Cat. no.	BNM no.	Area	Mound	Square	Context	Number	Remarks
DN.1		Shakhoura	A1-96-97	F2/F3	Tomb	27	
DN.2	3721-2-91-3	Saar	5-91-92	2			
DN.3	30	Hamad Town	1-94-95	D2	Tomb	2-D2	
DN.4	3873-2-91-3	Saar	12-91		Tomb	16	Figure 613.
DN.5	2434-2-90	Saar	5-87-88	E5	Tomb	58	
DN.6	87	Saar	5-95-96	D5	Tomb	74	
DN.7	4268-2-91-3	Saar	1-90				
DN.8	3838-2-91-3	Saar	6-91-92	4			
DN.9	51	Shakhoura	5-92-93		Tomb	3	
DN.10	3801-2-91-3	Saar	5-91-92	1	Tomb	37	
DN.11	5222-2-91-3	Saar	10-91	4	Tomb	1	
DN.12	316	Saar	11-95-96		Tomb	14	Figure 614.
DN.13	4716-2-90-3	Saar	2-87		Tomb	2	
DN.14	A719	Hamad Town	110-84-85				
DN.15	A5840	Hamad Town	149-84-85		Tomb	19	
DN.16	A3442		96-97				
DN.17	IMA535						
DN.18	IMA452						
DN.19		Karranah	1-1992		Tomb	C-IV-2	
DN.20	FM-A-985.T	Unplaced	T158-4		Tomb	1	

Table 340. Context information for vessels of Type DN.

Cat. no.	BNM no.	Area	Mound	Square	Context	Number	Remarks
NON.41		Unplaced	Higham		Tomb	41	Fragment.
NON.42	554	Al-Maqsha	1991-92	D5	Tomb	92A	
NON.43	12	Saar	53-91-92		Tomb	1	
NON.44	208	Al-Maqsha	1992-93	L6	Mound fill		
NON.45	2210-2-90	Shakhoura	1990	B2			
NON.46	3738-2-91-3	Saar	6-91-92	2	Tomb	4	
NON.47	10175-2-91	Hamad Town	106-84-85		Tomb	1	
NON.48	5176-2-91-3	Saar	2-91-92	C2/C3	Tomb	22	

Table 341. Context information for the unique bowls.

Number	Height, min.	Height, max.	Rim dia., min.	Rim dia., max.
11	3.5	6	17	21

Table 342. Description of vessels of Type DO. Measurements in centimetres.

sibly Phase III material (cat. no. DN.12). The last mentioned vessel was found with a Phase I vessel and a Phase III bowl. This information suggests that the type was in use over a rather long period of time and it is a possibility that the examples found in the Gulf are imported from Seleucia or central Mesopotamia.

Unique bowls
Eight unique bowls in Plain Ware were recorded. None of them are illustrated.

Dating evidence and discussion
Three of the unique bowls were found with other material. Cat. no. NON.47 was found with a Phase I bottle and cat. nos NON.46 and NON.48 with Phase III material.

Plain ware plates
Type DO: Fish plate
A varied group of plates with a thickened or overhanging rim. Some of the vessels have internal incised rings.

Cat. no.	BNM no.	Area	Mound	Square	Context	Number	Remarks
DO.1	227	Saar	9-91	1	Tomb	6	
DO.2	7245-2-91	Al-Maqsha	1991		Tomb	6	Figure 615.
DO.3	203	Al-Hajar	6-92-93	D4	Tomb	15	
DO.4	5672-2-91	Um Al-Hasam					
DO.5	7186-2-91	Um Al-Hasam					
DO.6	142	Saar	5-95-96	D3	Tomb	44	Figure 616.
DO.7	12	Saar	3-96	D4	Tomb	5	
DO.8	160	Saar	7-95-96	E4			
DO.9	91-2-12	Saar	1-91		Tomb	22	
DO.10	A4836	Hamad Town	73-85-86		Tomb	52	
DO.11	A109	Saar	10-99-01	B			

Table 343. Context information for vessels of Type DO.

Number	Height, min.	Height, max.	Rim dia., min.	Rim dia., max.
6	19	27	N/A	N/A

Table 344. Description of the incense burners. Measurements in centimetres.

Cat. no.	BNM no.	Area	Mound	Square	Context	Number	Remarks
NON.49	498-2-88						No context information. Figure 617.
NON.50	9402-2-91	Ali	101-88-89		Tomb	16	
NON.51	9749-2-91	Ali	103-88-89	C2	Tomb	1	
NON.52	A195	Shakhoura	1-92-93	B4	Tomb	35	
NON.53	IMA119						
NON.54	IMA122						

Table 345. Context information for the incense burners.

Cat. no.	BNM no.	Area	Mound	Square	Context	Number	Remarks
DP.1	A1751		00-01				

Table 346. Context information for vessels of Type DP.

Dating evidence and discussion

The fish plates in plain ware are related to Type CY fish plates in glazed ware. The Attic fish plate inspired this type. It is attested at Qala'at al-Bahrain in Period Va, Vb and Vd (Højlund & Andersen 1994: figs 1295–1296, 1333–1334, 1342, 1379–1380, 1451, 1613–1617). On Failaka the fish plates are also well attested in plain ware (Hannestad 1983: nos 453–458).

The fish plates in plain ware are very common in most of Period V at Qala'at al-Bahrain and four vessels from the tombs (cat. nos DO.2, DO.6, DO.7 and DO.10) have been found with Phase II and III material.

Plain ware incense burners

A varied group of six pedestal incense burners in plain ware was recorded.

Dating evidence and discussion

No pedestal burners have been published from Qala'at al-Bahrain, whereas cubical burners are well known from earlier periods (Højlund & Andersen 1994: 363; 1997: 183–186).[17] Cat. nos NON.50 and NON.51 have been found with other vessels.

Plain ware lamps

Type DP: Oil lamp

One lamp in plain ware similar in shape to the glazed ware lamps was recorded.

Dating evidence and discussion

The one plain ware lamp is closely related to the lamps in glazed ware. A fragment of a lamp in plain ware was found in a Period Va context at Qala'at al-Bahrain (Højlund & Andersen 1994: fig. 1336).

---

[17] The incense burners have not been studied in detail, but it would appear that pedestal burners are quite rare in the region.

Conclusion

In this chapter, 1827 complete vessels have been recorded and analyzed and 116 types of pottery have been described and defined. For ninety-three of the types accounting for 1607 vessels (88 % of the vessels) it has been possible to suggest a likely dating within one of the phases defined by the study of the glass vessels presented in Chapter 2. The attribution of the pottery types to these phases is of course an estimate, since the lifespan of a type does not necessary follow the artificial phases. The attribution must therefore be understood as the most likely dating of a type (see p. 107).

The collection of pottery from the tombs is unique for the time being, since it is the first quantified collection of pottery from the Tylos period on Bahrain and only a very few comparable collections have been published from the region, e.g. Kush, with only one phase dating within the Tylos period, and Thaj, where absolute datings and typological developments of the pottery are missing.

The good dating evidence from the Bahraini tombs from Phases II and III in particular, where a significant amount of well-dated glass vessels have been

Type	Ware	Numbers
Type Z: Echinus bowl.	Plain	67
Type Y: Bowl with flaring sides and vertical rim.	Plain	45
Type B: Hollow-based bowl.	Glazed	40
Type AB: Saucer with flaring sides.	Plain	35
Type D: Echinus bowl.	Glazed	32
Type X: Thin-walled bowl.	Sand-tempered	30
Type K: Mesopotamian amphora.	Glazed	20
Type O: Echinus bowl.	Red	18
Type R: Echinus bowl.	Grey	18
Type S: Bowl with angular profile.	Grey	16
Type J: Bottle with two shoulder-attached loop-handles.	Glazed	15
Type N: Carinated bowl.	Red	15
Type C: Bowl with flaring sides and offset lip	Glazed	14
Type M: Hemispheric bowl.	Red	14
Type G: Plate with internal thickened rim.	Glazed	11
Type A: Hemispheric bowl.	Glazed	8
Type F: Bowl with angular profile and out-turned rim.	Glazed	8
Type P: Bowl with three feet.	Grey	5
Type U: Amphora with strap-handles.	Grey	4
Type E: Miniature echinus bowl.	Glazed	4
Type V: Bottle with two shoulder-attached loop-handles.	Grey	4
Type L: Bowl with three feet.	Red	3
Type AA: Saucer with vertical rim.	Plain	3
Type Q: Carinated bowl.	Grey	2
Type T: Rounded bowl.	Grey	2
Type I: Handleless bottle.	Glazed	2
Type H: Lagynos.	Glazed	2

Table 347. List of types dating to Phase I and number of vessels of each type.

found with the local pottery, may also have some chronological implications for some of the other sites mentioned in the introduction to this chapter. In the following I will discuss the pottery assemblage phase by phase, summarizing the discussions of each type made in the previous presentation of the pottery types, and compare the assemblage with the material from other excavations in the region.

Phase I

The most common ware in Phase I (*c.* 200 to 50 BC) is the glazed ware, closely followed by the plain. (See table 348). The best-represented types are the echinus bowl (Type Z), the bowl with flaring sides and vertical rim (Type Y) and the saucer with flaring sides (Type AB) in plain ware, and the hollow-based bowl (Type B) and the echinus bowl (Type D) in glazed ware. All the vessels in sand tempered ware are thin-walled bowls (Type X).

Ware	Numbers	Frequency	Types
Glazed	156	36%	11
Grey	51	12%	7
Plain	150	34%	4
Red	50	11%	4
Sand-tempered	30	7%	1
Total	437	100%	27

Table 348. Number of vessels and types of the different wares in Phase I.

Phase I has been defined as the pre-glass phase, although a single core-formed glass flask (cat. no. 1.3) has been found with Phase I pottery, but no parallels and thus no dating have been found for that vessel. The pottery inventory illustrates a great similarity with Period Vb at Qala'at al-Bahrain, where the echinus bowls (Type Z), the bowls with flaring sides and vertical rim (Type Y) and the saucers with flaring sides (Type AB) in plain ware are common types (Højlund & Andersen 1994: 265-266). The thin-walled bowls in sand-tempered ware date at Qala'at al-Bahrain to Period Vb and Vc (Højlund & Andersen 1994: figs 1434–1435, 1497–1500). Characteristic vessels of Period Va from Qala'at al-Bahrain seem to be lacking, indicating that the earliest burials of the Tylos period cannot be dated earlier than Period Vb at Qala'at al-Bahrain for which a second-century BC date has been suggested (Andersen 2002; Højlund & Andersen 1994: 299). Similarities with the inventory from Period I in the Danish excavations in the Seleucid fortress on Failaka also exist. The echinus bowl and the bowl with

flaring sides and offset lip in glazed ware, and the echinus bowl and the saucer with flaring sides in plain ware are all fairly common in Phase I and Period I on Failaka (Hannestad 1983). Because of the similarities between the pottery from Failaka and the pottery from Bahrain, a close relation between these two islands has been suggested (Salles 1987; Højlund & Andersen 1994: 480), but an apparent difference in the collections exist. Lamps, which may reflect aspects of a wider socio-cultural behaviour, rather than plain bowls and plates, are common on Failaka (Hannestad 1983: nos 690–706), but almost absent on Bahrain.

Although the sand-tempered ware, the red ware and the grey ware do not account for a very significant proportion of the pottery in Phase I, it is in this phase that they are most common and only very few vessels may belong to later phases.

The relatively low frequency of grey and red ware vessels in the tombs on Bahrain has been a surprise, since it has been put forward that these wares could be east Arabian (Hannestad 1983: 49–50). The grey ware and the red ware are well represented at Qala'at-Bahrain in most of the sub-periods of Period V and it seems that the grey and red wares were more common in the settlement than as grave goods. However, the assemblage from the Danish excavations at Qala'at al-Bahrain has not been quantified in the publications and it is difficult to suggest any frequencies of certain wares on the basis of a selection of published sherds. A similar situation exists for the collections of pottery from the Arabian mainland and before proper comparable material is discovered and published, final conclusions cannot be made. Nevertheless, the grey and red wares are distributed on both sides of the Gulf (see pp. 104-105) and their frequencies in literature seem to reflect the amount of archaeological investigations carried out in various areas. It is the hope that surveys currently undertaken on the Iranian side of the Gulf will shed light on the possibility that red ware and grey ware may in fact have been produced there.

The types produced in grey ware are a mixture of Near Eastern shapes and types influenced by Attic black glazed pottery. Although the grey surface could be understood as an imitation of the black glaze, this cannot be the case, since grey ware is already attested in layers dating to the Achaemenid period at Qala'at al-Bahrain (Højlund & Andersen 1994: 212–213, 226–228) and uses an inventory of shapes that cannot be associated with Attic black glazed pottery. The grey ware is therefore a Near

Eastern tradition, which adopts some of the new shapes introduced by the Greeks after Alexander the Great's conquest of the Achaemenid Empire. The class does not seem to adopt the Roman shapes, which strongly influenced the shapes produced in glazed ware in Phases II and III (see below). This is quite reasonable, since grey ware vessels are becoming rare in these phases.

The sand-tempered ware seems to be well distributed in north-east Arabia with a high frequency in Thaj (see Type X) and it is likely that this city was the production centre or the source of inspiration for the thin-walled bowls (Type X), which account for the majority of sand-tempered ware vessels in the Bahraini tombs. The archaeological investigations at the site have been limited and have not yet revealed any production facilities. The dating of the main occupation at Thaj is also insecure, but the majority of dated finds seem to belong in the early "Tylos" period, which could explain why sand-tempered ware is best represented in Phase I of the tombs. Sand-tempered wares as such are common in Bahrain and most other Gulf sites for cooking pots and other utility vessels, but the combination of shape and ware points towards an inland origin.

Plain ware seems to be most common in Phase I and all of the types dated to this phase also find good parallels at Qala'at al-Bahrain. Some, e.g. the echinus bowl and the saucer with flaring sides, also find close parallels on Failaka. The echinus bowl and the fish plate are likely to have been inspired by vessels in Attic black glazed ware.

It has now long been established that many forms in glazed ware in the Seleucid period were influenced by Greek/Attic prototypes. This influence can still be seen in the glazed pottery of Phase I, but it is the same types or slight variations of types, which were introduced in the early Hellenistic period, and the material does not illustrate a continued western influence in the second century BC.

The overall impression of the assemblage from Phase I is that of a mixed collection of vessels representing a number of traditions, some of which can be assigned to specific areas, whereas others lack comparable material. There is a significant proportion of vessels influenced by Greek pottery, but also of vessels of types of Near Eastern and Arabian traditions.

Phase II

Phase II (c. 50 BC to AD 50) is defined as the period before the invention of the blowing of glass flasks. It is mainly dated by four vessels found in the first phase of Shakhoura Mound A1 1996–1997, from where two wooden coffins have also been C[14]-dated[18] to the time around the beginning of our era (Andersen et al. 2004). The pottery associated with the Phase is only glazed ware, although a few of the types dated to Phase I may have continued into Phase II and some of the types assigned to Phase III are likely to have been introduced during Phase II (i.e. Types AN, AZ, BU and CC).

Type	Ware	Numbers
Type AC: Shallow hollow-based bowl.	Glazed	81
Type AH: Cup with angular profile.	Glazed	50
Type AE: Crater with three feet.	Glazed	43
Type AF: Cup with incurving rim.	Glazed	35
Type AI: Lagynos.	Glazed	23
Type AL: Bottle with two vertical handles.	Glazed	18
Type AD: Saucer with vertical rim.	Glazed	18
Type AJ: Cosmetic pot.	Glazed	8
Type AG: Cup with angular profile.	Glazed	6
Type AK: Handleless bottle.	Glazed	2
Type AM: Vessel imitating core-formed glass unguentaria	Fine	1

Table 349. List of types dating to Phase II and number of vessels of each type.

[18] Three samples provided the following dates: AD 31–53, 36 BC–AD 1 and 50 BC.

Ware	Numbers	Frequency	Types
Glazed	284	100%	10
Fine	1	0%	1
Total	285	100%	11

Table 350. Number of vessels and types of the different classes in Phase II.

The most common shape in Phase II is the shallow hollow-based bowl (Type AC) of which a complete profile has been found at Qala'at al-Bahrain in a Period Vd context. The type is found in relatively large numbers in Period II at Failaka, indicating that the BI-ware is contemporary with Phase II. Types AE and AH have also been found in Period Vd contexts at Qala'at al-Bahrain, which indicates that Period Vd is contemporary with Phase II. It has been argued that Period Vd at Qala'at al-Bahrain is contemporary with Period II at Failaka (Højlund & Andersen 1994: 299). This observation is now supported by the material from the Bahraini tombs. However, the suggested dating of Phase II is lower than the first- and second-century AD dating suggested for Period Vd at Qala'at al-Bahrain (Højlund & Andersen 1994: 299). If the original dating of Period Vd is to be maintained, similarities with the pottery from Phase III should be expected. Nevertheless, except for the four types that has been dated to Phase III, but were likely to have been introduced already in Phase II, the two collections are rather different. In Phases I, II and IV correlation exists between the grave goods and the finds from the settlements, which makes it unlikely that the situation in Phase III would be very different. The high number of types and vessels in Phase III and the fairly large collection from Period Vd should thus have produced more correlations. It should also be noted that three of the eleven types dating to Phase II find exact parallels in the Period Vd assemblage and no Roman glass vessels, which are common finds in the tombs in Phase III and in the tombs and settlement in ed-Dur, have been reported from the Danish or the French excavations at Qala'at al-Bahrain. The types from Qala'at al-Bahrain, which indicate that Period Vd should be dated into the second century AD are rimfragments of bowls in common ware, which find parallels dated to the late Parthian period in Susa (Højlund & Andersen 1994: 299). It is possible that such utility vessels are evidence of a limited settlement, but it should also be noted that the chronology of Susa has been criticized, since only a very few finds provide absolute dates between the Achaemenid floors and Islamic layers (Boucharlat 1993: 44–46). There are pottery types from the

Period Vd inventory, which find good parallels in ed-Dur, but nothing suggests that these types were not used in the first half of the first century AD and thus within the suggested dating of Phase II. This indicates that the majority of material from Period Vd layers should be dated prior to the introduction of large quantities of blown glass probably in the middle of the first century AD and therefore slightly earlier than suggested by Højlund. This dating corresponds well with the dating initially suggested for Period II on Failaka (Hannestad 1983: 78).

A significant difference in the preservation of the glaze between Periods I and II on Failaka was noted (Hannestad 1983) and this difference can also be seen on some of the Bahraini vessels. The glaze in Phase I seems to be preserved as more greyish or white, whereas the vessels from Phase II has more often decayed into an irrisident or golden appearance (See Figure 618). In Phase III both types of glaze seem common.

Fig. 618. Cat. no. AH.47. Phase II vessel where the glaze has decayed into a golden appearance.

None of the types from Phase II finds any exact parallels outside the Gulf region. The assemblage gives a very coherent impression. Most of the types and by far the most popular ones are strongly influenced by Roman or eastern Mediterranean pottery in this phase. It would appear that every new type in the inventory can find very good prototypes in the West and only a couple of poorly represented types can be understood as developments of older types, i.e. Types AD, AJ and AK.

That potters in the East in this period again looked to the West for inspiration comes as no surprise. It has earlier been suggested that the crater with three feet could possibly have been inspired by similar vessels in terra sigillatae, although it was not concluded which way the influence ran (Salles 1990).

In Seleucia Roman influence has been noted (Valtz 1993) and on Failaka (Hannestad 1983: 21), but for the first time we now have a significant and well-dated assemblage that clearly reflects the adoption of a variety of terra sigillatae shapes in the Gulf region. Because of the relatively secure dating of Phase II, it is very likely that the adoption of Roman types by potters in the East and consumers choosing these new shapes, started or gained momentum in the middle of the first century BC, corresponding with the Roman expansion in the East after the victories of Sulla, Pompey and Octavian.

Type	Ware	Numbers
Type AQ: Hollow-based bowl.	Glazed	155
Type BE: Cup with vertical rim.	Glazed	82
Type BF: Cup with vertical rim.	Glazed	78
Type BQ: Bottle with one handle.	Glazed	45
Type BL: Jar.	Glazed	44
Type BU: Mesopotamian amphora.	Glazed	42
Type CC: Little jug with one handle.	Plain	32
Type BV: Bottle with two neck-attached loop-handles.	Glazed	30
Type BO: Cosmetic pot.	Glazed	23
Type BA: Stemmed cup with projecting foot.	Glazed	23
Type AP: Hollow-based bowl.	Glazed	23
Type BX: Pilgrim flask.	Glazed	22
Type BM: Jug.	Glazed	16
Type AO: Shallow hemispheric bowl.	Glazed	16
Type AT: Bowl with angular profile.	Glazed	15
Type BC: Plain stemmed cup.	Glazed	15
Type AR: Miniature of hollow-based bowl.	Glazed	13
Type AN: Hemispheric bowl.	Glazed	11
Type BY: Bottle with two handles.	Glazed	11
Type BR: Bottle with one handle.	Glazed	11
Type BG: Miniature of cup with vertical rim.	Glazed	10
Type BB: Miniature of stemmed cup with projecting foot.	Glazed	9
Type BI: Cup with angular profile.	Glazed	9
Type AX: Saucer with flaring rim.	Glazed	8
Type BJ: Fish plate.	Glazed	8
Type BN: Jug.	Glazed	8
Type BD: Stemmed cup with handles.	Glazed	7
Type BK: Miniature fish plate.	Glazed	7
Type BZ: Bottle with two vertical handles.	Glazed	7
Type CB: Hemispheric bowl	Sand-tempered	6
Type BH: Cup with angular profile.	Glazed	5
Type AV: Miniature of bowl with angular profile.	Glazed	5
Type BS: Bottle with one handle.	Glazed	4
Type AU: Bowl with angular profile.	Glazed	4
Type AY: Saucer with moulded rim.	Glazed	3
Type BP: Cosmetic pot.	Glazed	3
Type AS: Bowl with rounded body and out-turned lip.	Glazed	2
Type BT: Bottle with one handle.	Glazed	2
Type AZ: Kantharos.	Glazed	2
Type CA: Unguentarium.	Fine	2

Table 351. List of types dating to Phase III and number of vessels of each type.

Phase III

The dating of Phase III (c. AD 50–150) originates from a large number of well-dated glass vessels mainly of east Roman production. More than half of the pottery vessels from the tombs date from this rather brief period. Glazed ware is by far the most common class, accounting for 95.5 % of the vessels in this period.

Ware	Vessels	Frequency	Types
Plain ware	32	4%	1
Glazed ware	778	95%	37
Sand-tempered ware	6	1%	1
Fine	2	0	1
Total	818	100%	37

Table 352. Number of vessels and types of the different classes in Phase III.

Many of the finds from Phase III have good parallels at ed-Dur in the UAE and it is most likely that the main occupation at this site corresponds with Phase III. As in Phase II, many of the new types introduced in Phase III find convincing prototypes in the west. The footed bowls with vertical rims are the most common, but for other new types I have found no acceptable parallels in the West, which could indicate that other sources of influence came into play during this period.

Fig. 619. Cat. no. AQ.22. Type AQ, Hollow-based bowl, is the most common types from the Tylos period tombs with 155 vessels recorded.

Types of glazed ware that find good parallels in Babylonia or north Mesopotamia or illustrate manufacturing or stylistic details from that area are only represented in very low numbers (e.g. Types BS and BT). On the other hand the best represented types in the Bahraini collection are not attested in Babylonia or north Mesopotamia, but may only find parallels at coastal sites along the Gulf (e.g. Types AQ, BE and BF). This could indicate a production of glazed

ware pottery in Bahrain, but the actual evidence for such a production in the Tylos period is confined to a waster found at Qala'at al-Bahrain, which is a rather thin argument, since a waster could easily have been overseen in a shipment of pots. However, evidence in the form of tripods used to stack glazed ware vessels in the kiln have been found in Islamic contexts, but that does not document a production in pre-Islamic times either. The best evidence for production centres at present is thus the frequencies of various types and the distribution patterns. This indicates that the majority of glazed ware vessels were produced in one or more centres, maybe on Bahrain or in the vicinity, but surely at a coastal site in the Gulf region. The undiscovered site of Charax Spasinou, the capital of the Characenian kingdom, is a likely candidate as an economic and industrial centre where glazed ware pottery was produced.

The high number of vessels (both imported glass and local Gulf pottery) dating to Phase III indicates more burials than in the other phases, either because of a higher population density and therefore more deaths; or a larger part of the population adopted the beliefs and traditions manifested in the tomb burials; or there was generally more wealth among the population, which enabled more resources to be spent on grave construction and more grave goods to be placed in the tombs. The material from Phase III gives the impression of prosperity.

Phase IV

The ceramic material from Phase IV (c. AD 150–450) is very limited and dominated mainly by jugs in hard-fired ware. Four types in glazed ware also belong in this phase and they are probably developments of earlier types known in the Bahraini collection.

The dating of the hard-fired ware seems to be fairly secure, since a relatively large number of vessels in this class have been found with Phase IV glass vessels. There are, however, a few combinations with Phase III material, which may be the result of residuality, reuse of tombs, Phase III types continuing into Phase IV or hard-fired ware being introduced in small quantities in Phase III. However, the thin grey ware from ed-Dur strongly indicates that the class was in circulation in the first century AD in the region, but only became common at a later stage in Bahrain. With the glass of Phase IV, the possibility of a dating of the entire collection of vessels to c. the fourth century AD was mentioned. This could also be applied to the pottery. Very few well-dated and published assemblages exist from this period in the Gulf, but the similarity of Type CI with beakers in

Type	Ware	Numbers
Type CL: Jug with trefoil rim.	Hard-fired	11
Type CN: Jug with flaring rim.	Hard-fired	10
Type CO: Jug with horizontal rim.	Hard-fired	9
Type CF: Amphora.	Glazed	9
Type CD: Hollow-based bowl.	Glazed	6
Type CQ: Amphora.	Hard-fired	5
Type CE: Bowl with angular profile.	Glazed	4
Type CI: Beaker.	Hard-fired	3
Type CR: Non-diagnostic jugs.	Hard-fired	2
Type CJ: Jar.	Hard-fired	2
Type CG: Bottle with two handles.	Glazed	2
Type CP: Globular jug.	Hard-fired	1
Type CM: Jug with vertical rim.	Hard-fired	1
Type CK: Jar.	Hard-fired	1
Type CH: Bowl.	Hard-fired	1

Table 353. List of types dating to Phase IV and number of vessels of each type.

Ware	Vessels	Frequency	Types
Hard-fired ware	46	69%	11
Glazed ware	21	31%	4
Total	67	100%	15

Table 354. Number of vessels and types of the different classes in Phase IV.

fine orange painted ware and Type CL with a vessel from Khatt dated to the fifth century (Kennet 1998), and the close similarities between the Phase IV material from Bahrain with the collection from the cemetery in Area F in ed-Dur, suggest a dating within the period from the third to the fifth century AD.

The vessels dating to Phase IV are mainly jugs, probably used for serving beverage and often found with conical or hemispherical glass beakers. A few beakers in hard-fired ware were also found. Their profile is very close to beakers in fine orange painted ware, of which some fragments have been found at Qala'at al-Bahrain, and at most sites dating to the Sasanian period on the Oman peninsula. The fine orange painted ware is believed to have been produced in Iran (Potts 1998). The jugs may also imitate Sasanian metal jugs, as indicated by the knob on top of the handle on many of the jugs with trefoil rim. This is a common detail on metal jugs. The style of the vessels in hard-fired ware does not seem to originate in the West as most of the new types did in the previous periods. The beakers find good prototypes in Iran and the jugs possible ones. The beginning of Phase IV is defined as starting in the middle of the second century AD, but bearing in mind that we have no positive evidence for vessels dating to the second and third centuries AD, the possible Iranian influence on the pottery in Phase IV does not necessarily start in the middle of the second century AD, but can safely be associated with the rise of the Sasanians at the beginning of the third century AD and their successful expansion over the next decades. The possible lack of finds from the second and third centuries AD will be discussed in Chapter 5.

Phase V
No pottery vessels can be dated to this phase.

The chronological perspectives

4

In the previous chapters, a chronological system was established. Furthermore, possible changes in production and trade patterns, as well as indications of shifting stylistic origin of the glass and pottery types, were documented. It is the aim of this chapter to establish a more general view of the Tylos period burials. The investigations will emphasize the chronological perspectives of the material in order to see if the variety of glass and pottery vessels changed significantly during the Tylos period or remained rather constant. This may indicate whether any significant changes in burial custom and possible belief took place during the almost 800 year-long period during which the Tylos period cemeteries were used. It is, however, beyond the analytic and methodical framework of this study to attempt reconstructions of the burial rites that created the contextual setting for the grave goods.

The dated glass and pottery vessels presented in Chapters 2 and 3 will be used for analysis. The overall form is assumed to be indicative of function (see p. 106) and the chronological changes in the variety of form will be the first characteristic to be investigated. This analysis can be supplemented with the material (glass or ceramic) to see whether the invention of glass-blowing in Phases II and III had an effect on the assemblage. The last parameter to be investigated is the geographical distribution of dated vessels on Bahrain. Since we know of only very few settlements the distribution of tombs may give an indication of settlement patterns.

The sample

In Chapters 2 and 3, 2148 vessels or fragments of glass and pottery vessels were presented and 1917 of them could be dated to one of the five phases, keeping in mind that types have a lifespan independent of the artificial phases (see p. 107). For the following analysis of form and ware, the total population is the 1917 vessels for which a likely dating has been suggested. The information is summarized in Table 355. Due to the limited number of vessels in Phase V, the results here must be regarded as pre-

liminary, whereas the remaining periods provide a good statistical foundation.

For the geographical analysis, we also need the area information and since this information is missing for some of the dated vessels, the population is smaller (1684 vessels).

Form and function versus time

Due to the high degree of Mediterranean influence on the shape of the pottery, which was documented in Chapter 3, it is reasonable to suggest that it was not only the form that was copied, but also the function of that specific vessel. For the Mediterranean pottery, this is often known from written sources or contextual evidence. By summarizing the information from Appendix 1, we obtain the numbers in table 356.

From Figure 620 it is clear that the frequency of bowls illustrates a steady decline from Phases I to V and the proportion of bottles increases. The cups are absent in Phase I and the frequency of jugs is also very low. This changes in Phases II to IV where cups and jugs are relatively common. If we add a further interpretative level to the shape of the vessels, it may be reasonable to suggest that bottles are (mainly) used in relation to personal adornment, by assuming they have served as containers for oils and other liquids such as unguents, lotions and pigments. A primary function of bowls and plates may have been to serve food, and jugs and cups may have been related to drinking. This leaves us with three possible situations in which the glass and pottery vessels could have been used, i.e. personal adornment, eating and drinking. If we add the above figures for bowls and plates and cups and jugs together, we obtain the development of possible use illustrated in figure 621.

The graphs indicate a possible and very interesting development. In Phase I vessels that can be associated with eating are by far the most common. In Phases II and III, vessels for drinking become more frequent and in Phases IV and V, vessels used in re-

221

Type	Ware	Function	Phase	Numbers
Type 1: Core-formed bottle.	Glass	Bottle	II	3
Type 2: Marbled unguentarium.	Glass	Bottle	II	4
Type 3: Linear incised bowl.	Glass	Bowl	II	1
Type 4: Pillar moulded bowl.	Glass	Bowl	II	2
Type 5: Unique bowl.	Glass	Bowl	II	1
Type 6: Plain unguentarium.	Glass	Bottle	III	43
Type 7: Plain unguentarium.	Glass	Bottle	III	5
Type 8: "Baby feeding" bottle.	Glass	Bottle	III	1
Type 9: Miniature jug.	Glass	Bottle	III	2
Type 10: Amphoriskos.	Glass	Bottle	III	6
Type 11: Amphoriskos with pointed base.	Glass	Bottle	III	3
Type 12: Aryballos.	Glass	Bottle	III	20
Type 13: Amphoriskos.	Glass	Bottle	III	17
Type 14: Miniature transport amphora.	Glass	Bottle	III	5
Type 15: Date-flask.	Glass	Bottle	III	23
Type 16: Hexagonal bottle.	Glass	Bottle	III	2
Type 17: Lenticular bottle.	Glass	Bottle	III	1
Type 18: Scroll or lozenges decorated bottle.	Glass	Bottle	III	8
Type 19: Squat bottle with two handles.	Glass	Bottle	III	2
Type 20: Bottle, imitating a bunch of grapes.	Glass	Bottle	III	1
Type 21: Beaker with applied decoration.	Glass	Cup	III	2
Type 22: Bowl with cut-out ridge.	Glass	Bowl	III	2
Type 23: Mould-blown conical beaker.	Glass	Cup	III	1
Type 24: Flask with funnel mouth.	Glass	Bottle	IV	4
Type 25: Bulbous flask..	Glass	Bottle	IV	22
Type 26: Unguentarium with indented body.	Glass	Bottle	IV	6
Type 27: Candlestick unguentarium.	Glass	Bottle	IV	6
Type 28: Bell-shaped unguentarium.	Glass	Bottle	IV	15
Type 29: Unguentarium with globular body and long neck	Glass	Bottle	IV	2
Type 30: Unguentarium with pinched-out ribs.	Glass	Bottle	IV	1
Type 31: Unguentarium with conical body.	Glass	Bottle	IV	1
Type 32: Toilet bottle.	Glass	Bottle	IV	1
Type 33: Unguentarium with applied thread.	Glass	Bottle	IV	1
Type 34: Ointment jar.	Glass	Bottle	IV	28
Type 35: Miniature jug.	Glass	Bottle	IV	5
Type 36: Globular jug.	Glass	Bottle	IV	1
Type 37: "Mercury bottle".	Glass	Bottle	IV	1
Type 38: Mould-blown unguentarium.	Glass	Bottle	IV	1
Type 39: Optic blown vessel.	Glass	Bottle	IV	4
Type 40: Conical beaker.	Glass	Cup	IV	10
Type 41: Hemispheric bowl.	Glass	Cup	IV	13
Type 42: Plain little bowl.	Glass	Bowl	IV	11
Type 43: Little bowl with coil base.	Glass	Bowl	IV	3
Type 44: Flask with funnel mouth.	Glass	Bottle	V	9
Type 45: Bulbous flask.	Glass	Bottle	V	4
Type 46: Elongated flask.	Glass	Bottle	V	5
Type 47: Miniature jug.	Glass	Bottle	V	1
Type A: Hemispheric bowl.	Glazed	Bowl	1	8
Type B: Hollow-based bowl.	Glazed	Bowl	1	40

Type	Ware	Function	Phase	Numbers
Type C: Bowl with flaring sides and offset lip.	Glazed	Bowl	1	14
Type D: Echinus bowl.	Glazed	Bowl	1	32
Type E: Miniature echinus bowl.	Glazed	Bowl	1	4
Type F: Bowl with angular profile and out-turned rim.	Glazed	Bowl	1	8
Type G: Plate with internal thickened rim.	Glazed	Plate	1	11
Type H: Lagynos.	Glazed	Jug	1	2
Type I: Handleless bottle.	Glazed	Bottle	1	2
Type J: Bottle with two shoulder-attached loop-handles.	Glazed	Bottle	1	15
Type K: Mesopotamian amphora.	Glazed	Bottle	1	20
Type L: Bowl with three feet.	Red	Bowl	1	3
Type M: Hemispheric bowl.	Red	Bowl	1	14
Type N: Carinated bowl.	Red	Bowl	1	15
Type O: Echinus bowl.	Red	Bowl	1	18
Type P: Bowl with three feet.	Grey	Bowl	1	5
Type Q: Carinated bowl.	Grey	Bowl	1	2
Type R: Echinus bowl.	Grey	Bowl	1	18
Type S: Bowl with angular profile.	Grey	Bowl	1	16
Type T: Rounded bowl.	Grey	Bowl	1	2
Type U: Amphora with strap-handles.	Grey	Bottle	1	4
Type V: Bottle with two shoulder-attached loop-handles.	Grey	Bottle	1	4
Type X: Thin-walled bowl.	Sand-tempered	Bowl	1	30
Type Y: Bowl with flaring sides and vertical rim.	Plain	Bowl	1	45
Type Z: Echinus bowl.	Plain	Bowl	1	67
Type AA: Saucer with vertical rim.	Plain	Bowl	1	3
Type AB: Saucer with flaring sides.	Plain	Bowl	1	35
Type AC: Shallow hollow-based bowl.	Glazed	Bowl	II	81
Type AD: Saucer with vertical rim.	Glazed	Bowl	II	18
Type AE: Crater with three feet.[19]	Glazed	Jug	II	43
Type AF: Cup with incurving rim.	Glazed	Cup	II	35
Type AG: Cup with angular profile.	Glazed	Cup	II	6
Type AH: Cup with angular profile.	Glazed	Cup	II	50
Type AI: Lagynos.	Glazed	Jug	II	23
Type AJ: Cosmetic pot.	Glazed	Bottle	II	8
Type AK: Handleless bottle.	Glazed	Bottle	II	2
Type AL: Bottle with two vertical handles.	Glazed	Bottle	II	18
Type AM: Vessel imitating core-formed glass unguentaria	Fine	Bottle	II	1
Type AN: Hemispheric bowl.	Glazed	Bowl	III	11
Type AO: Shallow hemispheric bowl.	Glazed	Bowl	III	16
Type AP: Hollow-based bowl.	Glazed	Bowl	III	23
Type AQ: Hollow-based bowl.	Glazed	Bowl	III	155
Type AR: Miniature of hollow-based bowl.	Glazed	Bowl	III	13
Type AS: Bowl with rounded body and out-turned lip.	Glazed	Bowl	III	2
Type AT: Bowl with angular profile.	Glazed	Bowl	III	15
Type AU: Bowl with angular profile.	Glazed	Bowl	III	4
Type AV: Miniature of bowl with angular profile.	Glazed	Bowl	III	5

[19] Assuming that the function of the Type AE crater with three feet *was* as a crater, i.e. a bowl for serving wine, the function is the same as the jugs and they will thus be analysed together.

Type	Ware	Function	Phase	Numbers
Type AX: Saucer with flaring rim.	Glazed	Bowl	III	8
Type AY: Saucer with moulded rim.	Glazed	Bowl	III	3
Type AZ: Kantharos.	Glazed	Cup	III	2
Type BA: Stemmed cup with projecting foot.	Glazed	Cup	III	23
Type BB: Miniature of stemmed cup with projecting foot.	Glazed	Cup	III	9
Type BC: Plain stemmed cup.	Glazed	Cup	III	15
Type BD: Stemmed cup with handles.	Glazed	Cup	III	7
Type BE: Cup with vertical rim.	Glazed	Cup	III	82
Type BF: Cup with vertical rim.	Glazed	Cup	III	78
Type BG: Miniature of cup with vertical rim.	Glazed	Cup	III	10
Type BH: Cup with angular profile.	Glazed	Cup	III	5
Type BI: Cup with angular profile.	Glazed	Cup	III	9
Type BJ: Fish plate.	Glazed	Plate	III	8
Type BK: Miniature fish plate.	Glazed	Plate	III	7
Type BL: Jar.	Glazed	Jug	III	44
Type BM: Jug.	Glazed	Jug	III	16
Type BN: Jug.	Glazed	Jug	III	8
Type BO: Cosmetic pot.	Glazed	Bottle	III	23
Type BP: Cosmetic pot.	Glazed	Bottle	III	3
Type BQ: Bottle with one handle.	Glazed	Bottle	III	45
Type BR: Bottle with one handle.	Glazed	Bottle	III	11
Type BS: Bottle with one handle.	Glazed	Bottle	III	4
Type BT: Bottle with one handle.	Glazed	Bottle	III	2
Type BU: Mesopotamian amphora.	Glazed	Bottle	III	42
Type BV: Bottle with two neck-attached loop-handles.	Glazed	Bottle	III	30
Type BX: Pilgrim flask.	Glazed	Bottle	III	22
Type BY: Bottle with two handles.	Glazed	Bottle	III	11
Type BZ: Bottle with two vertical handles.	Glazed	Bottle	III	7
Type CA: Unguentarium.	Fine	Bottle	III	2
Type CB: Hemispheric bowl.	Sand-tempered	Bowl	III	6
Type CC: Little jug with one handle.	Plain	Jug	III	32
Type CD: Hollow-based bowl.	Glazed	Bowl	IV	6
Type CE: Bowl with angular profile.	Glazed	Bowl	IV	4
Type CF: Amphora.	Glazed	Jug	IV	9
Type CG: Bottle with two handles.	Glazed	Bottle	IV	2
Type CH: Bowl.	Hard-fired	Bowl	IV	1
Type CI: Beaker.	Hard-fired	Cup	IV	3
Type CJ: Jar.	Hard-fired	Jug	IV	2
Type CK: Jar.	Hard-fired	Jug	IV	1
Type CL: Jug with trefoil rim.	Hard-fired	Jug	IV	11
Type CM: Jug with vertical rim.	Hard-fired	Jug	IV	1
Type CN: Jug with flaring rim.	Hard-fired	Jug	IV	10
Type CO: Jug with horizontal rim.	Hard-fired	Jug	IV	9
Type CP: Globular jug.	Hard-fired	Jug	IV	1
Type CQ: Amphora.	Hard-fired	Jug	IV	5
Type CR: Non-diagnostic jugs.	Hard-fired	Jug	IV	2

Table 355. List of types of glass and pottery vessels specifying ware, function and dating.

Function/Time	I	II	III	IV	V
Bottle	45	36	341	101	19
Bowl	379	103	263	25	0
Cup	0	91	243	26	0
Jug	2	66	100	51	0
Plate	11	0	15	0	0
Total	437	296	962	203	19

Table 356. Number of vessels in each category versus phase.

Func./Phase	I	II	III	IV	V
Bottle	10 %	12 %	35 %	50 %	100 %
Bowl	87 %	35 %	27 %	12 %	0 %
Cup	0 %	31 %	25 %	13 %	0 %
Jug	0 %	22 %	10 %	25 %	0 %
Plate	3 %	0 %	2 %	0 %	0 %
Total	100 %	100 %	100 %	100 %	100 %

Table 357. Frequency of vessels in each category versus phase.

lation to personal adornment are the most frequent. As it is problematic to separate vessels used for drinking and eating (see p. 106) the above indications should be simplified further, before including the material of the vessels in the analysis. By adding together the figures for vessels used for drinking and eating, the results illustrated in figure 622 are obtained.

It is still very clear that a graduate change from a preference for vessels associated with eating and drinking to vessels associated with personal adornment took place. In the following, the material of the vessels will be added.

Material	Type	I	II	III	IV	V
Ceramic	Adornment	45	29	202	2	0
Ceramic	Eat/Drink	392	256	616	65	0
Glass	Adornment	0	7	139	99	19
Glass	Eat/Drink	0	4	5	37	0
		437	296	962	203	19

Table 358. Number of vessels associated with adornment, and eating and drinking, sorted by material, versus time.

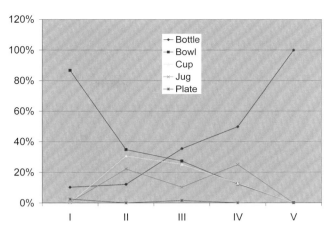

Fig. 620. Diagram of frequencies of vessels in general categories of shape versus phase.

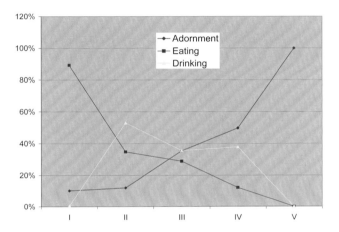

Fig. 621. Diagram of frequencies of vessels in categories of function versus phase.

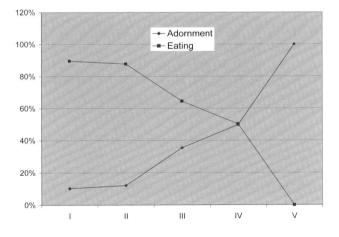

Fig. 622. Diagram of frequencies of vessels associated with adornment, and eating and drinking versus time.

Material	Type	I	II	III	IV	V
Ceramic	Adornment	10%	10%	21%	1%	0%
Ceramic	Eat/Drink	90%	86%	64%	32%	0%
Glass	Adornment	0%	2%	14%	49%	100%
Glass	Eat/Drink	0%	1%	1%	18%	0%
		100%	100%	100%	100%	100%

Table 359. Frequencies of vessels associated with adornment, and eating and drinking, sorted by material, versus time.

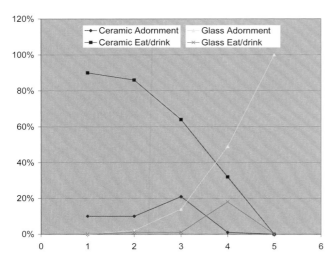

Fig. 623. Diagram of frequencies of vessels associated with adornment, and eating and drinking, sorted by material, versus time.

From Figure 623 it is evident that ceramic vessels associated with eating and drinking decline steadily, but in Phase IV these vessels are supplemented with a significant corpus of glass vessels. The perfume bottles in ceramic are most frequent in Phase III, and thus at a time when glass bottles were beginning to enter the tombs in a significant number, but in Phase IV only very few bottles in ceramic were deposited. This could indicate that glass replaced ceramic as the material used for bottles in the centuries after the invention of glass-blowing, but at this stage bottles were already becoming more frequent as grave goods in Bahrain, as indicated by the increased frequency of ceramic bottles in Phase III. The glass tableware supplement the ceramics in Phase IV, but further development is difficult to determine due to the limited sample from Phase V.

Demography

With dated material from a large part of Bahrain, we are now able to draw a map of possible settlement patterns on Bahrain in the Tylos period, and examine whether the decline of Qala'at al-Bahrain at the beginning of the Christian era is repeated in the adjacent cemeteries. The empirical background is the dated glass and pottery vessels presented in Chapters 2 and 3 and their contextual association with various areas. It has been suggested that cemeteries from the Tylos Period have been found on the Islands of Muharraq, Nabih Saleh and Umm an-Hassan (Herling 2003: 441–446), but no finds in the Main Store at Bahrain National Museum support this, and there is no documentation confirming that tombs dating to this period were excavated in these areas. There is, however, the possibility that only plastered tombs — normally dated to the Tylos period by Bahraini archaeologists — were found, which did not contain any grave goods. For the time being, we must conclude that the burials seem confined to the main island of Bahrain.

Area definitions and descriptions

Finds recorded from excavations of cemeteries in the Bahrain areas are listed in Table 360. The areas are named after the nearest village or in the case of Hamad Town and Isa Town, after these new foundations. All the cemeteries are situated close to fairly fertile farmland and the majority along the north coast, where a 4–5 km broad fertile coastal plain with freshwater wells enables efficient allotment farming. The size of the regions defined below, is no larger than the cemeteries within it could theoretically have been used by the inhabitants of only one settlement, if one accepts a funeral procession of up to c. 3 km to be reasonable. However, until settlements from the period have been identified, a more secure model for the relation between settlements and cemeteries can not be made, and more detailed discussions of settlement patterns in geographical areas smaller than the proposed regions will be of a very speculative nature.

North-eastern region

Only a few cemeteries are known from the eastern part of the northern coastal plain, which is a peninsula and now covered by the modern capital of Al-Manama. These sites were excavated rather early after the establishment of the Department for Archaeology and National Heritage in 1969, and at a time when the modern city had already expanded significantly into the surrounding farmland. In the south-western part of the modern city evidence of an ancient settlement dating back to the very early Islamic period was excavated at Bilad al-Qadim, but no finds from the Tylos period were encountered (Insoll 2005).

Area	Region	I	II	III	IV	V
Abu Arshira	North-east			22		
Abu-Saybi	North/ Shakhoura	1	6	35		
Al-Hajar	North	62	31	41	1	6
Ali	Central	29	1	7	4	
Al-Manama Suq Magasis	North-east		3	1		
Al-Maqsha	North	9	4	9	1	11
Barbar	North-west	4				
Buri	Central		3	3		
Dar Kulayb	South-west			2	15	
Hamad Town	South-west	32	13	104	53	
Isa Town	Central	2		1		
Jannussan	North	7	1	2		
Karranah	North	23	1	22		
Karzakan	South-west	1		1		
Maqabah	North-west	1	2	6	2	
Shakhoura	North/ Shakhoura	39	90	287	3	
Saar	North-west	174	97	303	92	1
Um Al-Hasam	North-east	3	4	5	1	
Total		387	256	851	172	18

Table 360. *List of areas in which material from the Tylos period has been recovered by the Department for Archaeology and National Heritage and by foreign expeditions, and the general region where these areas are situated. The information is supplemented with the number of vessels from each period.*

Northern region and Shakhoura

In his account of the first year of the Danish excavations, Bibby described the landscape from Al-Manama along the new Budaiya Road:

"But after the village of Jidd Hafs the desert begins to intrude between the plantations and the road, and for the next three miles the route is bordered by a half-mile wide strip of sand. This long narrow stretch of desert is sown with countless tumuli – perhaps a thousand all told – of a very different character than the Bronze Age mounds..." (1954: 137).

These mounds have almost disappeared now; bulldozing and leisure digging took place before the establishment of the Department of Archaeology and National Heritage and after the Department had carried out numerous excavations in that area to clear land for developments. Now a few groups

of mounds still stand along the Budaiya Road, the largest being near the village of Shakhoura.

North of Budaya Road towards the coast and just south of the modern village of Janussan, there is a line of significantly higher mounds. French excavations have dated these mounds to the Tylos period and it has been suggested that they developed on top of older "clearings mounds" made of sand and rubble cleaned out from the allotments. Furthermore, a column capital was found, indicating that there may have been some kind of settlement in the vicinity. A dating of the capital to the second or third century AD has been suggested (Boulos 1984).

The cemeteries in the northern region (i.e. at Al-Maqsha, Al-Hajar, Jannussan, Jidd Hafs and Karranah) are near Qala'at al-Bahrain, which is the most significant settlement from the Tylos period so far identified on Bahrain. These cemeteries could have been used by the inhabitants of Qala'at al-Bahrain, although there could have been other settlements in the region. The cemeteries around Shakhoura and Abu-Saybi are situated more than 3 km from the settlement at Qala'at al-Bahrain and they were thus likely to have served another settlement and will be dealt with independently. Significant material from both the cemeteries closer to Qala'at al-Bahrain mentioned above and the Shakhoura and Abu-Saybi cemeteries, has been recovered.

A chronological system for Qala'at al-Bahrain in the Tylos period has been described by Højlund (Højlund & Andersen 1994; 1997) augmented by the present writer (Andersen 2001; 2002) and reviewed in this study (see pp. 214–216). It is evident that a significant corpus of material exists from the earliest Tylos periods at Qala'at al-Bahrain and until just after the beginning of our era, thereafter finds are few. No securely dated finds dating to the final part of the Tylos period and the earlier Islamic periods have been found, which strongly indicates that a hiatus in occupation occurred, probably from the fourth to perhaps the twelfth century AD. A Sasanian phase of the occupation of the so-called Coastal Fortress at Qala'at al-Bahrain has been suggested (Lombard & Kervran 1993: 137–138). The related pottery features only one sherd (*ibid.* fig. 16.1) which can be referred to the Sasanian period with some certainty, and the argument seems therefore at present to be rather unconvincing. The majority of finds relating to the fortress can be dated to the Islamic period (Højlund & Andersen 1994: 293; Frifelt 2001: 37–46). A collection of fine orange painted ware, datable to the third to fourth century AD, has been found at Qala'at al-Bahrain, but it is not related to any architecture (Højlund & Andersen: 1997: 213–215). Fragments of hard-fired ware, which have been identified from many trenches, are likely to be the remnants of the accompanying coarse ware (Andersen 2001). A capital, reused as building material for the walls at the Bahrain Fort, could belong to the Sasanian period, but no parallels have been found (Boulos 1984: 161).

North-western region

From the north-western region a very large quantity of material has been recovered mainly from cemeteries around the modern village of Saar where recent urban developments have required the removal of many mounds. North of Saar a mound has been excavated near Maqabah and another near the Barbar village.

The area west and south of Saar also featured a very large group of burial mounds from the Bronze Age, and south of the city a Bronze Age settlement and a burial complex of interlocking graves have been excavated (Killick & Moon 2005). On top of the burial complex, an isolated house or possibly a fire temple was excavated by the Department of Antiquities. Within a rectangular building a coin dating to the fifth century AD and a few sherds were recovered, but the amount of finds from this site is very limited (Crawford, Killick & Moon 1997: 20; Lombard & Kervran 1993: 138; Killick & Moon 2005: 2).

The pottery found above the Bronze Age Temple at Barbar indicates activity at the site from around the third century until the ninth or tenth century AD, and the recovery of some sculpture fragments indicates that the site could have been a place of some religious or secular importance, possibly in the third or fourth century AD (Andersen & Kennet 2003).

Central region

The material from the central area is limited, but since that area has not undergone vast development either before or after the establishment of the Department for Archaeology and National Heritage, and hardly any mounds dating to the Tylos period are visible in the landscape today, the few finds probably reflect that the area was not densely occupied in the Tylos period.[20]

---

[20] During surveys and visits to the area by the present writer, mounds with the irregular shape so typical of the tumuli dating to the Tylos period have not been seen, and Bahraini archaeologists have not mentioned the existence of such mounds.

South-western region

The south-western region was mainly excavated in the 1980s to clear land for the foundation of Hamad Town. This was created in a Bronze Age mound-landscape, but mounds from the Tylos period were scattered in between. Arable land is also present along the west coast, but the coastal plain is narrower than along the north coast, approximately 1–2 km. The cemeteries, both from the Tylos period and the Bronze Age are situated behind the fertile areas, whereas along the north coast the cemeteries from the Tylos period are scattered between the allotments. The most southerly area occupied in the Tylos period seems to be around the modern village of Dar Kulayb, which is situated halfway down the west coast.

The eastern and southern part of the island may have been in ancient times as deserted as it is now, with only some pastoralism and minor settlements around a few wells, and no cemeteries from the Tylos period have been excavated or reported in these regions.

Distribution of sites through time

By looking at the frequencies of dated finds from the regions defined above, a broad picture of the distribution of sites through time should develop. So far, only the settlement at Qala'at al-Bahrain has provided a chronological development, whereas the finds from Saar and Barbar are too few to attempt any detailed reconstruction of the development of the site. Assuming that the cemeteries from the northern region were used by the inhabitants from Qala'at al-Bahrain, the decline of that settlement from Phase III postulated above should be repeated in a decline of burials in the northern region.

Region	I	II	III	IV	V
North-east	3	7	28	1	
North	101	37	74	2	17
North / Shakhoura	40	96	322	3	
North-west	179	99	309	94	1
Central	31	4	11	4	
South-west	33	13	107	68	

Table 361. Number of datable finds from the various regions.

Region	I	II	III	IV	V
North-east	1%	3%	3%	1%	0%
North	26%	14%	9%	1%	94%
North / Shakhoura	10%	38%	38%	2%	0%
North-west	46%	39%	36%	55%	6%
Central	8%	2%	1%	2%	0%
South-west	9%	5%	13%	40%	0%

Table 362. Frequencies of datable finds from the various regions.

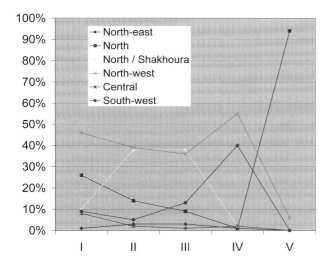

Fig. 624. Graph illustrating the development in various regions. The figures from Phase V are very tentative due to the few finds from that period.

From the figure above it is evident that the figures from the central and the north-east regions are constantly very low. It is likely that two different factors are responsible for that. Modern development in the north-east region before the establishment of the Department of Archaeology and National Heritage may have caused the destruction of many mounds there, whereas the central region is not as fertile as the coastal plains, and a less dense population is therefore likely to explain the relatively low numbers of burials in the Tylos period.

The north-west region has rich material through all periods and in Phase IV where the sites at Barbar and Saar indicate other activities, although it is still unclear if these sites were of a religious or a secular nature. The south-west region seems to have had its heyday in Phase IV with only relatively few finds in the earlier periods.

The northern region excluding the Shakhoura cemeteries illustrates a steady decline from producing

a third of the material in Phase I to producing only *c.* 2% in Phase IV. That corresponds very well with the impression from Qala'at al-Bahrain, where many finds can be dated to Phase I and II, a little to Phase III and IV and nothing to Phase V. The Shakhoura and Abu-Saybi cemeteries have produced many finds from Phases II and III, but declined rapidly between Phases III and IV.

Conclusion

In this chapter, two themes were investigated. Since we have a sequence of dated finds with different functions from various areas in Bahrain, it is now possible to illustrate developments in the composition of grave goods and possible settlement patterns.

The invention of glass-blowing and the following spread of the technique seems to have affected the composition of the grave goods. Glass flasks became the dominant choice as containers for unguents in Phase IV and glass tableware became more frequent as well. This was at a time when a production of glass in the East was well established (see pp. 96-97), which is likely to have affected the availability of such vessels in the Gulf region. However, glass seems only to replace pottery as a material, since an increased use of vessels used for personal adornment was noted from Phases I to III and thus prior to the period when glass became the preferred choice of grave goods.

It is evident that a change in the choice of grave goods took place during the Tylos period, where vessels used for eating were slowly being replaced with vessels associated with personal adornment. Together with the intermediate phase, where vessels associated with drinking were common, this development may indicate a change in notions of the afterlife. Initially it was most important to provide provision for the journey to the underworld (i.e. expressed in vessels associated with eating), then social life became important and equipment used for banquets became common grave goods (i.e. vessels associated with drinking). Finally, self-presentation in the group was emphasized by an increased number of vessels associated with personal adornment. This could indicate a graduate change from emphasising individuality towards more communal notions. The composition of the grave goods could thus indicate a change from an individual to a communal attitude towards the social aspect of burial. This hypothesis needs more evidence to be well founded, but other observations point in the same direction (see Salman & Andersen, forthcoming).

The tombs from the Tylos period are situated in relation to the fertile and arable coastal plains along the north and north-west coast of the main island of Bahrain, Awal. This corresponds well with the study of skeletal remains from the Hamad Town and Saar cemeteries conducted by Littleton (1998), since many skeletons showed deformations generated by physical work. The finds from the cemeteries around the ancient urban centre of Bahrain at Qala'at al-Bahrain illustrate a steady decline from Phases I to IV, which supports the interpretation of the pottery assemblage from the settlement (see pp. 214-216). However, both at Saar and Shakhoura, where a very significant proportion of the finds from Phase II and III in particular have been found, no settlements have been identified. A possibility of settlements being hidden under more recent and still occupied areas exists, but no obvious settlement sites are visible in relation to the cemeteries in Shakhoura and Saar, whereas other modern villages are situated on top of well-defined mounds. Very good examples of this can be seen in ed-Deir, on the island of Muharraq, Jidd Hafs, just south of Qala'at al-Bahrain and Dumistan on the west coast.

The historical reconstruction of the Tylos period

5

In the following, a reconstruction will be attempted of the historical setting in which the new burial tradition started, how it developed and became the main source of information of the period on Bahrain and how it declined and disappeared. Although directly comparable material from a large quantity of excavated tombs is lacking, a number of excavations and studies have provided information, making a reconstruction of the cultural and historical setting in eastern Arabia possible. However, the material has its limitations. Relevant written and archaeological evidence supplementing the results of the study of the glass and pottery vessels placed in the Bahraini tombs will be introduced and discussed in the following sections. The evidence presented is by no means intended to be a complete list of the work conducted in eastern Arabia, but it is most important for the understanding of the Tylos period on Bahrain.

The periods defined, on the basis of the analysis of the glass in Chapter 2, will form the framework but with some modifications, since the phasing of other sites and historical epochs/eras have other subdivisions. The first section will cover the period from the fourth century BC to the end of Phase I at around 50 BC. The next section will include both Phases II and III, i.e. the period from *c.* 50 BC until AD 150, and the last two sections deal with Phases IV (*c.* AD 150–450) and V (*c.* AD 450–700).

Eastern Arabia in the period from *c.* 400 to 50 BC

The Achaemenid and early Tylos periods on Bahrain are well attested in the archaeological remains from Qala'at al-Bahrain. That material shows that significant changes took place after the fall of the Achaemenids, and before discussing the origin of the burial tradition, which was introduced a century later, the situation on Bahrain and in eastern Arabia should be summarized.

Qala'at al-Bahrain in the Achaemenid and early Tylos periods

From the Achaemenid period (Period IVc–d in the Qala'at al-Bahrain pottery sequence) substantial finds were made at Qala'at al-Bahrain.[21] The city wall was maintained and a building with a clear defensive function was built up against the front of the city wall, east of the gate on the northern part (Højlund & Andersen 1994: 477–478). Inside the walls, a rather advanced urban architecture was revealed with houses made of well-cut ashlars and including toilets and underground drains. Although of different size, none of these houses was especially prominent and they must therefore be interpreted as houses for citizens (Højlund & Andersen 1997: 210–211). A hoard of silver weighing 1.2 kg found under the floor in one of the houses may indicate that the inhabitants of Qala'at al-Bahrain were fairly wealthy. The hoard consists of fragments of jewellery and ingots and some fragments of metal sheeting with letters in South Arabian script (Højlund & Andersen 1997: 175–182). Amongst other finds, which probably belonged to the occupants of these houses, *c.* 100 fragments of figurines, with the most common type being a horse or donkey often with a seated rider, should be mentioned. None of the animals was positively identified as camel (Højlund & Andersen 1997: 187–193). A complete variant of this type of figurine was found in the al-Maqsha cemetery just outside Qala'at al-Bahrain (Lombard 1999: fig. 202). Ten cuboid incense burners document the use of incense (Højlund & Andersen 1997: 183–186). In two houses in Danish Excavation 519, twenty-nine and ten "snake bowls" respectively were buried below the floors in two of the rooms. The vessels used for these offerings were common tableware stylistically closely related to Achaemenid metal vessels. Each vessel contained the skeleton of a snake and often between one and three beads, and sometimes another vessel served as a lid (Højlund & Andersen 1997: 134–144). Also below the floors in Excavations 519 and 520, several pot and bathtub burials were found (Højlund & Andersen 1994:

---

[21] A Period IVe does also belong in the Achaemenid period, but is only defined by a limited number of pot- and bathtub-burials (Højlund & Andersen 1997: 209).

364; 1997: 145–159). Burials within the city are a unique feature only seen in this very limited period at Qala'at al-Bahrain, but they were very common in Babylonia in the same period, and in the following centuries (Reuther 1968).

The evidence strongly indicates that Qala'at al-Bahrain in the Achaemenid period was a prosperous city with close ties to Babylonia, which was situated within the Achaemenid Empire, and also with connections to South Arabia. The caravan trade across the desert developed during the first half of the first millennium BC (Salles 1987: 89) and Bahrain is situated off the coast where one of the possible main routes from the south terminates. It is therefore quite possible that Qala'at al-Bahrain served as a port for ships bringing goods to the head of the Gulf and thus closer to the cities of Mesopotamia. The bathtub burials could well be the physical remains of a diaspora of Babylonian merchants or their descendants. Altogether, the finds from Qala'at al-Bahrain indicate that very close ties existed between Bahrain and the north. Bahrain could perhaps have been situated within the Achaemenid Empire, but no secure evidence exists for this hypothesis at present (Højlund & Andersen 1994: 478–479). An acceptable interpretation could be that Qala'at al-Bahrain was a Babylonian emporium playing a significant role in the trade and distribution of incense from South Arabia to Babylonia and other urban centres in the north. This trade may also have been supplemented with other commodities, local as well as imported.

The Greek conquest of the Achaemenid Empire was very quickly reflected in the material culture at Qala'at al-Bahrain. From the earliest Tylos period (Period Va1 in the Qala'at al-Bahrain pottery sequence) the pottery found in a pit deposit and dated to the first quarter of the third century, based on sherds of imported Attic black glazed vessels, illustrates that the new shapes brought to the Near East by the Greeks were quickly adopted by local potters. The wares, the manufacturing techniques and the functions were, however, the same as in Period IVd (Andersen 2002). This suggests that it was the same people as before, who produced and used these vessels, but responded quickly to fashion changes in the north. Period Va pottery has been found in the upper layers in the building with a military function built on the outside of the city wall in the Achaemenid period. Other finds, mainly of pottery from Period Va to Vc, were made in a smaller building inside the wall. During this period the city wall, which had been maintained and developed during the Achaemenid period was aban-

doned. A precise dating of this has not been made but in Period Vd, houses were built on the outside of the wall and the wall itself was heavily plundered (Højlund & Andersen 1994: 479). The finds from the early Tylos period at Qala'at al-Bahrain do not illustrate the same complexity as the material from the Achaemenid period, but seem to be much more modest. Furthermore, no bathtub burials can be assigned to the Tylos Period. It would appear that the settlement at Qala'at al-Bahrain began a decline after the fall of the Achaemenids. Apart from the pottery mentioned above very few other finds from this period at Qala'at al-Bahrain have been made. A few Greek inscriptions, or rather single words, have been found at Qala'at al-Bahrain, but dating to various periods.

A single outstanding find dates to the early Tylos Period and indicates that wealth was still accumulated at Qala'at al-Bahrain. A coin hoard dating to the end of the third century BC is the most important find from the Tylos period at Qala'at al-Bahrain. It consists of c. 300 silver coins of eastern Arabian issues imitating Alexander tetradrachms. They are of two series and the large number of dies used for striking the coins indicates that the minting was considerable. The coins of Type 1A illustrate a seated god on the reverse, but rather than being identified with Zeus, as he would be on the prototypes, a South Arabian inscription identifies him with *Shamash*, a sun god of Semitic origin popular among the Arabs (Callot 1994). The coin hoard from Qala'at al-Bahrain is not an isolated phenomenon, since we see an increased circulation of north-eastern Arabian coinage towards the end of the third century BC in north-eastern Arabia (Salles 1987: fig. 2c), suggesting that the region became monetarized following the Greek tradition. It has been suggested that some of these coins may have been struck on Bahrain (Callot 1994: 356), but taking the archaeological evidence into consideration Gerrha/Thaj may be a more likely place (see below). This was also originally suggested by Mørkholm (1973).

Thaj/Gerrha and the rise of a north-east Arabian entity

The City of Gerrha is well known from ancient sources and was said

> ...to be inhabited by Chaldaeans, exiles from Babylon.
> (Strabo 16.3.3).

Written evidence for trans-shipment of goods exists in Strabo's account of Gerrha. In this passage

Strabo is partly relying on Aristobulos, who was a contemporary of Alexander the Great.

> ... the Gerrhaeans traffic by land, for the most part, in Arabian merchandise and aromatics, though Aristobulus says, on the contrary, that the Gerrhaeans import most of their cargoes on rafts to Babylonia, and thence sail up the Euphrates with them, and then convey them by land to all parts of the country.
> (Strabo 16.3.3).

Gerrha seems to have benefited from a strategic position between the desert routes and the sea, which in principle is similar to the role of Qala'at al-Bahrain in the Achaemenid period (see above). It is likely that Gerrha also played a role in the caravan trade between South Arabia and the cities within the Achaemenid Empire, but the archaeological evidence is not yet as clear as on Bahrain. The above passage indicates that a change in trade pattern, from a transhipment of goods from caravan to ships to overland transport only, took place sometime after the fall of the Achaemenids and before Strabo was writing around the beginning of our era (Potts 1990: 91). This change from seaborne to overland transport may also explain the decline of Qala'at al-Bahrain as the position on the coast became less important.

A likely location of Gerrha is the site of Thaj, by far the most significant site that has been discovered within the possible location of Gerrha. No definite finds have yet proved this hypothesis and the question remains therefore unsolved (Potts 1990: 85–98). However, the site of Thaj is beyond discussion within the realm of Gerrha and the historical setting can safely be linked with the archaeological remains found there. The site is situated at a so-called *sabkha*, which is a salt flat, *c.* 90 km inland from the nearest accessible point on the coast of the Gulf and lying *c.* 160 km west-north-west of Dhahran. The main feature at the site is a large fortified settlement measuring *c.* 700 x 575 m with building remains within the walls. Traces of further buildings were noted to the south of the fortified settlement and to the north is the *sabkha*. Around the settlement are a vast number of tumuli and some stone-lined wells. In the 1960s the site was used seasonally by bedouins, who owned some ruined houses and palm groves (Bibby 1973: 10).

The site has been known by European scholars since the nineteenth century but systematic investigations were first carried out by a Danish expedition, which made brief surveys in 1962 and 1964, and followed in 1968 by a larger survey and exploratory excavations at the site (Bibby 1973: 10–28, 1996: 222–236). These investigations shed light on the construction of the city wall, documented occupation and destruction layers and produced a vast amount of finds, notably pottery fragments, figurines and offering bowls. One of the tumuli also underwent investigation, and a tomb orientated north–south and made of ashlars was found. It had been previously robbed, but a stone plate inscribed with South Arabian script was reused for the construction (1973: 25–26). Similar inscriptions have been found earlier and later and a rather significant corpus now exists. They have been dated on palaeographic evidence to the period from *c.* 350–100 BC and are mainly funeral inscriptions (Potts 1990: 69–85). In 1983, a team from Freie Universität Berlin in co-operation with the Saudi Arabian Department of Antiquities conducted further excavations at Thaj. Probably the most important discovery were sherds of Attic black glazed pottery found in the foundation trench for the city wall, dating it to after *c.* 300 BC (Potts 1990; 1993a). These excavations have been followed by investigations conducted by the Saudi Arabian Department of Antiquities (Eskoubi & al-Aila 1985).

The dating of Thaj is problematic. The local pottery found in the excavations in the settlement seems to be quite coherent, indicating that the site did not have a long lifespan as a major settlement. Potts tried to describe a sequence but the numbers of each type are very low and the typological development is not clear. His periods I–III were also assigned to the Seleucid era, whereas Period IV was suggested to extend into the first century AD. The dating of this later phase was mainly suggested due to an apparent similarity between Roman sigillatae cups and a type of local pottery closely related to Type X bowls in sand-tempered ware (1993a). This is, however, unlikely since thin-walled bowls in sand-tempered ware predate the sigillatae cups (see Chapter 3). There seems, rather, to be a general absence of both Greek and Roman influence on the style of the pottery from Thaj, unlike the pottery from Bahrain. As well as the local pottery, there is a large group of sherds of Attic black glazed pottery (Bibby 1973: fig. 6; Potts 1993: pl. 2a; and an unpublished surface collection stored at Moesgård Museum). The great majority of these sherds can be dated to the late fourth or first half of the third century BC. A large quantity of figurines of mainly two types has been found. One group represents animals (camels) and the other humans (females) (Bibby 1973: 17–19). The style and rendering of the female figurines are close to figurines common in Mesopotamia since the Bronze Age (e.g. Hoffmann 1996: nos 4–8). A few Roman and Sasanian coins found on the surface document later activities, but they have not been associated with stratified material or architectural remains (Potts 1990: 203). Recently a team from the Saudi Arabian Department of Antiquities excavated a tumulus in the Thaj Oasis. They found an unrobbed tomb with spectacular grave goods, including a gold mask, probably dating to the first century AD (al-Hashash *et al.* 2001). The grave construction was similar to the one excavated by the Danes.

The above evidence suggests that a new political and cultural entity in north-east Arabia was established in Thaj in the third century BC. This entity was a highly developed organization capable of constructing major public works such as a 2.5 km-long city wall and importing Attic pottery, among other wares. The inhabitants buried their dead in hundreds of stone-lined cists each with a tumulus, which together must have made a significant impact on the landscape. Commercial contacts between Bahrain and Gerrha are indicated by the coin hoard from Qala'at al-Bahrain, but it appears that the urban structure at Thaj, e.g. the city wall, was constructed when similar structures at Qala'at al-Bahrain began to be neglected. It could very well be that the inhabitants of Thaj took over the trade and redistribution of goods centred on the Babylonian emporium at Qala'at al-Bahrain in the Achaemenid period.

Failaka and the Seleucids

It has been suggested that the Seleucids inherited the Gulf region and thus Bahrain after the Achaemenids, and paid an active interest in the trade by securing the waters with a fleet and founding colonies (Salles 1987: 89). Nevertheless, there is very little concrete evidence for this along the east Arabian coastline, apart from the foundation of the fortress on the island of Failaka off the Kuwaiti coast.

First Danish, and later French, excavations have uncovered a fortress with temples on Failaka. The most significant architectural remains are a walled enclosure with square turrets (the fortress). Two temples were found inside. Temple A was built as a typical Greek temple with some oriental details in the rendering of the architectural ornaments. Temple B seems to have been less decorated and was built after Temple A. From Failaka there is written evidence of sanctuaries for Artemis, Apollon and "Soteria",

which could be a surname for Artemis, but has also been associated with other female deities. The most important was, however, Artemis (Jeppesen 1960). The remaining open space within the enclosure was slowly used to build dwellings (1989). Outside the fortress three other structures have been found, the "terracotta workshop" and two sanctuaries. The finds from Failaka illustrate a mixture of Greek and Oriental elements (Salles 1987: 84–85).

The chronology has been outlined in L. Hannestad's study of the pottery from the Hellenistic fortress (F5). She described two assemblages of pottery representing two periods of occupation. The first period was dated by a coin hoard dating to the late third century BC, stamped Rhodian amphora handles dated to 225–200 BC and finally two Attic black glazed sherds, one of which can be dated to 285–250 BC. She suggested that Period I lasted from "around or not much before the middle of the 3rd century BC to the very late 2nd or early 1st century BC", and the construction of the fortress was thus dated to "around or not much before the middle of the 3rd century BC". The second period is defined by a limited collection of pottery found in the upper levels in the area in front of Temple A and tentatively dated to the beginning of our era (Hannestad 1983). Generally, a foundation date of the fortress to the middle of the first half of the third century BC has been accepted (Hannestad 1994: 590).

The most important find on Failaka was a long inscription, which documents that Alexander the Great's successors in the East, the Seleucids, had direct interests in the island (Jeppesen 1989: 82–114). The dating of the inscription has been disputed, but most scholars accept a dating around the initial dating suggested by Jeppesen, i.e. *c.* 240 BC (Hannestad 1994: 587). A passage in the inscription mentions that the moving of the temple, which was the main topic of the inscription, was the intention of the ancestors of the Seleucid king, who actually ordered it. This evidence indicates that Seleucid interests on Failaka did begin sometime before *c.* 240 BC and could be connected with the foundation of the fortress (Hannestad 1994: 591). Similarities between the pottery from Qala'at al-Bahrain and Failaka, the known Seleucid interest on Failaka and a tentative interpretation that levels below the so-called Coastal Fortress at Qala'at al-Bahrain belong to a Seleucid fortress, led Salles to suggest the existence of a Seleucid naval base or garrison on Bahrain (1987: 102–105). This view is questioned by Potts, as he argues that there is no evidence of Bahrain being a dependency of the Seleucid Kingdom and the Hellenistic influence is only a result of Bahrain's position close to Hellenized western Asia (Potts 1990: 152–52). Nevertheless, in the publication of the finds from Excavation 520 Højlund maintains the hypothesis put forward by Salles, and argues that the similarities between Failaka and Bahrain and the difference between Bahrain and Thaj indicate that Bahrain was under Seleucid supremacy (Højlund & Andersen 1994: 480).

It has now been documented that the coastal fortress was not a Seleucid foundation, but dates to the Sasanian period (Lombard & Kervran 1993) or the Islamic period (Højlund & Andersen 1994: 293) and therefore cannot support the hypothesis of a Seleucid presence. The only similarities we have in the third century BC are in fact the similarities of the local pottery, a handful of fragments of Attic black glazed sherds and the existence of coin hoards in both places. The hoards consist of mainly east Arabian coins, although the hoards from Failaka did contain Seleucid issues too. Any positive evidence for an active Seleucid presence on Bahrain in the third century BC has not been found. That the pottery in Bahrain and Failaka shares great similarities cannot be any surprise as pots are easily transportable in large quantities by ship, whereas overland transport to an inland site e.g. Thaj, can be regarded as much more expensive and not relevant for any quantities of inexpensive goods. In the collections of ceramics from the two sites a notable difference also exists, which may hint that the socio-cultural situation was different at the two sites. Lamps are common finds on Failaka (Hannestad 1983: 73), but extremely rare on Bahrain. The above does, however, not exclude the possibility of a Seleucid governor sitting on Bahrain with a small garrison. No tombs, which could serve as prototypes for the Bahraini ones, have been found on Failaka.

The tombs and their origin

The pottery vessels from the earliest phase of the tombs (Phase I), indicate that this phase should be dated to the period from *c.* 200 to 50 BC and illustrates a mixture of Arabian, Greek and Mesopotamian stylistic traditions.

The prototypes for the tombs introduced to Bahrain are likely to be found in the new political and cultural entity in north-east Arabia. In Thaj, we have evidence of stone-lined cists covered by a tumulus and dating, on palaeographic evidence, from probably the late fourth century BC (Potts 1990: 69–85). These tombs are very similar to the earliest tombs on Bahrain (see Salman & Andersen, forthcoming,

for a more detailed description of the tombs). It would be reasonable to suggest that the contacts - commercial, political or private - between Bahrain and Thaj/Gerrha influenced the choice of burial tradition made by the inhabitants of Bahrain or, more likely, by a segment of the population. The introduction of a new burial tradition probably in the late third or early second century BC on Bahrain can be understood in relation to the state formations in eastern Arabia indicated by the coins and written evidence presented above. Tombs similar to the ones from Bahrain have been found along the northeast coast of Saudi Arabia (Bowen 1950; Potts *et al.* 1978: 18), supporting the notion that the tradition was related to some sort of state formation and/or ethnic grouping in north-east Arabia. Although the general concept of an individual tomb with a tumulus can reflect relations with Thaj, elements attested in the Bahraini tombs do not find parallels in the rather limited material published from cemeteries in north-east Arabia. For instance, tombstones of a simple anthropomorphic type were used on Bahrain in this phase (see Figure 625). They most frequently have a rectangular body with concave sides and a round or oval piece on top forming a head. Two of these tombstones have been inscribed in Greek. The inscriptions give the names and patronymics of the deceased. The names are Semitic, one inscription also gives the year and probably the ethnic origin of the deceased, as line 3 reads "of Alexandria". However, that line is very worn and the reading insecure. The year is 195 and most likely in the Seleucid era giving a date of 118/117 BC (Gatier, Lombard & al-Sindi 2002: 226–229). The other inscription states that the deceased was a captain (*ibid.* 2002: 229). Related tombstones have been found in Yemen in funeral contexts tentatively dated to the third to second century BC (Vogt 2002: nos 265, 267) and in Phoenicia related pieces have been reported from Lebanon (Sader 2005: nos 9, 50). Further away, closely related tombstones are also known from Chersonesos on the Crimea peninsula (Ivanova, Cubova & Kolesnikova 1976: nos 113–118) where the type has been dated to the fourth to second century BC and traditionally taken as evidence of Hellenistic influence (Kolesnikova 1977), although this dating is currently debated (V. Stolba, pers. communication, 2005). Nevertheless, anthropomorphic tombstones appear not to have been used in Thaj, where inscriptions were preferred. Elements of the material culture of north-east Arabia and Bahrain in particular can be traced to the Greek world and the Seleucid Empire, and also to Babylonian traditions and South Arabia. This is not surprising, since similar developments on the fringes of the desert can be seen in Petra and Palmyra where nomads settled and developed urban civilizations using components and stylistic expressions from foreign civilizations (cf. Colledge 1976; Odenthal 1983; Weber & Wenning 1997).

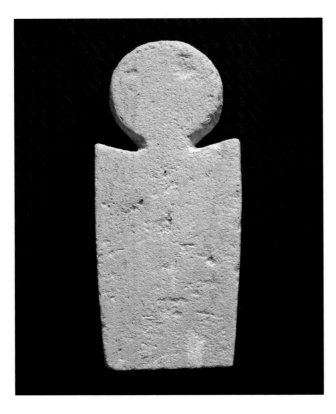

Figure 625. Tombstone of the simple anthropomorphic type from the mound fill of Shakhoura, Mound 1-1991-92, Trench B6.

This process may have continued on Bahrain, as it is evident that the strong relation, which existed in the Achaemenid period between people living in Qala'at al-Bahrain and in the cities to the north, was continued to some extent, and surely a knowledge of Greek/Macedonian burial traditions could have affected some aspects. But where, for instance, the temples on Failaka were Greek in their idea, but elaborated with Oriental architectural details, the burials on Bahrain may have been Arabian in their core, but spiced with a few Greek components.

Mleiha and the settlement pattern on Bahrain
The site of Mleiha in the UAE has produced a significant proportion of evidence. Earlier works by an Iraqi team have been published (Taha 1974; Madhloom 1974) and although the more recent French excavations are not yet published in full, their results have recently been summarized in a first

volume (Mouton 1999: 9–32). The occupation has been divided into five phases and covers the period from late Iron Age[22] to the third or fourth century AD, and thus spans several phases of the Bahraini tombs. From Phase I at Mleiha,[23] only a few sherds in coarse ware have been recovered from layers below the more substantial layers of Mleiha II. Very quickly, the site reached its maximum extent of *c.* 1.5 x 1 km during Mleiha II and was built up with lightly-built dwellings where only the post holes remain. This was not the local building technique in the previous period, where mud brick was the preferred material for houses in the small villages that were scattered all over the UAE. These villages disappeared probably during Mleiha II and so far Mleiha is the only known settlement from this period in the UAE. However, mud bricks were used to build tombs, constructed as massive towers with a quadrangular plan, decorated with crenellated battlements and covering a rectangular underground burial chamber. The burial chambers were intended for individual burials, which were richly furbished with weapons and various imported objects. Around these premier tombs, less elaborate burials were placed. The phase has been dated to the third century (or possibly only the second half) and the first half of the second century BC. The dating was mainly based on stamped Rhodian amphora handles and moulded glass of eastern and east Mediterranean origin. The change in settlement pattern between the Iron Age cultures and the rise of Mleiha has been understood as the result of migration from central Arabia to the periphery of the desert, with parallel developments in Petra in Jordan and Qaryat al-Fau in south-west Saudi Arabia where architectural features of the tombs are similar. This is believed to indicate a common origin for the people living at these sites (Mouton 1999: 21).

The relation between south-east and north-east Arabia has been discussed in a recent review of coinage from south-east Arabia. It was suggested that northeast merchants acted as intermediaries in the trade between south-east Arabia and the West in this early period because of the lack of a harbour in southeast Arabia (Haerinck 1998). It appears, therefore, that the north-east entity centred at Gerrha/Thaj gained increased commercial and political influence not only in the coastal areas of north-east Arabia

---

[23] The chronological periods at Mleiha have also been called "Phases" and to avoid confusion with the Bahraini phases, the ones at Mleiha will be termed Mleiha I, II etc, instead of Phase I, II etc.

and Bahrain, but extended its influence in the whole of east Arabia in the century following the fall of the Achaemenids.

A significant proportion of finds dating to Phase I of the Bahraini tombs was found in the Saar cemeteries, where no settlements of this period have been identified in the vicinity. Nor have any finds dating to the Achaemenid and earliest Tylos periods been published, although significant remains from the Bronze Age have been uncovered (the Saar Settlement and numerous cemeteries). This indicates that a new settlement must have been founded, but it was of a nature such that there are very few remains, if any at all. The foundation and nature of the settlement at Mleiha provides us with a contemporary model, which could be a convincing explanation for the lack of identified settlements adjacent to most of the Bahraini cemeteries. Due to a much denser population on Bahrain than in the UAE since antiquity, the few remains (e.g. post holes from lightly-built dwellings) are likely to have been disturbed and erased. Domestic rubbish spread by intense cultivation over the past 2000 years is likely never to enter the archaeological record. The lack of identified settlements on Bahrain cannot be a surprise, if they were of a nature similar to what has been revealed at Mleiha. It has been suggested that the people settling at Mleiha migrated from central Arabia, and the sites of Petra and Qaryat al-Fau were founded on the same process. Indeed, migrations from the Najd region to the coastal areas are well-known phenomena, evident in historical sources and linguistic components of modern Arabia (Holes 2006). However, a significant difference existed between south-east and north-east Arabia in the third century BC, since in the north-east a well-organized entity existed, which was probably centred in Thaj. This entity could interact with possible immigrants, whereas in the UAE the immigrants may have been able to maintain and develop their own traditions more independently of previous conditions. The rarity of weapons in the Bahraini tombs is in sharp contrast to burials on the Oman peninsula where weapons are common grave goods (see Yule 2001; Haerinck 2001). This evidence supports the view that cultural differences existed between the inhabitants of north-east and south-east Arabia.

Antiochos III and the Characenian Kingdom

It has been suggested that the Seleucid kings followed an Achaemenid policy, practised in inaccessible areas in Anatolia, Iran and north Arabia, of not attempting to conquer and bring these areas under direct rule. Rather, they preferred a system of "gift-giving" and provision of military contingents from those areas, which in return maintained their freedom (Sherwin-White & Kuhrt 1993: 17–18, 97).

In 205 BC, Antiochos III was said to have paid a visit to Gerrha:

> The Gerraeans begged the king not to abolish the gifts the gods had bestowed on them, perpetual peace and freedom. The king, when the letter had been interpreted to him, said that he granted their request…
> When their freedom had been established, the Gerraeans passed a decree honouring Antiochus with the gift of five hundred talents of silver, a thousand talents of frankincense and two hundred talents of the so-called "stacte". He then sailed to the island of Tylus and left for Seleucia. The spices were from the Persian Gulf.
> (Polybius 13.9.4–5).

This episode has been understood by others as the Seleucids obtaining control over north-east Arabia (Callot 1994) and a recently discovered stele with an inscription could support that view. The stele was found during the 1996–1997 excavation of Mound A1 in Shakhoura where it was reused as the capstone of a tomb dating to the time around the beginning of our era (Gatier, Lombard & Al-Sindi 2002; Salman & Andersen, forthcoming).

> In the name of King Hyspaosinos and of Queen Thalassia, Kephisodoros, strategos of Tylos and of the Islands (has dedicated) the temple, to the Dioscuri Saviours, in ex-voto. (Gatier, Lombard & Al-Sindi 2002: 223)

The dedicatory inscription from Shakhoura tells us that there was a temple (or shrine) on Bahrain to the Dioscuri Saviours, who were the Greek protectors of seafarers. The inscription was written in Greek, and the name of the governor was Kephisodoros, which is of Greek origin (derived from the river Κηφισός, Fick 1894: 161). This indicates that in the second half of the second century BC at least a segment (which may be confined to only the governor and a garrison) of the population on Bahrain read Greek and worshipped the Greek pantheon.

King Hyspaosinos was the founder of the Characenian kingdom in southern Mesopotamia in the middle of the second century BC and the inscription thus documents that Bahrain was under Characenian supremacy at that time; it has therefore been suggested that the Characenian kingdom inherited the Gulf region from the Seleucids (Gatier, Lombard & Al-Sindi 2002). In any case, the evidence suggests that sometime before or in the middle of the second century, Bahrain came under direct Mesopotamian rule. At the same time, it appears that Thaj declined, since most datable finds date to the Seleucid era and only sporadic evidence attests to activities in the following centuries, as noted above.

Eastern Arabia in the period from *c.* 50 BC to AD 150

The burial tradition of the Tylos period is now well established on Bahrain. Although Phases II and III are rather short periods, a very significant proportion of the grave goods dates to these periods. The frequency of grave goods (glass and pottery vessels) from the cemeteries around Qala'at al-Bahrain declines, whereas grave goods from Shakhoura become much more abundant. The variety of grave goods in Phases II and III illustrates a change from Phase I, since vessels associated with drinking became relatively popular.

In Phase II, glass vessels from the eastern Mediterranean region began to be placed in the tombs. These vessels are widely distributed types from just before the invention of glass-blowing and very early blown types. In Phase III, glass vessels became common grave goods. They are also well dated, imported vessels and this phase can be safely dated to the period from the middle of the first century AD to the middle of the second century AD. A new range of shapes in glazed ware was introduced on Bahrain in Phase II and the other wares almost went out of use. The new shapes rely on prototypes in terra sigillatae and other Mediterranean wares, and the situation in the typological development of the pottery seems comparable to the earliest Tylos period, where inspiration from Greek/Attic pottery has been well documented (Hannestad 1983). This continues in Phase III, where the pottery was mainly glazed ware and most of the new types assigned to this phase rely on prototypes from the West, although a few cannot be understood as developments of earlier types or to have been inspired by Roman pottery.

The Characenian kingdom

Characenian interest in Bahrain may have continued from the middle of the second century BC, where the Shakhoura inscription cited above documents the existence of a Characenian governor on Bahrain, until at least the beginning of the second century AD. This is indicated by a bilingual inscription in Greek and Palmyrene discovered at the Palmyrene Agora during the 1939–1940 season of excavation.

> Iaraios son of Nebouzabad son of Salamallath son of Akkadanos and citizen in the Hadrianic Palmyra, Satrap over the Thilouans for Meredatos, King of Spasinou Charax – The merchants in Spasinou Charax (dedicated this) in his honour, in the month of April, year 442. (Seyrig 1941: 253 [PAT 1374, Inv. 1038]. Author's translation)

The dedication was made in 442 in the Seleucid era (AD 131) to honour a Palmyrene citizen, but the most important part was his title as the Characenian satrap of the Thilouans. Herzfeld pointed out the interpretation of the Thilouans as the inhabitants of Tylos (1968: 62) and this interpretation is now generally accepted (Potts 1990: 146). Another Palmyrene inscription may also refer to the Thilouans, but is badly preserved (T. Keizer, pers. communication, 2005).

Rome's eastern trade

The beginning of Phase II and the Roman imports and influence on style, in the middle of the first century BC corresponds well with the eastern expansion of the Roman Empire. The increased import of east Mediterranean glassware and the adoption of Roman types of pottery by local potters could well be the result of increased contacts between northeast Arabia and the Roman Empire. Since we have no evidence for an active Roman policy in eastern Arabia, the driving force of the contacts is likely to have been commercial. We have very good written evidence for trade between eastern Arabia and the Mediterranean via the Nabataeans or via the Characenian kingdom in southern Mesopotamia and Palmyra (Schuol 2000; Young 2001). At this time, the north-east Arabian entity may have lost some importance. Coins of north-east Arabian issues are rare (Callot 1994), and the urban centre at Thaj seems not to have produced the same quantity of finds as before. On the other hand perhaps Characenian influence and control had been strengthened, since the south Mesopotamian kingdom benefitted from the loose federation of the Parthian Empire (Frye 2000: 18). Furthermore, the kingdom was situated in a strategic position on one of the main roads between East and West where ships with goods from India entered the Mesopotamian rivers and caravan tracks (and were thus taxable), on their way to the new Roman markets with their many consumers. In this setting Bahrain happened to play a role in Rome's eastern trade, being on the road to India, but also the possible provider of transport, seamen and pearls. In return, they obtained luxury items, which were often placed in the tombs, and also a good knowledge of life and fashions in the Roman Empire. Some aspects were adopted, as indicated by the *andron* excavated at Qala'at al-Bahrain and dating to this period, and the large number of drinking cups and jugs being placed in the tombs. The impression from the tombs is that society on Bahrain, or that segment of society represented in the tombs, was egalitarian and could afford some splendour in its burial practices, but was also heavily involved in physical work, as indicated by the analyses of skeletal remains (Littleton 1998).

In south-east Arabia, a situation similar to the one on Bahrain has been found. In Mleiha, mud bricks were now being used for building houses. They were enclosed units, separated by "a few dozen metres" (Mouton 1999: 23). Funerary monuments also became larger and now had one or two chambers with an access passage and stairs. The superstructures at the beginning of the period were not that well preserved and it is not possible to say if they were towers, as in the previous period, or platforms. Later in the period, installations for funeral ceremonies were built instead of the towers (Mouton 1999). A settlement was founded at ed-Dur towards the end of the first century BC. The chronology of the site has been discussed in Chapters 2 and 3 and can be summarized into a main phase dating from the late first century BC to the beginning of the second century AD and a second occupation dating to the third century AD, although there may have been limited activities between the two phases (see Chapter 2). The main occupational phase at ed-Dur is characterized by a modest settlement situated in-between the tombs. These are single tombs quite similar to the ones on Bahrain, or vaulted subterranean tombs intended for collective burials. The two types seem to have been used at the same time. Ed-Dur and Mleiha are believed to have been closely integrated, ed-Dur being a coastal site providing food from the sea and harbour facilities, whereas Mleiha provided agricultural products. They may thus have formed one entity (Haerinck 2001: 4). A lot of glass from the eastern Roman Empire has been found at ed-Dur and so have fragments of terra sigillatae.

It has been suggested that the merchants from the south-east entity centred in Mleiha and ed-Dur became independent from north-east Arabian intermediaries, who were now bypassed, and south-east merchants played a more direct role in seaborne trade (Haerinck 1998: 25). Comparing the evidence from the UAE with the available material from north-east Arabia, i.e. the settlements at Qala'at al-Bahrain and Thaj, and the coins, this conclusion seems very reasonable. The information brought to light from the Bahraini tombs indicates, however, that the general economic situation in south-east and north-east Arabia was, indeed, very similar in the late first century BC and first century AD and both areas seemed to prosper from international trade, as indicated by the fairly large quantity of imported objects.

From the first century AD, we have an abundance of evidence for Roman trade with India (Meyer 1992; Turner & Cribb 1996; Young 2001) and the prosperity in eastern Arabia indicated by the archaeological remains can well be assumed to be the result of the local economy being stimulated by the international trade passing through the Gulf.

Religious beliefs in eastern Arabia in the Seleucid and Parthian periods

The simple anthropomorphic tombstones are still used in Phases II and III, but new types were being introduced in this period. One type finds its nearest parallels in reliefs from Palmyra, whereas another type relies on the iconography of Phoenician tombstones. This type illustrates a male figure in frontal pose, with his right arm raised with the palm forward and the left hand holding the drapery (Figure 626). The rendering of a few of the faces is closely related to late Parthian sculpture (see Lombard 1999: no. 361), but the iconography does not find any precise parallels in Mesopotamia. However, exact parallels are common in Phoenician cemeteries both in the eastern Mediterranean region (e.g. Louvre inv. no. AO 29410 from Syria), but also in the western colonies as for instance Carthage (Moscati 2001: 367). This is particularly interesting since Strabo, who writes around the beginning of our era and thus exactly in Phase II, observes a connection between Tylos and Phoenicia:

> On sailing farther, one comes to other islands, I mean Tyre and Aradus, which have temples like those of the Phoenicians. It is asserted, at least by the inhabitants of the islands, that the islands and cities of the Phoenicians which bear the same names are their own colonies. (Strabo 16.3.4)

Nevertheless, evidence for religious beliefs in Bahrain in the Tylos period is very limited. For the earlier half of the Tylos period (Phases I to III/c. 300 BC–AD 150) we only have the dedication inscription by Kephisodoros documenting a cult for the Dioscuri Saviours and the passage by Strabo cited above. A bronze plaque attached to a wooden plank depicting Asklepios, the Greek god of medicine, was found off the northern coast of Bahrain (Vine 1993: 63). Together with the temples to Artemis and Apollon on Failaka, where the cult may have continued at this time, these discoveries indicate that at least a part of the Greek pantheon was worshipped in the Gulf region. The use of "Charon's" coin also indicates some knowledge of Greek notions of death and burial, but this is not conclusive (see Penglase 1995; Salman & Andersen, forthcoming).

Figure 626. Tombstone of the "Phoenician" type from the mound fill of Shakhoura, Mound 1-1992-93, Trench J3.

The east Arabian coins of Type 1A found at Qala'at al-Bahrain imitating Alexander's tetradrachms illustrate a seated god on the reverse, but rather than being identified with Zeus, as he would be on the prototypes, a South Arabian inscription identifies him with *Shamash*, a sun god of Semitic origin (Callot 1994: 335). *Shamash* is also known from ed-Dur where a temple was dedicated to him (Haerinck, Metdepenninghen & Stevens 1991: 32–39). Although the stelae using a distinctive Phoenician iconography are difficult to date precisely, they also belong to this period. On their own, they are insufficient to document the adoption of aspects of east Mediterranean religious beliefs. Together with the statement by Strabo (16.3.4) and the evidence of cults for Mediterranean deities mentioned above, the presence of "Phoenician"-type tombstones could perhaps indicate that the contacts with the Mediterranean region had an impact upon the lives of the inhabitants of Bahrain beyond just providing a bit of exotic luxury. However, "local" deities still played a significant role in eastern Arabia and the degree of adoption of east Mediterranean beliefs may not have gone further than the use of stylistic and iconographic elements in a local context, as illustrated by the coins. The "Phoenician" stelae seem to be confined in eastern Arabia to Bahrain, indicating that more local ethnic or religious groupings developed.

Eastern Arabia in the period from *c.* AD 150 to 450

Between Phases III and IV, significant changes took place and a hiatus in the material may be present in the second and third century AD. However, the same cemeteries remained in use and the overall variety of grave goods did not change, although unguentaria became more frequent. At the beginning of the period a few tombstones may still have been made, since the style of the rendering of some of the faces relies on late Parthian sculpture, but the tradition of tombstones appears to die out.

Decline in Rome's eastern trade?

Toward the end of the first century AD or in the first half of the second century AD, it appears that close contact with the Mediterranean came to a sudden halt. Thereafter we no longer find the abundance of Roman wares or their important influence on the style of the pottery, and the few finds now originate in the region to the east of the Roman Empire. A similar picture has been described for the typological development of Parthian sculpture, which originated stylistically in the Greek tradition, but developed an independent expression towards the end of the Parthian rule (Mathiesen 1992: 14). However, not only did the style and possible origin of the grave goods change, the number of grave goods also fell significantly and few grave goods were placed in the tombs in the second and third century AD. It would appear that the whole pattern of trade and distribution changed, and the inhabitants on Bahrain no longer received the same share of the profit as in the previous periods. Multiple burials and the reuse of tombs became very common (Salman & Andersen, forthcoming), perhaps indicating that the resources available for building new tombs were limited. Another possibility is indicated by the composition of the grave goods, which may document a change from an individual to a communal attitude to burials (see the end of Chapter 4). The cemeteries remained the same as before, however, and a radical change in belief and thus burial custom seems not to have taken place. A decline in the number of finds also occurred at ed-Dur and Mleiha and possibly in most of eastern Arabia, indicating that the pattern was regional rather than an isolated phenomenon on Bahrain (Kennet 2005).

It has been suggested that the trade and economic development was moved to the Iranian coast by the Sasanians (Howard-Johnston 1995). Nevertheless, it is not possible to explain the changes in eastern Arabia with the rise of the Sasanians, since they only came to power in the second quarter of the third century AD and thus a century later than the beginning of the recession on the Arabian side.

Most of the commodities imported to the Roman Empire from the East would not have been preserved in the archaeological record, but many of the best precious stones used for engraved gems and intaglios have been imported from the East (Hening 1978: 31), and it has been observed that, "Gems enjoyed great popularity in the early imperial times..." (Richter 1956: 61). Looking at the very large cameos often used for royal portraiture (e.g. the Gemma Augustea) the number of preserved ones from the first century AD also seems much higher than from the following century. In the third and fourth centuries AD, they seemed to have gained some popularity again (based on a count in Richter 1971: 91–128).[24]

The trade routes may have been affected by Parthian intervention in the Characenian Kingdom in the middle of the second century AD (Young 2001). The possible decline of Roman imports of eastern products in the second century AD, as indicated by the engraved gems, and the decline of imports from the Roman Empire in eastern Arabia could thus be understood as a result of the trade routes via the Gulf being cut off. However, two main routes existed for the Roman trade with India: one was via the Gulf and the other via Egypt and the Red Sea (see Chapter 2). As security against the Gulf route being cut off, the Red Sea route should have been developed and would thus have prospered to accommodate increased trade, but one of the two main ports in Egypt (Myos Hormus) was also abandoned, most likely during the second century AD (Meyer 1992), and only the harbour at Berenike remained in use. On the other hand there is evidence that a canal between the upper Red Sea and the Nile delta was being restored by the emperor Trajan (AD 98–117) (Sidebotham 1996: 291–292). Finally, numismatic evidence from India indicates that most trade with the West dates to the first half of the first century AD (Turner & Cribb 1996: 318). The above evidence altogether suggests that the trade between Rome and the East had its heyday in the first century AD and declined afterwards.

A decline in the demand of eastern products by Roman consumers would be a very simple and obvious explanation, and indeed likely, since the Romans at the beginning of the second century AD would have been accustomed to eastern products, which therefore may no longer have possessed the same aura of luxury, as they had a century earlier.

The Sasanian influence

In previous periods, Roman types inspired the style of the pottery, and the glass vessels were of well-distributed types, where types similar to the ones found on Bahrain have been found throughout the Roman Empire. In Phase IV, the distribution pattern of glass changed and the vessels only find parallels in the eastern Mediterranean region and the East. The style of the pottery also changed, since the imitation of Roman types stopped and a new fabric, i.e. the hard-fired ware, was introduced with a new range of shapes.

It is likely that at some point Bahrain came under Sasanian supremacy, and was periodically ruled indirectly via the Lakhmid at al-Hira (Frye 1983; Potts 1990: 150–152; Morony 2001–2002: 26). We know of at least two possible occasions where Sasanian kings directed military expeditions against Arabia, the first being Ardasir's campaign in c. AD 240 against north-eastern Arabia (al-Tabari 1999: 15–16) and the other the campaign by Sapur II in c. AD 325, which was led in retaliation to an Arabian campaign along the Persian coast (1999: 50–56). Since the shapes of some of the vessels in hard-fired

---

[24] I am grateful to Prof. Niels Hannestad (University of Aarhus) for pointing out the chronological development of the quantity and quality of engraved gems within the Roman Empire.

ware rely on prototypes from Iran, i.e. the Type CI beaker in hard-fired ware, it is likely that the expansion of the Sasanian Empire affected the material culture in the Gulf region from the third century AD.

The trade may also have increased again in late antiquity, although it never reached the quantity of the first century AD. The lack of distinctive second- and third-century AD glass vessels in the Gulf material and the possibility of all vessels of Phase IV being of a fourth-century AD date, suggests that during this period there was again an increase in trade, which is also indirectly indicated by the increased number of late antique gems, as mentioned above. Economic activities in the Gulf in the fourth century AD are furthermore attested by Ammianus Marcellinus, a contemporary Roman historian, who wrote:

> All along the coast is a throng of cities and villages, and many ships sail to and fro. (23.6.11)

The Bahraini evidence may thus provide the key for a more detailed understanding of the economic development in the Gulf in the Sasanian period.

Changing settlement patterns in eastern Arabia

The south-west cemeteries have produced most finds from this period, but many vessels have also been found in the north-west region. Although the general picture is of decline and recession in Phase IV, we also find new foundations of possible settlements at Saar, Barbar and Qala'at al-Bahrain. These seem not to be farmers' dwellings, since the walls at Saar look too massive to be those of an ordinary house and fragments of a human-sized sculpture were recovered at Barbar. At Qala'at al-Bahrain fragments of beakers imported from Iran and a column capital were found, but the nature of the site in the Sasanian period has yet to be explained. A further indication for a new site of this period is a column capital found by a French team near Jannussan. A dating to the second or third century AD for the capital has been suggested, because of similarities with a capital from Hatra (Boulos 1984: 160).

The picture of new foundations and changing settlement patterns seems to be repeated in south-east Arabia. The site of Kush situated in Ras al-Khaimah in the UAE may be a new foundation. It was discovered by Beatrice de Cardi in 1977 and excavated from 1994 to 2001 by a British team in co-operation with Ras al-Khaimah Museum. So far a pottery sequence covering the period from the fourth or fifth century AD to the late thirteenth century AD has

been published (Kennet 2004) together with preliminary reports and studies (Kennet 1997; 2002). Period I and II are pre-Islamic periods, whereas the following periods fall within the Islamic era. Period I is characterized by mud-brick architecture densely built up. The nature of the site in this phase is not clear, and neither is it clear whether earlier layers partly underlie these structures. In Period II, which dates to the very late pre-Islamic or earliest Islamic periods, a massive mud-brick tower was constructed. It may have been a stronghold for a Sasanian or Arabian feudal property owner (Kennet 2004: 12–13). Not far from Kush at the site of Khatt an assemblage of pottery, probably dating to the fourth and fifth century AD, has been excavated but the nature of the occupation is not clear (Kennet 1998).

The settlements at both ed-Dur and Mleiha changed from being open and egalitarian in nature, and were replaced by fort-like structures probably in the second or third century AD. In Mleiha, a densely built-up town of mud-brick houses with walled enclosures remained between a fort, which may have been a "place of political power", and a fortified building in the north end of the settlement. No tombs dating to this period have been excavated in Mleiha (Mouton 1999: 26–28). At ed-Dur at the beginning of the third century AD, a fortress was built on top of a dune close to the lagoon, which gave access to the sea. From the second half of the third century to the first half of the fourth century AD, the fortress was used as a cemetery. It has therefore been suggested that the function of the building may have been religious (Lecomte 1993).

Although the interpretation of these sites has varied from strongholds to religious monuments, the appearance of larger structures is very different from the previous periods, where only a few buildings have any monumental value (e.g. the *Shamash* temple at ed-Dur). The new foundations may be indicative of a segmentation of society and the rise of a local or regional elite (Kennet 2005).

Eastern Arabia in the period from c. AD 450 to 700

In the last centuries before the coming of Islam the number of burials in the cemeteries of the Tylos Period is clearly very limited and only a few glass vessels provide evidence that the traditions of the earlier phases were maintained. These few vessels illustrate, however, that an independent stylistic tradition had developed in the East during the Sasanian period and the material culture in the Gulf region was no longer using Western prototypes, as it had in an earlier part of the Tylos period.

The Nestorian church, and hence Christianity, had gained a foothold in Arabia probably in the fourth century AD and the church became better established over the following centuries in north-east Arabia (Vine 1980: 59, 76–78). From the fifth century AD, we have evidence that a bishop was appointed on Bahrain (Potts 1990: 150–151). Nevertheless, archaeological evidence of a Christian community has not been found on Bahrain, but impressive monasteries have been found elsewhere in the Gulf, e.g. on the island of Khārg (Steve 2003: 85–154) and on the island of Sir Bani Yas off the coast of Abu Dhabi in the UAE (Elders 2003). The name of the modern village ed-Deir on the island of Muharraq suggests, however, that a monastery also existed on Bahrain, since in the early twentieth century the village was known as Der ar-Rahib, which means "the monk's monastery" (Holes 2002: 273). The above evidence strongly suggests that a Christian community was present on Bahrain from the fourth or fifth century AD and probably remained there until and into the early Islamic era. The disappearance of the "Tylos burials" could thus be a result of a larger part of the population adopting the Christian faith with a more modest burial tradition and an abandonment of earlier pagan cemeteries.

Appendix 1

List of tombs containing more than one glass or pottery vessel.

Tomb No.	Area	Mound	Context	No.	Cat. nos
1	Abu Arshira	1973	Tomb	89	BO.10, BV.13
2	Abu-Saybi	1983	Tomb	1	7.4, BR.5
3	Abu-Saybi	5-97	Tomb	6	BM.1, AQ.48, BL.21
4	Al-Hajar	1-92-93	Tomb	1	K.12, DA.6, B.24, F.2
5	Al-Hajar	1-92-93	Tomb	4	Z.4, B.14
6	Al-Hajar	1-92-93	Tomb	5	X.21, B.32
7	Al-Hajar	1-92-93	Tomb	8	AB.24, Y.29
8	Al-Hajar	1-94	Tomb	5	BQ.21, BX.7, BE.50
	Al-Hajar	1-94	Outside tomb	9	47.1, 46.2, 45.2, 44.1, 44.5, 46.1
9	Al-Hajar	1979	Tomb	1	AH.38, Z.43, Z.47, Z.21
10	Al-Hajar	1979	Tomb	2	Z.48, Z.13, AB.6, Z.25
11	Al-Hajar	1981	Tomb	1	AC.74, AQ.123
12	Al-Hajar	2-1971	Tomb	1A	7.2, 18.8, 14.2
13	Al-Hajar	2-1971	Tomb	1B	10.6, 12.19, 12.7, 18.2, 21.1, 6.28, 18.5, 20.1, 6.43, 2.4
14	Al-Hajar	2-92	Tomb	11	AC.42, AI.3
15	Al-Hajar	2-92	Tomb	6	AD.5, AN.8
16	Al-Hajar	2-92	Tomb	9	AI.4, AC.52
	Al-Hajar	2-92-93	Tomb	31	DB.7, CS.18
	Al-Hajar	2-92-93	Tomb	33	AC.12, AK.1
17	Al-Hajar	2-92-93	Tomb	46	F.8, X.22
	Al-Hajar	2-93	Outside tomb	48	D.5, NON.23
18	Al-Hajar	3-93	Tomb	8	AC.22, AH.27
19	Al-Hajar	6-92-93	Tomb	10	B.21, AI.14
	Al-Hajar	6-92-93	Tomb	35	B.15, DB.9
20	Al-Hajar	7-92-93	Tomb	2	BX.9, AD.18
21	Al-Hajar	7-92-93	Outside tomb	8	D.22, CS.13, Z.28
	Ali	101-88-89	Tomb	16	BP.3, CB.4, CS.21, BO.17, NON.50, BP.1
22	Ali	103-88-89	Tomb	1	CR.1, CQ.3, NON.51
23	Ali	105-89-90	Tomb	1	CX.9, BV.8
	Ali	1988	Tomb	41	M.9, U.3
24	Ali	60-88-89	Tomb	10	K.3, AB.28, AR.2
25	Ali	60-88-89	Tomb	17	Q.2, H.2, B.7
	Ali	60-88-89	Tomb	21	DD.2, X.24
26	Ali	60-88-89	Tomb	29	J.13, K.11, CT.6
27	Ali	60-88-89	Tomb	36	J.2, AB.30
28	Ali	60-88-89	Tomb	5	Y.40, N.12
29	Al-Manama Suq Magasis	1989	Tomb	2	AC.38, AE.18
	Al-Maqsha	1978	Tomb	12	46.4, 45.4, 45.3, 44.9, 44.4, 25.11
	Al-Maqsha	1991	Tomb	6	BT.2, DO.2
30	Al-Maqsha	1992-93	Tomb	1	AI.1, AC.37
31	Al-Maqsha	1992-93	Tomb	4	AQ.155, BN.8
32	Al-Maqsha	1992-93	Tomb	4	Z.1, P.4
33	Barbar	1996	Tomb	8	AB.18, D.24
34	Dar Kulayb	24-93-94	Tomb	1	CD.2, 41.10, NON.30, 31.1, CD.1, DA.2, DA.3, CE.2, CE.3, 25.9, BM.4, 25.10
35	Dar Kulayb	24-93-94	Tomb	2	41.3, 41.2, NON.19, 40.7, 37.1, 41.4
	Hamad Town	106-84-85	Tomb	1	J.7, NON.47

Tomb No.	Area	Mound	Context	No.	Cat. nos
36	Hamad Town	10-89-90	Tomb	41	CR.2, CL.10, CO.9, NON.6, NON.4, 40.8, NON.5, 40.9, 28.9, NON.3, NON.7
37	Hamad Town	1-94-95	Tomb		BU.37, AQ.29
	Hamad Town	1-94-95	Tomb		CE.1, 43.1
38	Hamad Town	1-94-95	Tomb		BL.17, BQ.18, AQ.101
39	Hamad Town	1-94-95	Tomb		AC.53, AE.36
40	Hamad Town	1-94-95	Tomb		CL.3, CO.2
41	Hamad Town	1-94-95	Tomb		AE.39, AD.1
42	Hamad Town	1-94-95	Tomb		6.24, DF.3, 15.16, BO.7
	Hamad Town	1-94-95	Tomb		CP.1, DE.1, BI.2
43	Hamad Town	1-94-95	Tomb		CO.1, CJ.1, CL.1
	Hamad Town	1-94-95	Tomb		NON.11, BB.7
44	Hamad Town	1-94-95	Tomb		AJ.1, BA.1, CD.5
45	Hamad Town	1-94-95	Tomb		K.15, BV.17, BO.8
	Hamad Town	1-94-95	Tomb		34.16, 25.1, BE.61,13.16, 34.1, 25.7
46	Hamad Town	1-94-95	Tomb		BL.16, BE.32
	Hamad Town	1-94-95	Tomb		D.15, BU.13
47	Hamad Town	1-94-95	Tomb		BQ.7, 6.38
48	Hamad Town	1-94-95	Tomb		6.11, 2.3
49	Hamad Town	1-94-95	Tomb		BL.30, BE.41
50	Hamad Town	1984-85	Tomb	E47	Z.58, DA.9
	Hamad Town	30-84-85	Tomb	21	BV.22, J.3
	Hamad Town	30-84-85	Tomb	41	BL.18, CX.6
51	Hamad Town	70A-85-86	Tomb	1	18.1, CC.2
52	Hamad Town	70A-85-86	Tomb	6	CL.5, CN.9, BQ.40
53	Hamad Town	73-85-86	Tomb	1	CL.7, 41.5, 38.1, 41.12, CN.10, CO.4, 12.8, AQ.150, 25.6, 33.1, CN.3, CN.7, 34.27
	Hamad Town	73-85-86	Tomb	12	NON.24, CC.9
54	Hamad Town	73-85-86	Tomb	27	DG.3, 7.5
55	Hamad Town	73-85-86	Tomb	44	CD.6, NON.1, 32.1, 41.7
56	Hamad Town	73-85-86	Tomb	51	BY.7, 12.13
57	Hamad Town	73-85-86	Tomb	52	AQ.153, DO.10
58	Hamad Town	73-85-86	Tomb	54	CC.10, 10.4, AO.14
	Hamad Town	83-85-86	Tomb	31	CQ.4, A.7
59	Hamad Town	83-85-86	Tomb	42	BL.9, BE.28
60	Hamad Town	83-85-86	Tomb	44	NON.18, CQ.2, CQ.1,25.3, 30.1, 25.8, DA.10
	Hamad Town	88-85-86	Tomb	4	CL.9, AP.23, Z.61
	Hamad Town	A70-95-96	Tomb	6	CG.2, CG.1
61	Karranah	1-1992	Tomb		AQ.3, BV.1
62	Karranah	1-1992	Tomb		DN.19, D.31
63	Karranah	1-1992	Tomb		AB.35, Y.44
64	Maqabah	1989	Tomb	1	B.12, 12.6, AC.16
65	Maqabah	1989	Tomb	2	AO.1, AF.31
66	Maqabah	1989	Tomb	7	12.9, 14.4, AQ.51
67	Shakhoura	13-00-01	Tomb	15	BL.36, AQ.140
68	Shakhoura	13-00-01	Tomb	23	BX.15, BV.23
69	Shakhoura	1-87	Tomb	9	AE.4, AP.11
70	Shakhoura	1-91	Tomb	4	AB.5, CX.4
71	Shakhoura	1-91-92	Tomb	12	BD.5, BK.4, AT.8, CC.19
72	Shakhoura	1-91-92	Tomb	2	DA.1, AH.21
73	Shakhoura	1-92-93	Tomb	108	AQ.18, 13.13, 6.40, AY.3
74	Shakhoura	1-92-93	Tomb	111	BY.1, AO.7
75	Shakhoura	1-92-93	Tomb	121	BQ.3, BL.6
76	Shakhoura	1-92-93	Tomb	123	AQ.60, 13.1, BE.53
77	Shakhoura	1-92-93	Tomb	13	BF.29, AQ.24, BL.31

Tomb No.	Area	Mound	Context	No.	Cat. nos
78	Shakhoura	1-92-93	Tomb	136	AQ.16, BF.5, AQ.54
	Shakhoura	1-92-93	Tomb	138	BM.10, DH.2
79	Shakhoura	1-92-93	Tomb	156	13.7, AQ.61, AQ.38, AQ.98
80	Shakhoura	1-92-93	Tomb	166	AQ.110, 19.2, 15.23, 6.39, 15.7, BC.8, 15.22, 15.21, 15.20
81	Shakhoura	1-92-93	Tomb	169	AQ.52, BR.4, BF.12
82	Shakhoura	1-92-93	Tomb	170	18.6, AQ.81, 15.8, BE.11
83	Shakhoura	1-92-93	Tomb	175	AQ.85, BC.4, 6.2, 11.1, 11.2, 15.1
84	Shakhoura	1-92-93	Tomb	26	19.1, 14.3, AQ.102
85	Shakhoura	1-92-93	Tomb	28	BM.8, AQ.91
86	Shakhoura	1-92-93	Tomb	29	BF.17, AQ.19, BA.14, BL.2
87	Shakhoura	2-01-02	Tomb	14	BU.27, BF.40
88	Shakhoura	2-01-02	Tomb	16	BN.5, BF.74, BQ.34
89	Shakhoura	2-01-02	Tomb	26	BE.39, BC.5
90	Shakhoura	25-01	Tomb	26	21.2, BQ.38
91	Shakhoura	25-01	Tomb	3	AO.13, AX.4, BU.28
92	Shakhoura	29-00-01	Tomb	17	NON.12, B.37, BK.7
	Shakhoura	29-00-01	Tomb	19	AC.81, CX.11
93	Shakhoura	29-00-01	Tomb	20	D.6, AN.10
94	Shakhoura	2-91	Tomb	3	6.19, BO.5
95	Shakhoura	2-91-92	Jar	1	15.13, BK.6
96	Shakhoura	2-91-92	Tomb	11	BX.6, AN.3, BL.4
97	Shakhoura	2-91-92	Tomb	14	AB.2, M.2
98	Shakhoura	2-91-92	Tomb	15	M.11, AA.2
99	Shakhoura	2-91-92	Tomb	23	15.12, CT.3, BO.6
100	Shakhoura	2-91-92	Tomb	26	BZ.3, O.5
101	Shakhoura	2-91-92	Tomb	47	6.33, BV.12, AQ.103
102	Shakhoura	2-92	Tomb	55	AE.6, AH.5
103	Shakhoura	2-92	Tomb	56	AE.26, AC.56
104	Shakhoura	2-92	Tomb	57	AJ.6, CB.2, BX.4, BB.2
105	Shakhoura	2-92	Tomb	65	AP.9, AE.9
13	Shakhoura	2-94	Tomb	13	AP.8, BL.7
107	Shakhoura	30-98-99	Tomb	27	BM.13, AF.27
108	Shakhoura	30-98-99	Tomb	3	BX.17, AL.16
	Shakhoura	30-98-99	Tomb	6	BV.28, DB.14
109	Shakhoura	3-1969	Tomb	1	AO.10, AQ.121
110	Shakhoura	3-91	Tomb	3	CB.3, BO.13
111	Shakhoura	4-91	Tomb	1	13.10, BL.13
112	Shakhoura	4-92-93	Tomb	21	BR.8, AQ.97
113	Shakhoura	4-92-93	Tomb	5	K.2, C.1, Z.8
	Shakhoura	6-92-93	Tomb	9	Y.25, G.6
114	Shakhoura	7-93	Tomb	114	AE.20, AH.41, AC.27
115	Shakhoura	7-93	Tomb	25	AD.10, AC.14
116	Shakhoura	7-93	Tomb	30	BF.60, AC.20, AE.28
117	Shakhoura	7-93	Tomb	46	AE.11, AH.3, AC.17
118	Shakhoura	7-93	Tomb	5	BF.23, BA.20
119	Shakhoura	7-93	Tomb	58	AE.29, AC.71, AH.26
120	Shakhoura	7-93	Tomb	59	BA.12, AC.19
121	Shakhoura	7-93	Tomb	61	AC.63, AF.16, K.7, E.1
122	Shakhoura	7-93	Tomb	62	AC.58, BM.5, AE.35
123	Shakhoura	7-93	Tomb	75	AH.31, CS.12
124	Shakhoura	7-93	Tomb	8	AF.10, BM.3
	Shakhoura	7-93	Tomb	82	6.1, DB.12
125	Shakhoura	A1-96-97	Tomb	1	AF.17, BA.10
126	Shakhoura	A1-96-97	Tomb	12	AC.24, BM.2, AE.13

Tomb No.	Area	Mound	Context	No.	Cat. nos
	Shakhoura	A1-96-97	Tomb	14	CS.17, BA.11
127	Shakhoura	A1-96-97	Tomb	15	AF.24, AH.9
128	Shakhoura	A1-96-97	Tomb	2	1.1, AJ.3
129	Shakhoura	A1-96-97	Tomb	27	DN.1, AC.1
130	Shakhoura	A1-96-97	Tomb	36	NON.27, AQ.32, BL.15, BG.4
131	Shakhoura	A1-96-97	Tomb	45	BL.10, AQ.41
132	Shakhoura	A1-96-97	Tomb	47	BU.26, 3.1, 1.2
	Shakhoura	A1-96-97	Tomb	63	BM.15, BQ.27
134	Shakhoura	A1-96-97	Tomb	65	BZ.2, BU.35, CC.13, BL.34, BE.22, BF.34, BQ.32, AT.15, CC.16
	Shakhoura	A1-96-97	Tomb	66	BX.3, CA.1
136	Shakhoura	A1-96-97	Tomb	74	AQ.28, BL.14, BM.6, BF.46
137	Shakhoura	A1-96-97	Tomb	84	AQ.44, 26.3
138	Shakhoura	A1-96-97	Tomb	87	6.9, BO.2
139	Saar	10-91	Tomb	1	B.10, DN.10, AP.2
140	Saar	10-91	Tomb	2	X.20, Z.34
141	Saar	10-91	Tomb	3	V.2, Y.8
	Saar	10-99-01	Tomb	1	CS.24, BV.30
142	Saar	10-99-01	Tomb	100	BL.41, BM.11
143	Saar	10-99-01	Tomb	110	AL.17, CX.10
144	Saar	10-99-01	Tomb	30	BF.11, 15.14
145	Saar	10-99-01	Tomb	33	BC.2, Z.63
146	Saar	10-99-01	Tomb	39	BD.2, AO.3
147	Saar	10-99-01	Tomb	4	AX.6, BL.42
148	Saar	10-99-01	Tomb	43	BR.10, J.15
149	Saar	10-99-01	Tomb	45	BU.36, 22.2, BL.40
150	Saar	10-99-01	Tomb	46	BR.11, 6.31
151	Saar	11-95-96	Tomb	10	AL.11, AI.13, S.6, AJ.7, AC.70
152	Saar	11-95-96	Tomb	18	O.8, AE.31, AC.66
153	Saar	11-95-96	Tomb	25	2.2, AQ.104, 6.6, 34.3, 6.12, 26.5
154	Saar	11-95-96	Tomb	34	AV.3, AN.1
155	Saar	11-95-96	Tomb	40	BK.5, CC.11
156	Saar	11-95-96	Tomb	7	BU.9, BV.5, BU.6
157	Saar	11-95-96	Tomb	9	AL.15, BU.10
158	Saar	1-1960	Tomb	1	C.14, Y.45
	Saar	1-1960	Tomb	2	S.16, CS.28
159	Saar	1-1960	Tomb	3	O.18, K.20
	Saar	12-91	Tomb	15	AL.6, 42.6
160	Saar	12-91	Tomb	16	Z.20, DN.3
161	Saar	12-91	Tomb	6	41.13, 34.23, S.10, 34.24, 25.22
162	Saar	12-91	Tomb	7	B.26, S.7
	Saar	12-91	Tomb	8	BN.2, CS.3
163	Saar	12-95-96	Tomb	12	AC.2, AI.5
164	Saar	12-95-96	Tomb	22	39.4, 34.18, 25.17, AQ.26
165	Saar	12-95-96	Tomb	34	AQ.33, AE.12
166	Saar	12-95-96	Tomb	35	AQ.106, BL.26
167	Saar	12-95-96	Tomb	39	AO.4, 12.18
168	Saar	12-95-96	Tomb	5	AE.34, AQ.23
169	Saar	163-91-92	Tomb	19	BL.12, AQ.96
170	Saar	163-91-92	Tomb	20	AQ.83, BL.23
171	Saar	163-91-92	Tomb	28	AE.14, AP.5
172	Saar	163-91-92	Tomb	4	24.2, 34.9, 27.1, 27.4, 28.1
173	Saar	163-91-92	Tomb	6	AQ.27, BL.8
	Saar	163-91-92	Tomb	8	AG.4, AE.27
174	Saar	176-1988	Tomb	7	27.2, 29.1

Tomb No.	Area	Mound	Context	No.	Cat. nos
175	Saar	1-91	Tomb	15	BC.1, BI.1, BQ.15
176	Saar	1-91	Tomb	18	AC.47, AE.1, B.20
177	Saar	1-91	Tomb	19	BU.18, AB.22, L.1
178	Saar	1-91	Tomb	2	F.5, X.26
179	Saar	1-91	Tomb	21	AH.28, AE.7
180	Saar	1-91	Tomb	3	K.1, B.17, J.1
181	Saar	1-91	Tomb	30	A.6, C.2, Z.35
182	Saar	1-91	Tomb	4	AQ.11, AR.7, AR.3, R.2, Z.37, N.9
	Saar	1-91	Tomb	5	AH.19, AH.46
183	Saar	1-91-92	Tomb	5	K.17, AC.67
184	Saar	1-96	Tomb	7	BH.2, 26.4, CF.2, 34.15
	Saar	2-87	Tomb	2	CC.25, DN.12
185	Saar	2-91-92	Tomb	22	BS.2, BV.11, BV.3, NON.31, V.1, NON.48, 13.4, 15.19
186	Saar	3-90-91	Tomb	2	Y.6, AB.1
187	Saar	3-96	Tomb	12	M.5, N.10, K.5, I.2
188	Saar	3-96	Tomb	4	N.4, B.9
189	Saar	3-96	Tomb	5	AC.80, DO.7
190	Saar	3-96	Tomb	6	N.8, Y.22
191	Saar	4-91-92	Tomb	14	DB.1, DB.15, Y.26, 1.3, E.2, J.11, DB.17
	Saar	4-91-92	Tomb	17	DJ.3, CC.24
	Saar	4-91-92	Tomb	30	CY.1, AI.20
	Saar	4-91-92	Tomb	33	CD.3, DB.16
192	Saar	4-91-92	Tomb	36	13.14, 6.29, BQ.17
193	Saar	4-91-92	Tomb	46	CX.8, DG.2
	Saar	5-85-86	Tomb	1	CC.22, NON.33, CS.20
194	Saar	5-87-88	Tomb	11	AE.19, AP.15
195	Saar	5-87-88	Tomb	13	R.9, AC.48
196	Saar	5-87-88	Tomb	22	AD.16, AL.2
197	Saar	5-87-88	Tomb	24	AC.5, AF.33
198	Saar	5-87-88	Tomb	25	BE.5, BO.3
199	Saar	5-87-88	Tomb	27	CN.5, BO.12
	Saar	5-87-88	Tomb	31	R.12, R.10
200	Saar	5-87-88	Tomb	35	BU.8, BH.5
201	Saar	5-87-88	Tomb	42	AN.6, BD.4
202	Saar	5-87-88	Tomb	49	28.5, 25.2, 26.6, 36.1, 27.6, 25.4, 34.12
	Saar	5-87-88	Tomb	51	CS.8, AC.54
	Saar	5-87-88	Tomb	56	AV.4, CS.4
203	Saar	5-87-88	Tomb	7	AC.30, AL.1
204	Saar	5-87-88	Tomb	83	AE.23, BF.68, AP.17
205	Saar	5-87-88	Tomb	94	AQ.66, 13.2
206	Saar	5-91-92	Tomb	16	AC.7, Y.28, F.6
207	Saar	5-91-92	Tomb	4	Y.30, Y.20, J.10, B.11, AL.8
208	Saar	5-91-92	Tomb	8	B.30, AL.10, S.11
	Saar	5-95-96	Tomb	10	X.12, DL.2
209	Saar	5-95-96	Tomb	12	12.14, NON.8, 42.9, 25.19
210	Saar	5-95-96	Tomb	24	34.10, 25.18, 26.1, 34.11
211	Saar	5-95-96	Tomb	36	35.5, 40.10, 34.26, 24.3
	Saar	5-95-96	Tomb	43	AV.1, 40.3
212	Saar	5-95-96	Tomb	44	AC.31, DO.6
213	Saar	5-95-96	Tomb	55	35.3, 28.13, 35.4, 34.20, 34.22, 25.21, 28.11, 28.14, 28.15, 34.21, 25.20, 40.1, 28.12, 28.10
214	Saar	5-95-96	Tomb	57	BE.74, BU.5
215	Saar	5-95-96	Tomb	78	BV.2, AQ.25
216	Saar	5-95-96	Tomb	83	40.6, CF.1
217	Saar	5-96-97	Tomb	39	AE.32, AQ.86

Tomb No.	Area	Mound	Context	No.	Cat. nos
218	Saar	5-96-97	Tomb	5	AT.1, BU.25, BU.3
219	Saar	5-96-97	Tomb	7	6.22, AQ.88, BL.37
220	Saar	6-91-92	Tomb	14	41.6, 29.2
221	Saar	6-91-92	Tomb	15	Z.16, BU.7
222	Saar	6-91-92	Tomb	4	BU.12, NON.46, BZ.6
223	Saar	6-96	Tomb	33	15.3, AD.14
224	Saar	7-91	Tomb	1	Y.7, AI.22, O.16
225	Saar	7-95-96	Tomb	118	BV.16, BL.24
226	Saar	7-95-96	Tomb	119	42.5, BE.7
	Saar	7-95-96	Tomb	12	AT.11, DF.1
227	Saar	7-95-96	Tomb	130	BC.13, AQ.39
228	Saar	7-95-96	Tomb	137	18.4, 13.3, AY.1, 6.15
229	Saar	7-95-96	Tomb	15	AC.4, AI.12
230	Saar	7-95-96	Tomb	20	AD.8, AP.10
231	Saar	7-95-96	Tomb	21	AI.6, BF.13
232	Saar	7-95-96	Tomb	22	P.2, AE.10
233	Saar	7-95-96	Tomb	28	AX.8, 40.4, CF.6
234	Saar	7-95-96	Tomb	3	BR.2, 10.3
235	Saar	7-95-96	Tomb	38	CF.8, BU.24
236	Saar	7-95-96	Tomb	39	BO.14, BV.4
237	Saar	7-95-96	Tomb	4	AQ.37, BD.1
	Saar	7-95-96	Tomb	44	BD.3, 8.1
	Saar	7-95-96	Tomb	5	6.36, 9.2
238	Saar	7-95-96	Tomb	55	40.5, CF.4
239	Saar	7-95-96	Tomb	57	AE.17, AQ.14
240	Saar	7-95-96	Tomb	67	BI.6, BL.29, AQ.107
241	Saar	7-95-96	Tomb	68	CC.12, BG.7
242	Saar	7-95-96	Tomb	7	CC.18, 6.17
243	Saar	7-95-96	Tomb	77	15.9, 13.5
244	Saar	8-97	Tomb	38	BC.11, BE.68, AE.37, BU.31
245	Saar	8-97	Tomb	5	BE.47, BV.7
246	Saar	9-91	Tomb	1	B.33, S.5, K.13
247	Saar	9-91	Tomb	2	AB.21, Y.32
248	Saar	9-91	Tomb	3	Z.46, K.9
249	Unplaced	Higham	Tomb	36	4.1, BO.1, BX.1, 2.1, 5.1
250	Unplaced	T158-2	Tomb	1	T.2, Z.65
	Unplaced	T158-2	Tomb	3	L.3, Z.66
251	Unplaced	T158-4	Tomb	2	CS.27, A.8, D.32
	Unplaced	T158-5	Tomb	1	NON.28, 12.17, CV.9, CU.7, CU.8, CU.9, 34.13, 34.14

Appendix 2

The composition of a number of glass samples has been analysed on a scanning electron microscope by Ulrich Schnell, Nationalmuseet, Copenhagen. The samples were collected in Bahrain and brought to Denmark for analysis. Since it was not desirable to break samples of complete vessels, the samples were most often from fragmented and rather weathered vessels. Due to the weathering of some of the surfaces and as the soil in Bahrain contains salts and gypsum, some samples may also be contaminated by these minerals.

The aim of these analyses was to investigate whether the change in style and appearance of the vessels between Phases III and IV were a result of a change in the place of production and not just a result of chronological development (see pp. 96-97). Previously tested samples from ed-Dur all seem to be natron-based glass, which is characteristic of a Western production (Brill 1998: 70–71) and since many of the vessels from Phase III find exact stylistic parallels in ed-Dur, there are no reasons to believe that they should be from different sources. This is confirmed by the sample tested from cat. no. 6.5. This sample has low values of MgO and K_2O, which is characteristic of natron-based glass (Brill 1998: 70; 2005: 67). So-called Sasanian glass produced further east was using soda from plant-ashes and is characterized by relatively high values of MgO and K_2O (Brill 2005: 67). The remaining samples from Bahrain have relatively high values of these two minerals and it is therefore likely that these vessels were produced in the East. It is interesting that examples of Type 11, 12, 13 and 15 were also made of plant-ash glass; since these types probably date within Phase III, it is therefore most likely that the plant-ash production (eastern production) began to distribute its products in Phase III.

Cat. no.	6.5	11.1	12.8a	12.8b	12.8c	13.5	15.20	25.5	28.3	34.26	35.5	40.3	41.1	41.9	45.2
Na2O	3,39	2,86	6,58	4,13	12,07	1,59	0,71	0,50	12,48	2,03	0,48	1,52	0,04	1,13	2,77
MgO	0,49	10,30	4,19	5,38	5,19	32,11	19,77	19,75	4,44	3,17	14,67	6,24	22,92	9,43	10,31
Al2O3	8,32	1,09	5,27	5,33	5,53	0,82	2,17	2,78	1,61	5,25	2,66	2,99	0,67	2,27	1,03
SiO2	84,31	76,77	68,86	57,45	71,53	62,63	74,79	72,45	71,20	84,73	36,87	82,60	72,23	84,15	79,73
SO3	0,48	0,54	1,76	1,04	0,11	0,74	0,30	1,29	0,91	0,88	2,85	0,71	0,60	0,35	0,49
K2O	1,46	1,25	1,60	1,88	1,48	0,28	0,47	0,55	1,86	0,37	0,55	0,90	0,47	0,60	1,35
CaO	1,10	6,22	1,32	4,87	0,90	1,36	0,61	0,94	6,44	1,75	40,48	3,89	2,15	0,25	3,31
TiO2	0,05	0,10	0,34	0,38	0,05	0,07	0,13	0,20	0,10	0,24	0,13	0,14	0,08	0,18	0,11
MnO	0,02	0,03	8,80	17,87	2,33	0,06	0,03	0,32	0,00	0,03	0,09	0,02	0,06	0,00	0,01
FeO	0,38	0,83	0,83	1,62	0,82	0,33	0,92	1,22	0,91	1,56	1,21	0,99	0,71	1,58	0,89
SrO	0,00	0,00	0,45	0,05	0,00	0,00	0,10	0,00	0,04	0,00	0,00	0,00	0,09	0,06	0,00
	100,00	99,99	100,00	100,00	100,01	99,99	100,00	100,00	99,99	100,01	99,99	100,00	100,02	100,00	100,00

Table 363. Composition of a number of glass samples.

Bibliography

Adams, R.M. (1981): *Heartland of Cities, Surveys of Ancient Settlements and Land Use on the Central Floodplain of the Euphrates.* Chicago & London.

Ammianus Marcellinus/transl. J.C. Rolfe (1963-1971): The Loeb Classical Library. London & Cambridge, Mass.

Andersen, H.H. & Højlund, F. (2003): *The Barbar Temples.* Jutland Archaeological Society Publications, vol. 48. Aarhus.

Andersen, S.F. (2001): *An investigation of the pottery from c. 300 BC to c. 600 AD from the Danish excavations at Qala'at al-Bahrain.* MA thesis, University of Aarhus. [In Danish, unpublished].

——————— (2002): The Chronology of the earliest Tylos period on Bahrain. *Arabian Archaeology and Epigraphy* 13/2: 234–245.

Andersen, S.F. & Kennet, D. (2003): The Sasanian and Islamic Pottery. Pages 307–310 in Andersen & Højlund 2003.

Andersen, S.F. & Salman, M.I. (2006): The Tylos burials in Bahrain. *Proceedings of the Seminar for Arabian Studies* 36: 111–124.

Andersen, S.F., Salman M.I., Strehle, H. & Tengberg, M. (2004): Two wooden coffins from the Shakhoura Necropolis, Bahrain. *Arabian Archaeology and Epigraphy* 15/2: 219–228.

al-Ansary, A.R. (1982): *Qaryat al-Fau: a portrait of pre-islamic civilisation in Saudi-Arabia.* London.

Antonini, S. (ed.) (2000): *Yemen. Nel paese della Regina di Saba.* Rome.

Arnold, W. & Bobzin, H. (eds) (2002): *"Sprich doch mit deinen Knechten aramäisch, wir verstehen es", 60 Beiträge zur Semitistik, Fest-*schrift für Otto Jastrow zum 60. Geburtstag. Wiesbaden.

Ball, W. & Harrow, L. (eds) (2002): *Cairo to Kabul, Afghan and Islamic Studies.* London.

Bernard, P. (1973): *Fouilles d'Ai Khanoum, vol. I.* Mémoires de la délégation Archéologique Française en Afghanistan. Paris.

Bernard, V., Gachet, J. & Salles, J-F. (1990): Apostilles en marge de la céramique des États IV et V de la forteresse. Pages 241–285 in Calvet & Gachet 1990.

Bibby, T.G. (1954): Fem af Bahrains hundrede tusinde gravhøje. *Kuml* 1954: 116–141.

——————— (1958): Bahrains oldtidshovedstad gennem 4000 år. *Kuml* 1957: 128–163.

——————— (1967): Arabian Gulf Archaeology. *Kuml* 1966: 75–95.

——————— (1973): *Preliminary Survey in East Arabia 1968.* Jutland Archaeological Society Publications, vol. XII. Copenhagen.

——————— (1996): *Looking for Dilmun.* London.

Blondé, F., Ballet, P. & Salles, J-F. (eds) (2002): *Céramiques hellénistiques et romaines. Productions et diffusion en Méditerranée orientale (Chypre, Égypte et côte syro-palestinienne).* Travaux de la Maison de l'Orient Méditerranéen, no 35. Lyon.

Boehmer, R.M., Pedde, F. & Salje, B. (1995): *Uruk, Die Gräber.* Ausgrabungen in Uruk-Warka, Endberichte, Band 10. Mainz am Rhein.

Boucharlat, R. (1987): Les niveaux Post-Achéménides à Suse, Secteur Nord. *Cahiers de la Délégation Archéologique Française en Iran* 15: 145–311.

————— (1993): Pottery in Susa during the Seleucid, Parthian and early Sasanian periods. Pages 41–58 in Finkbeiner 1993.

Boucharlat, R. & Mouton, M. (1993): Mleiha. Pages 219–250 in Finkbeiner 1993.

————— (1994): Mleiha (Emirate of Sharjah, UAE) at the beginning of the Christian Era. *Proceedings of the Seminar for Arabian Studies* 24:13–25.

Boucharlat, R. & Salles J-F. (eds) (1984): *Arabie orientale, Mésopotamie et Iran méridional de l'Age du Fer au début de la période islamique*. Paris.

Boucharlat, R. & Salles J-F. (1989): The Tylos Period (300 BC–600 AD). Pages 83–131 in Lombard & Kervran 1989.

Boulos, R. (1984): Un chapiteau de Janussan. Pages 159–161 in Lombard & Salles 1984.

Bowen, R.L.B. (1950): *The Early Arabian Necropolis of 'Ain Jawan*. Bulletin of the American Schools of Oriental Research, Supplementary Studies, 7–9.

Brill, R.H. (1998): Chemical Analyses of Selected Fragments. Pages 69–76 in Whitehouse 1998.

————— (2005): Chemical Analyses of Some Sasanian Glasses from Iraq. Pages 65–88 in Whitehouse 2005.

Callot, O. (1994): Un trésor de monnaies d'argent et monnaies diverses. Pages 351–360 in Højlund & Andersen 1994.

Calvet, Y. & Gachet, J. (eds) (1990): *Failaka Fouilles Françaises 1986–1988*. Travaux de la maison de l'Orient, no. 18. Lyon.

Cameron, A. (ed.) (1995): *The Byzantine and Early Islamic Near East III*. Princeton.

Campbell, S. & Green A. (eds) (1995): *The Archaeology of Death in the Ancient Near East*. Oxbow Monograph, 51. Exeter.

Carboni, S. (2002): An Anthropomorphic Glass Rhyton. Pages 58–61 in Ball & Harrow 2002.

Carboni, S. & Whitehouse, D. (2001): *Glass of the Sultans*. New York.

Christensen, A.P. & Johansen, C.F. (1972): *Hama: fouilles et recherches de la Fondation Carlsberg, 1931–1938. III/2: Les poteries hellénistiques et les terres sigillées orientales*. Nationalmuseets skrifter. Copenhagen.

Clairmont, C.W. (1963): *The Glass Vessels*. The Excavations at Dura-Europos, Final report IV, part V. New Haven, CT.

Colledge, M.A.R. (1976): *The Art of Palmyra*. London.

Cool, H.E.M. & Price, J. (1995): *Roman glass vessel from excavations in Colchester, 1971–85*. Colchester Archaeological Report, 8. Colchester.

Cox, D.H. (1949): *The Greek and Roman Pottery*. The Excavations at Dura-Europos, Final report IV, Part 1, Fascicle 2. New Haven, CT.

Crawford, H. Killick, R. & Moon, J. (eds) (1997): *The Dilmun Temple at Saar*. London & New York.

Curtis, J.E. (ed.) (2000): *Mesopotamia and Iran in the Parthian and Sasanian Periods: Rejection and Revival c. 238 BC–AD 642*. London.

Curtis V.S. & Andersen S.F. (forthcoming): A Sasanian site at Barbar, Bahrain. In Kennet & Luft (forthcoming).

Daems, A. & Haerinck, E. (2001): Excavations at Shakhoura (Bahrain). *Arabian Archaeology and Epigraphy* 12/1: 90–95.

Daems, A. Haerinck, E. & Rutten, K. (2001): A burial mound at Shakhoura (Bahrain). *Arabian Archaeology and Epigraphy* 12/2: 173–182.

Debevoise N.C. (1934): *Parthian Pottery from Seucia on the Tigris*. University of Michigan Studies, Humanistic Series, vol. XXXII. Ann Arbor, MI.

de Cardi, B. (1975): Archaeological Survey in Northern Oman 1972. *East and West (Rome)* 25/1–2: 9–75.

de Cardi, B. Kennet, D & Stocks, R.L. (1994): Five thousand years of settlement at Khatt, UAE. *Proceedings of the Seminar for Arabian Studies* 24: 35-95.

de Tommaso, G. (1990): *Ampullae Vitreae, Contenitori in vetro di unguenti e sostanze aromatiche dell'italia Romana (I sec. A.C.–III sec. D.C.)*. Archaeologica, 94. Rome.

Doppelfeld, O. (1966): *Römisches und fränkisches Glas in Köln*. Cologne.

Dornemann, R.H. (1983): *The archaeology of the Transjordan in the Bronze and Iron Ages*. Milwaukee, WI.

During Caspers, E.C.L. (1972–1974): The Bahrain Tumuli. *Persica, Annuaire de la Société Néerlando-Iranienne* 6: 131–156.

————— (1980): *The Bahrain Tumuli, an illustrated catalogue of two important collections*. Leiden.

Dyson, S.L. (1968): *The Commonware Pottery. The Brittle Ware*. The Excavations at Dura-Europos, Final report IV, Part 1, Fascicle 2. New Haven, CT.

Elders, J. (2003): The Nestorians in the Gulf: Just Passing Through? Recent Discoveries on the Island of Sir Bani Yas, Abu Dhabi Emirate, U.A.E. Pages 229–236 in Potts, Naboodah & Hellyer 2003.

Eskoubi, K.M. & al-Aila, S.R.A. (1985): Thaj Excavations. Second Season 1404/1984. *Atlal* 9: 41–53.

Ess, M. van & Pedde, F. (1992): *Uruk, Kleinfunde II*. Ausgrabungen in Uruk-Warka Endberichte, Band 7. Mainz am Rhein.

Ettlinger, E., Hedinger, B., Hoffmann, B., Kenrick, P.M., Pucci, G., Roth-Rubi, K., Schneider, G., von Schnurbein, S., Wells, C.M. & Zabenlicky-Scheffengger, S. (1990): *Conspectus formarum terrae sigillatae italico modo confectae*. Bonn.

Fick, A. (1894): *Die Griechischen Personennamen nach ihrer Bildung erklärt and systematisch geordnet* (Zweite Auflage). Göttingen.

Field, H. (1951): Reconnaissance in Southwestern Asia. *Southwestern Journal of Anthropology* 7/1: 86–102. Albuquerque, NM.

Finkbeiner, U. (1991): Keramik der seleukidischen und parthischen Zeit aus dn Grabungen in Uruk-Warka. I. Teil. *Baghdader Mitteilungen* 22: 537–638.

————— (1992): Keramik der seleukidischen und parthischen Zeit aus dn Grabungen in Uruk-Warka. II. Teil. *Baghdader Mitteilungen* 23: 473–581.

Finkbeiner, U. (ed.) (1993): *Materialien zur Archäologie der Seleukiden- und Partherzeit im südlichen Babylonien und im Golfgebiet*. Tübingen.

Fleming, S.J. (1999): *Roman Glass*. Philadelphia, PA.

Fossing, P. (1940): *Glass Vessels before Glass-Blowing*. Copenhagen.

Frifelt, K. (1984–1985): Burial Mounds near Ali Excavated by the Danish Expedition. *Dilmun, Journal of the Bahrain Historical and Archaeological Society* 12: 11–14.

————— (2001): *Islamic Remains in Bahrain*. Jutland Archaeological Society Publications, vol. 37. Moesgård.

Frye, R.N. (1983): Bahrain under the Sasanians. Pages 167–170 in Potts 1983.

————— (2000): Parthian and Sasanian History of Iran. Pages 17–22 in Curtis 2000.

Gatier, P-L., Lombard, P. & Al-Sindi, K. (2002): Greek Inscriptions from Bahrain. *Arabian Archaeology and Epigraphy* 13/2: 223–233.

Gawlikowski, K. & As'ad K. (1994): The Collection of Glass Vessels in the Museum of Palmyra. *Studia Palmyre'skie* 9: 5–39.

Ghirshman, R. (1976): *Terrasses Sacrées de Bard-è Néchandeh et Masjid-i Solaiman, vols 1 & 2*. Mémoires de la Délégation Archéologique en Iran, Tome XLV. Paris.

Glob, P.V. (1968): *Al-Bahrain. De danske ekspeditioner til oldtidens Dilmun*. Copenhagen.

Goldstein S. M. (2005): *Glass. From Sassanian Antecedents to European Imitations*. London.

Goethert-Polaschek, K. (1977): *Katalog der römischen Gläser des Rheinischen Landesmuseums Trier*. Trier Grabungen und Forschungen, Band IX. Mainz am Rhein.

Grose, D.F. (1974): Roman Glass of the first century AD. A dated deposit of glassware from Cosa, Italy. *Annales du Congrès de l'Association Internationale pour l'Histoire du Verre* 6: 31–52.

————— (1989): *Early Ancient Glass, core-formed, rod-formed, and cast vessels and objects from the late Bronze Age to the early Roman Empire, 1600 B.C. to A.D. 50.* The Toledo Museum of Art. New York.

Haerinck, E. (1983): *La Céramique en Iran pendant la Période Parthe (ca. 250 av. J.C. à ca. 225 après J.C.): Typologie, Chronologie et Distribution.* Iranica Antiqua, supplément II. Gent.

————— (1998): The shifting pattern of overland and seaborne trade in SE-Arabia, foreign pre-islamic coins from Mleiha (Emirate of Sharjah, U.A.E.). *Akkadica* 106: 22–40.

————— (2001): *Excavations at ed-Dur (Umm al-Qaiwain, United Arab Emirates)/the University of Ghent South-East Arabian archaeological project.* vol. 2. *The tombs.* Leuven.

Haerinck, E., Metdepenninghen, C. & Stevens, K.G. (1991): Excavations at ed-Dur (Umm al-Qaiwain, U.A.E.). Preliminary report on the second Belgian season (1988). *Arabian Archaeology and Epigraphy* 2: 31–60.

————— (1992): Excavations at ed-Dur (Umm al-Qaiwain, U.A.E.). Preliminary report on the third Belgian season (1989). *Arabian Archaeology and Epigraphy* 3: 44–60.

Haerinck, E., Phillips, C.S., Potts, D.T. & Stevens, K.G. (1993): Ed-Dur, Umm al Qaiwain (U.A.E). Pages 183–194 in Finkbeiner 1993.

Hannestad, L. (1983): *Ikaros — The Hellenistic Settlement.* vol. 2. *The Hellenistic Pottery from Failaka.* Jutland Archaeological Society Publications, vol. XVI. Aarhus.

————— (1994): The chronology of the hellenistic fortress (F5) on Failaka. *Topoi* 4/2: 587–595.

Hansman, J. (1967): Charax and the Karkheh. *Iranica Antiqua* 7: 21: 58.

————— (1984): The Land of Meshan. *Iran* 22: 161–166.

Harden, D.B. (1936): *Roman glass from Karanis.* Ann Arbor, MI.

————— (1964): Some Tomb Groups of Late Roman Date in the Ammam Museum. *Annales du Congrès de l'Association Internationale pour l'Histoire du Verre* 3: 48–55.

————— (1968): The Canosa Group of Hellenistic Glasses in the British Museum. *Journal of Glass Studies* 10: 21–47.

————— (1981): *Catalogue of Greek and Roman Glass in the British Museum.* vol 1. London.

al-Hashash, A.M., al-Zayer, W.A., al-Saif, Z.A., al-Sanna, S.H. & al-Hajri, M.Y. (2001): Report on the Archaeological Excavations at Thaj. *Atlal* 16: 23–26.

Hayes, J.W. (1975): *Roman and Pre-Roman Glass in the Royal Ontario Museum.* Toronto.

————— (1997): *Handbook of Mediterranean Roman pottery.* London.

Henig, M. (1978): *A Corpus of Roman Engraved Gemstones from British Sites.* British Archaeological Reports, British Series, 8. (Second edition). Oxford.

Herling, A. (2003): *Tyloszeitliche Bestattungspraktiken auf der Insel Bahrain.* Bd I–III. Göttingen.

Herling, A. & Salles, J-F. (1993): *Hellenistic Cemeteries in Bahrain.* Pages 161–182 in Finkbeiner 1993.

Herling, A., Latzel, M., Littleton, J., Möllering, I., Schippmann, K. & Velde, C. (1993): *Excavation at Karranah Mound I (1992).* [Unpublished report].

Herling, A. & Velde C. (1994): Excavations at Karranah Mound I, Bahrain. A preliminary report. *Iranica Antiqua* 29: 225–239.

Herrmann, G., Kurbansakhatov, K., Simpson, S.J. et al. (1999): The International Merv Project: Preliminary Report on the Seventh Season (1998). *Iran* 37: 1–24.

Herzfeld, E. (1968): *The Persian Empire, Studies in Geography and Ethnography of the Ancient Near East.* Wiesbaden.

Hochuli-Gysel, A. (1977): *Kleinasiatische glasierte Reliefkeramik (50 v. Chr. bis 50 n. Chr.) und ihre oberitalischen Nachamungen*. Acta Bernensia 7. Bern.

Hoffmann, C. (1996): *Glimt af den Nære Orients oldtid, Mesopotamisk kunst fra en dansk privat-samling*. Ny Carlsberg Glyptotek. Copenhagen.

Højlund, F. & Andersen, H.H. (1994): *Qala'at al-Bahrain*. vol. 1. Jutland Archaeological Society Publications, vol. XXX/1. Aarhus.

——————— (1997): *Qala'at al-Bahrain*. vol. 2. Jutland Archaeological Society Publications, vol. XXX/2. Aarhus.

Holes, C. (2002): Non-Arabic Semitic elements in the Arabic dialects of eastern Arabia. Pages 269–280 in Arnold & Bobzin 2002.

——————— (2006): The Arabic dialects of Arabia. *Proceedings of the Seminar for Arabian Studies* 36: 25–34.

Howard-Johnston, J. (1995): The two great powers in late antiquity: a comparison. Pages 157–226 in Cameron 1995.

Insoll, T. (2005): *The Land of Enki in the Islamic Era: Pearls, Palms and Religious Ideology in Bahrain*. London.

Invernizzi, A. & Salles, J-F. (eds) (1993): *Arabia Antiqua, Hellenistic Centres around Arabia*. Serie Orientale Roma, vol. LXX/2. Rome.

Isings, C. 1957: *Roman Glass from dated finds*. Archaeologica Traiectina. Groningen.

Israeli, Y. (1991): The Invention of Blowing. Pages 46–55 in Newby & Painter 1991.

Ivanova, A.P., Cubova, A.P. & Kolesnikova, L.G. (1976): *Antichnaja skulptura Chersonesa*. Kiev.

Jensen, S.T. (2003): Tylos burials from three different sites on Bahrain. *Arabian Archaeology and Epigraphy* 14/2: 127–163.

Jeppesen, C. (1960): Et kongebud til Ikaros, De hellenistiske templer på Failaka. *Kuml*: 153–198.

——————— (1989): *Ikaros — The Hellenistic Settlement*. vol. 3. *The Sacred Enclosure in the Early Hellenistic Period*. Jutland Archaeological Society Publications, XVI/3. Aarhus.

Kennet, D. (1997): Kush: a Sasanian and Islamic-period archaeological tell in Ras al-Khaimah (U.A.E.). *Arabian Archaeology and Epigraphy* 8: 284–302.

——————— (1998): Evidence for 4th/5th -century Sasabian occupation at Khatt, Ras al-Khaimah. Pages 105–116 in Phillips, Potts & Searight 1998.

——————— (2002): The development of Northern Ras al-Khaimah and the 14th-century Hormuzi economic boom in the lower Gulf. *Proceedings of the Seminar for Arabian Studies* 32: 151–164.

——————— (2004): *Sasanian and Islamic Pottery from Ras al-Khaimah. Classification, chronology and analysis of trade in the Western Indian Ocean*. British Archaeological Reports, International Series, 1248. Oxford.

——————— (2005): On the eve of Islam: archaeological evidence from Eastern Arabia. *Antiquity* 79/303: 107–118.

Kennet D. & Luft P. (eds) (forthcoming): *Recent advances in Sasanian archaeology and history. Proceedings of a conference held at the University of Durham, November 3rd & 4th, 2001*. British Archaeological Reports, International Series.

Kervran, M. (1984): Les Niveaux Islamiques du Secteur Oriental du Tépé de L'Apadana, III. Les objets en verre, en pierre et en métal. *Cahiers de la Délégation Archéologique Française en Iran* 14: 211–235.

Killick, R. & Moon, J. (eds) (2005): *The Early Dilmun Settlement at Saar*. Ludlow.

Kolesnikova, L.G. (1977): Znacenie i mesto antropomorphnych nadgrobij v nekropole Chersonesa. *Sovetskaja archeologija* 2: 87–99.

Kröger, J. (1995): *Nishapur, Glass of the Early Islamic Period*. New York.

Kuhrt, A. & Sherwin-White, S. (eds) (1987): *Hellenism in the East. The interaction of Greek and non-Greek civilizations from Syria to Central Asia after Alexander*. London.

Kunina, N. (1997): *Ancient Glass in the Hermitage collection*. St Petersburg.

Lamberg-Karlovsky, C.C. (1970): *Excavation at Tepe Yahya, Iran 1967–1969, progress report 1*. Bulletin 27, American School of Prehistoric research. Cambridge, MA.

Lamm, C.J. (1929–1930): *Mittelalterliche Gläser und Steinschnittarbeiten aus dem Nahen Osten*. Berlin.

———— (1931): Les Verres Trouvés a Suse. *Syria* 12: 358–367.

Lapp, P.W. (1963): Observations on the Pottery from Thaj. *Bulletin of the American Schools of Oriental Research* 172: 20–22.

Larsen, C.E. (1983): *Life and Land Use on the Bahrain Islands*. Chicago, IL.

Lecomte, O. (1993): Ed-Dur, les occupations des 3e et 4e s. ap. J.-C.: Contexte des trouvailles et matériel diagnostique. Pages 195–218 in Finkbeiner 1993.

Littleton, J. (1998): *Skeletons and Social Composition, Bahrain 300 BC–AD 250*. British Archaeological Reports, International Series, 703. Oxford.

———— (2003): Unequal in life? Human remains from the Danish excavations of Tylos tombs. *Arabian Archaeology and Epigraphy* 14/2: 164–193.

Lombard, P. (1994): The French Archaeological Mission at Qala'at al-Bahrain, 1989–1994: Some results on Late Dilmun and later periods. *Dilmun, Journal of The Bahrain Historical and Archaeological Society* 16: 26–42.

Lombard, P. (ed) (1999): *Bahreïn, La civilisation des deux mers, de Dilmoun à Tylos*. Ghent.

Lombard, P. & Kervran M. (1993): Les niveaux "Hellénistiques" du Tell de Qal'at al-Bahrain. Données préliminaires. Pages 127–161 in Finkbeiner 1993.

Lombard, P. & Kervran M. (eds) (1989): *A Selection of Pre-islamic Antiquities from Excavations 1954–1975*. Bahrain National Museum Archaeological Collections, vol. I. Bahrain.

Lombard, P. & Salles J-F. (1984): *La Nécropole de Janussan*. Travaux de la maison de l'Orient, no. 6. Lyon.

Lunde, P. & Porter, A. (eds) (2004): *Trade and Travel in the Red Sea Region, Proceedings of Red Sea Project I, Held in the British Museum, Oct. 2002*. British Archaeological Reports, International Series, 1269. Oxford.

McCown, D.E., Haines, R.C. & Biggs, R.D. (1978): *Nippur, excavations of the Joint Expedition to Nippur of the University Museum of Philadelphia and the Oriental Institute of the University of Chicago. The North Temple and the sounding E*. Vol. 2. Chicago, IL.

MacDonald, K.C. (2003): The domestic chicken in the Tylos burial of Bahrain. *Arabian Archaeology and Epigraphy* 14/2: 194–195.

Mackay, E., Harding, L. & Petrie, F. (1929): *Bahrein and Hemamieh*. British School of Archaeology in Egypt, vol. 47. London.

McNicoll, A. & Roaf, M. (1975): *Archaeological Investigations in Bahrain 1973–1975*. [Unpublished manuscript].

Madhloom, T. (1974): Excavations of The Iraqi Mission At Meleha, Sharjah U.A.E. *Sumer* 30: 149–158.

Mathiesen, H.E. (1992): *Sculpture in the Parthian Empire, a study in chronology*. Aarhus.

Meyer, C. (1992): *Glass from Quseir al-Qadim and the Indian Ocean Trade*. The Oriental institute of the University of Chicago, Studies in Ancient Oriental Civilizations, no 53. Chicago, IL.

Miroschedji, P. (1987): Fouilles du chantier Ville Royale II à Suse (1975–1977). Niveaux d'époques achéménide, séleucide, parthe et islamique. *Cahiers de la Délégation Archéologique Française en Iran* 15: 11–143.

Moorey, P.R.S. (1978): *Kish Excavations 1923–1933*. Oxford.

Mørkholm, O. (1973): En hellenistisk møntskat fra Bahrain. *Kuml* 1972: 183–202.

Morony, M.G. (2001–2002): The Late Sasanian Economic Impact on the Arabian Peninsula.

International Journal of Ancient Iranian Studies 1/2: 25–37.

Moscati, S. (2001): *The Phoenicians*. London & New York.

Mouton, M. (1992): *La Péninsule d'Oman de la fin de l'Age du fer au début de la Période Sassanide*. PhD thesis, University of Paris. [Unpublished].

——————— (1999): *Mleiha I, Environnement, stratégies de subsistance et artisanats*. Travaux de la Maison de l'Orient Méditerranéen, no. 29. Lyon & Paris.

Negro Ponzi, M.M.M. (1968–1969): Sasanian Glassware from Tell Mahuz (North Mesopotamia). *Mesopotamia* 3–4: 293–384.

——————— (1970–1971): Islamic Glassware from Seleucia. *Mesopotamia* 5–6: 67–71.

——————— (1972): Glassware from Abu Skhair (Central Iraq). *Mesopotamia* 7: 215–238.

——————— (1984): Glassware from Choche (Central Mesopotamia). Pages 33–40 in Boucharlat & Salles 1984.

——————— (1987): Late Sasanian Glassware from Barada. *Mesopotamia* 22: 265–275.

——————— (2002): The glassware from Seleucia (Central Iraq). *Parthica* 4: 63–156.

——————— (2005): Mesopotamian Glassware of the Parthian and Sasanian period: Some notes. *Annales du Congrès de l'Association Internationale pour l'Histoire du Verre, Annales du 16e congrès, London 2003*: 141–145.

Nenna, M-D. (1999): La verrerie. Pages 181–201 in Lombard 1999.

Newby, M. & Painter, K. (eds) (1991): *Roman Glass: Two Centuries of Art and Invention*. Occasional Papers from the Society of Antiquaries of London, vol. XIII. London.

Nicholson, P.T. (1999): The Glass. Pages 231–241 in Sidebotham & Wendrich 1999.

——————— (2000): The Glass. Pages 203–210 in Sidebotham & Wendrich 2000.

Oates, D. & Oates, J. (1958): Nimrud 1957: The Hellenistic Settlement. *Iraq* 20: 114–57.

Odenthal, J. (1983): *Syrien, Hochkulturen zwischen Mittelmeer una Arabischer Wüste 5000 Jahre Geschichte im Spannungsfeld von Orient und Okzident*. DuMont Kunst-Reiseführer. Cologne.

Peacock, D.P.S. (1993): The site of Myos Hormos, a view from space. *Journal of Roman Archaeology* 6: 226–232.

Penglase, C. (1995): *Some Concepts of Afterlife in Mesopotamia and Greece*. Pages 192–195 in Campbell & Green 1995.

Perkins, A. (1973): *The Art of Dura-Europos*. Oxford.

Petocz, D. & Hart, S. (1981): *Report of the Australian team working for the Bahrain Department of Antiquities 1979–1980*. [Unpublished report].

Petrie, C. (2002): Seleucid Uruk: An analysis of ceramic distribution. *Iraq* 64: 85–124.

Phillips, C.S., Potts, D.T. & Searight, S. (eds) (1998): *Arabia and her Neighbours. Essays on prehistorical and historical developments presented in honour of Beatrice de Cardi*. Turnhout.

Polybius/transl. by Paton, W.R. (1960): *The Histories*. The Loeb Classical Library. London and Cambridge, Mass.

Potts, D.T. (1990): *The Arabian Gulf in Antiquity*. vol. II. Oxford.

——————— (1993a): The Sequence and Chronology of Ayn Jawan. Pages 111–126 in Finkbeiner 1993.

——————— (1993b): The Sequence and Chronology of Thaj. Pages 87–110 in Finkbeiner 1993.

——————— (1998): Namord ware in South-eastern Arabia. Pages 207–220 in Phillips, Potts & Searight 1998.

Potts, D.T. (ed.) (1983): *Dilmun: new studies in the archaeology and early history of Bahrain*. Berlin.

Potts, D.T., Al Naboodah, H. & Hellyer, P. (eds) (2003): *Archaeology of the United Arab Emirates*. London.

Potts, D.T., Mughannum, A.S., Frye, J. & Sanders, D. (1978): Preliminary report on the second phase of the Eastern Province survey 1397/1977. *Atlal* 2: 7–27.

Price, J. & Cottam, S. (1998): *Romano-British glass vessels: A Handbook*. Practical Handbooks in Archaeology, no 14. York.

Price, J. & Worrell, S. (2003): Roman, Sasanian, and Islamic Glass from Kush, Ras al-Khaimah, United Arab Emitates: A preliminary survey. *Annales du Congrès de l'Association Internationale pour l'Histoire du Verre. Annales du 15e Congrès, 2001*: 153–157.

Reade, J. (ed) (1996): *The Indian Ocean in Antiquity*. London.

Reuther, O. (1968): *Die Innenstadt von Babylon (Merkes)*. Leipzig.

Ricciardi, R.V. (1967): Pottery from Coche. *Mesopotamia* 2: 93–104, figs 131–191.

———— (1970-71): Sasanian pottery from Tell Mahuz. *Mesopotamia* 5-6: 427-428.

Rice, M. (1972): The grave complex at Al Hajjar, Bahrain. *Proceedings of the Seminar for Arabian Studies* 2: 66-75.

Richter, G.M.A. (1956): *Catalogue of Engraved Gems, Greek, Etruscan, and Roman*. Metropolitan Museum of Art, New York. Rome.

———— (1971): *Engraved Gems of the Romans*. The engraved Gems of the Greeks, Etruscans and Romans, Part II. Edinburgh.

Rotroff, S. (1982): *Hellenistic Pottery, Athenian and imported moldmade bowls*. The Athenian Agora, vol. XXII. Princeton, NJ.

———— (1997): *Hellenistic Pottery, Athenian and imported wheelmade Table Ware and related Material*. The Athenian Agora, vol. XXIX. Princeton, NJ.

Sader, H. (2005): *Iron Age Funerary Stelae from Lebanon*. Cuadernos de Arqueología Mediterránea, 11. El Prat de Llobregat.

Saldern, A. von (1963): Achaemenid and Sassanian Cut Glass. *Ars Orientalis* 5: 7–16.

Salles, J-F. (1984): Céramiques de surface à Ed-Dour, Émirats Arabes Unis. Pages 241–270 in Boucharlat & Salles 1984.

———— (1987): The Arab-Persian Gulf under the Seleucids. Pages 75–109 in Kuhrt & Sherwin-White 1987.

———— (1990): Questioning the BI-ware. Pages 303–334 in Calvet & Gachet 1990.

Salles, J-F. & Lombard, P. (1999): La céramique. Pages 162–175 in Lombard 1999.

Salman, M.I. & Andersen S.F. (forthcoming): *The Tylos period Burials on Bahrain*. Vol. 2. *The Shakhoura and Hamad Town Cemeteries*.

Scanlon, G.T. & Pinder-Wilson, R. (2001): *Fustat Glass of the Early Islamic Period, Finds excavated by The American Research Center in Egypt 1964–1980*. London.

Scatozza, H. & Lucia, A. (1986): *I Vetri Romani di Ercolano*. Rome.

Schuol, M. (2000): *Die Charakene, Ein mesopotamisches Königreich in hellenistisch-parthischer Zeit*. Stuttgart.

Seyrig, H. (1941): Antiquités Syriennes, Inscriptions grecques de l'agora de Palmyra. *Syria* 22: 223–270.

Sherwin-White, S. & Kuhrt, A. (1993): *From Samarkhand to Sardis, A new approach to the Seleucid empire*. London.

Sidebotham, S.E. (1996): Roman Interests in the Red Sea and Indian Ocean. Pages 287–308 in Reade 1996.

———— (2004): Reflections of ethnicity in the red sea commerce in antiquity: evidence of trade goods, languages and religions from the excavations at Berenike. Pages 105–115 in Lunde & Porter 2004.

Sidebotham, S.E. & Wendrich, W.Z. (eds) (1999): *Report of the 1997 Excavations at Berinike and the Survey of the Egyptian Eastern Desert, including Excavations at Shenshef.* Leiden.

—————— (2000): *Report of the 1998 Excavations at Berinike and the Survey of the Egyptian Eastern Desert, including Excavations in Wadi Kalalat.* Leiden.

Simpson, StJ. (1995): Death and burial in the Late Islamic Near East: Some Insights from Archaeology and Ethnography. Pages 240–251 in Campbell & Green 1995.

—————— (2005): Sasanian Glass from Nineveh. *Annales du Congrès de l'Association Internationale pour l'Histoire du Verre, Annales du 16e congrès, London 2003*: 146–151.

Simpson, StJ. (ed.) (2002): *Queen of Sheba, Treasures from Ancient Yemen.* Barcelona.

Stern, E.M. (1995): *Roman Mould-blown Glass, The first through sixth centuries.* The Toledo Museum of Art. Rome.

Steve, M-J. (2003): *L'Île de Khãrg.* Neuchâtel.

Strabo/transl. H.L. Jones (1960–1969): *Geography.* (8 volumes). Loeb Classical Library. London & Cambridge.

Strommenger, E. (1967): *Gefässe aus Uruk von der Neubabylonischen Zeit bis zu den Sasaniden.* Ausgrabungen der deutschen forschungemeinschaft in Uruk-Warka, band 7. Berlin.

al-Tabari/transl. and ed. C.E. Bosworth (1999): *The History of al-Tabari, The Sasanids, the Byzantines, the Lakhmids, and Yemen.* New York.

Taha, M.Y. (1974): Pottery From United Arab Emirates. *Sumer* 30: 159–174.

Toll, N.P. (1943): *The Green Glazed Pottery.* The Excavations at Dura-Europos, Final Report IV, Part 1, Fascicle 1. New Haven, CT.

—————— (1946): *The Excavations at Dura-Europos.* Part II. *The Necropolis.* London.

Triantafyllidis, P. (2003): Achaemenid Glass Production. *Annales du Congrès de l'Association Internationale pour l'Histoire du Verre, Annales du 15e Congrès, 2001*: 13–17.

Turner, P.J. & Cribb, J. (1996): Numismatic Evidence for the Roman Trade with Ancient India. Pages 309–319 in Reade 1996.

Valtz, E. (1984): Pottery from Seleucia on the Tigris. Pages 41–48 in Boucharlat & Salles 1984.

—————— (1991): New observations on the Hellenistic pottery from Seleucia-on-the-Tigris. *Internationale Archaeologie* 6: 45–56.

—————— (1993): Pottery and exchange: Imports and local production at Seleucia-Tigris. Pages 167–182 in Invernizzi & Salles 1993.

—————— (2000): Cosmetic Containers from Seleucia on the Tigris. *Münstersche Beiträge z. antiken Handelsgeschichte* 19: 59–69.

—————— (2002): Ceramica Invetriata, Caratteristiche ed Evoluzione della Produzione di Seleucia ad Tigrim. Pages 331–338 in Blondé, Ballet & Salles 2002.

Vessberg, O. & Westholm, A. (1956): *The Hellenistic and Roman Periods in Cyprus.* The Swedish Cyprus Expedition, vol. IV, part 3. Stockholm.

Vickers, M. (1994): Nabataea, India, Gaul, and Carthage: Reflections on Hellenistic and Roman Gold Vessels and Red-Gloss Pottery. *American Journal of Archaeology* 98: 231–248.

Vine, A.R. (1980): *The Nestorian Churches.* (Reprint of the 1937 edition). London.

Vine, P. (1986): *Pearls in Arabian waters, the heritage of Bahrain.* London.

—————— (1993): *Bahrain National Museum.* London.

Vogt, B. (2002): Dead and Funerary Practices. Pages 180–207 in Simpson 2002.

Watt J.C.Y., Jiayao, A., Howard, A.F., Marshak, B.I., Bai, S. & Feng, Z. (2004): *China. Dawn of a Golden Age, 200-750 AD.* New Haven & London.

Weber, T. & Wenning, R. (eds) (1997): *Petra, antike Felsstadt zwischen arabischer Tradition und griechischer Norm*. Mainz am Rhein.

Weinberg G.D. (ed.) (1988): *Excavations at Jalame. Site of a Glass Factory in the Late Roman Palestine*. Colombia.

Whitcomb, D.S. (1985): *Before the Roses and Nightingales, Excavations at Qasr-i Abu Nasr, Old Shiraz*. New York.

Whitehouse, D. (1997): *Roman Glass in the Corning Museum of Glass*. vol. 1. New York.

——————— (1998): *The Glass Vessels*. The University of Ghent South-East Arabian Archaeological Project, Excavations at ed-Dur (Umm al-Qaiwain, United Arab Emirates). Leuven.

——————— (2000): Ancient glass from ed-Dur (Umm al-Qaiwain, U.A.E.) 2. Glass excavated by the Danish expedition. *Arabian Archaeology and Epigraphy* 11/1: 87–128.

——————— (2001): *Roman Glass in the Corning Museum of Glass*. vol. 2. New York.

——————— (2005): *Sasanian and Post-Sasanian Glass in the Corning Museum of Glass*. New York & Manchester.

Woolley, C.L. & Randall-MacIver, D. (1910): *Karanòg, The Romano-Nubian cemetery*. Philadelphia, PA.

Worrell, S. & Price, J. (2003): *The Glass from Kush, Ra's al-Khaimah*. Pages 247–252 in Potts, Al Naboodah & Hellyer 2003.

Young, G.K. (2001): *Rome's Eastern Trade, International commerce and imperial policy, 31 BC–AD 305*. London & New York.

Yule, P. (2001): *Die Gräberfelder in Samad al Shān (Sultanat Oman) — Materialien zu einer Kulturgeschichte-Text & Tafeln*. Orient-Archäologie, Band 4. Rahden/Westf.

Zarins, J., Mughannum, A.S. & Kamal, M. (1984): Exacavations at Dhahran South — The Tumuli Field (208–92) 1403 A.H. 1983. *Atlal* 8: 25–54.